BARRON'S

TOEIC®

Essential Words

SEVENTH EDITION

Lin Lougheed, Ed.D.

Teachers College
Columbia University

ACKNOWLEDGMENTS

I would like to acknowledge Chris Oliver and his students at Sophia University Junior College Division, Kanagawa, Japan, for their assistance in perfecting the Barron's TOEIC Preparation books.

Published by Kaplan, Inc., d/b/a Barron's Educational Series
750 Third Avenue
New York, NY 10017
www.barronseduc.com

ISBN: 978-1-5062-7344-0

10 9 8 7 6 5 4 3 2 1

Kaplan, Inc., d/b/a Barron's Educational Series print books are available at special quantity discounts to use for sales promotions, employee premiums, or educational purposes. For more information or to purchase books, please call the Simon & Schuster special sales department at 866-506-1949.

Contents

LESSONS 16–20: PURCHASING

LESSONS 21–25: FINANCING AND BUDGETING

LESSONS 26–30: MANAGEMENT ISSUES

LESSONS 31–35: RESTAURANTS AND EVENTS

LESSONS 36–40: TRAVEL

LESSONS 41–45: ENTERTAINMENT

LESSONS 46–50: HEALTH

Introduction

WHAT THE BOOK IS ABOUT

This book teaches you vocabulary that will help you when you take the TOEIC (Test of English for International Communication). The TOEIC measures the English proficiency of people working in international business or planning to use English to communicate with others. Although the exam does not specifically test specialized vocabulary, the items on the exam are in specialized contexts.

This book will help you understand specialized contexts that are often used on the TOEIC. Each chapter focuses on a particular context that has appeared on the TOEIC. The contexts are specialized, but the words are not. The words are general vocabulary. They can be used in many contexts. You will learn these words in contexts that are used on the TOEIC.

At the end of the book, you will find a TOEIC practice test. It will give you the opportunity to practice your vocabulary in the context of a TOEIC test. The practice test follows the new TOEIC format. This new format has the same question types as the old TOEIC, plus some new question types. TOEIC tests in this new format are already being administered in some countries. They will also be administered in other countries over the next few years. Please visit the ETS TOEIC website (*ets.org/toeic*) to find out when the new TOEIC will be administered in your country.

HOW TO USE THIS BOOK

This book contains 50 lessons, and each lesson introduces you to 12 new words in a specific context. If you study one lesson every day, in 50 days you can learn 600 new words. You will practice these words by doing exercises that look just like the questions on the TOEIC.

Word List

On the first page of each lesson, you will see a list of 12 words. For each word you will see the definition of the word and two sentences using the word in context.

This page

- Introduces you to the words for the lesson
- Shows you the words in context
- Serves as a reference anytime you need to check the meaning of a word

Word Families

On this page, you will see the verb, noun, adjective, and adverb forms of six words selected from the word list.

Example

verb	popularize
noun	popularity
adjective	popular

You will also see sentences using these words in context.

On this page, you will

- Learn more words
- Learn to recognize words in their different forms
- Learn about word endings that change words into nouns, verbs, adjectives, and adverbs

Words in Context

Next you will see a paragraph called Words in Context. You will have the opportunity to see and use the words for the lesson in context.

- Complete the paragraph using words from the word list.
- Read the paragraph over to see all the words for that lesson used in context.
- Return to the paragraph as often as you like to reinforce the meanings of the words.

Listening Comprehension

In this section, you will practice the words for the lesson by doing exercises that are just like the listening questions on the TOEIC.

PART 1—You will see a photo. You will choose the statement that best describes the photo.
PART 2—You will listen to a question or statement and choose the best response.
PART 3—You will listen to a conversation and answer three questions about it.
PART 4—You will listen to a talk and answer three questions about it.

You will practice the words for the lesson in context because the questions, conversation, and talk all use words from the word list for each lesson. You will also practice listening skills and test-taking skills that you will need when you take the TOEIC.

Reading Comprehension

In this section, you will practice the words for the lesson by doing exercises that are just like the reading questions on the TOEIC.

PART 5—You will choose the best word to complete each sentence.
PART 6—You will read a paragraph and choose words to complete it.
PART 7—You will read a passage, or two related passages, and answer comprehension questions.

You will practice the words for the lesson in context because the reading passages all use words from the word list for each lesson. You will also practice reading skills and test-taking skills that you will need when you take the TOEIC.

STRATEGIES TO IMPROVE YOUR VOCABULARY

One of the best ways to improve your vocabulary is to read, and read often. When you read, you

- See words in context
- Expose yourself to new words

The more you read, the more words you will see. The more words you see, the more you will learn. Reading can be a very enjoyable experience, so make sure you read things that are interesting to you. Then you will have fun, improve your vocabulary, and build skills you will need for the TOEIC, all at once. When you read, there are several strategies you can use to improve your vocabulary.

1. Analyze Word Parts

Words can be made of roots, prefixes (before the root), and suffixes (after the root).

Example

re (prefix) + *circula* (root) + *tion* (suffix) = *recirculation*

In English, many of these roots, prefixes, and suffixes come from Greek and Latin words. Learning the meanings of different roots, prefixes, and suffixes will help you increase your vocabulary.

Example

re means *again*

reunite	bring together again
reconsider	think about again
retrain	train again

This book will expose you to many words that use common roots, prefixes, and suffixes.

2. Recognize Prefixes

Prefixes add to or change the meaning of the root word in some way. Learning the meanings of different prefixes will help you expand your vocabulary.

Some common prefixes in English:

Prefix	Meaning	Examples
out-	more or better	outperform, outsell
over-	too much	overwork, overdo
re-	again	rewrite, regain
fore-	before, in front	foretell, forehead
pre-	before	prepay, pretest
inter-	between	international, interact
in-	not	incorrect, inconvenient
multi-	many	multicolored, multilevel

3. Recognize Suffixes

Suffixes can tell you whether a word is a noun, verb, adjective, or adverb. As you learn to recognize different suffixes, they will help you understand the meanings of new words.

Some common suffixes in English:

VERBS

Suffix	Examples
-ize	prioritize, authorize
-ate	refrigerate, hesitate
-en	lighten, widen
-fy	magnify, verify

NOUNS

Suffix	Examples
-tion, -sion	nation, conclusion
-ment	government, arrangement
-ance, -ence	importance, independence
-er, -or	manager, refrigerator
-ity	ability, community
-ness	happiness, weakness
-ship	membership, friendship
-ee	employee, attendee

ADJECTIVES

Suffix	Examples
-y	easy, wavy
-ous	mountainous, ridiculous
-able, -ible	presentable, terrible
-ic, -ical	athletic, musical
-ful	beautiful, wonderful
-less	careless, joyless
-ive	productive, creative
-ant, -ent	important, dependent

ADVERBS

Suffix	Examples
-ly	easily, importantly

4. Recognize Word Families

Word families are related groups of words that have the same root but different suffixes.

Example
depend (verb)
depend*ence* (noun)
depend*able* (adjective)
depend*ably* (adverb)

By adding different suffixes to the original word, *depend*, new words are formed. The meaning of each word is similar to the others, but each one has a different grammatical form.

When you learn a new word, it is very easy to understand the other words that are part of the same word family. In each chapter of this book, you will see examples of word families.

5. Make Your Own Word Journal

When you read, you will come across many new words, and you will need an organized way to record them.

- Use a special notebook just for recording your new words.
- Make a new page each day or each time you read a new article or story.
- For each new word, write the word, a synonym, a definition, the original sentence where you found the word, and then make up your own sentence using the word.
- Every day, review the pages from the previous days.
- Photocopy the chart on the next page to make the pages for your Word Journal.

Example

New Word	Synonym	Definition	Original Sentence	My Sentence
consider	think about	To think carefully about something	After considering all the difficulties, they decided to go ahead with the project.	I considered different schools before I chose this one.

New Word	Synonym	Definition	Original Sentence	My Sentence

6. Keep a Daily Reading Log

It is important to read something in English every day, aside from class assignments. It is important to read things that are interesting to you. You will get more out of the experience this way. It is also important to read many different kinds of things. This keeps you from getting bored, and, more important, it helps you learn a wider variety of vocabulary.

- Read for 20–30 minutes each day.
- Read things that are interesting to you.
- Read on a variety of topics.
- Read books, magazines, newspapers, and webpages.

The following steps will help you read in a way that will improve your vocabulary:

1. Read without stopping. Do not stop to look up unknown words. You can understand the general idea of a passage without understanding every word.
2. Underline or highlight unknown words, or write them on a separate piece of paper.
3. Guess the meaning of unknown words. Use the context and your knowledge of prefixes and suffixes and word families to do this.
4. Choose five key words and write them in your reading log. These should be unknown words that are important for understanding the meaning of the passage.
5. Look up the five key words in your dictionary.
6. Write a one-paragraph summary of the passage. Try to use the five key words in your summary.

Photocopy the chart below to make pages for your reading log.

Title: ____________________

Date: ____________________

No. of pages read: ____________________

Source (book, web, magazine, etc.): ____________________

Key words:

____

____

____

____

____

Summary:

____

____

____

____

____

____

____

____

____

____

____

____

____

____

____

____

____

STUDY CONTRACT

It takes a lot of discipline to learn a foreign language. You need to formalize your commitment by signing a contract with yourself. This contract will obligate you to spend a certain number of hours each week learning English for a certain period of time. Sign the contract below to make your commitment.

- Print your name below on line 1.
- Write the time you will spend each week studying English on lines 4–8. Think about how much time you have to study every day and every week and make your schedule realistic.
- Sign your name and date the contract on the last line.
- At the end of each week, add up your hours. Did you meet the requirements of your contract?

TOEIC STUDY CONTRACT

I, ________________________, promise to study for the TOEIC. I will begin my study with *Barron's Essential Words for the TOEIC* and I will also study English on my own.

I understand that to improve my English I need to spend time on English.

I promise to study English ________________________ hours per week.

I will spend ________ hours per week listening to English.

I will spend ________ hours per week writing English.

I will spend ________ hours per week speaking English.

I will spend ________ hours per week reading English.

This is a contract with myself. I promise to fulfill the terms of this contract.

________________________ ________________________

Signed Date

STRATEGIES TO PRACTICE YOUR VOCABULARY

Now that you have signed the contract, you are committed to studying English for a certain amount of time each week. The best way to do this is to pick a time when you will practice every day. Establishing a routine is part of developing good study habits. Here are some ways that you can practice the vocabulary you learn in this book.

1. Review Every Day

Every time you sit down to work with this book, you should look over the words from the previous lesson. Do the same every time you work with your Word Journal or Daily Reading Log.

- Review words from previous lessons
- Note words that you are unsure of
- Include these words in the following suggested practice activities

2. Read Out Loud

Saying your vocabulary words out loud is another way to reinforce them. You can read word lists out loud, and you can also read the passages that contain your vocabulary words. You can read out loud

- The word lists from each lesson in this book
- The Words in Context paragraphs in this book
- The passages you read for your Daily Reading Log
- The word lists in your Word Journal

3. Categorize Words

Make a list of words that you want to review. Be sure to include the words that have given you difficulty. Divide the words into categories. For example, you could make a list of things you have or do at home, things you have or do at an office, things you see or do at a store. Any one word might appear in more than one category.

- Choose a list of words to review
- Divide the list into categories
- Use the words from each category to write a paragraph
- Using the same words, think of new categories and make new lists

4. Associate Words

Choose a word from your list of words to review and list words you associate with it.

Examples

Word	search
Associations	Things you search for:
	keys
	money
	jobs
	parking spaces
Word	warning
Associations	Places where you see warnings:
	elevators
	electric wires
	subways
	cigarette packages

Extra Activities

In addition to studying this book, there are many ways that you can study on your own. You should listen to and read English as much as you can. You should also practice speaking and writing. Here are some ways you can practice your listening, reading, speaking, and writing skills in English. Check the ones you plan to try and add some ideas of your own.

INTERNET-BASED SELF-STUDY ACTIVITIES

Listening

- ☐ Podcasts on the Internet
- ☐ News websites: CNN, BBC, NBC, ABC, CBS
- ☐ Movies in English
- ☐ YouTube
- ☐ ____________________
- ☐ ____________________

Speaking

- ☐ Use Skype to talk with English speakers
- ☐ ____________________
- ☐ ____________________

Writing

- ☐ Write e-mails to website contacts
- ☐ Write a blog
- ☐ Leave comments on blogs and YouTube
- ☐ Post messages in a chat room
- ☐ Use Facebook and Twitter
- ☐ ____________________
- ☐ ____________________

Reading

- ☐ Read news and magazine articles online
- ☐ Do web research on topics that interest you
- ☐ Follow blogs that interest you
- ☐ ____________________
- ☐ ____________________

OTHER SELF-STUDY ACTIVITIES

Listening

- ☐ Listen to CNN and BBC on the radio
- ☐ Watch movies and TV in English
- ☐ Listen to music in English
- ☐ ____________________
- ☐ ____________________

Speaking

- ☐ Describe what you see and do out loud
- ☐ Practice speaking with a conversation buddy
- ☐ ____________________
- ☐ ____________________

Writing

- ☐ Write a daily journal
- ☐ Write a letter to an English speaker
- ☐ Make lists of the things you see every day
- ☐ Write descriptions of your family and friends
- ☐ ______________________________
- ☐ ______________________________

Reading

- ☐ Read newspapers and magazines in English
- ☐ Read books in English
- ☐ Read graphic novels in English
- ☐ ______________________________

Examples of Self-study Activities

Whether you read an article in a newspaper or on a website, you can use that article in a variety of ways to practice reading, writing, speaking, and listening in English.

- Read about it.
- Paraphrase and write about it.
- Give a talk or presentation about it.
- Record or make a video of your presentation.
- Listen to or watch what you recorded. Write down your presentation.
- Correct your mistakes.
- Do it all again.

PLAN A TRIP

Go to *www.fodors.com* or another travel website.

Choose a city, then choose some sites to visit there (*reading*). Write a report about the city (*writing*). Tell why you want to go there and when you want to go. Tell what sites you plan to visit. Where will you eat? How will you get around?

Now write a letter to someone recommending this place (*writing*). Pretend you have to give a lecture on your planned trip (*speaking*). Make a video of yourself talking about this city. Then watch the video and write down what you said. Correct any mistakes you made and record the presentation again. Then choose another city and do this again.

SHOP FOR AN ELECTRONIC PRODUCT

Go to *www.cnet.com*

Choose an electronic product and read about it (*reading*). Write a report about the product. Tell why you want to buy one. Describe its features.

Now write a letter to someone recommending this product (*writing*). Pretend you have to give a talk about this product (*speaking*). Make a video of yourself talking about this product. Then watch the video and write down what you said. Correct any mistakes you made and record the presentation again. Then choose another product and do this again.

DISCUSS A BOOK OR A CD

Go to *www.amazon.com*

Choose a book or CD or any product. Read the product description and reviews (*reading*). Write a report about the product. Tell why you want to buy one or why it is interesting to you. Describe its features.

Now write a letter to someone recommending this product (*writing*). Pretend you have to give a talk about this product (*speaking*). Make a video of yourself talking about this product. Then watch the video and write down what you said. Correct any mistakes you made and record the presentation again. Then choose another product and do this again.

DISCUSS ANY SUBJECT

Go to *http://simple.wikipedia.org/wiki/Main_Page*

This website is written in simple English. Pick any subject and read the entry (*reading*).

Write a short essay about the topic (*writing*). Give a presentation about it (*speaking*). Record the presentation. Then watch the video and write down what you said. Correct any mistakes you made and record the presentation again. Choose another topic and do this again.

DISCUSS ANY EVENT

Go to *http://news.google.com*

Google News has a variety of links. Pick one event and read the articles about it (*reading*).

Write a short essay about the event (*writing*). Give a presentation about it (*speaking*). Record the presentation. Then watch the video and write down what you said. Correct any mistakes you made and record the presentation again. Then choose another event and do this again.

REPORT THE NEWS

Listen to an English-language news report on the radio or watch a news program on TV (*listening*). Take notes as you listen. Write a summary of what you heard (*writing*).

Pretend you are a news reporter. Use the information from your notes to report the news (*speaking*). Record the presentation. Then watch the video and write down what you said. Correct any mistakes you made and record the presentation again. Then listen to another news program and do this again.

EXPRESS AN OPINION

Read a letter to the editor in the newspaper (*reading*). Write a letter in response in which you discuss whether you agree with the opinion expressed in the first letter. Explain why (*writing*).

Pretend you have to give a talk explaining your opinion (*speaking*). Record yourself giving the talk. Then watch the video and write down what you said. Correct any mistakes you made and record the presentation again. Then read another letter to the editor and do this again.

REVIEW A BOOK OR MOVIE

Read a book (*reading*). Think about your opinion of the book. What did you like about it? What didn't you like about it? Who would you recommend the book to and why? Pretend you are a book reviewer for a newspaper. Write a review of the book with your opinion and recommendations (*writing*).

Give an oral presentation about the book. Explain what the book is about and what your opinion is (*speaking*). Record yourself giving the presentation. Then watch the video and write down what you said. Correct any mistakes you made and record the presentation again. Then read another book and do this again.

You can do this same activity after watching a movie (*listening*).

SUMMARIZE A TV SHOW

Watch a TV show in English (*listening*). Take notes as you listen. After watching, write a summary of the show (*writing*).

Use your notes to give an oral summary of the show. Explain the characters, setting, and plot (*speaking*). Record yourself speaking. Then watch the video and write down what you said. Correct any mistakes you made and record the presentation again. Then watch another TV show and do this again.

LISTEN TO A LECTURE

Listen to an academic or other type of lecture on the Internet. Go to any of the following or similar sites and look for lectures on topics that are of interest to you:

https://academicearth.org/playlists/

http://podcasts.ox.ac.uk

http://freevideolectures.com

www.ted.com/talks

Listen to a lecture and take notes as you listen. Listen again to check and add to your notes (*listening*). Use your notes to write a summary of the lecture (*writing*).

Pretend you have to give a lecture on the same subject. Use your notes to give your lecture (*speaking*). Record yourself as you lecture. Then watch the video and write down what you said. Correct any mistakes you made and record the lecture again. Then listen to another lecture and do this again.

Lesson 1: Contracts

WORDS TO LEARN

- abide by
- agreement
- assurance
- cancellation
- determine
- engage
- establish
- obligate
- party
- provision
- resolve
- specific

Study the following definitions and examples.

1. **abide by** v., to comply with; to conform
   a. The two parties agreed to abide by the judge's decision.
   b. For years he has abided by a commitment to annual employee raises.
2. **agreement** n., a mutual arrangement; a contract
   a. The landlord and tenant were in agreement that the rent should be prorated to the middle of the month.
   b. According to the agreement, the caterer will also supply the flowers for the event.
3. **assurance** n., a guarantee; confidence
   a. We should not begin the work without the assurance of a signed contract.
   b. He spoke with assurance about the skills of his contract lawyer.
4. **cancellation** n., annulment; stopping
   a. Work on the project had to stop because of the cancellation of the contract.
   b. The cancellation clause appears at the back of the contract.
5. **determine** v., to find out; to influence
   a. After reading the contract, I was still unable to determine if our company was liable for back wages.
   b. The skill of the union bargainers will determine whether the automotive plant will open next week.
6. **engage** v., participate; involve
   a. Before engaging in a new business, it is important to do thorough research.
   b. He engaged us in a fascinating discussion about current business law.
7. **establish** v., to institute permanently; to bring about
   a. When this company was established, the owners signed contracts with all their employees.
   b. The contract establishes a relationship between the company and the service provider.
8. **obligate** v., to bind legally or morally
   a. The contractor was obligated by the contract to work 40 hours a week.
   b. The agreement with the company obligates us to pay 50% of the total fee before work can begin.
9. **party** n., a person or group participating in an action or plan; the persons or sides concerned in a legal matter
   a. The parties agreed to a settlement in their contract dispute.
   b. The party that prepares the contract has a distinct advantage.
10. **provision** n., a measure taken beforehand; a stipulation
    a. Carefully read all the provisions of the contract before signing it.
    b. The contract contains a provision to deal with how payments are made if John loses his job.
11. **resolve** v., to find a solution; to make a firm decision
    a. The mediator was able to resolve the problem to everyone's satisfaction.
    b. The businessman resolved to clean out all the files by the end of the week.
12. **specific** adj., particular
    a. The customer's specific complaint was not addressed in his e-mail.
    b. In a contract, one specific word can change the meaning dramatically.

WORD FAMILIES

verb	agree	If both parties agree to the terms, we can finalize the contract.
noun	agreement	As soon as the labor agreement was signed, the factory resumed production of new cars and vans.
adjective	agreeable	The parties are agreeable to the terms.

verb	assure	I assure you that the contract was reviewed by our lawyer.
noun	assurance	What assurance is there that the company will stay in business during the life of the contract?
adverb	assuredly	He spoke assuredly about the terms of the contract.

verb	cancel	We can cancel the contract, but that will cause a number of problems.
noun	cancellation	A cancellation fee is usually included in a writer's contract in case the article isn't published.
adjective	canceled	The canceled contract ended up costing our company a good deal of money.

verb	obligate	The terms of the contract obligate us to work for at least one more month.
noun	obligation	According to the contract, the company has the obligation to provide child care for employees' families.
adjective	obligatory	Agreeing to the terms of the contract is obligatory if you want to work here.

verb	provide	Since the machine is very reliable, why don't we cancel the service contract they provided?
noun	provider	We must negotiate a new contract with our Internet service provider.
noun	provision	The provision for canceling the contract is in the last clause.

verb	specify	The contract specifies an annual salary raise.
noun	specification	The work was done according to the specifications of the contract.
adjective	specific	There is no specific part of the contract that prevents us from hiring extra help.

WORDS IN CONTEXT

Read the following passage and write the words in the blanks below.

abide by	cancel	establish	provide
agreement	determine	obligates	resolve
assurance	engaging	parties	specifies

Contracts are an integral part of the workplace. The purpose of a contract is to (1) ________________ an (2) ________________ between two or more (3) ________________. The contract (4) ________________ the terms and (5) ________________ the parties to follow them. Contracts often include the amount that a client will pay contractors and what services will be provided. For example, in your office, you may have a contract that provides (6) ______________ that your copier machine or phones will be repaired within a certain amount of time. A contract often states ways to (7) ______________ if the quality of work delivered is acceptable. Well-written contracts usually (8) ______________ ways to (9) ______________ problems like these when they happen. Before (10) ______________ in a contract, both parties should think carefully, as they will have to (11) ______________ the conditions specified in it. A contract usually specifies how the two parties can (12) ______________ it if either party fails to meet the terms.

WORD PRACTICE

Listening Comprehension

Track 2

PART 1 PHOTO

Look at the picture and listen to the sentences.
Choose the sentence that best describes the picture.

1. Ⓐ Ⓑ Ⓒ Ⓓ

PART 2 QUESTION–RESPONSE

Listen to the question and the three responses. Choose the response that best answers the question.

2. Ⓐ Ⓑ Ⓒ

3. Ⓐ Ⓑ Ⓒ

PART 3 CONVERSATION

Listen to the dialogue. Then read each question and choose the best answer.

4. What problem do the speakers have with the computer company?
   (A) It won't renew the contract.
   (B) It can't repair the computer.
   (C) It sends incorrect bills.
   (D) It charges them for extra spare parts.

5. When will the contract run out?
   (A) In two months
   (B) In nine months
   (C) In one year
   (D) In four years

6. What does the woman suggest doing?
   (A) Asking the company to write a new contract
   (B) Canceling the contract
   (C) Renewing the contract
   (D) Waiting until the contract runs out

PART 4 TALK

Listen to the talk. Then read each question and choose the best answer.

7. Who is talking?
   (A) A lawyer
   (B) An upset signer of the contract
   (C) A secretary
   (D) Someone who has canceled his agreement

8. Which part of the contract are they looking at?
   (A) A cancellation clause
   (B) The assurance of quality
   (C) The agreement on payment
   (D) A provision in case of bankruptcy

9. When can the parties sign the contract?
   (A) In two days
   (B) At the end of the week
   (C) Next week
   (D) In thirty days

Reading

PART 5 INCOMPLETE SENTENCES

Choose the word that best completes the sentence.

10. The two sides were no closer to a final ____ at midnight than they were at noon.
    (A) agreement (C) agree
    (B) agreeable (D) agreed

11. Ms. Smith ____ to bring up her concerns about the contract at the next meeting.
    (A) resolved (C) assured
    (B) abided by (D) established

12. If you ____ your reservation 48 hours in advance, you will not be billed.
    (A) oblige (C) engage
    (B) cancel (D) determine

13. I don't feel any ____ to give my boss more than two weeks' notice when I leave.
    (A) oblige (C) obliged
    (B) obligatory (D) obligation

14. The ____ for terminating the contract were not discussed.
    (A) provide (C) provider
    (B) provisions (D) provisioning

15. The contract calls for the union to ____ who their bargaining representative will be.
    (A) specific (C) specifying
    (B) specification (D) specify

PART 6 TEXT COMPLETION

Choose the word or phrase that best completes the sentence.

Rental Property for Everyone

Whether you have a small apartment in your house to rent or decide to invest in an apartment or office building, rental property can provide extra income for you and your family. What does every landlord need to know?

Leases: A lease is an ____ (16.) between a landlord and a tenant. Standard leases are available on the Internet, and many property owners find them quite satisfactory. Read the standard lease carefully to determine if it meets the needs of your situation. You may want to make some additional ____ (17.). You may want to add a pet clause, for example, or make different specifications pertaining to the security deposit. If you decide to make changes to the standard lease, you should meet with a lawyer. ____ (18.) When you have a lease written by a lawyer, you ____ (19.) that you have the protection you need in case of disagreements.

16. (A) agree
    (B) agreed
    (C) agreeable
    (D) agreement

17. (A) provisions
    (B) resolutions
    (C) obligations
    (D) engagements

18. (A) Your lease should clearly state how much the tenant should pay towards the security deposit.
    (B) The lease is the most important tool you have for resolving disputes with your tenant.
    (C) The only parties who should sign the lease are you and your tenant.
    (D) A standard lease is usually not longer than two or three pages.

19. (A) assure
    (B) will assure
    (C) are assuring
    (D) are assured

PART 7 READING COMPREHENSION

Questions 20–24 refer to the following letter and form.

Santos Office Cleaners

112 Main St.
Windsor, Ontario

December 15, 20—

Mr. James Harrison
17 Hartland Road
Windsor, Ontario

Dear Mr. Harrison,

We are very sorry that you have decided to cancel your cleaning service contract with us. In order to assure that we provide our customers with the best possible service, we always try to determine the reasons for contract cancellations. Please take a few minutes to fill out the enclosed form. This is for our information only; completing the form does not obligate you to buy any product or enter into any new agreement with our company. We appreciate your cooperation. If at any time in the future you decide to renew your contract with us, please don't hesitate to contact me.

Sincerely,

Rosa Santos

Rosa Santos
Owner

Santos Office Cleaners
Customer Questionnaire

Date contract signed: March 23, 20—

Type of facility:
- ☑ single office
- ☐ office building
- ☐ private home
- ☐ other

Frequency of service:
- ☐ daily
- ☑ weekly
- ☐ monthly
- ☐ other

Reason for contract cancellation (choose one):
- ☐ no longer need service
- ☐ signed contract with a different company
- ☑ payment dispute not satisfactorily resolved
- ☐ specific complaint not resolved
- ☐ other

Comments: I was always satisfied with the service provided by your employees. However, I am frustrated by your inability to resolve the payment issues.

20. What is the purpose of the letter?
    (A) To find out why Mr. Harrison no longer wants this service
    (B) To ask Mr. Harrison to renew his contract
    (C) To advertise new services provided by the company
    (D) To offer the customer a better contract

21. What is Ms. Santos's business?
    (A) Customer relations
    (B) Cleaning service
    (C) Contract review
    (D) Conflict resolution

22. Why did this customer cancel the contract?
    (A) The company damaged something in his office.
    (B) The employees provided unsatisfactory service.
    (C) He had a disagreement about his bill.
    (D) He doesn't want this type of service anymore.

23. The word *assure* in letter one, line 3, is closest in meaning to
    (A) guarantee.
    (B) discover.
    (C) prove.
    (D) advertise.

24. The word *specific* in form two, line 15, is closest in meaning to
    (A) personal.
    (B) important.
    (C) repeated.
    (D) particular.

Lesson 2: Marketing

WORDS TO LEARN

- attract
- compare
- competition
- consume
- convince
- currently
- fad
- inspiration
- market
- persuasion
- productive
- satisfaction

Study the following definitions and examples.

1. **attract** v., to draw by appeal
   a. The display attracted a number of people at the convention.
   b. The new advertising attracts the wrong kind of customer into the store.
2. **compare** v., to examine similarities and differences
   a. Once the customer compared the two products, her choice was easy.
   b. The price for this brand is high compared to the other brands on the market.
3. **competition** n., a contest or struggle
   a. In the competition for afternoon diners, Hector's has come out on top.
   b. In order to keep up with the competition, we need to market our product better.
4. **consume** v., to absorb; to use up
   a. The business plans consumed all of Fritz's attention this fall.
   b. Marketing costs consume a good part of a company's budget.
5. **convince** v., to bring to believe by argument; to persuade
   a. The salesman convinced his customer to buy his entire inventory of pens.
   b. Before a business can convince customers that it provides a quality product, it must convince its marketing staff.
6. **currently** adv., happening at the present time; now
   a. Currently, we do most of our advertising on the Internet.
   b. Currently, customers are demanding big discounts for bulk orders.
7. **fad** n., a practice followed enthusiastically for a short time; a craze
   a. The mini dress was a fad once thought to be finished, but now it is making a comeback.
   b. Classic tastes may seem boring but they have proven to resist fads.
8. **inspiration** n., a thing or person that arouses a feeling
   a. His work is an inspiration to the marketing department.
   b. Marta's high sales in Spain were an inspiration to other European reps.
9. **market** v., the course of buying and selling a product; n., the demand for a product
   a. When Omar first began making his chutneys, he marketed them door-to-door to gourmet shops.
   b. There was a good market for brightly colored clothing last year, but this year nobody seems interested in buying it.
10. **persuasion** n., the power to influence; a deep conviction or belief
    a. The seminar teaches techniques of persuasion to increase sales.
    b. Companies use different methods of persuasion to get people to buy their products.
11. **productive** adj., constructive; high yield
    a. Productive advertising results in many sales.
    b. Alonzo is excited about his productive marketing staff.
12. **satisfaction** n., happiness
    a. Your satisfaction is guaranteed or you'll get your money back.
    b. We will print the advertisement to your satisfaction.

WORD FAMILIES

verb	attract	The store's poor location did not help it attract customers.
noun	attraction	The live clown was the most successful attraction in the toy store.
adjective	attractive	Lou ran his store on an old-fashioned premise: quality merchandise at attractive prices.

verb	compare	She compared the prices before she made a decision.
noun	comparison	There was no comparison in the quality of the two brands.
adjective	comparable	To get an average for home costs, the agent sought prices on comparable homes.

verb	compete	In order to compete in today's market, companies need to advertise on the Internet.
noun	competition	A company must always be aware of what its competition is doing.
adjective	competitive	Companies keep their products competitive by making them available on the Internet as well as in stores.

verb	consume	The analyst was able to consume new information quickly.
noun	consumer	The government tracks consumer spending closely.
adjective	consumable	He ran a study of the use of consumable goods.

verb	market	The sales department disagreed about how to market their newest product.
noun	marketing	A good director of marketing can find a way to sell even an unattractive product.
adjective	marketable	Once the sales manager decided to change the packaging, the product became much more marketable.

verb	satisfy	The goal of marketing is to show that the product satisfies consumers' needs.
noun	satisfaction	Our highest priority is customer satisfaction.
adjective	satisfactory	All our products arrive in the stores in satisfactory condition.

WORDS IN CONTEXT

Read the following passage and write the words in the blanks below.

attract	consumers	fad	persuaded
compared	convince	inspiration	product
competes	current	market	satisfied

Yassir is getting ready to realize his dream: opening a business that sells plants on the Internet. After completing a business plan that helped him to determine that there was demand for his (1) ______________ in the (2) ______________, Yassir is ready to start promoting his business. Having (3) ______________ the bank that there was a market—that there were people willing to buy plants on the Internet—he needed to find these (4) ______________.

Once he has an established base, Yassir, like other business owners, will have to continually (5) ______________ new customers. At the same time, he must keep the customers he already has (6) ______________. To this end, he has to make sure that his (7) ______________ customers are happy with the products they buy. Yassir's job is to provide his customers with the (8) ______________ to keep bringing him their business. To do this, he will have to (9) ______________ consumers that he offers a good product at a fair price, especially when (10) ______________ to the businesses with which he (11) ______________. He hopes that Internet plant buyers are here to stay and not just part of a (12) ______________.

WORD PRACTICE

Listening Comprehension

Track 3

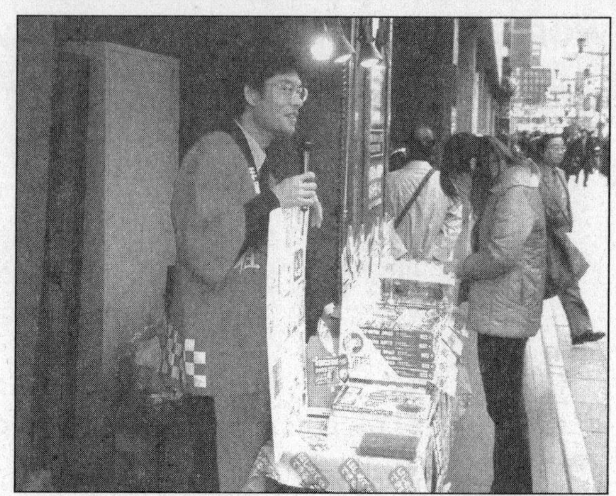

PART 1 PHOTO

Look at the picture and listen to the sentences. Choose the sentence that best describes the picture.

1. Ⓐ Ⓑ Ⓒ Ⓓ

PART 2 QUESTION–RESPONSE

Listen to the question and the three responses. Choose the response that best answers the question.

2. Ⓐ Ⓑ Ⓒ

3. Ⓐ Ⓑ Ⓒ

PART 3 CONVERSATION

Listen to the dialogue. Then read each question and choose the best answer.

4. Why does the store need to be more competitive?
   (A) There's currently a recession.
   (B) Productivity has dropped lately.
   (C) There's a new competitor nearby.
   (D) New employees have little experience.

5. How will the store attract more customers?
   (A) By giving them trial products
   (B) By giving them discounts
   (C) By selling new products
   (D) By featuring happy customers in ads

6. Who will the woman call?
   (A) A photographer
   (B) A photocopy salesperson
   (C) A customer
   (D) A marketing executive

PART 4 TALK

Listen to the talk. Then read each question and choose the best answer.

7. Who would listen to this talk?
   (A) Customers
   (B) Competitors
   (C) Students
   (D) Salespeople

8. What are they trying to identify?
   (A) Their weaknesses
   (B) How to price their service
   (C) Their strong points
   (D) Who the competition is

9. Where will the listeners be this afternoon?
   (A) At home
   (B) In a workshop
   (C) At a store
   (D) With a client

Reading

PART 5 INCOMPLETE SENTENCES

Choose the word that best completes the sentence.

10. Marketing specialists have conducted extensive studies of what _____ customers to a particular product.

    (A) attractive (C) attracts
    (B) attraction (D) attracting

11. Smart shoppers will _____ similar brands of an item before making a decision.

    (A) compare (C) comparative
    (B) comparison (D) comparable

12. If our work isn't to your _____, please notify us within 60 days.

    (A) satisfy (C) satisfaction
    (B) satisfactory (D) satisfied

13. Manufacturers like to know what features _____ find useful.

    (A) consumers (C) consumption
    (B) consume (D) consumable

14. A company can lose big money if it invests too much money in a product that turns out to be just a passing _____.

    (A) inspiration (C) market
    (B) persuasion (D) fad

15. We will not be able to _____ in this market unless we price our products correctly.

    (A) produce (C) persuade
    (B) compete (D) convince

PART 6 TEXT COMPLETION

Choose the word or phrase that best completes the sentence.

Dear Valued Customer,

Smart consumers like yourself are concerned about your family's nutrition. Health is a top priority, and so is value. ____ (16.). That's why we are introducing Farm Fresh, our new line of 100% natural and organic frozen dinners. We know you'll love the great natural taste of Farm Fresh dinners such as Turkey and Wild Rice, Wild Salmon with Spring Greens, and Country Chicken with Vegetables. Farm Fresh dinners are ____ (17.) packaged with 100% recyclable materials. But we don't have to use a lot of fancy words to convince you to enjoy Farm Fresh frozen dinners. We will let their great taste ____ (18.) you to keep coming back for more. Please use the enclosed coupons to buy up to six Farm Fresh dinners of your choice at 25% off the usual retail price. We know you ____ (19.) by the great taste and the great price.

Sincerely,

Rosa Martello

National Frozen Foods, Inc.

16. (A) It is important to stay healthy by exercising regularly.
    (B) You want high-quality food products at competitive prices.
    (C) Many families feel a vegetarian diet offers better nutrition.
    (D) Consumers often feel that fresh food is more healthful than frozen.

17. (A) attract
    (B) attractive
    (C) attractively
    (D) attraction

18. (A) convince
    (B) compete
    (C) consume
    (D) compare

19. (A) satisfy
    (B) satisfied
    (C) will satisfy
    (D) will be satisfied

PART 7 READING COMPREHENSION

Questions 20–24 refer to the following report.

Catherine Cosmetics Company
Sales Department Meeting Report
March 29, 20—

We reviewed the sales figures for the past quarter. We are currently experiencing a significant drop in sales in our hair care products. This has been going on since the beginning of the year when we introduced the improved version of our top-selling hair care line, Catherine's Curls. Our advertising has not been successful in convincing more consumers to buy these products. We know there is a market for products such as these manufactured with 100% natural ingredients and no testing on animals. In fact, our competitors are doing quite well in this area and have been for a number of years. We know from our research that the popularity of all-natural cosmetic products is more than just a passing fad, and this is why we decided to branch out into this area. We have carefully compared our products to those of our three largest competitors. We have looked at product ingredients, packaging, target consumers, pricing, and sales strategies. Our product is similar, or even better, in all ways but one. Our packaging is significantly less eye-catching than that of our competitors, and it does not convey the important aspects of the products to the consumer, that is, that these products are entirely made with natural ingredients. Therefore, in order to attract more customers, we recommend employing a new designer to create better packaging for the Catherine's Curls line of products.

20. When did the sales department have a meeting?
    (A) At the beginning of the year
    (B) In March
    (C) A quarter of a year ago
    (D) At the end of last year

21. Which of the following might be part of the Catherine's Curls line of products?
    (A) Shampoo
    (B) Hand lotion
    (C) Nail polish
    (D) Lipstick

22. According to the report, why are fewer people buying Catherine's Curls products?
    (A) The prices are too high.
    (B) The ingredients aren't natural.
    (C) The packages aren't attractive.
    (D) The type of product is not popular.

23. The word *market* in line 5 is closest in meaning to
    (A) product.
    (B) factory.
    (C) purchase.
    (D) demand.

24. The word *fad* in line 9 is closest in meaning to
    (A) need.
    (B) fashion.
    (C) event.
    (D) wish.

Lesson 3: Warranties

WORDS TO LEARN

- characteristic
- consequence
- consider
- cover
- expire
- frequently
- imply
- promise
- protect
- reputation
- require
- variety

Study the following definitions and examples.

1. **characteristic** adj., revealing of individual traits; n., an individual trait
   a. It is characteristic of this company to provide only a limited warranty with its products.
   b. That salesperson has an annoying characteristic—he pushes his customers to buy the warranty.
2. **consequence** n., that which follows necessarily
   a. The consequence of not following the service instructions for your car is that the warranty is invalidated.
   b. Rachael did not buy an extended warranty and, as a consequence, had to pay for the repairs herself.
3. **consider** v., to think about carefully
   a. I considered buying the computer until I learned that the warranty coverage was very limited.
   b. After considering all the options, Della decided to buy a used car.
4. **cover** v., to provide protection against
   a. The warranty covers the cost of all repairs for a period of one year.
   b. An extended warranty covers the product for a longer period of time.
5. **expire** v., to end
   a. Our contract with the cleaning company will expire next month.
   b. After the warranty expires, you will have to pay for repairs yourself.
6. **frequently** adv., occurring commonly; widespread
   a. Appliances frequently come with a one-year warranty.
   b. Warranties for this kind of appliance are frequently limited in their coverage.
7. **imply** v., to indicate by inference
   a. The salesperson implied that the warranty covered all damages to the equipment for one year.
   b. The warranty implies that repairs will take several weeks.
8. **promise** n., a pledge, a commitment; v., to pledge to do, bring about, or provide
   a. A warranty is a promise the manufacturer makes to the consumer.
   b. The sales associate promised that our new mattress would arrive by noon on Saturday.
9. **protect** v., to guard
   a. The warranty protects the consumer against a defective product.
   b. The warranty will protect you from spending a lot of money in repairs.
10. **reputation** n., the overall quality of character
   a. The salesperson showed me an unfamiliar product, but I bought it because of the reputation of the manufacturer.
   b. The company knew that the reputation of its products was the most important asset it had.
11. **require** v., to deem necessary or essential
   a. A car warranty may require the owner to have it serviced by a certified mechanic.
   b. The law requires that each item clearly display the warranty information.
12. **variety** n., many different kinds
   a. There's a variety of standard terms that you'll find in warranties.
   b. A variety of problems appeared after the product had been on the market for about six months.

WORD FAMILIES

verb	characterize	A warranty is characterized by the length of its terms.
adjective	characteristic	It is characteristic of many companies to offer an extended warranty for a fee.
adverb	characteristically	A warranty characteristically provides for replacement or repair within certain time limits.

verb	consider	You should consider carefully whether a product will meet your needs.
noun	consideration	After long consideration, Heloise decided that the five-year warranty would be sufficient.
adjective	considerable	The fee for the extra year of protection was a considerable expense.

verb	imply	The salesperson implied that the cost of the extended warranty would be low.
noun	implication	The implication is that if you drop the product and it breaks, the repairs aren't covered by the warranty.
adjective	implicit	Correct use of the product by the consumer is implicit in the terms of the warranty.

verb	protect	Juan protected the warranty by taking excellent care of his lawn mower.
noun	protection	For your own protection, you should have a warranty that provides for a replacement product.
adjective	protective	Alfredo is very protective of the condition of his car and gets all the preventive maintenance his warranty requires.

noun	reputation	The good reputation of the manufacturer inspired Maria Jose to try the new product.
adjective	reputable	Because the company had a reputable name, I did not spend sufficient time reading the details of the warranty.
adjective	reputed	The new store is reputed to carry items that are not of the highest quality.

verb	require	The warranty requires that you send the product to an approved repair shop to have it fixed.
noun	requirement	The terms of the warranty divulge the legal requirement the manufacturer has to the consumer.
adjective	requisite	The warranty spelled out the requisite steps to take to request a replacement product.

WORDS IN CONTEXT

Read the following passage and write the words in the blanks below.

characteristics	covers	implies	reputations
consequences	expire	promise	required
consider	frequently	protect	variety

Warranties are a seller's (1) _______________ to stand behind its products. Most major purchases such as computers or cars come with a warranty, as do smaller purchases such as stereos or other electronic housewares. Warranties are not (2) _______________ by law, but are (3) _______________ found on products. If you are making a purchase, you should (4) _______________ the individual (5) _______________ of a warranty, as not all warranties are the same. In fact, there is a great (6) _______________ among them. Check the warranty to see what repairs it (7) _______________ and for what amount of time. At the minimum, warranties are required to promise that the product will do what it (8) _______________ that it will do; for example, that a blender will blend or a hair dryer will dry hair. Most warranties are good for a fixed time, then they (9) _______________. You can (10) _______________ yourself by buying products from companies with good (11) _______________ and by taking good care of your new purchase. There are (12) _______________ to not taking care of a product, as most warranties require that you use the product in a certain manner.

WORD PRACTICE

Listening Comprehension

Track 4

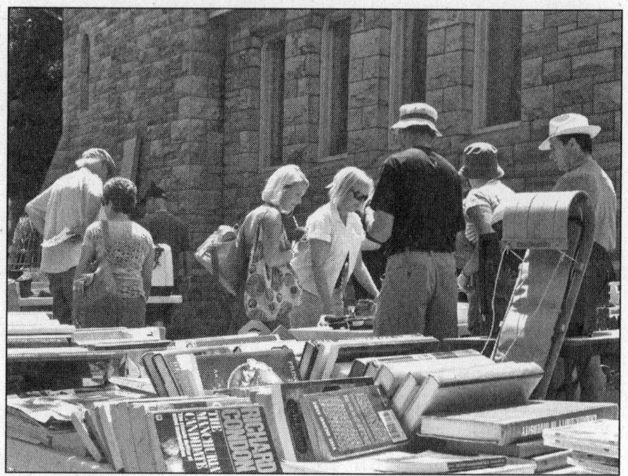

PART 1 PHOTO

Look at the picture and listen to the sentences. Choose the sentence that best describes the picture.

1. Ⓐ Ⓑ Ⓒ Ⓓ

PART 2 QUESTION–RESPONSE

Listen to the question and the three responses. Choose the response that best answers the question.

2. Ⓐ Ⓑ Ⓒ 3. Ⓐ Ⓑ Ⓒ

PART 3 CONVERSATION

Listen to the dialogue. Then read each question and choose the best response.

4. How long is the basic warranty effective?
   (A) Thirty days
   (B) Sixty days
   (C) One year
   (D) Two years

5. What will happen if the woman uses an unapproved mechanic?
   (A) There are no consequences.
   (B) The warranty is no longer effective.
   (C) Protection is decreased by 50%.
   (D) She will have full coverage.

6. What does the woman decide to do?
   (A) Take her car to an approved mechanic
   (B) Buy the extended warranty
   (C) Refuse the basic warranty
   (D) Buy a different car

PART 4 TALK

Listen to the talk. Then read each question and choose the best answer.

7. What is the point of the talk?
   (A) Items under warranty must be fixed.
   (B) If an item is misused, the warranty may be invalidated.
   (C) Machines with unusual wear are difficult to repair.
   (D) Customers often don't understand warranties.

8. Who is the audience for this talk?
   (A) A factory repairperson
   (B) A customer
   (C) Someone who rents machines
   (D) Buyers

9. How can a customer receive money back for a defective product?
   (A) Follow the directions on the package
   (B) Return it to the place of purchase
   (C) Repackage it carefully
   (D) Return it within 30 days

Reading

PART 5 INCOMPLETE SENTENCES

Choose the word that best completes the sentence.

10. The timing belt ______ shows signs of wear after about 180,000 miles.
    (A) character (C) characterize
    (B) characteristic (D) characteristically

11. Jacques and Louisa will only ______ purchasing appliances that come with a money-back guarantee.
    (A) consideration (C) considering
    (B) consider (D) considerable

12. If there is any ______ of the director's involvement, we need to follow up swiftly and thoroughly.
    (A) imply (C) implicated
    (B) implicit (D) implication

13. The level of _____ implied by the warranty was misleading.
    (A) protect (C) protection
    (B) protective (D) protector

14. When planning a major purchase, look for a _____ company that sells high-quality products.
    (A) reputable (C) requisite
    (B) considerable (D) implicit

15. If the appliance breaks down within two years of purchase, the manufacturer is _____ to send you a replacement at no charge.
    (A) considered (C) expired
    (B) protected (D) required

PART 6 TEXT COMPLETION

Choose the word or phrase that best completes the sentence.

One-Year Limited Warranty

This warranty ____ (16.) the purchaser from all malfunctions of the product due to defects in materials or workmanship. Only the original purchaser of the product is covered. Resale of the product automatically invalidates this warranty. This warranty ____ (17.) the manufacturer to repair any defective product or to refund the full purchase price to the purchaser, at the manufacturer's discretion. The manufacturer's liability does not exceed the purchase price of the product. This warranty does not imply that the purchaser has any rights in the case of a defective product beyond those stated herein. This warranty ____ (18.) one year from the date of purchase.

____ (19.).

16. (A) protects
    (B) implies
    (C) promises
    (D) considers

17. (A) require
    (B) requires
    (C) is requiring
    (D) has required

18. (A) should expire
    (B) might expire
    (C) will expire
    (D) can expire

19. (A) Customers frequently misunderstand the terms of a warranty.
    (B) Most warranties expire after one year, although some can be extended.
    (C) It is always a good idea to make sure that your purchase is protected by a warranty.
    (D) A receipt or other proof of purchase is required in order to make claims under the terms of this warranty.

PART 7 READING COMPREHENSION

Questions 20–24 refer to the following two letters.

Kitchen Electronics, Inc.

October 12, 20—

Mrs. Sophie Bordeaux
118 Montrose Street
Stoneybrook, MI

Dear Mrs. Bordeaux,

We received the defective toaster which you returned to us asking for a full refund under the terms of the one-year warranty. Unfortunately, the warranty on the toaster expired a month ago. The terms of the warranty do not cover your product once it has expired. Consequently, we will not be able to send you a refund. However, we will be able to send you a refurbished toaster of the same model in exchange for the defective one if you desire. Please let us know if such an arrangement would be satisfactory to you.

Please don't hesitate to contact me if you have any questions. We appreciate your business.

Sincerely,

Matthew Bodine

Matthew Bodine
Customer Service Manager

November 1, 20—

Matthew Bodine
Customer Service Manager
Kitchen Electronics, Inc.
194294 Honeywell Boulevard
Victoria Springs, AL

Dear Mr. Bodine,

I have received your letter offering to send me a refurbished toaster in place of my defective one. I had not realized that my warranty had already expired. After considering the matter, I have decided to accept the refurbished toaster. Your company has a good reputation, and I frequently use your products. In fact, this is the first time I have ever had a problem with anything I have purchased from you. Therefore, I am sure that the refurbished toaster will work as well as a brand new one. However, I would like to be assured that the refurbished toaster will be protected by a warranty, just as a new toaster would be. If this is the case, then please send me the toaster as soon as possible. Thank you.

Sincerely,

Sophie Bordeaux

Sophie Bordeaux

20. Why did the customer return the toaster?
    (A) It doesn't work.
    (B) It was too expensive.
    (C) She wants a brand new one.
    (D) She prefers a different model.

21. When did she purchase the toaster?
    (A) A month ago
    (B) Last October
    (C) Exactly one year ago
    (D) A little over a year ago

22. What will she get in place of the returned toaster?
    (A) Nothing
    (B) A refund
    (C) A brand new toaster
    (D) A different, repaired toaster

23. The word *considering* in line 4 of the second letter is closest in meaning to
    (A) reading about.
    (B) thinking about.
    (C) talking about.
    (D) worrying about.

24. The word *frequently* in line 7 of the second letter is closest in meaning to
    (A) often.
    (B) rarely.
    (C) never.
    (D) occasionally.

Lesson 4: Business Planning

WORDS TO LEARN

- address
- avoid
- demonstrate
- develop
- evaluate
- gather
- offer
- primarily
- risk
- strategy
- strengthen
- substitution

Study the following definitions and examples.

1. **address** n., a formal speech; v., to direct attention to
   a. The article praised her address to the steering committee.
   b. Marco's business plan addresses the needs of small business owners.
2. **avoid** v., to stay clear of; to keep from happening
   a. To avoid going out of business, owners should prepare a proper business plan.
   b. Lloyd's errors in accounting could have been avoided by a business consultation with his banker.
3. **demonstrate** v., to show clearly and deliberately; to present by example
   a. Alban's business plan demonstrated that he had put a lot of thought into making his dream a reality.
   b. The professor demonstrated through a case study that a business plan can impress a lender.
4. **develop** v., to expand, progress, or improve
   a. Lily developed her ideas into a business plan by taking a class at the community college.
   b. The restaurant Wanda opened ten years ago has developed into a national chain.
5. **evaluate** v., to determine the value or impact of
   a. It's important to evaluate your competition when making a business plan.
   b. The lenders evaluated our credit history and decided to loan us money.
6. **gather** v., to accumulate; to conclude
   a. We gathered information for our plan from many sources.
   b. I gather that interest rates for small businesses will soon change.
7. **offer** n., a proposal; v., to propose; to present in order to meet a need or satisfy a requirement
   a. Devon accepted our offer to write the business plan.
   b. Jackie must offer her banker new statistics in order to encourage the bank to lend her money toward her start-up business.
8. **primarily** adv., first; most importantly
   a. We are primarily concerned with convincing the board of directors to apply for the second loan.
   b. The developers are thinking primarily of how to enter the South American market.
9. **risk** n., the chance of loss or damage
   a. The primary risk for most start-up businesses is insufficient capital.
   b. Expanding into a new market is a big risk.
10. **strategy** n., a plan of action
    a. A business plan is a strategy for running a business and avoiding problems.
    b. Let's develop a strategy for promoting our ice cream parlor.
11. **strengthen** v., make stronger or more powerful
    a. You can strengthen your plan by including the possibility of rising costs.
    b. We are working on a plan to strengthen sales over the next two quarters.
12. **substitution** n., replacement
    a. Your substitution of fake names for real ones makes the document seem insincere.
    b. There is no substitution for hard work and perseverance.

WORD FAMILIES

verb	avoid	It is best to avoid get-rich-quick schemes.
noun	avoidance	Your avoidance of these issues will not make them go away.
adjective	avoidable	Many problems are avoidable with careful planning.

verb	demonstrate	A business plan demonstrates how the business will make money and pay expenses.
noun	demonstration	The business professor gave a demonstration of how to develop a business plan.
adjective	demonstrative	The failure of that business is demonstrative of what can happen when there is no business plan.

verb	develop	Our assignment is to develop a sample business plan.
noun	development	The plan is under development and will not be ready for a while.
noun	developer	The plan developers worked hard to make sure they had considered all the possibilities.

verb	evaluate	Please review these articles and evaluate their usefulness for our plan.
noun	evaluation	Yoko feared the professor's evaluation of her business plan.
noun	evaluator	The independent evaluator reviewed our business plan and gave us good feedback.

verb	strategize	Instead of going into a panic, let's strategize the best way to meet the deadline.
noun	strategy	The business plan lays out a strategy for future growth.
adjective	strategic	The handout outlined the strategic points to cover in a business plan.

verb	substitute	No amount of intelligence can substitute for good planning.
noun	substitution	The substitution of one amount for another made a big difference in their business plan.
adjective	substituted	The substituted amount was much larger than the original amount.

WORDS IN CONTEXT

Read the following passage and write the words in the blanks below.

address	develop	offered	strategy
avoid	evaluation	primary	strengthen
demonstrate	gathering	risks	substitute

Every business must (1) _______________ a business plan. The business plan's (2) _______________ purpose is to improve the entrepreneur's control over the business and to help him (3) _______________ common mistakes. There is no (4) _______________ for a well-prepared business plan. It is the way to (5) _______________ the business and help it improve in all areas. The business plan documents the (6) _______________ for growing the business. Think of the business plan as a road map that describes in which direction the company is going, what its goals are, and how it is going to get there.

In developing the plan, the entrepreneur will conduct research to determine a systematic and realistic (7) _______________ of the company's chances for success in the marketplace. In creating the plan, the entrepreneur must research the company's target market and define its potential. The entrepreneur must be able to prove through research that customers in the market need the good or service that is (8) _______________ and that a sufficient number of potential customers exists to support the business.

A business plan also looks at the (9) _______________ the business faces. Chief among these is competitors. The business plan must analyze the company's competition by (10) _______________ information on competitors' market share, products, and strategies. The plan should (11) _______________ what distinguishes the entrepreneur's products or services from others already in the market. It is also common for businesses to fail because the owner fails to invest or seek sufficient capital to run the business. A good business plan should (12) _______________ this issue as well.

WORD PRACTICE

Listening Comprehension

Track 5

PART 1 PHOTO

Look at the picture and listen to the sentences. Choose the sentence that best describes the picture.

1. Ⓐ Ⓑ Ⓒ Ⓓ

PART 2 QUESTION–RESPONSE

Listen to the question and the three responses. Choose the response that best answers the question.

2. Ⓐ Ⓑ Ⓒ

3. Ⓐ Ⓑ Ⓒ

PART 3 CONVERSATION

Listen to the dialogue. Then read each question and choose the best response.

4. How do the speakers feel about Alexa's business plan?
   (A) She has gathered too much data.
   (B) She has taken on too much risk.
   (C) She has made many obvious mistakes.
   (D) She is serious-minded and cautious.

5. How will the man help Alexa?
   (A) By doing market research
   (B) By searching for an office
   (C) By pointing out her mistakes
   (D) By nominating her for an award

6. According to the man, what is the most important strategy for success?
   (A) Investing in a good sound system
   (B) Having a good business plan
   (C) Eliminating all risk
   (D) Studying the market

PART 4 TALK

Listen to the talk. Then read each question and choose the best answer.

7. What is the topic of the talk?
   (A) Long-term growth plans
   (B) An offer for a leveraged buyout
   (C) How to minimize risk
   (D) Where to borrow funds

8. How will the company fund its growth?
   (A) Bank loans
   (B) Profits
   (C) Sale of stocks
   (D) Owner investment

9. When will the evaluation begin?
   (A) At the end of this year
   (B) At the beginning of next year
   (C) In two years
   (D) In a few years

Reading

PART 5 INCOMPLETE SENTENCES

Choose the word that best completes the sentence.

10. Many problems are _____ if you take the time to create a solid business plan.

(A) avoidable (C) strategic
(B) primary (D) risky

11. I don't want to intrude, but would you like me to _____ how to use that machine?

(A) demonstrate (C) demonstrative
(B) demonstration (D) demonstrator

12. While you are _____ your business plan, it is a good idea to keep a resource library of valuable materials.

(A) develop (C) developing
(B) development (D) developer

13. After you turn in your business plan, you will receive a written _____ of your work within two weeks.

(A) evaluator (C) evaluate
(B) evaluative (D) evaluation

14. If we think _____, we can come up with a plan that promises success.

(A) strategize (C) strategically
(B) strategic (D) strategist

15. If you are not available to chair this month's business association meeting, another member of the committee could _____ for you.

(A) substitute (C) gather
(B) address (D) offer

Memo

To: Stephen Saunders, President
From: Willa Richardson, Marketing Department
Re: Changes in market

In order to address the changes that are currently taking place in the market, I believe we need to modify our business plan. I have been ____ data for the past several months.
16.

The information clearly shows that younger and younger people are becoming interested in purchasing products such as ours. We need to develop a ____ to reach this younger
17.

age group. We need to redirect some of our resources toward this goal. I think if we make this a priority over the next year, we will be able to ____ our position against our
18.

competitors. ____. I would like to share the results of my research with you.
19.

It demonstrates the need to focus our energy toward this younger age group. Please let me know if we can meet this week to discuss it.

16. (A) substituting
    (B) addressing
    (C) avoiding
    (D) gathering

17. (A) strategy
    (B) risk
    (C) demonstration
    (D) substitution

18. (A) strong
    (B) strength
    (C) strengthen
    (D) strengthened

19. (A) We must develop products that are attractive to younger people.
    (B) If we don't, we risk losing the market share that we already have.
    (C) These types of products are primarily of interest to older consumers.
    (D) We offer a greater variety of products than most of our competitors.

PART 7 READING COMPREHENSION

Questions 20–24 refer to the following article.

When developing a plan for a new business, the entrepreneur quite naturally wants to eliminate all risk. While it is impossible to avoid some risk, the goal is to minimize it as much as possible. How can we do this? Thorough research and careful planning are the keys. There are two parts to good research. First, you must demonstrate that there is a need for the product or service you plan to offer. Are there enough people out there who would be willing to pay for it? Second, you must look at your competition. What do you have to offer that your competitors do not? Is your product or service of better quality in some way? Is it cheaper or more easily available? Is there a niche in the market that your competitors are not addressing? If what you have to offer is identical to what your competitors are offering, your business is not likely to be successful. These are some things to consider when evaluating how well you can measure up against the competition. Once you have evaluated a need for your product or service and determined how yours will be different from your competitors', you are ready to begin the next part of your plan—financing.

20. What is this article mostly about?
    (A) Financing new businesses
    (B) How to price products
    (C) The need for research
    (D) The best marketing strategies

21. What does the author say about risk?
    (A) We should try to reduce it.
    (B) We must avoid it.
    (C) We can eliminate it with careful planning.
    (D) It is the key to success.

22. According to the article, what can lead to the failure of a new business?
    (A) Offering a cheaper product
    (B) Selling the exact same product that the competitors sell
    (C) Selling only to a niche in the market
    (D) Offering only services and not products

23. The word *addressing* in line 13 is closest in meaning to
    (A) focusing on.
    (B) calling on.
    (C) giving up.
    (D) staying away from.

24. The word *demonstrate* in line 6 is closest in meaning to
    (A) feel.
    (B) create.
    (C) remove.
    (D) show.

Lesson 5: Conferences

WORDS TO LEARN

- accommodate
- arrangement
- association
- attend
- get in touch
- hold
- location
- overcrowded
- register
- select
- session
- take part in

Study the following definitions and examples.

1. **accommodate** v., to fit; to provide with something needed
   a. The meeting room was large enough to accommodate the various needs of the groups using it.
   b. Because the deadline for reserving rooms was past, the hotel could not accommodate us.
2. **arrangement** n., a plan or organization
   a. The travel arrangements were taken care of by Sara, Mr. Billings's capable assistant.
   b. The arrangement of speakers was alphabetical to avoid any hurt feelings.
3. **association** n., an organization of persons or groups having a common interest; a relationship or society
   a. Membership in a professional association provides business contacts and mutual support.
   b. Because of his association with the conference director, we were able to get good prices for the rooms.
4. **attend** v., to go to; to pay attention to
   a. We expect more than 100 members to attend the annual meeting.
   b. The hotel manager attended to all our needs promptly.
5. **get in touch** v., to make contact with
   a. When we arrive at the hotel, we will get in touch with the manager about the unexpected guests.
   b. The registration desk is a good central location for people to get in touch with each other.
6. **hold** v., to contain; to conduct
   a. This meeting room holds at least 80 people comfortably.
   b. She holds an annual seminar that is very popular.
7. **location** n., a position or site
   a. The location of the meeting was changed from the Red Room to the Green Room.
   b. Disney World is the perfect location for the meeting since members could bring their families.
8. **overcrowded** adj., too crowded
   a. When the guests entered the dining room, Sue could see that the room would become overcrowded.
   b. To avoid being overcrowded, we limited the number of guests that members could bring.
9. **register** n., a record; v., to record
   a. According to the register, more than 250 people attended the afternoon seminar.
   b. Hotels ask all guests to register and give a home address.
10. **select** v., to choose from a group; adj., specially chosen
   a. The conference participant selected the marketing seminar from the various offerings.
   b. The winners were a select group.
11. **session** n., a meeting
   a. The morning sessions tend to fill up first, so sign up early.
   b. Due to the popularity of this course, we will offer two sessions.
12. **take part in** v., to join and participate in
   a. The session is very informal, which makes it easier for people to take part in the discussion.
   b. We could not get enough people to take part in the meeting, so we canceled it.

WORD FAMILIES

verb	accommodate	The hotel staff was able to accommodate our many needs for the conference.
noun	accommodation	The accommodations at the hotel include a swimming pool, gym, and restaurant.
adjective	accommodating	The conference center manager was extremely accommodating and tried to make our stay pleasant.

verb	arrange	We will arrange the chairs in a circle.
noun	arrangement	Nobody could understand the seating arrangement.

verb	associate	Do you think customers will associate the failed upstart with ours?
noun	association	Any association with the former company will put us in a negative light.
adjective	associated	The associated costs will put this project out of our reach.

verb	attend	Gillian attended the reception for visiting ambassadors.
noun	attendee	More than 500 attendees packed the ballroom.
noun	attendance	Attendance was low for this year's annual meeting.

verb	register	You can register for the conference by going to the conference website.
noun	register	The hotel's register showed that only half the attendees had arrived.
noun	registration	Registration is very easy because all the information and forms can be found on the conference website.

verb	select	Since there are overlapping workshops, participants will have to select which one most appeals to them.
noun	selection	His dinner selection of stuffed quail sounded better on the menu than it looked on the plate.
adjective	selective	The planning committee was very selective about who received invitations.

WORDS IN CONTEXT

Read the following passage and write the words in the blanks below.

accommodate	attending	location	select
arrangements	get in touch	overcrowded	sessions
associations	hold	register	take part in

Many (1) ______________ and organizations hold annual conferences so that their members can (2) ______________ with each other and (3) ______________ educational programs. When planning a conference, event coordinators try to have a variety of (4) ______________ so people (5) ______________ can (6) ______________ a workshop or meeting that best suits their needs. When making (7) ______________ for a conference, they look for a site that will (8) ______________ all their needs. They want to (9) ______________ the conference at a place that is large enough for the number of people expected to attend, without the meeting rooms being (10) ______________. Good event coordinators tour the site before making a final decision because brochures cannot show all the necessary details. Having meetings in a fun (11) ______________ can really encourage people to (12) ______________ for the meeting.

WORD PRACTICE

Listening Comprehension

Track 6

PART 1 PHOTO

Look at the picture and listen to the sentences.
Choose the sentence that best describes the picture.

1. Ⓐ Ⓑ Ⓒ Ⓓ

PART 2 QUESTION–RESPONSE

Listen to the question and the three responses. Choose the response that best answers the question.

2. Ⓐ Ⓑ Ⓒ   3. Ⓐ Ⓑ Ⓒ

PART 3 CONVERSATION

Listen to the dialogue. Then read each question and choose the best response.

4. Why are they having difficulty arranging a site for the conference?
   (A) It's a busy time of year.
   (B) They procrastinated.
   (C) Their group is large.
   (D) The coordinator has been sick.

5. When will the conference take place?
   (A) At the end of this month
   (B) Next month
   (C) At the end of this year
   (D) Next year

6. How many people do they expect at the conference?
   (A) Two hundred
   (B) Four hundred
   (C) Five hundred
   (D) Ten hundred

PART 4 TALK

Listen to the talk. Then read each question and choose the best answer.

7. What is the topic of the talk?
   (A) Accommodating people with disabilities
   (B) Legal responsibility for off-site events
   (C) Arranging conferences
   (D) Preparing convention catalogs

8. What is true of the facility belonging to the speaker's company?
   (A) It's inconvenient for those with disabilities.
   (B) It can't accommodate people with hearing loss.
   (C) It is only available for certain types of events.
   (D) It is accessible to people with disabilities.

9. How should attendees request a special interpreter?
   (A) By asking for one at the time of registration
   (B) By getting in touch with the head of the facility
   (C) By registering ahead of the other attendees
   (D) By requesting one when they arrive at a session

Reading

PART 5 INCOMPLETE SENTENCES

Choose the word that best completes the sentence.

10. The banquet room can _____ up to 750 people for dinner.

    (A) select
    (B) hold
    (C) attend
    (D) arrange

11. Helen made the final _____ for use of the conference room with the hotel's general manager.

    (A) arranging
    (B) arrange
    (C) arrangement
    (D) arranged

12. For most people, Samco is _____ with computer chip production.

    (A) associate
    (B) associated
    (C) associating
    (D) association

13. We expect that fewer guests will _____ the evening gala.

    (A) attend
    (B) attending
    (C) attention
    (D) attendance

14. The association's members were asked to _____ for the special session well in advance because space in the lecture hall was limited.

    (A) register
    (B) accommodate
    (C) crowd
    (D) attend

15. By adding more class _____, the staff was able to please more members.

    (A) select
    (B) selective
    (C) selecting
    (D) selections

PART 6 TEXT COMPLETION

All members of the Countywide Small Business Owners Association are invited to take part in our annual conference, to be held on March 31 at the Grand Hotel in Marysville.

The conference begins at 8:30 A.M. with an address by this year's guest, Cynthia Quinn, owner of Designs by Cynthia, Inc., and winner of numerous business and community awards. Morning small group sessions begin at 9:30. Attendees can ____ (16.) a variety of sessions including Financing Your New Business; Selecting the Best Location; and Formulas for Success. Lunch will be served at 12:30, followed by afternoon small group sessions at 2:00.

This is the Association's most popular event, so ____ (17.) early to assure your place. Complete the registration form and make your payment at *csboa.com/conference_reg* before March 1. Follow the same link to arrange your overnight ____ (18.) at the Grand Hotel and receive the special conference discount price. ____ (19.).

16. (A) take part in
    (B) arrange
    (C) locate
    (D) get in touch

17. (A) will register
    (B) must register
    (C) registering
    (D) register

18. (A) accommodate
    (B) accommodating
    (C) accommodations
    (D) accommodates

19. (A) At the same time, you can let the hotel know if you are interested in sharing a room with another conference attendee.
    (B) It is common practice for hotels to offer discounts to those attending local conferences.
    (C) The Grand Hotel is a good location for a conference as it has many rooms in which sessions can be held.
    (D) The hotel café serves breakfast until 10:00 am and offers a wide selection of pastries and other breakfast options.

PART 7 READING COMPREHENSION

Questions 20–24 refer to the following two e-mails.

To: Max Sullivan
From: Martha Reynolds
Subj: Conference

Max,

I have been working on the arrangements for our upcoming conference. I've looked into the City Convention Center, and I think it is the most convenient location. It is close to public transportation and hotels. The accommodations are also excellent. The rooms are large, and we can reserve up to ten meeting rooms. However, the price is almost 50% more than we agreed we could spend. The other choice is the Mayfield Hotel. Many associations hold their conventions there. It is a nice place, and the price is reasonable. However, it is not close to the subway. Also, it is much smaller than the Convention Center. I think we could only get three meeting rooms. Would that be enough? Please get in touch with me today to let me know what you think. I need to reserve a place soon.

Martha

To: Martha Reynolds
From: Max Sullivan
Subj: Re: Conference

Martha,

In regard to selecting a location for the conference, I think the Convention Center is better than the Mayfield Hotel. The hotel is much too small. Remember, we plan to hold at least five sessions at a time. We couldn't do that at the hotel. We expect more people to take part in the convention this year, so it is important to have a space that can accommodate everyone. About the price, I think we can rearrange the budget a bit in order to be able to pay for it. So go ahead and reserve the space at the Convention Center.

Max

20. What are these e-mails about?
    (A) The date of the conference
    (B) The conference site
    (C) The topics of the conference sessions
    (D) The number of conference attendees

21. How many meeting rooms will they need?
    (A) Only three
    (B) At least five
    (C) Up to ten
    (D) Almost 50

22. What does Max prefer about the Convention Center?
    (A) The price
    (B) The location
    (C) The size
    (D) The people

23. The words *get in touch* in line 16 of the first e-mail are closest in meaning to
    (A) offer.
    (B) discuss.
    (C) provide.
    (D) contact.

24. The word *selecting* in line 1 of the second e-mail is closest in meaning to
    (A) choosing.
    (B) reserving.
    (C) comparing.
    (D) seeking.

WORD REVIEW #1
LESSONS 1–5 GENERAL BUSINESS

Choose the word that best completes the sentence.

1. Although negotiating a new contract was complicated, both parties came to an ______ that satisfied them.

   (A) address
   (B) engagement
   (C) agreement
   (D) implication

2. The local business ______ was formed as a way for local business owners to help and learn from each other.

   (A) accommodation
   (B) location
   (C) market
   (D) association

3. When the family decided to open a restaurant, they had to find a ______ that would attract business.

   (A) locate
   (B) locator
   (C) locating
   (D) location

4. A ______ company will honor the terms set forth in its warranty.

   (A) repute
   (B) reputedly
   (C) reputation
   (D) reputable

5. The goal of marketing is to ______ customers, to persuade them to buy a product or service.

   (A) attract
   (B) specify
   (C) compare
   (D) consume

6. Once both parties have agreed to a contract, they have also agreed to abide by every ______ provision.

   (A) specify
   (B) specific
   (C) specification
   (D) specificity

7. Good business planning includes developing an overall ______, addressing likely objections, and demonstrating why potential buyers need the product or service.

   (A) strategy
   (B) strategic
   (C) strategically
   (D) strategize

8. When you register for out-of-town conferences, make room ______ as soon as you decide to attend.

   (A) accommodate
   (B) accommodations
   (C) accommodating
   (D) accommodated

9. Marketers must avoid making promises they can't keep while they ______ the quality of their product or service.

   (A) demonstrate
   (B) demonstration
   (C) demonstrative
   (D) demonstrable

10. A consultant must adhere carefully to his contract if he wants to ______ a good business reputation.

    (A) establish
    (B) establishment
    (C) established
    (D) establishing

Choose the one word or phrase that best completes each sentence.

Are you looking for a place __________ your next conference? The Littleton Convention Center offers a

11. (A) to register
    (B) to provide
    (C) to assure
    (D) to hold

convenient location at an affordable price. Whether your event is big or small, our site can accommodate your needs. We offer meeting rooms, several auditoriums, and a large exhibition hall. Catering services are also available. Get __________ touch with us at 555-0964 to make arrangements for your event. We know

12. (A) on
    (B) in
    (C) at
    (D) to

you'll __________ with our services.

13. (A) satisfy
    (B) satisfied
    (C) be satisfied
    (D) be satisfying

Smart __________ compare prices before they buy. That's why nine out of ten shoppers

14. (A) attenders
    (B) consumers
    (C) competitors
    (D) developers

choose Star Brand household cleaning products. Star Brand products are the most efficient cleaning products around. They can clean even the toughest stains and dirt because they are __________ with bleach. Every Star Brand

15. (A) strengthened
    (B) strengths
    (C) strongly
    (D) strong

product comes with the company promise: If you are not 100% satisfied, your money will be returned with no questions asked. Next time you are shopping for cleaning products, __________ Star Brand. We know you'll be happy you did.

16. (A) consideration
    (B) considering
    (C) consider
    (D) considers

When purchasing a new appliance, check to make sure that a warranty is included. This __________ important protection to you, the consumer. If you decide to return a product

17. (A) offer
    (B) offers
    (C) are offering
    (D) have offered

that is under warranty, you will have __________ that any damage was not caused by

18. (A) demonstration
    (B) demonstrative
    (C) demonstrator
    (D) to demonstrate

misuse or mishandling. Also, make certain that you return a damaged product before the warranty __________. Companies do not have to accept products that are returned

19. (A) inspires
    (B) implies
    (C) expires
    (D) persuades

after the date stated in the warranty.

Lesson 6: Computers and the Internet

WORDS TO LEARN

- access
- allocate
- compatible
- delete
- display
- duplicate
- failure
- figure out
- ignore
- search
- shut down
- warning

Study the following definitions and examples.

1. **access** n., the ability or right to enter or use; v., to obtain; to gain entry
   a. You can't gain access to the files unless you know the password.
   b. We accessed the information on the company's website.
2. **allocate** v., to designate for a specific purpose
   a. The office manager did not allocate enough money to purchase software.
   b. We will need to allocate more space on the website for advertising.
3. **compatible** adj., able to function together
   a. This operating system is not compatible with this model computer.
   b. Users of software applications want new versions to be compatible with current versions.
4. **delete** v., to remove; to erase
   a. The technicians deleted all the data on the disk accidentally.
   b. This button on the keyboard deletes the characters from the screen.
5. **display** n., what is visible on a monitor; v., to show
   a. The light on the LCD display is too weak.
   b. The webpage does not display secure information such as passwords and credit card numbers.
6. **duplicate** v., to produce something equal; to make identical
   a. I think the new word processing program will duplicate the success of the one introduced last year.
   b. Duplicate the file and save it in another place.
7. **failure** n., an unsuccessful work or effort
   a. Your failure to inform us about the changed password cost the company a day's work.
   b. The repeated failure of her printer baffled the technician.
8. **figure out** v., to understand; to solve
   a. By examining all of the errors, the technicians figured out how to fix the problem.
   b. We figured out that it would take us at least ten minutes to download the file.
9. **ignore** v., not to notice; to disregard
   a. When the director is working at the computer, she ignores everything around her.
   b. Don't ignore the technician's advice when connecting cables.
10. **search** n., investigation; v., to look for
    a. Our search of the database produced very little information.
    b. If you search the Internet, I'm sure you'll find all the information you need.
11. **shut down** v., to turn off; to cease operations
    a. Please shut down the computer before you leave.
    b. We decided to shut down the blog after receiving so many bad comments.
12. **warning** n., an alert to danger or problems
    a. The red flashing light gives a warning to users that the battery is low.
    b. Flashing images on a webpage are warnings to attract users' attention.

WORD FAMILIES

verb	access	In many cafés you can access the Internet free of charge.
noun	access	You need a password to gain access to the online database.
adjective	accessible	Some people are so busy that they are accessible only by e-mail.

verb	allocate	Maria didn't allocate enough time to train the new staff members on our computer system.
noun	allocation	We need to change our allocation of resources so that we can spend more money on building our website.
adjective	allocated	The allocated money was never spent on new computers.

verb	duplicate	As we introduce this year's new line of products, we hope to duplicate the success we had with last year's products.
noun	duplicate	You should delete all duplicates from your computer.
noun	duplication	We want our website to be completely original and to avoid the duplication of sites that are already online.

verb	fail	We failed to tell you that your records were deleted.
noun	failure	The power failure caused the system to shut down.
adjective	fallible	Everyone can make a mistake. Even a computer is fallible.

verb	ignore	Unfortunately, she ignored the warning about the virus.
noun	ignorance	His ignorance of this word processing program surprised everyone.
adjective	ignorant	Tom was ignorant of the decision to change passwords and couldn't understand why he was unable to log into his account.

verb	warn	We were warned that our e-mail was not private.
noun	warning	The warning was written on the box.
adjective	warning	The warning signs were all there; we should have paid attention to them.

WORDS IN CONTEXT

Read the following passage and write the words in the blanks below.

access	deleted	failed	search
allocate	display	figure out	shut down
compatible	duplicate	ignore	warning

When I try to (1) _______________ my computer, a (2) _______________ pops up that says "Low Memory." From there, I can't (3) _______________ what to do. The computer won't let me (4) _______________ any of my files, so I can't (5) _______________ for those that I could delete. I've already (6) _______________ all of my (7) _______________ files, and I can't believe that my remaining files are using up so much memory. I'd be happy to (8) _______________ the computer's warning, but I have no option, since the (9) _______________ is frozen on this message. Do you think I've (10) _______________ to understand something about the operations of this computer? If you can, would you please (11) _______________ a few minutes in your busy schedule to help me solve this dilemma? As I said before, I'm sure that my software is (12) _______________ and is not the source of this problem.

WORD PRACTICE

Listening Comprehension

Track 7

PART 1 PHOTO

Look at the picture and listen to the sentences. Choose the sentence that best describes the picture.

1. Ⓐ Ⓑ Ⓒ Ⓓ

PART 2 QUESTION–RESPONSE

Listen to the question and the three responses. Choose the response that best answers the question.

2. Ⓐ Ⓑ Ⓒ   3. Ⓐ Ⓑ Ⓒ

PART 3 CONVERSATION

Listen to the dialogue. Then read each question and choose the best response.

4. What happens when the man tries to access his e-mail?
   (A) The computer shuts down.
   (B) A warning appears on the screen.
   (C) He hears a beeping noise.
   (D) The screen turns black.

5. What will the man do now?
   (A) Turn off the computer
   (B) Get a new monitor
   (C) Use a different program
   (D) Wait some more time

6. What does the woman suggest doing?
   (A) Working harder
   (B) Taking the computer back to the store
   (C) Calling someone to fix the computer
   (D) Ignoring the problem

PART 4 TALK

Listen to the talk. Then read each question and choose the best answer.

7. What does the speaker suggest that listeners do?
   (A) Buy her software
   (B) Read the manual
   (C) Figure out the program by tinkering with it
   (D) Consult the competitor's manual to check for compatibility

8. What problems could users face?
   (A) Their warranties could be invalidated.
   (B) Their warning systems could malfunction.
   (C) Their computers could shut down without warning.
   (D) Their manuals could be inaccurate.

9. What does the speaker recommend doing with files?
   (A) Reading them
   (B) Accessing them
   (C) Deleting them
   (D) Copying them

Reading

PART 5 INCOMPLETE SENTENCES

Choose the word that best completes the sentence.

10. In order to _____ your e-mail messages, you must type in your password.

(A) access
(B) accessible
(C) accessed
(D) accessibility

11. Too many of our staff are having problems using this software, so we need to _____ more funds for training.

(A) search
(B) allocate
(C) delete
(D) ignore

12. The computer staff is responsible for making sure all system files are _____.

(A) duplication
(B) duplicated
(C) duplicator
(D) duplicate

13. _____ to maintain the website is the main reason why sales are down.

(A) Fail
(B) Failure
(C) Failed
(D) Fallible

14. She _____ the warning that the hard drive was full, and consequently they were unable to save the test data.

(A) ignore
(B) ignored
(C) ignoring
(D) ignorant

15. The computer will _____ you to save your work before quitting.

(A) warning
(B) warned
(C) warn
(D) warns

PART 6 TEXT COMPLETION

MEMO

To: All Office Staff
From: IT Department
Re: Avoiding Computer Problems

We are here to help you with any problems you may have with your computer. Please make our job easier by observing the following guidelines.

- If you have problems seeing the ____ (16.), check to make sure that your monitor is turned on.
- If your computer crashes, write down any warning message that appears. We can ____ (17.) a problem more easily if we have this information.
- ____ (18.). Some software is not compatible with what is already on the computer and can cause problems.
- Some parts of the company website are ____ (19.) without a password. If you need a password, please let us know and we will assign you one.

16. (A) keyboard
    (B) display
    (C) printer
    (D) controls

17. (A) figure out
    (B) ignore
    (C) warn
    (D) fail

18. (A) Please let us know if you need help learning how to use any of your software programs.
    (B) Software training workshops are available through the Human Resources department.
    (C) We plan to install new software over the course of the coming week.
    (D) Please do not install any new software without our approval.

19. (A) accesses
    (B) accessing
    (C) accessible
    (D) inaccessible

PART 7 READING COMPREHENSION

Questions 20–24 refer to the following note.

Jim,

I have decided to get a new computer for my home office, and I need your advice to help me select the right one. I have allocated a certain amount of money from my budget for this. I think it is enough for a completely new system including computer, monitor, printer, and scanner. I would like to continue using the software I already use, so I need a system that is compatible with my current system and software. However, I think I should get a different brand. I have had nothing but trouble with the computer I have now. It often shuts down without warning, and sometimes I can't access my files. I haven't been able to figure out the reason for these problems, and no one has been able to fix it for me.

I plan to go to some stores this Saturday and Sunday to search for my new computer. Would you be able to go with me? If not, I'll call you before the weekend to get your advice. I have a big project coming up next month, so I would like to get my new computer up and running soon. Let me know if you can help me this weekend.

Janet

20. What does Janet want Jim to help her with?
    (A) Finding money to buy a computer
    (B) Accessing her files
    (C) Choosing a new computer
    (D) Repairing her computer

21. What does Janet plan to do this weekend?
    (A) Call Jim
    (B) Go on a date with Jim
    (C) Look for a new computer
    (D) Figure out the reason for her problems

22. When will Janet's big project begin?
    (A) Saturday
    (B) Sunday
    (C) Before the weekend
    (D) Next month

23. The word *allocated* in line 3 is closest in meaning to
    (A) earned.
    (B) designated.
    (C) borrowed.
    (D) removed.

24. The word *access* in line 11 is closest in meaning to
    (A) save.
    (B) write.
    (C) close.
    (D) open.

Lesson 7: Office Technology

WORDS TO LEARN

- affordable
- as needed
- capacity
- durable
- in charge
- initiative
- physically
- provider
- recur
- reduction
- stay on top of
- stock

Study the following definitions and examples.

1. **affordable** adj., able to be paid for; not too expensive
   a. The company's first priority was to find an affordable phone system.
   b. Obviously, the computer systems that are affordable for a Fortune 500 company will not be affordable for a small company.
2. **as needed** adv., as necessary
   a. The courier service did not come every day, only as needed.
   b. The service contract states that repairs will be made as needed.
3. **capacity** n., the ability to contain or hold; the maximum that something can hold or do
   a. We need a room with the capacity to hold two photocopiers and shelves for paper and other supplies.
   b. The memory requirements of this software application exceed the capacity of our computers.
4. **durable** adj., sturdy, strong, lasting
   a. This printer is so durable that, with a little care, it will last another five years.
   b. The phone is very durable; I've dropped it several times and it still works well.
5. **in charge** adj., in control
   a. He appointed someone to be in charge of maintaining a supply of paper in the fax machine.
   b. Your computer should not be in charge of you, rather you should be in charge of your computer.
6. **initiative** n., the first step; an active role
   a. Employees are encouraged to take the initiative to discuss their technology needs with management.
   b. Our technology initiative involves a new database that will help revolutionize our customer service.
7. **physically** adv., with the senses; of the body
   a. The computer screen is making her physically sick.
   b. Physically moving your screen from one place on the desk to another can help reduce same-position-strain syndrome.
8. **provider** n., a supplier
   a. The department was extremely pleased with the service they received from the phone provider.
   b. We need to find a new provider of supplies for our photocopier.
9. **recur** v., to occur again or repeatedly
   a. The need for repairs to the photocopier recurs too often.
   b. The managers did not want that particular error to recur.
10. **reduction** n., a lessening; a decrease
    a. The outlet store gave a 20 percent reduction in the price of the shelves and bookcases.
    b. The reduction in office staff has made it necessary to automate more job functions.
11. **stay on top of** v., to know what is going on; to know the latest information
    a. It's important to stay on top of supplies for the printers and reorder them before they run out.
    b. In this industry, you must stay on top of current developments.
12. **stock** v., to keep on hand; n., a supply
    a. Please stock the shelves with a large supply of ink and paper for the printers.
    b. The office's stock of toner for the photocopier was quickly running out.

WORD FAMILIES

verb	afford	Our office really needs new printers, but we can't afford to buy them this year.
noun	affordability	We looked into the affordability of buying a photocopier with a larger capacity.
adjective	affordable	A lot of office technology that was expensive in the past has now become more affordable.

verb	initiate	The company will initiate the use of smartphones this year.
noun	initiative	The manager, knowing how concerned his employees were, took the initiative to provide training for them on the new equipment.
noun	initiation	The initiation of the new computer system was welcomed by the entire office staff.

noun	physique	Moving all that office equipment around will certainly help you develop a good physique.
adjective	physical	The physical presence of a computer engineer is much better than telephone tech support.
adverb	physically	Sitting at a computer all day may help you get your work done, but it isn't good for you physically.

verb	provide	The company provides a five-year warranty on its products.
noun	provider	As your provider of network services, I promise to give you the best prices and service.
noun	provision	Our provisions of supplies should last to the end of the quarter.

verb	recur	We don't want that problem to recur every month.
noun	recurrence	Every recurrence of the same problem costs us money.
adjective	recurring	Recurring problems waste time and money.

verb	reduce	Buying in bulk can help to reduce costs.
noun	reduction	Disconnecting the fax machine created a noticeable reduction in phone bills.
adjective	reducible	Although our system is working at capacity, the amount of information being processed is not reducible.

WORDS IN CONTEXT

Read the following passage and write the words in the blanks below.

affordable	durable	physical	reduce
as needed	in charge	provider	stays on top of
capacity	initiates	recurring	stock

Many companies have one person or a department that is (1) ______________ of running the office. If you have ever worked for a company that doesn't have an office manager, you very quickly learn to appreciate the importance of the job. Who is in charge of placing orders? Who services the fax machine or printer? Who makes sure that the office is presentable for customers? Are the new conference tables and shelves (2) ______________ enough to withstand heavy use? Are they (3) ______________ for the office budget?

It is the office manager's responsibility to maintain an efficient and smooth-running office. He or she looks for ways to (4) ______________ costs and minimize interruptions in the day-to-day operations. Whereas functional managers know the (5) ______________ of their employees, the office manager knows the (6) ______________ capacity of the office and the supplies and machines that are in the office.

The office manager (7) ______________ the ordering of furniture and supplies, and (8) ______________ changing office technology. Over time, he or she may notice (9) ______________ problems that require changing a service (10) ______________. Furniture and large items are ordered (11) ______________. Other frequently used materials, such as paper, folders, and mailing materials, are on an automatic ordering schedule and a (12) ______________ of those supplies is on hand at the office.

WORD PRACTICE

Listening Comprehension

Track 8

PART 1 PHOTO

Look at the picture and listen to the sentences. Choose the sentence that best describes the picture.

1. Ⓐ Ⓑ Ⓒ Ⓓ

PART 2 QUESTION–RESPONSE

Listen to the question and the three responses. Choose the response that best answers the question.

2. Ⓐ Ⓑ Ⓒ   3. Ⓐ Ⓑ Ⓒ

PART 3 CONVERSATION

Listen to the dialogue. Then read each question and choose the best response.

4. What is required for all new purchases?
   (A) A receipt
   (B) A charge card
   (C) Up-front payment
   (D) Approval

5. What is the purpose of this requirement?
   (A) To avoid delays
   (B) To help save money
   (C) To make purchasing a top priority
   (D) To reduce steps in the ordering process

6. What is the woman's opinion of this requirement?
   (A) It's annoying.
   (B) It's enjoyable.
   (C) It's a good idea.
   (D) It's boring.

PART 4 TALK

Listen to the talk. Then read each question and choose the best answer.

7. Why don't they order units on an as-needed basis?
   (A) They're more expensive.
   (B) The provider won't take individual orders.
   (C) Delivery time is too long.
   (D) Nobody takes the initiative to place the order.

8. What kind of provider could help them?
   (A) A less pushy provider
   (B) A more aggressive provider
   (C) One with better prices
   (D) One with a website

9. What does the speaker like about the suggested company's products?
   (A) The durability
   (B) The quality
   (C) The price
   (D) The size

Reading

PART 5 INCOMPLETE SENTENCES

Choose the word that best completes the sentence.

10. This copier is priced within our budget, but it doesn't have the ______ to handle large jobs.
    (A) stock
    (B) provisions
    (C) affordability
    (D) capacity

11. The office manager took the ______ to order more printers without discussing the matter with his boss.
    (A) initiated
    (B) initiating
    (C) initiative
    (D) initiation

12. This phone has more capacity than my old one even though its ______ size is actually smaller.
    (A) physical
    (B) physique
    (C) physicality
    (D) physically

13. As promised in our last meeting, this contract ______ you with the best prices.
    (A) provide
    (B) provides
    (C) provision
    (D) provider

14. We have to get a more ______ machine, as this one always seems to be in need of repairs.
    (A) as needed
    (B) recurring
    (C) in charge
    (D) durable

15. The employee preferred to have a ______ in salary than to have to continue working with her outdated computer.
    (A) reducing
    (B) reduction
    (C) reduce
    (D) reduces

Memo

To: Miriam Ketonen, Office Manager
From: Jason Roberts, Assistant Office Manager
Re: Photocopier

There have been recurring problems with the office photocopier, particularly with paper jams. I believe the problem is with the type of machine we have. A machine of this size simply does not have the capacity to handle the amount of copying we normally do. Obviously we can't ___ (16.) the number of copies we make. I suggest that it's time to order a larger and ___ (17.) machine. I have looked through the catalogs and discovered several that I think would suit our needs. I have selected the most ___ (18.) ones, as I know we have a limited amount of money to spend. I have attached their descriptions. ___ (19.). Therefore, I will need your approval before I go ahead and place the order. Let me know which of the machines you think is best, and I will fill out the purchase order.

Thanks.

16. (A) reduce
    (B) recur
    (C) stock
    (D) initiate

17. (A) durable
    (B) durables
    (C) more durable
    (D) most durable

18. (A) costly
    (B) physical
    (C) attractive
    (D) affordable

19. (A) A durable machine would mean fewer breakdowns leading to interruption of work.
    (B) They all have the capacity to handle the amount of copying we do.
    (C) You are the one in charge of making large purchases like this.
    (D) I am really getting tired of this recurring problem.

PART 7 READING COMPREHENSION

Questions 20–24 refer to the following two letters.

Business Kitchens, Inc.

April 19, 20—

Dear Mr. Conner,

I am writing to follow up on our conversation of last Monday. You said you were looking for a new provider for kitchen supplies for your office, and that your particular need at this time was for a large-capacity coffeemaker. I have looked through the coffeemakers we have available, and believe I have found the best one to suit your needs. The primary advantage of the 300X Office Coffeemaker is that it reduces mess. The coffeemaker is filled with water daily. Then, to make a cup of coffee, the user simply inserts a premeasured package of coffee into the machine and presses the "on" button. The coffee is ready in one minute. There are no pots to clean or filters to change. The machine can make tea and other hot drinks as well. The 300X is also the most durable machine on the market.

I am enclosing a description of the machine and price information. We can also deliver refills of coffee and tea to you on a weekly or monthly basis. In addition, we stock other kitchen appliances such as microwave ovens and office-sized refrigerators. Please let me know if you are interested in purchasing such items.

Sincerely,

Laura Baker

Laura Baker
Sales Manager

Johnson Research Affiliates

April 26, 20—

Dear Ms. Baker,

Thank you for the information on the 300X Office Coffeemaker. I think it will meet our needs for large-capacity coffeemakers at an affordable price. Our office is large, so I would like to order two at this time. I don't think we will need the regular deliveries of coffee and tea. Our use of these varies so much from week to week that it is better to order them as needed. My assistant is good at staying on top of these things, so we don't have to worry about running out. Currently we don't have a need for ovens or refrigerators although we may in the near future. I will keep you informed. Meanwhile, we will send you a purchase order for the coffeemakers. Thank you for your help.

Sincerely,

Matthew Conner

Matthew Conner
Office Manager

20. What will Mr. Conner buy now?
    (A) Coffeemakers
    (B) Ovens
    (C) Microcomputers
    (D) Refrigerators

21. What does he say that he likes about the product he has selected?
    (A) It reduces mess.
    (B) It is durable.
    (C) It is not expensive.
    (D) It will be delivered regularly.

22. How often will he order refills?
    (A) Once a day
    (B) Once a week
    (C) Every month
    (D) When he needs them

23. The word *provider* in line 2 of the first letter is closest in meaning to
    (A) consumer.
    (B) supplier.
    (C) maker.
    (D) designer.

24. The word *stock* in line 17 of the first letter is closest in meaning to
    (A) have.
    (B) repair.
    (C) buy.
    (D) use.

Lesson 8: Office Procedures

WORDS TO LEARN

- appreciation
- bring in
- casually
- code
- expose
- glimpse
- made of
- out of
- outdated
- practice
- reinforce
- verbally

Study the following definitions and examples.

1. **appreciation** n., recognition; understanding; thanks
   a. In appreciation of your hard work, the department will hold a lunch party on November third.
   b. Your appreciation of my efforts inspired me through the final stages of the construction.
2. **bring in** v., to hire or recruit; to cause to appear
   a. The company president wanted to bring in an efficiency consultant.
   b. The company brought in a new team of project planners.
3. **casually** adv., informally
   a. On Fridays, most employees dress casually.
   b. Martin spoke casually, as if he were chatting with friends.
4. **code** n., rules of behavior
   a. The new employees observed the unwritten code of conduct in their first week on the job.
   b. Even the most traditional companies are changing their dress code to something less formal.
5. **expose** v., to make aware; to give experience
   a. Mergers require that employees be exposed to different business practices.
   b. The new hires' week in each department exposed them to the various functions in the company.
6. **glimpse** n., a quick look
   a. I haven't met the new client yet, but I caught a glimpse of her as she was leaving the office.
   b. After one year with the company, he still felt he had only a glimpse of the overall operations.
7. **made of** v., consisting of; produced from
   a. This job will really test what you are made of.
   b. People say that the negotiator has nerves made of steel.
8. **outdated** adj., obsolete; not currently in use
   a. The purpose of the seminar is to have employees identify outdated methods and procedures.
   b. Before you do a mailing, make sure that none of the addresses is outdated.
9. **practice** n., method of doing something; v., to repeat in order to learn
   a. The manager started her practice of weekly breakfast meetings more than twenty years ago.
   b. Bill practiced answering the office telephone until he felt he could do it right.
10. **reinforce** v., to strengthen; support
    a. The financial officer's unconventional method of analyzing data was reinforced by the business journal article.
    b. Employees reinforced their learning with practice in the workplace.
11. **run out of** v., to use up; to no longer have
    a. Orders should be placed before you run out of the supplies.
    b. The presenter ran out of time before he reached his conclusion.
12. **verbally** adv., in spoken form
    a. She verbally reprimanded the new hire in front of his entire team.
    b. The guarantee was made only verbally.

WORD FAMILIES

verb	appreciate	We appreciate the time that you have put into this project, but we need to see more positive results.
noun	appreciation	In appreciation for your hard work, we are giving you a top-priority project.
adjective	appreciative	Everyone was appreciative of the intern's assistance.

noun	casualness	Her boss was unhappy with the casualness of her manner.
adjective	casual	The casual atmosphere at the office made everyone feel relaxed.
adverb	casually	The office dress code allows people to dress casually on Fridays.

verb	expose	As a matter of company policy, we try to expose all managers to the challenging work of telephone sales through hands-on experience.
noun	exposure	Exposure to the elements will corrode the container for the sensor.
adjective	exposed	Mr. Lee was exposed to Chinese business practices during his three-year assignment as a manager in Beijing.

verb	practice	All managers are expected to practice caution in their spending until the end of the year.
noun	practice	He was surprised at the difference in office practices from one local office to another.
adjective	practical	We need a practical solution to this common problem.

verb	reinforce	Reading the employee handbook will reinforce your understanding of office procedures.
noun	reinforcement	All employees need reinforcement from their supervisor.
adjective	reinforceable	The company dress code is reinforceable only if the managers follow it themselves.

verb	verbalize	Well-established procedures are often difficult to verbalize.
adverb	verbally	No employees should be verbally reprimanded in front of their peers.
adjective	verbal	They had a verbal agreement, but there was no written contract.

WORDS IN CONTEXT

Read the following passage and write the words in the blanks below.

appreciation	casually	made of	practices
been exposed to	code	ran out of	reinforced
brought in	glimpse	outdated	verbalize

How many employees show any (1) ______________ for their corporate culture? How many executives appreciate what their corporate culture is and what it is (2) ______________? It is often (3) ______________ by the office procedures and routines that have been established over the years. A manager made her mark twenty years ago by dressing (4) ______________, thereby forever changing the dress (5) ______________. A director bought from the competition when he (6) ______________ stock and the practice soon became standard. These examples add to a company's culture.

Good employees know what the standard procedures are. This is an important element in recruiting new employees, as well as training workers. When training workers, it is often important to have them read the procedures, write their reactions, and (7) ______________ their opinions about these practices. This promotes a sense of cooperation between those who establish the (8) ______________ and those who must follow them.

Employees who have been with a company for many years may not be able to identify (9) ______________ practices because they haven't (10) ______________ anything else. What happens when a department needs an extra hand? Is a "temp" (11) ______________, or is someone borrowed from another department? The new recruits often ask the questions that allow more senior employees to get a (12) ______________ of the corporate culture.

WORD PRACTICE

Listening Comprehension

Track 9

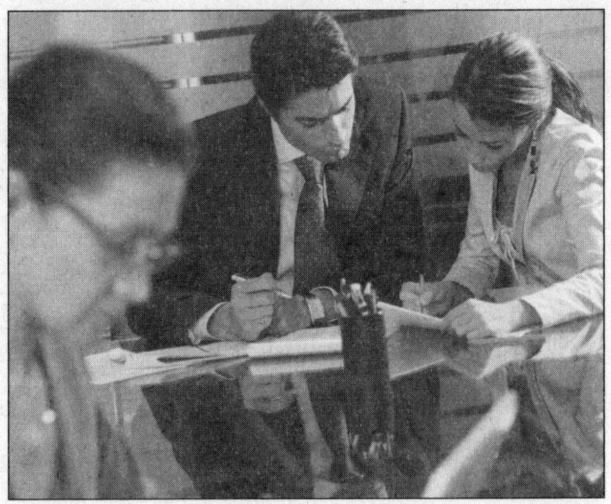

PART 1 PHOTO

Look at the picture and listen to the sentences. Choose the sentence that best describes the picture.

1. Ⓐ Ⓑ Ⓒ Ⓓ

PART 2 QUESTION–RESPONSE

Listen to the question and the three responses. Choose the response that best answers the question.

2. Ⓐ Ⓑ Ⓒ   3. Ⓐ Ⓑ Ⓒ

PART 3 CONVERSATION

Listen to the dialogue. Then read each question and choose the best response.

4. What will the woman tell the man about?
   (A) Hiring policies
   (B) Company practices
   (C) How to make a schedule
   (D) The employee's communication problems

5. What problem has the man had?
   (A) No one can explain things to him clearly.
   (B) He never has time for anything.
   (C) No one has time to talk to him.
   (D) He isn't familiar with his coworkers.

6. How does the woman suggest he reinforce their discussion?
   (A) By talking to other employees
   (B) By practicing what he hears
   (C) By reviewing the schedule
   (D) By looking at the handbook

PART 4 TALK

Listen to the talk. Then read each question and choose the best answer.

7. Who is the speaker?
   (A) A software trainer
   (B) A hardware salesman
   (C) A new computer owner
   (D) A scientist from R&D

8. What will they do today?
   (A) Choose new software
   (B) Review their computer skills
   (C) Hire a specialist
   (D) Take apart the CPU

9. What will they do after the speaker finishes?
   (A) Spend a lot of time practicing
   (B) Watch a television program
   (C) Have lunch
   (D) Attend a board meeting

Reading

PART 5 INCOMPLETE SENTENCES

Choose the word that best completes the sentence.

10. Ms. Handa was unable to express her _____ for all that her colleagues had done for her.

(A) appreciation (C) appreciating
(B) appreciated (D) appreciates

11. Roger made a mistake when he greeted the client so _____.

(A) casual (C) causality
(B) casually (D) casualness

12. _____ to more experienced staff members helps new employees learn the procedures.

(A) Expose (C) Exposing
(B) Exposure (D) Will expose

13. I have only had a quick _____ of the document but will read it more thoroughly tonight.

(A) code (C) casualness
(B) practice (D) glimpse

14. Human Resources tries to _____ employees' understanding by offering workshops twice a year.

(A) reinforce (C) reinforced
(B) reinforcing (D) reinforcement

15. The use of formal forms of address, such as "Sir" and "Madam," may be considered _____ in more modern workplaces.

(A) verbal (C) exposed
(B) outdated (D) casual

NOTICE—CASUAL FRIDAYS

A number of staff members have expressed an interest in Casual Friday. I realize that this custom ____ in many offices nowadays. I appreciate the fact that many of you
16.

have discussed this matter with me ____, and pointed out that our strict dress
17.

code is outdated. Because so many people have expressed an interest in dressing casually once a week, we will have Casual Friday in this office starting next week. While we want to be relaxed, we do not want to ____ our coworkers to styles of
18.

dress that may make them feel uncomfortable. ____. Shoes and shirts are required,
19.

and beach and gym attire are unacceptable.

Amanda Jones, Director

16. (A) practices
    (B) practiced
    (C) is practiced
    (D) is practicing

17. (A) verb
    (B) verbal
    (C) verbally
    (D) verbalize

18. (A) expose
    (B) practice
    (C) reinforce
    (D) appreciate

19. (A) Nobody minds if you wear outdated styles of clothing.
    (B) Please remember to dress comfortably and for the weather.
    (C) Everyone has their own taste in clothing and their own way of dressing.
    (D) So, while the dress code will be relaxed, it does not mean that you can wear anything you want.

PART 7 READING COMPREHENSION

Questions 20–24 refer to the following article.

When you bring in a new employee, it is important to make sure that he or she understands the usual office procedures as well as the codes of behavior. These things should be outlined clearly in the employee handbook. New employees should understand that they are expected to do more than just glimpse at the handbook and then hide it in a drawer. A thorough reading of it will help them understand many things they need to know about the workplace culture. Employees also appreciate verbal reinforcement. Supervisors should let them know when they have completed a job well, or if they are bending the rules too far. More experienced coworkers can be asked to support new employees while they are getting used to their new positions and explain procedures to them, but ultimately it is the supervisor's responsibility to make sure that the normal office practices are carried out. When everyone understands what is expected, then the office procedures run more smoothly. In fact, it is not a bad idea to review the codes and procedures with the entire staff from time to time. This can be done on a regular basis at staff meetings, or it can be part of a training session.

20. What should new employees do with the handbook?
    - (A) Read it quickly.
    - (B) Study it completely.
    - (C) Hide it in a drawer.
    - (D) Share it with coworkers.

21. What should the supervisor do when an employee breaks a rule?
    - (A) Punish her
    - (B) Fire her
    - (C) Tell her
    - (D) Retrain her

22. How can experienced coworkers help new employees?
    - (A) By writing a new handbook
    - (B) By explaining office procedures
    - (C) By inviting them to staff meetings
    - (D) By telling the supervisor when a rule has been broken

23. The words *bring in* in line 1 are closest in meaning to
    - (A) invite.
    - (B) train.
    - (C) hire.
    - (D) meet.

24. The word *codes* in line 3 is closest in meaning to
    - (A) rules.
    - (B) lessons.
    - (C) mistakes.
    - (D) types.

Lesson 9: Electronics

WORDS TO LEARN

- device
- facilitate
- network
- popularity
- process
- replace
- revolution
- sharp
- skill
- software
- store
- technically

Study the following definitions and examples.

1. **device** n., a tool or machine used for a specific task
   a. A cell phone is a small device that is easy to carry around.
   b. You can connect this device to your computer and use it to store your files.
2. **facilitate** v., to make easier
   a. The computer program facilitated the scheduling of appointments.
   b. The director tried to facilitate the transition to the new policy by meeting with all staff.
3. **network** v., to connect; to broadcast; to engage in informal communication; n., an interconnected group or system over a radio or TV
   a. The recent graduate networked with her mother's coworkers.
   b. We set up a new network in my office to share files.
4. **popularity** n., the state of being widely admired, sought after, or accepted
   a. After the new commercials began running, the popularity of the batteries increased significantly.
   b. This brand of computer enjoys widespread popularity among college students.
5. **process** v., a series of actions or prescribed procedure; n., a series of operations or actions to bring about a result
   a. I've processed the data I collected and have gotten some interesting results.
   b. There is a process for determining why your computer is malfunctioning.
6. **replace** v., to put back in a former place or position; to take the place of
   a. I've replaced the hard drive that was malfunctioning.
   b. We have been looking for months and have found no one to replace our former administrator.
7. **revolution** n., a sudden or important change in a situation
   a. We see a revolution in the computer field almost every day.
   b. Cell phones have caused a revolution in communication.
8. **sharp** adj., abrupt or acute; smart
   a. There was a sharp decline in calls to the help desk after we upgraded each employee's computer.
   b. The new employee proved how sharp she was when she mastered the new program in a few days.
9. **skill** n., a developed ability
   a. The software developer has excellent technical skills and would be an asset to our software team.
   b. Salman's job as designer of electronic tools makes good use of his manual dexterity skills.
10. **software** n., the programs for a computer
   a. This software allows me to integrate tables and spreadsheets into my reports.
   b. The computer came preloaded with the basic software.
11. **store** v., to keep
   a. You can store more data on a zip drive.
   b. You can store hundreds of songs on your smartphone.
12. **technically** adv., with specialized skill or knowledge
   a. Technically speaking, the virus infected only script files.
   b. We find that our younger employees tend to be more technically skilled.

WORD FAMILIES

verb	popularize	The Internet has popularized last-minute travel.
noun	popularity	The popularity of the product was extremely short-lived, and it soon disappeared from the store shelves.
adjective	popular	The new computer program was extremely popular, and people asked for it at all the stores.

verb	replace	I'd like to replace my cell phone with a newer model.
noun	replacement	Look online to see if you can find an affordable replacement for this damaged computer.
adjective	replaceable	Make copies of all your files as they are not easily replaceable.

verb	revolutionized	Using diamond has revolutionized the pressure sensor industry during the last decade.
noun	revolution	The revolution in electronics technology has allowed products such as phones to get smaller and more portable.
adjective	revolutionary	The Internet is revolutionary in how it has changed the way we communicate.

noun	skill	Jason didn't get the job because he didn't have the necessary computer skills.
adjective	skilled	Margaret is a skilled computer programmer.
adverb	skillfully	He skillfully replaced the broken computer screen.

verb	store	I store the phone numbers of all my business contacts in my personal cell phone.
noun	store	We keep a store of computer supplies in that closet.
noun	storage	We need a computer with greater storage capacity.

noun	technician	Even a skilled technician couldn't repair that machine.
adjective	technical	At least a small amount of technical knowledge is required for most jobs these days.
adverb	technically	People who are technically trained have an easier time finding jobs.

WORDS IN CONTEXT

Read the following passage and write the words in the blanks below.

devices	popular	revolutionized	software
facilitated	processing	sharply	stored
networks	replaced	skills	technical

By the mid-1980s, virtually all U.S. businesses owned at least one computer. Prices of computers declined (1) _______________ over the next few years, resulting in a surge in popularity. At the same time, offices started to rely on (2) _______________, which (3) _______________ the sharing and processing of data. Such data (4) _______________ was made possible by improvements in both the hardware and software industries.

Today, virtually all office workers are trained to use the most (5) _______________ word processing (6) _______________ and most information is (7) _______________ in computer files. In fact, electronics have completely (8) _______________ the workplace. These days, workers rely on computers, cell phones, and other electronic (9) _______________ to carry out their job responsibilities. The job (10) _______________ needed today are very different from those needed in the past since now workers need to be comfortable with using electronics. Companies have to hire (11) _______________ workers to maintain their computers and other electronic equipment. People who were hired to do boring, repetitive jobs in the past have been (12) _______________ by computers, which can do such jobs faster and more cheaply.

WORD PRACTICE

Listening Comprehension

Track 10

PART 1 PHOTO

Look at the picture and listen to the sentences. Choose the sentence that best describes the picture.

1. Ⓐ Ⓑ Ⓒ Ⓓ

PART 2 QUESTION–RESPONSE

Listen to the question and the three responses. Choose the response that best answers the question.

2. Ⓐ Ⓑ Ⓒ   3. Ⓐ Ⓑ Ⓒ

PART 3 CONVERSATION

Listen to the dialogue. Then read each question and choose the best response.

4. Why can't the woman retrieve her file?
   (A) She doesn't know how.
   (B) She forgot its name.
   (C) It was accidentally deleted.
   (D) She can't remember where it's stored.

5. Why does she need the file?
   (A) To do her accounts
   (B) To report the news
   (C) To finish her proposal
   (D) To get information about a store

6. What does the man suggest the woman should do?
   (A) Figure it out herself
   (B) Let him help her
   (C) Improve her skills
   (D) Get help from the IT department

PART 4 TALK

Listen to the talk. Then read each question and choose the best answer.

7. Who is this talk for?
   (A) Employees at a company
   (B) University students
   (C) Computer software developers
   (D) People planning to buy computers

8. What is suggested about the computers?
   (A) They are unfamiliar to most people.
   (B) They are difficult to carry around.
   (C) They are very easy to use.
   (D) They are popular with clients.

9. What will listeners do next?
   (A) Record a conversation
   (B) Meet with clients
   (C) Take photos
   (D) Use the Internet

Reading

PART 5 INCOMPLETE SENTENCES

Choose the word that best completes the sentence.

10. A smartphone is such a handy little ______ and has become an indispensable part of our daily lives.

    (A) replacement (C) network
    (B) storage (D) device

11. We will ______ all of our outdated software with the newest versions.

    (A) facilitate (C) store
    (B) process (D) replace

12. There is a ______ approach to software design integration that all the big software developers are currently learning.

    (A) revolutionized (C) revolution
    (B) revolutionary (D) revolt

13. While Fabio's ______ with computers surpasses that of the technicians, he is unable to communicate his personal needs to the office manager.

    (A) skill (C) skillful
    (B) skilled (D) skillfully

14. A smartphone is an electronic ______ that is used for much more than just making phone calls.

    (A) devise (C) device
    (B) division (D) deviance

15. The newspaper article on the development of new fiber-optic cables was so full of ______ language that nobody could understand it.

    (A) technical (C) technicality
    (B) technically (D) technique

PART 6 TEXT COMPLETION

Computer technology has brought about a ____ in the workplace. ____ .
16. 17.

This phenomenon is called telecommuting and has been made possible by the widespread use of the Internet. Telecommuting has become ____ among employees, although the reactions of
18.

employers are mixed. Some like telecommuting and some don't. But most agree that it facilitates work for employees who live at a distance from the worksite. Telecommuting enables companies to keep skilled employees who move out of the area or who have family obligations that require them to stay close to home. ____ the regular nine-to-five office job? Probably not entirely, but we
19.

are sure to see more and more of it in the future.

16. (A) revolted
    (B) revolution
    (C) revolutionary
    (D) revolutionize

17. (A) Now employees all around the country do all or part of their jobs from home.
    (B) Today's jobs require greater technical skills than were needed in the past.
    (C) Employees can store a large amount of data on company computers.
    (D) Different kinds of devices are available to get the job done.

18. (A) sharp
    (B) technical
    (C) popular
    (D) replaceable

19. (A) It replaces
    (B) It will replace
    (C) Will it replace
    (D) Will it be replaced by

PART 7 READING COMPREHENSION

Questions 20–24 refer to the following two e-mails.

To: mary@acme.com
From: fred@acme.com
Subject: software training

Mary,

As you know, we have decided to replace our old software with a new program that will facilitate our work better. Although the new software is not technically difficult to use, it is significantly different from our old software. The entire staff will need to be trained to use it. Of course, not everyone can attend a training session together, because we need some staff members to be in the office at all times. The trainer suggests that each person attend one training session and one follow-up session. The sessions will last three to four hours each. The trainer can be here once a week. Please develop a training schedule so that everyone can be trained over the next two months. Thank you.

Fred

To: fred@acme.com
From: mary@acme.com
Subject: re: software training

Fred,

I have written up a schedule that will facilitate the training process. There will be eight weekly training sessions all together. Since we have four departments, the easiest way is to send one person from each department to each training session during the first month. Of course, it will be a different person each week. We can repeat the process during the second month for the follow-up sessions. This way everyone will have a chance to develop his or her skills on the new software. I am attaching a copy of the schedule. Please let me know what you think.

Mary

20. What is true about the new software?
    (A) It's difficult to use.
    (B) It's very different from the old software.
    (C) It requires many months of training.
    (D) It's very expensive.

21. Which staff members will be trained to use the new software?
    (A) Just one from each department
    (B) Fred and Mary only
    (C) Only four of them
    (D) All of them

22. How many training sessions will each person attend?
    (A) One
    (B) Two
    (C) Four
    (D) Eight

23. The word *skills* in line 11 of the second e-mail is closest in meaning to
    (A) abilities.
    (B) opportunities.
    (C) tasks.
    (D) ideas.

24. The word *replace* in line 1 of the first e-mail is closest in meaning to
    (A) sell.
    (B) change.
    (C) keep.
    (D) locate.

Lesson 10: Correspondence

WORDS TO LEARN

- assemble
- beforehand
- complication
- courier
- distribute
- express
- fold
- layout
- mention
- petition
- proof
- revise

Study the following definitions and examples.

1. **assemble** v., to put together; to bring together
   a. Her assistant copied and assembled the documents.
   b. The mail room clerk read the directions before assembling the parts to the new postage printer.
2. **beforehand** adv., in advance; in anticipation
   a. To speed up the mailing, we should prepare the labels beforehand.
   b. The goods could have been shipped today had they given us the order beforehand.
3. **complication** n., difficulty; complex situation
   a. There was a complication with the delivery because the address was written incorrectly.
   b. Complications always arise when we try to cover too many topics in one letter.
4. **courier** n., a messenger; an official delivery person
   a. We hired a courier to deliver the package.
   b. The courier service will clear the goods through customs.
5. **distribute** v., to pass out to a variety of people
   a. We no longer distribute our newsletter by mail because everyone reads it online.
   b. We plan to distribute copies of the announcement throughout the building.
6. **express** adj., fast and direct
   a. It's important that this document be there tomorrow, so please send it express mail.
   b. Express mail costs more than regular mail service, but it is more efficient.
7. **fold** v., to bend paper
   a. Fold the letter into three parts before stuffing it into the envelope.
   b. Don't fold the document if it doesn't fit the envelope.
8. **layout** n., a format; the organization of material on a page
   a. We had to change the layout when we changed the size of the paper.
   b. The layout for the new brochure was submitted by the designer.
9. **mention** n., something said or written; v., to refer to
   a. There was no mention of the cost in the proposal.
   b. You should mention in the letter that we can arrange for mailing the brochures as well as printing them.
10. **petition** n., a formal, written request; v., to make a formal request
   a. The petition was photocopied and distributed to workers who will collect the necessary signatures.
   b. We petitioned the postal officials to start delivering mail twice a day in business areas.
11. **proof** v., to look for errors
   a. This letter was not proofed very carefully; it is full of errors.
   b. Please proof the memo one more time before you distribute it.
12. **revise** v., to rewrite
   a. The brochure was revised several times before it was sent to the printer.
   b. We will need to revise the form letter since our address has changed.

WORD FAMILIES

verb	complicate	Don't try to complicate things by making two-sided copies; single-sided will do.
noun	complication	There are a few complications with your layout, but they can be easily solved.
adjective	complicated	The revisions in the document made it more complicated, rather than simpler.

verb	distribute	We generally distribute the mail early in the morning.
noun	distribution	As soon as these envelopes are addressed, they will be ready for distribution.
noun	distributor	The distributor of our products just sent an e-mail informing us that he is closing down his business.

verb	mention	As I mentioned in my note to you, you should try to be less wordy and more concise in your writing.
noun	mention	The mention of layoffs made us worry.
adjective	mentionable	No one considered the mediocre design a mentionable achievement.

verb	petition	The welders petitioned the factory to install air conditioning.
noun	petition	In order to be valid, the contents of the petition need to be printed at the top of each page that will contain signatures.
noun	petitioners	The petitioners spent the night outside of the courthouse.

verb	proof	It is your responsibility to proof your own work before sending it out.
noun	proofreader	The proofreader did not find the errors.
noun	proof	The editor checked the proof for errors before sending it to the printer.

verb	revise	After you revise the document, give it a new name so that we will still have access to both drafts.
noun	revision	You may have to do three or four full revisions to this document before it is acceptable.
adjective	revised	His revised memo was easier to read.

WORDS IN CONTEXT

Read the following passage and write the words in the blanks below.

assemble	courier	folding	petition
beforehand	distributed	layout	proofed
complicated	express	mention	revision

In small offices, it is often the executive assistant who must manage all the documents the firm produces. Documents must be carefully (1) _________ to make sure that they are free of errors. They must also be revised as necessary to make sure that the information is clear and correct. This (2) _________ should be done (3) _________ , of course, and not after the document has been printed and copied.

When preparing a mailing, the executive assistant must (4) _________ all the various attachments and documents that will be included in the envelope. If the mailing is going out to a large number of people, a photocopier can make the job much easier. It not only makes copies, but it also collates and staples them. And, the machine can also take care of (5) _________ the documents so that they fit into the envelopes. They can also be sent by e-mail or made available online.

There are several options for sending documents. Local, urgent correspondence can be hand-delivered by a (6) _________ service. Urgent documents and packages that are being sent farther away can go by (7) _________ mail, or they can be (8) _________ by a private delivery service instead of the mail system.

In addition to revising and proofing documents, an executive assistant may also have to act as a graphic designer, responsible for the (9) _____________, or design, of the documents. Did I (10) _____________ that this often requires learning (11) _____________ publishing software? It's a wonder that more executive assistants don't (12) _____________ their bosses for a raise.

WORD PRACTICE

Listening Comprehension

Track 11

PART 1 PHOTO

Look at the picture and listen to the sentences.
Choose the sentence that best describes the picture.

1. Ⓐ Ⓑ Ⓒ Ⓓ

PART 2 QUESTION–RESPONSE

Listen to the question and the three responses. Choose the response that best answers the question.

2. Ⓐ Ⓑ Ⓒ   3. Ⓐ Ⓑ Ⓒ

PART 3 CONVERSATION

Listen to the dialogue. Then read each question and choose the best response.

4. When will the meeting take place?
   (A) This afternoon
   (B) Tomorrow
   (C) In two days
   (D) On Tuesday

5. Why won't the woman help assemble the documents?
   (A) She's in a meeting.
   (B) She hurt her hand.
   (C) She's too busy.
   (D) She needs to revise them first.

6. What does the woman suggest that the man do?
   (A) Finish the work before the afternoon
   (B) Do the work himself
   (C) Ask another person for help
   (D) Remember to fold all the documents

PART 4 TALK

Listen to the talk. Then read each question and choose the best answer.

7. Where would you hear this talk?
   (A) A post office
   (B) A grocery store
   (C) A restaurant
   (D) An assembly line

8. What is the purpose of this talk?
   (A) To sell merchandise
   (B) To inform customers of a new service
   (C) To warn workers
   (D) To recognize a new employee

9. What time does the Courier Center close?
   (A) 2:00 P.M.
   (B) 4:00 P.M.
   (C) 6:00 P.M.
   (D) 8:00 P.M.

Reading

PART 5 INCOMPLETE SENTENCES

Choose the word that best completes the sentence.

10. I don't want to _____ matters, but have you considered using color to make your brochure stand out?

(A) complicate (C) complicated
(B) complication (D) complicating

11. Before you _____ the handouts for the meeting, make sure you have enough copies of each document.

(A) fold (C) mention
(B) assemble (D) express

12. The signatures on the _____ weren't all legible because rain had caused the ink to run.

(A) petition (C) petitioners
(B) petitioning (D) petitioned

13. To send out business letters without _____ them is unprofessional.

(A) proofing (C) proofreader
(B) proof (D) proofread

14. The memo _____ to the entire staff yesterday afternoon.

(A) distributed (C) was distributing
(B) was distributed (D) distribution

15. After each _____, you need to reread what you've written and note your suggestions for changes.

(A) revise (C) revision
(B) revised (D) will revise

PART 6 TEXT COMPLETION

MEMO

To: Production Staff
From: George Jones
Re: Document Preparation

In order to avoid extra work and waste of supplies, please observe the following guidelines when preparing documents for reproduction and distribution. The goal is to keep things simple and avoid ____.
16.

- When you work on the final revision of a document, pay special attention to the layout. ____.
17.
- Don't rush to the copier as soon as the final revision is complete. ____ each document carefully beforehand.
18.
- We have technology to help with the assembly of documents. The large copier on the second floor can ____ paper in addition to stapling. This will help you complete tasks efficiently.
19.
- If a document needs to be delivered the same day it is finished, please use a courier service.

16. (A) mentions
    (B) petitions
    (C) revisions
    (D) complications

17. (A) It is important to write in clear, easy to understand sentences.
    (B) The information in your document must be completely accurate.
    (C) The presentation of material is as important as the content itself.
    (D) This is because you want to make sure there are no spelling errors.

18. (A) Proof
    (B) Proofs
    (C) To proof
    (D) Proofing

19. (A) folder
    (B) folded
    (C) folds
    (D) fold

PART 7 READING COMPREHENSION

Questions 20–24 refer to the following advertisement.

Do you run a small business? If so, you likely don't have a large enough staff to deal with developing, reproducing, and mailing all your documents and correspondence. Why not let Office Systems, Inc., take care of this work for you? We provide the following services:

Editing

Don't send out your documents until you are sure they are absolutely perfect. We provide revision and proofreading services on all documents, large or small.

Design and Production

Our professional graphic designers work with you to develop the best format and layout for your documents. We also provide copying and assembling services, including folding, stapling, and packaging.

Delivery

We can connect you with several different delivery services, including the postal system and private courier companies. Is your correspondence urgent? Our express delivery service gets it to the recipient within 24 hours or less, guaranteed.

Visit any one of our branches to open up an account with us today. You can download an application from our website and fill it out beforehand to make the process go more smoothly. Don't let the details of correspondence and document development complicate your life. Let Office Systems, Inc., handle it all for you.

Visit *www.officesys.com* to find the branch nearest you.

20. Who is the audience for this advertisement?
    (A) Editors
    (B) Couriers
    (C) Corporate directors
    (D) Small business owners

21. Which of the following is a service offered by Office Systems, Inc.?
    (A) Accounting
    (B) Website development
    (C) Assembling documents
    (D) Reading letters

22. How can a customer open an account with Office Systems, Inc.?
    (A) By visiting a company branch
    (B) By sending an e-mail
    (C) By completing an online questionnaire
    (D) By writing a letter

23. The word *revision* in line 6 is closest in meaning to
    (A) copying.
    (B) rewriting.
    (C) delivery.
    (D) development.

24. The word *beforehand* in line 16 is closest in meaning to
    (A) by hand.
    (B) thoroughly.
    (C) in advance.
    (D) in person.

WORD REVIEW #2
LESSONS 6–10 OFFICE ISSUES

Choose the word that best completes the sentence.

1. Who is in charge _____ hiring?
   (A) by
   (B) on
   (C) of
   (D) for

2. Staff members can _____ the private pages on the website by typing in a password.
   (A) expose
   (B) allocate
   (C) duplicate
   (D) access

3. The office _____ samples of its products.
   (A) display
   (B) displayed
   (C) displaying
   (D) displayable

4. The staff expressed their _____ for the leadership of their boss.
   (A) appreciate
   (B) appreciated
   (C) appreciating
   (D) appreciation

5. Ms. Ming was pleased that the new employee showed such _____.
   (A) initiate
   (B) initiative
   (C) initiated
   (D) initiating

6. Before you send the letter, you should _____ it to make sure there are no errors.
   (A) proof
   (B) fold
   (C) petition
   (D) assemble

7. We always hire a private _____ to deliver sensitive documents.
   (A) code
   (B) courier
   (C) stock
   (D) search

8. Many office supply businesses specialize in furniture that is as _____ as it is affordable.
   (A) duration
   (B) durable
   (C) durability
   (D) durableness

9. The office manager finally figured _____ why the new software wasn't working properly.
   (A) in
   (B) for
   (C) out
   (D) about

10. The letter from our accountant _____ that our petty cash spending was almost equal to budgeted items.
    (A) mention
    (B) mentioned
    (C) mentioning
    (D) mentionable

Choose the one word or phrase that best completes each sentence.

The use of computers ________ the workplace. Thirty years ago, many people had never touched a computer.

11. (A) revolutionize
    (B) will revolutionize
    (C) had revolutionized
    (D) has revolutionized

Now almost everyone uses a computer for work. Computers facilitate work so that jobs can be completed more efficiently. Documents are easily duplicated and distributed with computers. The Internet has made it easy ________ for information. Computers have become very ________. Even the smallest businesses

12. (A) search
    (B) to search
    (C) searching
    (D) can search

13. (A) casual
    (B) durable
    (C) complicated
    (D) affordable

are able to buy them.

To: George Stanley
From: Marya Obermeyer
Subject: Photocopier issues

George,

We are almost out ________ paper for the photocopier. There is just one package left in the

14. (A) of
    (B) on
    (C) at
    (D) to

supply closet. I would appreciate your ordering a new box today. In the future, please stay on top of things like this. The order should have been made much sooner.

Also, we will have to ________ the photocopy machine sometime in the near future. We need

15. (A) reduce
    (B) recur
    (C) replace
    (D) reinforce

a new one that doesn't break down so often. Please start researching this and see if you can find one that is affordable. I would also like one that is not ________ to use.

16. (A) complicate
    (B) complicated
    (C) complicating
    (D) complication

Marya

MEMO

To: All office staff
From: Office Manager
Re: New photocopier

We have finally purchased a new photocopier. ____________, it is a great improvement over our

17. (A) Technical
(B) Technician
(C) Technicality
(D) Technically

old one. It can ____________ documents so you don't have to put them together yourself. It also

18. (A) assemble
(B) initiate
(C) revise
(D) practice

folds documents for mailing. However, it does not correct mistakes in your writing. When making multiple copies of a document, please __________ it beforehand and correct any errors. This will

19. (A) probe
(B) proof
(C) prove
(D) prompt

save us a great deal in both paper and time. Please let me know if you have any questions about using the new machine.

Lesson 11: Job Advertising and Recruiting

WORDS TO LEARN

- abundant
- accomplishment
- bring together
- candidate
- come up with
- commensurate
- match
- profile
- qualifications
- recruit
- submit
- time-consuming

Study the following definitions and examples.

1. **abundant** adj., plentiful; in large quantities
   a. The computer analyst was glad to have chosen a field in which jobs were abundant.
   b. The recruiter was surprised by the abundant number of qualified applicants.
2. **accomplishment** n., an achievement; a success
   a. The company was interested in hiring her because of her list of accomplishments.
   b. Finding the right applicant for the job is a big accomplishment.
3. **bring together** v., to join; to gather
   a. Every year, the firm brings together its top lawyers and its newest recruits for a training session.
   b. Our goal this year is to bring together the most creative group we can find.
4. **candidate** n., one being considered for a position, office, or award
   a. The recruiter will interview all candidates for the position.
   b. The president of our company is a candidate for the Outstanding Business Award.
5. **come up with** v., to plan; to invent; to think of
   a. In order to find good candidates for the position, we need to come up with a good advertising plan.
   b. How did the new employee come up with that cost-cutting idea after only one week on the job?
6. **commensurate** adj., in proportion to; corresponding; equal to
   a. Generally the first year's salary is commensurate with experience and education level.
   b. As mentioned in your packets, the number of new recruits will be commensurate with the number of vacancies at the company.
7. **match** n., a fit; a similarity; v.; to put together; to fit
   a. It is difficult to make a decision when both candidates seem to be a perfect match.
   b. A headhunter matches qualified candidates to suitable positions.
8. **profile** n., a group of characteristics or traits
   a. The recruiter told him that, unfortunately, he did not fit the job profile.
   b. As jobs change, so does the company's profile for the job candidate.
9. **qualifications** n., requirements, qualities, or abilities needed for something
   a. The job seeker had done volunteer work and was able to add it to his list of qualifications.
   b. The applicant had so many qualifications that the company created a new position for her.
10. **recruit** v., to attract people to join an organization or a cause; n., a person who is recruited
    a. When the consulting firm recruited her, they offered to pay her relocation expenses.
    b. The new recruits spent the entire day in training.
11. **submit** v., to present for consideration
    a. Submit your résumé to the human resources department.
    b. The applicant submitted all her paperwork in a professional and timely manner.
12. **time-consuming** adj., taking up a lot of time; lengthy
    a. Even though it was time-consuming, the participants felt that the open house was worthwhile.
    b. Five interviews later, Ms. Lopez had the job, but it was a time-consuming process.

WORD FAMILIES

noun	abundance	The company is growing fast and there is an abundance of job openings.
adjective	abundant	When jobs are scarce, job applicants are abundant.
adverb	abundantly	It was abundantly clear that the unemployment rate was not going to turn around anytime soon.

verb	accomplish	You can accomplish anything if you put your mind to it.
noun	accomplishment	The company is proud of our team's accomplishments.
adjective	accomplished	The accomplished artist had his paintings in all the major galleries.

verb	match	We need to match both job experience and personality for this position.
noun	match	The former marketing director is a good match for this position in public relations.
adjective	matching	The matching cushions look better on the chair.

verb	qualify	In order to qualify, you must have two years of work experience.
noun	qualifications	The manager made a list of qualifications for the vacant job position.
adjective	qualified	He applied for the position but he wasn't qualified for it.

verb	recruit	Large accounting firms recruit on college campuses every spring.
noun	recruitment	The company's recruitment resulted in ten highly qualified new employees.
noun	recruiter	As a recruiter, he traveled around the country speaking to recent college graduates.

verb	submit	Anyone who is interested in the position should submit a résumé and writing samples.
noun	submission	We have received your submission and will review it soon.
noun	submitter	The submitter of this résumé forgot to include his contact information.

WORDS IN CONTEXT

Read the following passage and write the words in the blanks below.

abundant	candidates	match	recruit
accomplishments	coming up with	profile	submit
bring together	commensurate	qualifications	time-consuming

Recruiting employees is a (1) ______________ and costly process. Therefore, employers want to (2) ______________ the right person with the right job the first time around. There are many ways to (3) ______________ good employees: advertising in newspapers and professional journals and online, recruiting on college campuses or at conferences, or getting referrals from headhunters.

Recruiting is a time for a company to brag about its (4) ______________ and excite people about its future. Each company is trying to (5) ______________ the best and the brightest, but they are not alone. Their competition is trying to do the same thing. When jobs are (6) ______________ and there is low unemployment, employers may face higher demands from job seekers. Conversely, when the economy is slowing down and jobs are few, employers are in a better position for attracting the best (7) ______________.

Employers look for certain characteristics and (8) ______________ in their employees. (9) ______________ a very specific (10) ______________ that fits the company culture and the specific job requirements is a difficult job. Employers want to see a well-rounded candidate and someone who has related work experience. They are willing to offer a salary that is (11) ______________ with that experience. Employers will make hiring and salary determinations based on the information candidates (12) ______________ throughout the application and interview process.

WORD PRACTICE

Listening Comprehension

Track 12

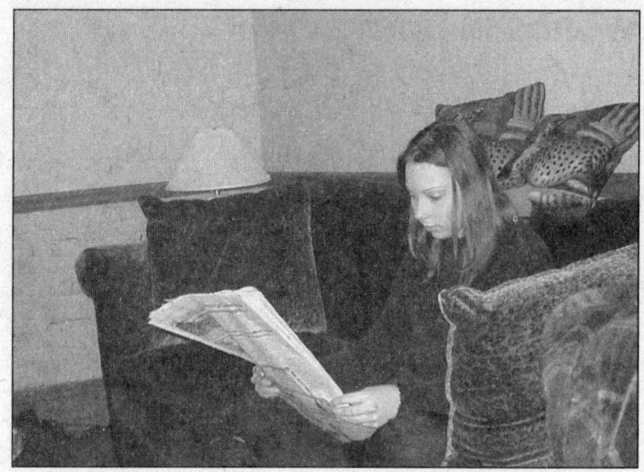

PART 1 PHOTO

Look at the picture and listen to the sentences. Choose the sentence that best describes the picture.

1. Ⓐ Ⓑ Ⓒ Ⓓ

PART 2 QUESTION–RESPONSE

Listen to the question and the three responses. Choose the response that best answers the question.

2. Ⓐ Ⓑ Ⓒ   3. Ⓐ Ⓑ Ⓒ

PART 3 CONVERSATION

Listen to the dialogue. Then read each question and choose the best response.

4. What has the woman been doing lately?
   (A) Fixing her drain
   (B) Earning money
   (C) Looking for matches
   (D) Searching for a job

5. How long has she been doing this?
   (A) Two months
   (B) Four months
   (C) Five months
   (D) Nine months

6. What did she do yesterday?
   (A) She had an interview.
   (B) She read a review.
   (C) She helped someone.
   (D) She accepted a new position.

PART 4 TALK

Listen to the talk. Then read each question and choose the best answer.

7. What should the résumé include?
   (A) Your major in college
   (B) Your grade point average
   (C) A current reference
   (D) A list of concrete achievements

8. What is the employer looking for?
   (A) Employees with long-term career plans
   (B) People to fill positions immediately
   (C) Aggressive marketers
   (D) People willing to accept minimum wage

9. Who should apply for a position now?
   (A) Accountants
   (B) Recruiters
   (C) School teachers
   (D) Apartment managers

Reading

PART 5 INCOMPLETE SENTENCES

Choose the word that best completes the sentence.

10. Your résumé shows you have _____ a great deal in your last position.

    (A) accomplish
    (B) accomplishment
    (C) accomplished
    (D) accomplishing

11. This program is used to scan résumés and search for key words that _____.

    (A) match
    (B) matched
    (C) matching
    (D) will match

12. It is illegal to _____ candidates based on gender or ethnicity.

    (A) profile
    (B) profiling
    (C) profiled
    (D) will profile

13. The applicants who _____ for the position will be flown to the corporate office and interviewed there.

    (A) recruit
    (B) qualify
    (C) bring together
    (D) come up with

14. Many people want to enter this profession but, unfortunately, job openings are not _____.

    (A) abundant
    (B) accomplished
    (C) time-consuming
    (D) recruited

15. After _____ all his materials, he had no option but to sit back and wait for some response.

    (A) submitting
    (B) submitted
    (C) submission
    (D) submit

ATTENTION JOB SEEKERS!

Attend the National Recruiting Fair to be held next Saturday, May 11, at the Hinton Hotel. This fair ____ representatives of over 150 major national corporations. They are all looking for
16.

qualified candidates to apply for thousands of currently available job openings. Attendees are advised to bring 15 copies of a current résumé that lists education, job experience, and professional ____. Many interviews will be conducted on site.
17.

Now you can stop that ____ job search, making call after call and sending out résumé
18.

after résumé. All the companies you want to work for will be together under one roof. ____. Admission is free.
19.

16. (A) bring together
    (B) brings together
    (C) brought together
    (D) to bring together

17. (A) accomplishes
    (B) accomplished
    (C) accomplishing
    (D) accomplishments

18. (A) time-consuming
    (B) submitting
    (C) recruiting
    (D) profiling

19. (A) The room is large enough to hold hundreds of people.
    (B) Many qualified people are looking for jobs these days.
    (C) List all of your professional qualifications on your résumé.
    (D) You are sure to find the company that is the best match for you.

PART 7 READING COMPREHENSION

Questions 20–24 refer to the following two e-mail messages.

To: Marjorie Morgan
From: Bill Smithers
Subject: Recruiting

Marjorie,

We need to start looking at recruiting some new staff members over the summer. Our company has gotten lots of new contracts recently. We have abundant work and need to take on two or three new employees to help with it. We should advertise the positions as entry-level with room for promotion. We should choose the job candidates carefully as I don't want to have to end up firing anyone who turns out to be a bad match. I would like the new staff members to start work by June 10. Therefore, we should ask interested candidates to submit their applications before the end of April so that we can start interviewing in early May. Please come up with a recruiting plan and let me know. Thanks.

Bill

To: Bill Smithers
From: Marjorie Morgan
Subject: re: Recruiting
Attachment: ad draft

Bill,

Here is my plan for recruiting new staff members for this summer. I will place ads in our local newspapers, in two major national papers, and on the major websites by April 1. The deadline for submission of applications will be April 30. We will start interviews on May 8. In the ads I will carefully outline the qualifications we are looking for. I am attaching a draft of the ad. Please look it over and send me your comments. I want to make sure it contains all the details you want.

Marjorie

20. Why does Mr. Smithers need to hire new staff members?
    (A) He has recently fired several employees.
    (B) His company has a lot of work.
    (C) Marjorie Morgan is leaving her job.
    (D) Several employees have been promoted.

21. What does Mr. Smithers ask Ms. Morgan to do?
    (A) Interview job candidates
    (B) Send him comments
    (C) Make a plan to recruit new employees
    (D) Read the major national newspapers

22. What will happen by April 30?
    (A) Job candidates will submit their applications.
    (B) Interviews will begin.
    (C) Two or three new staff members will be hired.
    (D) The new staff members will begin working.

23. The word *candidates* in line 8 of the first e-mail is closest in meaning to
    (A) advertisements.
    (B) descriptions.
    (C) recommendations.
    (D) applicants.

24. The word *qualifications* in line 8 of the second e-mail is closest in meaning to
    (A) quantities.
    (B) positions.
    (C) abilities.
    (D) salaries.

Lesson 12: Applying and Interviewing

WORDS TO LEARN

- ability
- apply
- background
- call in
- confidence
- constantly
- expert
- follow up
- hesitant
- interview
- present
- weakly

Study the following definitions and examples.

1. **ability** n., a skill; a competence
   a. The designer's ability was obvious from her portfolio.
   b. The ability to work with others is a key requirement.
2. **apply** v., to look for; to submit an application
   a. The college graduate applied for three jobs and received three offers.
   b. Everyone who is interested should apply in person at any branch office.
3. **background** n., a person's experience, education, and family history
   a. Your background in the publishing industry is a definite asset for this job.
   b. The employer did a complete background check before offering him the job.
4. **call in** v., to ask to come; to beckon
   a. The young woman was so excited when she was called in for an interview that she told everyone she knew.
   b. The human resources manager called in all the qualified applicants for a second interview.
5. **confidence** n., a belief in one's abilities; self-esteem
   a. Good applicants show confidence during an interview.
   b. He had too much confidence and thought that the job was his.
6. **constantly** adj., on a continual basis; happening all the time
   a. The company is constantly looking for highly trained employees.
   b. Martin constantly checked his messages to see if anyone had called for an interview.
7. **expert** n., a specialist
   a. Our department head is an expert in financing.
   b. The candidate demonstrated that he was an expert in marketing.
8. **follow up** v., to take additional steps; to continue; n., the continuation of a previous action
   a. Always follow up an interview with a thank-you note.
   b. As a follow up, the candidate sent the company a list of references.
9. **hesitant** adj., reluctant; with reservation
   a. Marla was hesitant about negotiating a higher salary.
   b. The recent college graduate was hesitant about accepting his first offer.
10. **interview** n., a meeting for getting information; v., to ask a series of questions
    a. It is very important to act professionally during a job interview.
    b. We had to interview a lot of people before we found the right one for the job.
11. **present** v., to introduce; to show; to offer for consideration
    a. The human resources director presents each candidate's résumé to the department supervisor for review.
    b. The candidate presented her qualifications so well that the employer offered her a job on the spot.
12. **weakly** adv., without strength; poorly
    a. Her hands trembled and she spoke weakly at the interview.
    b. She wrote so weakly we couldn't read it.

WORD FAMILIES

verb	apply	Your chances are better if you apply for a job in the spring.
noun	applicant	The manager selected him from all the applicants.
noun	application	The department can't process your application until all documents have been received.

noun	confidence	It's refreshing to see a manager with so much confidence in her employees.
adjective	confident	Don't be too confident until you actually have an offer.
adverb	confidently	The applicant confidently walked into the interview, sat down, and began to talk about himself.

noun	expert	That company has an opening for an information technology expert.
noun	expertise	They hired her because of her Internet expertise.
adjective	expert	As an expert negotiator, she should have no problem getting the salary that she wants.

verb	hesitate	Don't hesitate to call if you have any questions concerning the job.
noun	hesitation	Her hesitation about accepting the job made the department wonder if she was really interested.
adjective	hesitant	The applicant was hesitant to explain his reason for leaving his last job.

verb	present	I'd like to present my résumé for your consideration.
noun	presentation	The applicant's presentation made a favorable impression.
adjective	presentable	The applicant was well dressed and presentable.

noun	weakness	Interviewers often ask candidates about their strengths and weaknesses.
adjective	weak	She gave a weak description of her computer skills.
adverb	weakly	The applicant shook hands weakly, making me question her strength of character.

WORDS IN CONTEXT

Read the following passage and write the words in the blanks below.

abilities	called in	experts	interview
apply	confidence	follow up	present
backgrounds	constantly	hesitant	weaknesses

How many times in your life will you search for a new job? The (1) ____________ say probably more times than you think! Some people find the job search time-consuming and hard on their self- (2) ____________. The best job hunters are those who never stop looking and don't dwell on their (3) ____________. They network (4) ____________: at meetings, at social gatherings, and with people they meet on the street. They (5) ____________ periodically with contacts and acquaintances to keep up with new developments.

Good job hunters assess their (6) ____________ all the time. Before they even (7) ____________ for a position, they have researched the field and the specific companies they are interested in. They know where they could fit into the company and they tailor their résumés for each position. They try to show how their (8) ____________ match the job opening. Therefore, they're prepared to answer almost any question they may be asked in an (9) ____________. When they're finally (10) ____________ to meet their prospective employers, they're ready.

At the interview, these job hunters know that they must (11) ____________ themselves in the best way possible. This is their opportunity to shine. It is also their opportunity to see if this is truly the job that they want. If either party is (12) ____________ at the interview, it may be a sign that it isn't a good fit.

WORD PRACTICE

Listening Comprehension

Track 13

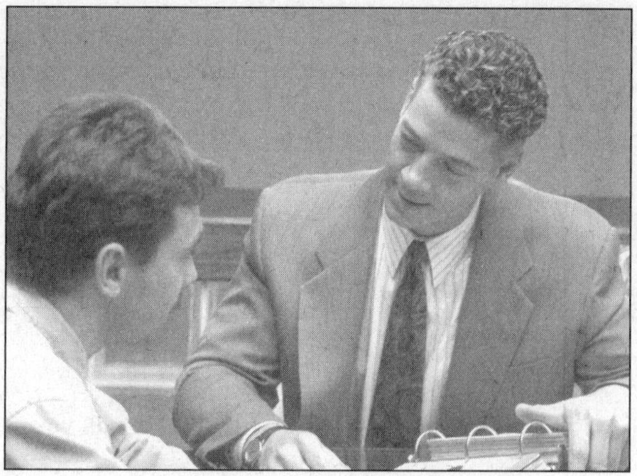

PART 1 PHOTO

Look at the picture and listen to the sentences.
Choose the sentence that best describes the picture.

1. Ⓐ Ⓑ Ⓒ Ⓓ

PART 2 QUESTION–RESPONSE

Listen to the question and the three responses. Choose the response that best answers the question.

2. Ⓐ Ⓑ Ⓒ   3. Ⓐ Ⓑ Ⓒ

PART 3 CONVERSATION

Listen to the dialogue. Then read each question and choose the best response.

4. What do people think about the woman now?
   (A) She has no confidence.
   (B) She is an expert.
   (C) She is a beginner at networking.
   (D) Her computer skills are weak.

5. What was the woman hesitant to do?
   (A) Apply for a job
   (B) Use a computer
   (C) Give a presentation
   (D) Go to a job interview

6. What does the man want the woman to do?
   (A) Help him with a workshop
   (B) Speak at a conference
   (C) Give him some change
   (D) Hire him

PART 4 TALK

Listen to the talk. Then read each question and choose the best answer.

7. Who would call in to this hotline?
   (A) An expert in Salvo's product line
   (B) An employer
   (C) A human resources presenter
   (D) A job seeker

8. What is the purpose of this recording?
   (A) To inform callers about Salvo
   (B) To explain to callers what they can do
   (C) To present the company's philosophy
   (D) To give background information about a product problem

9. What kind of people is Salvo currently looking for?
   (A) Fashion designers
   (B) Foreign language speakers
   (C) Human resource experts
   (D) Software users

Reading

PART 5 INCOMPLETE SENTENCES

Choose the word that best completes the sentence.

10. So many well-qualified people _____ for the position that we won't be able to make a decision for several weeks.
    (A) applying (C) applicant
    (B) application (D) applied

11. As the interview continued, the applicant began to feel nervous and he lost _____.
    (A) expertise (C) confidence
    (B) weakness (D) background

12. The applicant's unique _____ enabled her to have almost any job that she wanted.
    (A) expertise (C) expertly
    (B) experts (D) expert

13. She was hired for the position because she clearly had the _____ to do the job well.
    (A) hesitation (C) expert
    (B) follow up (D) ability

14. During an interview, it is important to _____ your weaknesses in a way that shows you are working to improve them.
    (A) presentation (C) presentable
    (B) present (D) presenting

15. Her handshake had always felt like a dead fish and it was taken as a sign of a _____ character.
    (A) weak (C) weakness
    (B) weakly (D) weakening

When you go on a job interview, the most important thing to remember is to present yourself well. ____ (16.). When you arrive, enter the interview room ____ (17.). Look the interviewer in the eye when you shake hands. When you talk about yourself, do not be shy about your abilities. You are there to prove that you can do the job. Explain your work and educational background briefly and discuss the skills you have developed through experience. ____ (18.) to point out areas in which you have expertise. The worst thing you can do is discuss your experience weakly. Remember, if you believe in yourself, other people will, too. Don't forget to ____ (19.) the interview with a thank-you note before a week has passed.

16. (A) Before you go, prepare yourself by dressing neatly and professionally.
    (B) Therefore, make sure you know how to get to the location of the interview.
    (C) You must be in good health at the time of the interview.
    (D) Afterwards, you can take time to relax and rest.

17. (A) confident
    (B) confidently
    (C) confide
    (D) confidence

18. (A) No hesitation
    (B) Not hesitating
    (C) Don't hesitate
    (D) Doesn't hesitate

19. (A) call in
    (B) apply to
    (C) be ready for
    (D) follow up

PART 7 READING COMPREHENSION

Questions 20–24 refer to the following e-mail message.

From: Samuel Rutherford
To: Matilda Moreno
Subject: Job Opening

Dear Ms. Moreno,

I understand that you are looking for a marketing research assistant. I am interested in applying for the marketing research assistant position. I have the background and abilities you are looking for. I have recently graduated from a four-year university program with a degree in Marketing. My work experience includes three months working as an intern for a local marketing firm, so I have on-the-job marketing experience in addition to my university training. I have also worked for the past two years as a part-time office manager while going to school. My experience at this job allowed me to develop important managerial and organizational skills.

I currently live in Deerfield but am interested in relocating to Riverdale. I will be visiting Riverdale during the first week of next month and am ready to come in for an interview any time during that week.

I am attaching my résumé and three letters of reference. Please don't hesitate to contact me if you have any questions or need further information. I believe I am a good match for your company, and I am confident that I can do the job. I look forward to hearing from you.

Sincerely,

Samuel Rutherford

20. What kind of job is Mr. Rutherford looking for?
    (A) Office manager
    (B) Human resources director
    (C) Marketing research assistant
    (D) Newspaper reporter

21. When does he want to have an interview?
    (A) Sunday
    (B) Next week
    (C) Next month
    (D) In three months

22. What attachments does he include with his e-mail?
    (A) A copy of his university degree
    (B) Three reference books
    (C) A job description
    (D) His résumé and three letters of reference.

23. The word *background* in line 2 is closest in meaning to
    (A) experience.
    (B) location.
    (C) position.
    (D) age.

24. The word *confident* in line 14 is closest in meaning to
    (A) afraid.
    (B) lucky.
    (C) glad.
    (D) sure.

Lesson 13: Hiring and Training

WORDS TO LEARN

- conduct
- generate
- hire
- keep up with
- look up to
- mentor
- on track
- reject
- set up
- success
- training
- update

Study the following definitions and examples.

1. **conduct** v., to hold; to take place
   a. We plan to conduct the training session in the auditorium.
   b. The interviews were conducted over a period of three weeks.
2. **generate** v., to create; to produce
   a. The new training program generated a lot of interest among employees.
   b. The job fair at the college campus should generate interest in our company.
3. **hire** n., an employee; v., to employ; to offer a job or position
   a. The new hire has integrated well with his colleagues.
   b. She was hired after her third interview.
4. **keep up with** v., to stay equal with
   a. The workers were told that they must keep up with the changes or they would be without jobs.
   b. Employees are encouraged to take courses in order to keep up with new developments.
5. **look up to** v., to admire; to think highly of
   a. Staff members looked up to the director because he had earned their respect over the years.
   b. There are few people in this world that I look up to as much as I look up to you.
6. **mentor** n., a person who guides and instructs; a resource
   a. The mentor helped her make some decisions about combining career and family.
   b. Many programs are problematic because mentors don't feel invested in the progress of the employees.
7. **on track** adj., on schedule; focused
   a. If we stay on track, the meeting should be finished at 9:30.
   b. You have a lot of work; if you can't stay on track, let me know immediately.
8. **reject** n., something that has been turned down; v., to turn down; to say no; to not accept
   a. We put the rejects in this box.
   b. Even though Mr. Lukin rejected their offer, they remained in contact.
9. **set up** v., to establish; to arrange
   a. Check with your supervisor to make sure that your office has been set up before you begin work.
   b. Set up a time and place for the meeting and then inform everyone who is involved.
10. **success** n., an accomplishment; the reaching of a goal
    a. The director's success came after years of hiring the right people at the right time.
    b. When the manager won an award, he attributed his success to his colleagues.
11. **training** n., the preparation or education for a specific job
    a. The new hire received such good training that, within a week, she was as productive as the other workers.
    b. The training is designed to prepare all workers for the changes that the company will face.
12. **update** v., to make current
    a. He updated the employees on the latest personnel changes.
    b. We update the calendar weekly.

WORD FAMILIES

verb	generate	The newspaper article generated a lot of interest in working for our company.
noun	generation	The new job advertisements have resulted in the generation of hundreds of applications.
noun	generator	The personnel director was the generator of the ideas behind our new hiring policy.

verb	hire	The personnel director needed to hire 15 people within a week.
noun	hire	The new hire quickly gained a reputation for excellent work.

verb	reject	The candidate rejected the offer the first time, but the second time she accepted it.
noun	rejection	Rejections are difficult, but you can learn something from them.

verb	succeed	In order to succeed in this business, you must be persistent.
noun	success	Don't let success go to your head!
adjective	successful	The trainers were very successful with this last group of new hires.

verb	train	Even though you were trained on a Mac, you'll have to learn how to use a PC.
noun	trainer	The trainer stayed after the meeting to answer any questions.
noun	trainee	Each new employee spends six weeks as a trainee.

verb	update	One of the job responsibilities is to update the blog at least once daily.
noun	update	According to the latest update, they are ready to start interviewing the candidates.
adjective	updated	That schedule is old; let me get you an updated schedule.

WORDS IN CONTEXT

Read the following passage and write the words in the blanks below.

conducted	keep up with	on track	successfully
generate	look up to	rejected	training
hires	mentor	set up	update

After the ads have been placed, and the interviews have been (1) _______________, decisions have to be made. Who should the company bring onboard? Job offers are extended and they are either accepted or (2) _______________. For those who accept the offer, the job search has been completed (3) _______________. But for both the employer and the new hire, the job has just begun.

Companies want new employees to (4) _______________ new business and new ideas as soon as possible. Before they can do that, the new (5) _______________ need some (6) _______________. All companies have unique expectations and methods of operating. Company trainers conduct workshops and seminars for both experienced and new workers. All employees must prepare for the future and continually (7) _______________ themselves in their field. Nowadays, workers are expected to (8) _______________ the latest trends and information. Otherwise, they fall behind.

Many companies (9) _______________ a mentoring program for new employees. The (10) _______________ is usually an experienced manager or employee and should be someone whom the new employee can (11) _______________. Mentors often review goals and objectives with their mentorees and help them to stay (12) _______________.

WORD PRACTICE

Listening Comprehension

Track 14

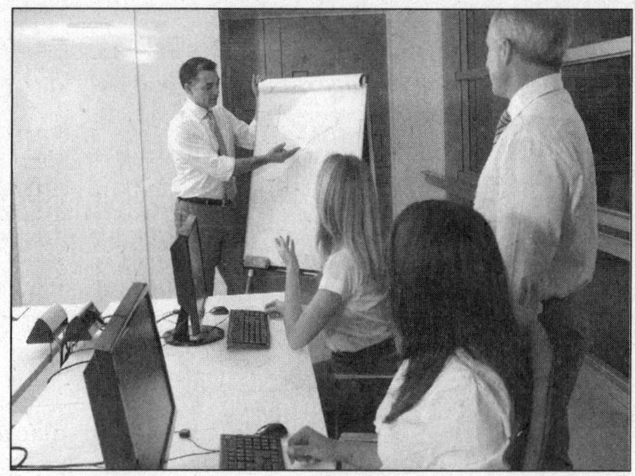

PART 1 PHOTO

Look at the picture and listen to the sentences. Choose the sentence that best describes the picture.

1. Ⓐ Ⓑ Ⓒ Ⓓ

PART 2 QUESTION–RESPONSE

Listen to the question and the three responses. Choose the response that best answers the question.

2. Ⓐ Ⓑ Ⓒ 3. Ⓐ Ⓑ Ⓒ

PART 3 CONVERSATION

Listen to the dialogue. Then read each question and choose the best response.

4. What is the response to the training program?
   (A) Boredom
   (B) Confusion
   (C) Chaos
   (D) Enthusiasm

5. How long will the training program last?
   (A) One week
   (B) Two weeks
   (C) Three weeks
   (D) Four weeks

6. What will the woman do now?
   (A) Join a discussion
   (B) Set up the room
   (C) Look for seating
   (D) Write a letter

PART 4 TALK

Listen to the talk. Then read each question and choose the best answer.

7. Who is listening to this talk?
   (A) New workers
   (B) Annual trainers
   (C) Patients
   (D) New mentors

8. What will they do first?
   (A) Select participants for the program
   (B) Think of traits of good teachers
   (C) Generate a list of rules
   (D) Hear an update on sales figures

9. How long will they spend on the first activity?
   (A) Two minutes
   (B) Three minutes
   (C) Four minutes
   (D) Five minutes

Reading

PART 5 INCOMPLETE SENTENCES

Choose the word that best completes the sentence.

10. The presentation was __________ for the benefit of the new hires.

(A) conduct
(B) conducted
(C) conducting
(D) conductor

11. At next week's meeting we hope to __________ some new ideas for recruiting job applicants.

(A) generated
(B) generate
(C) generates
(D) generating

12. He is not new to his profession, but he continues to take classes to __________ his skills.

(A) set up
(B) on track
(C) update
(D) succeed

13. Unfortunately, not all candidates can be offered a job; some have to be __________.

(A) rejected
(B) hired
(C) conducted
(D) generated

14. The __________ of the program depends on the active participation of everyone.

(A) successfully
(B) succeed
(C) successful
(D) success

15. In all my years as a __________, I have never seen such a motivated group of new hires.

(A) trainee
(B) trainer
(C) trained
(D) training

MENTORING

In order to ensure the ____ of new hires, many companies have
16.
implemented a mentor program. This is a formal way to provide new hires with the guidance they need to understand their responsibilities, to ____, and
17.
to keep from falling behind. With a mentor in place, the exactly whom to go to when confused about policies and procedures. In addition, many mentors conduct regular meetings with the people they are responsible for. This way they can make sure that no serious problems arise. A mentor does not necessarily replace formal ____ programs. In fact, they often go hand in hand. ____.
18. 19.
Mentors are a good way to provide this.

16. (A) success
    (B) succeed
    (C) successful
    (D) successfully

17. (A) set up
    (B) look up to
    (C) put up with
    (D) stay on track

18. (A) train
    (B) trainer
    (C) trained
    (D) training

19. (A) New hires may need a lot of support initially.
    (B) It is not always easy to find the right people to hire.
    (C) Most new hires succeed at their jobs, but some inevitably fail.
    (D) People who have not been properly trained should not be hired.

PART 7 READING COMPREHENSION

Questions 20–24 refer to the following memo and e-mail message.

MEMO

To: All new hires
From: Edwin Mallory
Human Resources Director
Re: Training session

All new hires are required to attend a training session that will take place on Friday, October 12 from 9:30 A.M. until 3:30 P.M. The session will be conducted in Meeting Room 3, and lunch will be provided. During the session you will get an overview of company policies and procedures. You will also be updated on changes in the benefits package and learn about professional development opportunities you will be required to participate in so that you can keep up with changes in your field. Attendance at this training is mandatory for everyone hired since June of this year. There will be no excuses.

To: Edwin Mallory
From: Amelia Foote
Subject: Training session

Dear Mr. Mallory,

I just learned from your memo that I will be required to attend the training session on October 12. Unfortunately, I had already planned to be out of the office that week attending my niece's wedding. My supervisor has given me permission to take that time off, and I have already purchased my plane tickets. I didn't know about the date of the training session when I set up these plans, and it will be very difficult to change them now. My mentor suggested that I ask you for permission to miss this training session. I am willing to attend the next session instead. I hope you don't reject this offer. It is very important to me to be able to attend this family event. Thank you.

Amelia Foote

20. How long will the training session last?
    (A) Three hours
    (B) Six hours
    (C) Nine hours
    (D) Twelve hours

21. Who must attend the training session?
    (A) All company employees
    (B) Only members of the Human Resources Department
    (C) Mentors and supervisors
    (D) All new hires

22. Why doesn't Amelia Foote want to attend the training session?
    (A) She has an important family event.
    (B) She thinks it won't be useful.
    (C) She believes the next session will be better.
    (D) She doesn't have permission from her supervisor.

23. The word *conducted* in line 4 of the memo is closest in meaning to
    (A) announced.
    (B) informed.
    (C) learned.
    (D) held.

24. The word *reject* in line 12 of the e-mail is closest in meaning to
    (A) consider.
    (B) accept.
    (C) say no.
    (D) agree to.

Lesson 14: Salaries and Benefits

WORDS TO LEARN

- aware
- basis
- benefit
- compensate
- delicately
- eligible
- flexibly
- negotiate
- raise
- retire
- vested
- wage

Study the following definitions and examples.

1. **aware** adj., knowing or noticing something
   a. The new staff member wasn't aware of the company's position on working a second job.
   b. Are you aware of the new employee's past work history?
2. **basis** n., the main reason for something; a base or foundation
   a. The manager didn't have any basis for firing the employee.
   b. On the basis of my ten years of loyalty to this company, I feel that I deserve three weeks' vacation.
3. **benefit** n., an advantage provided to an employee in addition to salary; v., to take advantage of
   a. Although the analyst earned a better salary at his new job, his benefits were better at his previous job.
   b. We all benefit from the company's policy of semiannual reviews.
4. **compensate** v., to pay; to make up for
   a. The company compensates employees for overtime by paying double for extra hours.
   b. The company will compensate employees for any travel expenses.
5. **delicately** adv., with sensitivity
   a. Senior management is handling these contract negotiations delicately.
   b. The manager delicately asked about the health of his client.
6. **eligible** adj., able to participate in something; qualified
   a. Some employees may be eligible for the tuition reimbursement plan.
   b. I don't understand why I'm not eligible if I have been with the company for over a year.
7. **flexibly** adv., with the ability to change; loosely
   a. My manager thinks flexibly, enabling herself to solve many sticky problems.
   b. We need to respond flexibly if we want to keep customers in this competitive market.
8. **negotiate** v., to talk for the purpose of reaching an agreement, especially on prices or contracts
   a. You must know what you want and what you can accept when you negotiate a salary.
   b. The associate looked forward to the day that she would be able to negotiate her own contracts.
9. **raise** n., an increase in salary; v., to move up
   a. With his raise, Mr. Drvoshanov was able to afford to buy a new car.
   b. We need to raise the standard for timeliness.
10. **retire** v., to stop working; to withdraw from a business or profession
    a. She retired at the age of 64 but continued to be very active with volunteer work.
    b. Many people would like to win the lottery and retire.
11. **vested** adj., guaranteed as a right; involved
    a. The day that Ms. Weng became fully vested in the retirement plan, she gave her two weeks' notice.
    b. The company has a vested interest in the happiness of its employees.
12. **wage** n., the money paid for work done, usually hourly
    a. Hourly wages have increased by 20 percent over the last two years.
    b. The intern spends more than half of her wages on rent.

WORD FAMILIES

verb	base	We base promotions on seniority.
noun	basis	Salary raises are determined on the basis of performance alone.
adjective	basic	The basic problem with this job is that the wages are too low.

verb	benefit	In order to benefit from the plan, you must fill out the paperwork and submit it to the personnel office.
noun	benefits	The new employee's benefits went into effect three months after his start date.
adjective	beneficial	The service that the insurance has provided has been very beneficial.

verb	compensate	The company compensates its full-time employees well.
noun	compensation	Compensation will be based on your work performance over the past six months.
adjective	compensatory	Compensatory time is given in lieu of overtime pay.

noun	flexibility	His flexibility on benefits was one of the main reasons we were able to hire him at this time.
adjective	flexible	Younger workers tend to be more flexible with their work schedules.
adverb	flexibly	She approaches problems flexibly, looking at the situation from every different angle.

verb	negotiate	The employee prepared a list of her accomplishments to share with her supervisor so that she could negotiate a higher salary.
noun	negotiation	The director was very pleased that the negotiations brought about the end of the strike.
noun	negotiator	I should take lessons from Mr. Tarsa; he is such a skilled negotiator.

verb	retire	Many people don't know what to do with all their time when they retire from work.
noun	retirement	The administrator added more money to the fund for her retirement.
adjective	retired	The retired worker came back to the office from time to time to see his friends.

WORDS IN CONTEXT

Read the following passage and write the words in the blanks below.

aware	compensated	flexibility	retirement
basis	delicate	negotiated	vested
benefits	eligible	raise	wage

An important part of the job search often comes after an offer has been made. Papers should not be signed until you have successfully (1) _______________ your salary and (2) _______________. You want to make sure you will be adequately (3) _______________ for your skills, work, and time. This is a (4) _______________ and difficult area. You should be (5) _______________ of what the salary ranges are at the company and in the field.

Some workers are not on a salary; rather they work for an hourly (6) _______________. In some cases, workers who earn an hourly wage have more (7) _______________ with the hours they work. The trade-off is that the worker may not receive any benefits. For those workers on a salary, the base salary that is negotiated is critical, because most subsequent pay raises come in small incremental amounts. Most companies have a review process either on an annual or semiannual (8) _______________. As a result of the review, an employee may receive a (9) _______________.

Each employee has a unique situation. Health insurance coverage and (10) _______________ plans may be essential to some employees, whereas they are not important to others. Many companies will offer benefits in such a way that it is to the employee's advantage to stay with the company for a longer period of time. Employees may not be (11) _______________ to sign up for a retirement plan until they have been with the company for one year and are not fully (12) _______________ in these plans until they have five years of service under their belts. Some bonus plans are paid out over a period of years. Vacation time increases after more years of service.

WORD PRACTICE

Listening Comprehension

Track 15

PART 1 PHOTO

Look at the picture and listen to the sentences.
Choose the sentence that best describes the picture.

1. Ⓐ Ⓑ Ⓒ Ⓓ

PART 2 QUESTION–RESPONSE

Listen to the question and the three responses. Choose the response that best answers the question.

2. Ⓐ Ⓑ Ⓒ

3. Ⓐ Ⓑ Ⓒ

PART 3 CONVERSATION

Listen to the dialogue. Then read each question and choose the best response.

4. Why is the man disappointed?
   (A) His health coverage is poor.
   (B) He asked for too much compensation.
   (C) He doesn't know how to negotiate.
   (D) He doesn't earn enough money.

5. How long has he been working at the company?
   (A) Two months
   (B) Four months
   (C) Six months
   (D) Nine months

6. What benefit does he get?
   (A) Life insurance
   (B) Health insurance
   (C) Paid vacation
   (D) Regular raises

PART 4 TALK

Listen to the talk. Then read each question and choose the best answer.

7. How often are raises given?
   (A) Once a year
   (B) Twice a year
   (C) At an employee's request
   (D) Whenever an employee is eligible for a raise

8. Where should employees go to learn more about wage increases?
   (A) The Employee Handbook
   (B) Their paycheck stubs
   (C) Their contract
   (D) Their supervisor

9. How many days of paid vacation does each employee get?
   (A) Five
   (B) Ten
   (C) Fourteen
   (D) Forty-two

Reading

PART 5 INCOMPLETE SENTENCES

Choose the word that best completes the sentence.

10. John wasn't _____ that he was eligible for a salary raise until his co-worker told him.

(A) compensatory (C) aware
(B) delicate (D) vested

11. The only _____ at my new job is the annual two-week paid vacation.

(A) wage (C) benefit
(B) raise (D) basis

12. The tired employee hoped that she would be _____ for all the long hours she kept and weekends she worked.

(A) compensation (C) compensated
(B) compensates (D) compensate

13. Sometimes the manager is too _____ and his workers take advantage of him.

(A) flex (C) flexibly
(B) flexible (D) flexibility

14. If the _____ continue into the evening, we will break for dinner at six.

(A) negotiator (C) negotiate
(B) negotiations (D) negotiated

15. No one is sure what will happen to the company when the president finally _____.

(A) retires (C) retired
(B) retirement (D) retiree

PART 6 TEXT COMPLETION

To all union members:

Your union has been working for you. You may ____ (16.) aware that we have been negotiating with management for improvements in the benefits package. Yesterday an agreement was reached on the following points:

1) All employees of the company will be ____ (17.) for an increase in wages every six months, following a performance review. Reasons for refusal to give a raise must be carefully documented according to union guidelines.
2) Employees ____ (18.) at one and a half times their usual hourly wages for overtime hours. Any time worked beyond 40 hours a week counts as overtime.
3) Part-time employees can now receive full health benefits. It is each employee's responsibility to complete and submit the application forms. Part-time employees are also guaranteed five days of paid vacation per year. ____ (19.).

16. (A) be
    (B) is
    (C) are
    (D) were

17. (A) flexible
    (B) beneficial
    (C) eligible
    (D) negotiable

18. (A) will compensate
    (B) are going to compensate
    (C) will be compensated
    (D) have to compensate

19. (A) These two benefits apply to employees who work a minimum of 20 hours a week on a permanent basis.
    (B) We are aware that it is beneficial for all our employees to maintain a good state of health.
    (C) Employees should discuss their retirement plans with their supervisors in a timely manner.
    (D) Employees often choose to spend their vacation days at the beach.

PART 7 READING COMPREHENSION

Questions 20–24 refer to the following e-mail message.

To: James Porter
From: Helene Bourassa
Subject: Re: Benefits questions

Dear James,

I will try to clarify for you your questions about retirement benefits.

Time of retirement: The time at which an employee can retire is calculated on the basis of age and number of years of service to the company. An employee of the company can retire with full benefits at age 55 if he or she has worked a minimum of 30 years for the company. Employees can retire at age 60 or above with 25 years of service to the company. Since you are younger than 60 years old and have worked for the company for 22 years, you won't be eligible to retire for another few years.

Benefits for your spouse: I know this is a delicate matter, but it is important to know about. If you die before your spouse, she will continue to receive full retirement benefits for the rest of her life.

Health insurance: Retirees are eligible to receive health insurance. There are several packages to choose from, and I will send you brochures about them. Your spouse will also be eligible for health coverage when you retire. If you happen to have any dependent children under the age of 21 and living at home, they, too, will be eligible for health coverage.

I hope this answers your questions. Please don't hesitate to contact me if you need any further information.

Helene

20. How old is James Porter?
    (A) Between 22 and 25
    (B) 25
    (C) Younger than 60
    (D) Exactly 60

21. Who can receive retirement benefits after James dies?
    (A) His children
    (B) His wife
    (C) All of his dependents
    (D) Nobody

22. Who can get health coverage when James retires?
    (A) His 19-year-old son who lives at home
    (B) His 20-year-old daughter who lives with her spouse
    (C) Any of his children who want it
    (D) Only his wife

23. The word *basis* in line 2 is closest in meaning to
    (A) solution.
    (B) formula.
    (C) amount.
    (D) foundation.

24. The word *delicate* in line 7 is closest in meaning to
    (A) sensitive.
    (B) complicated.
    (C) necessary.
    (D) interesting.

Lesson 15: Promotions, Pensions, and Awards

WORDS TO LEARN

- achievement
- contribute
- dedication
- look forward to
- look to
- loyal
- merit
- obviously
- praise
- promote
- recognition
- value

Study the following definitions and examples.

1. **achievement** n., an accomplishment; a completed act
   a. Your main achievements will be listed in your personnel file.
   b. Joseph's achievements in R&D will go down in company history.
2. **contribute** v., to add to; to donate; to give
   a. Make sure your boss is aware of the work you contributed to the project.
   b. All employees are asked to contribute a few minutes of their spare time to clean up the office.
3. **dedication** n., a commitment to something
   a. The director's dedication to a high-quality product has motivated many of his employees.
   b. We would never be where we are today if it weren't for many long hours and so much dedication.
4. **look forward to** v., to anticipate; to be eager for something to happen
   a. The regional director was looking forward to the new, larger offices.
   b. We look forward to seeing you at the next meeting.
5. **look to** v., to depend on; to rely on
   a. The workers always looked to him to settle their disagreements.
   b. The staff is looking to their supervisor for guidance and direction.
6. **loyal** adj., faithful; believing in someone or something
   a. You have been such a loyal advisor for so many years, I'm not sure what I'll do without you.
   b. Even though your assistant is loyal, you have to question his job performance.
7. **merit** n., excellence; high quality
   a. Employees are evaluated on their merit and not on seniority.
   b. Your work has improved tremendously and is of great merit.
8. **obviously** adv., clearly; evidently
   a. Her tardiness was obviously resented by her coworkers.
   b. He was obviously working hard to get the promotion.
9. **praise** n., the expression of approval or admiration; v., to express approval or admiration
   a. John received a lot of praise for the article he wrote about business trends.
   b. It never hurts to praise an employee for a job well done.
10. **promote** v., to give someone a better job; to support; to make known
    a. Even though the sales associate had a good year, it wasn't possible to promote him.
    b. The assistant director promoted the idea that the director was incompetent.
11. **recognition** n., credit; praise for doing something well
    a. The president's assistant was finally given the recognition that she has deserved for many years.
    b. Recognition of excellent work should be routine for every manager.
12. **value** v., to consider to be important; to state the worth
    a. Employees value their colleagues' opinions.
    b. The expert valued the text at $7,000.

WORD FAMILIES

verb	achieve	Making a list of your objectives will help you achieve them.
noun	achievement	His achievements were noticed by the vice president and he was sent to the London office.
noun	achiever	Mr. Vadji always considered himself a high achiever.

verb	contribute	All employees were urged to contribute something useful at the staff meetings.
noun	contribution	Each of you has made a significant contribution to our team's success.
noun	contributor	As contributors to the company's outstanding year, all employees will receive an additional holiday bonus.

verb	dedicate	The manager dedicates too much time to reports and not enough time to the customer.
noun	dedication	Margo's dedication to the company was rewarded with a two-week trip to Hawaii.
adjective	dedicated	Before the change in management, he used to be a more dedicated worker.

noun	loyalty	Her loyalty to the company impressed even the owners.
adjective	loyal	He has been both a loyal coworker and a loyal friend.
adverb	loyally	Rosa always speaks loyally of her boss and never lets anyone say a word against him.

verb	promote	In order to move ahead in the company, you must promote yourself.
noun	promotion	Promotions are given to those who prove their worth.
noun	promoter	As the main promoter of the product, Ms. Ross was responsible for the marketing campaign.

WORDS IN CONTEXT

Read the following passage and write the words in the blanks below.

achievements	look forward	merits	promotions
contributions	look to	obvious	recognizes
dedicate	loyalty	praised	value

Congratulations. You have been chosen by your colleagues to receive the Keeler Award of Excellence. This prestigious award (1) ______________ employees who have made extraordinary (2) ______________ to the corporation over the years.

Your coworkers gave several reasons for selecting you. First, they mentioned your (3) ______________ in the marketing department. You have increased sales for our company every year during the past four years. In addition, you have received four (4) ______________ during the same period of time, taking on ever greater levels of responsibility, due to the (5) ______________ of your work in developing our image in new markets. Your (6) ______________ to the department is (7) ______________ to everyone who works with you. The extra hours you regularly put in never go unnoticed. You are a mentor to your coworkers, who often (8) ______________ you for advice. Your supervisor (9) ______________ your high productivity.

The Keeler Award acknowledges an employee's (10) ______________ with a $1,000 bonus. We (11) ______________ to the opportunity to (12) ______________ a rosebush in the company garden in each recipient's name.

The awards ceremony will be held on August 7 on the front lawn at 10:30 A.M. Again, congratulations.

WORD PRACTICE

Listening Comprehension

Track 16

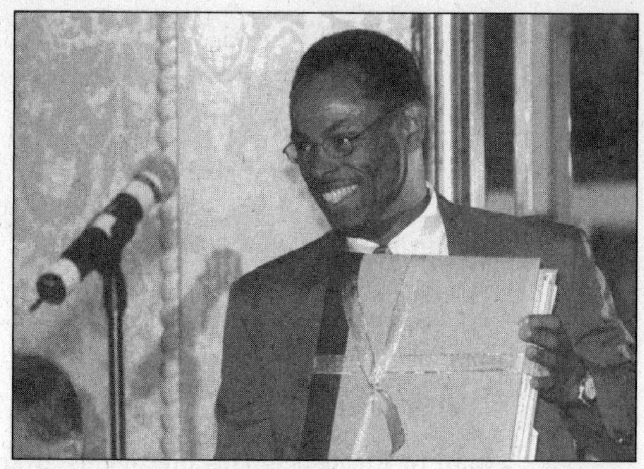

PART 1 PHOTO

Look at the picture and listen to the sentences. Choose the sentence that best describes the picture.

1. Ⓐ Ⓑ Ⓒ Ⓓ

PART 2 QUESTION–RESPONSE

Listen to the question and the three responses. Choose the response that best answers the question.

2. Ⓐ Ⓑ Ⓒ 3. Ⓐ Ⓑ Ⓒ

PART 3 CONVERSATION

Listen to the dialogue. Then read each question and choose the best response.

4. Why will the ceremony be held?
   (A) To honor Darrell
   (B) To boast about production figures
   (C) To celebrate the opening of a new office
   (D) To present awards

5. When will the ceremony be held?
   (A) Today
   (B) Tuesday
   (C) Tonight
   (D) Tomorrow

6. What is the speaker's opinion of Darrell?
   (A) He is loyal.
   (B) He is not productive.
   (C) He is unimpressive.
   (D) He is not a hard worker.

PART 4 TALK

Listen to the talk. Then read each question and choose the best answer.

7. Who is talking?
   (A) Two employees
   (B) An award presenter
   (C) Community volunteers
   (D) A professor

8. Who is the audience?
   (A) Students
   (B) Customers
   (C) Employees
   (D) Citizens

9. When did the company open?
   (A) 1965
   (B) 1975
   (C) 1985
   (D) 1995

Reading

PART 5 INCOMPLETE SENTENCES

Choose the word that best completes the sentence.

10. When he thought about his long career, he realized that his biggest ______ was in developing the new leaders of the company.

(A) achiever (C) achievement
(B) achieved (D) achieves

11. She has ______ so much time and energy to the project that her name should appear on the award.

(A) contributes (C) contributed
(B) contribution (D) contributor

12. Hard work and ______ will help you move up the corporate ladder.

(A) dedicated (C) dedication
(B) dedicates (D) dedicated

13. There is no reason to question her ______ to our company.

(A) loyal (C) loyalty
(B) loyally (D) laurels

14. A word of approval from Susan means a lot since she doesn't give out ______ very easily.

(A) value (C) dedication
(B) praise (D) contribution

15. Because of his many accomplishments and abilities, James was soon ______ to a supervisory position.

(A) promoted (C) achieved
(B) recognized (D) valued

Dear Harry,

____ (16.). Starting the first of next month, you will begin in your new position as manager of the Fulfillment Department. During your years as a member of the Fulfillment Department staff, you have made many ____ (17.) to the productivity and smooth operation of the department. We have always valued your dedication to your job, and now we are pleased to be able ____ (18.) your hard work and fine skills with this higher position. We know you will do a wonderful job. The Personnel Department will contact you soon regarding the changes in your salary and benefits. We ____ (19.) welcoming you to your new position next month.

Sincerely,

Madeline Kovacs

President

16. (A) We look forward to meeting you when you begin your new job.
    (B) We are pleased to inform you of your promotion within our company.
    (C) We are happy you have decided to leave your old company to come work with us.
    (D) We are proud of the many achievements of the entire Fulfilment Department staff.

17. (A) contribute
    (B) contributes
    (C) contributors
    (D) contributions

18. (A) recognize
    (B) to recognize
    (C) recognizing
    (D) will recognize

19. (A) look forward to
    (B) look in on
    (C) look for
    (D) look to

PART 7 READING COMPREHENSION

Questions 20–24 refer to the following memo and e-mail message.

To: All company staff
From: Claude Dubois, Personnel Manager
Re: Annual Awards Ceremony

It is time to start getting ready for the company's annual awards ceremony. It will take place at the Merrimack Hotel on Friday, November 10. Up to 15 staff members will receive awards from the company president that evening. We look to you, our company staff, to help us select deserving award recipients. Please send in your nominations for colleagues who you think merit the recognition of an award. Obviously, we would like to see names of people who have contributed more than average to the company. Send me your nominations by e-mail before October 15 so that we can have the list finalized before November 5.

Thank you.

To: claude_dubois@starco.com
From: marilyn_freeland@starco.com
Subject: nomination

Hi Claude,

I would like to nominate my coworker, Janet McGhee, assistant manager of the research department, for an award. Her dedication to her job is far above average. She always works long hours to make sure she gets her job done. If she is working on an important project, she will come into the office on weekends if she thinks it's necessary to complete her job on time. The rest of us in the department always look to Janet as an example of how to get a job done right. If anyone deserves the recognition of an award for loyalty and dedication, it's Janet. I hope you will consider her as an award recipient.

Thank you.

Marilyn

20. When will the awards ceremony be held?
    (A) October 15
    (B) November 5
    (C) November 10
    (D) November 15

21. Who will suggest award recipients?
    (A) The personnel manager
    (B) The company president
    (C) The assistant manager
    (D) The company staff members

22. Why does Marilyn Freeland think Janet McGhee deserves an award?
    (A) She works on important projects.
    (B) She always works long hours.
    (C) She looks to others as an example.
    (D) She manages the research department.

23. The word *Obviously* in line 9 of the memo is closest in meaning to
    (A) clearly.
    (B) quickly.
    (C) usually.
    (D) importantly.

24. The word *dedication* in line 4 of the e-mail is closest in meaning to
    (A) ability.
    (B) commitment.
    (C) knowledge.
    (D) attendance.

WORD REVIEW #3
LESSONS 11–15 PERSONNEL

Choose the word that best completes the sentence.

1. Coming _______ with a good ad is time-consuming.

    (A) up
    (B) to
    (C) by
    (D) on

2. To _______ the best and the brightest, companies have to be willing to pay well.

    (A) recruit
    (B) recruits
    (C) recruiting
    (D) recruitment

3. A qualified candidate usually exudes _______.

    (A) confident
    (B) confidence
    (C) confidential
    (D) confidentially

4. Any applicant is wise to follow _______ an interview with a note or a phone call.

    (A) after
    (B) behind
    (C) up
    (D) with

5. Workers are promoted on their _______ and merits.

    (A) achieve
    (B) achieved
    (C) achiever
    (D) achievements

6. The benefits package is an important aspect of contract _______.

    (A) negotiate
    (B) negotiable
    (C) negotiations
    (D) negotiated

7. Some employees have to wait years before they are fully _______ in the company pension plan.

    (A) valued
    (B) vested
    (C) retired
    (D) flexible

8. Health _______ are very important for an employee who develops a serious medical problem.

    (A) benefit
    (B) benefits
    (C) beneficial
    (D) beneficiary

9. A _______ and hardworking employee can look forward to rapid promotion.

    (A) background
    (B) delicate
    (C) hesitant
    (D) dedicated

10. An employee who does not meet expectations will _______ not get a promotion.

    (A) obvious
    (B) obviously
    (C) oblivious
    (D) obliviously

Choose the one word or phrase that best completes each sentence.

Thank you for your interest in working at Plytel Corporation. To apply for a position, please _______ a résumé

11. (A) submit
    (B) apply
    (C) negotiate
    (D) accomplish

and a letter explaining your background and interest. We will keep your information on file for a year. If your qualifications match available openings, we will call you _______ for an interview.

12. (A) on
    (B) in
    (C) to
    (D) at

Please do not call us; we will contact you if we have a position suited to your _______.

13. (A) able
    (B) ably
    (C) enable
    (D) abilities

When your company has a job opening, it is important to hire the right person for the job. The job interview offers you, the employer, an opportunity to get to know each _______ and assess his or her

14. (A) expert
    (B) mentor
    (C) supervisor
    (D) candidate

ability to do the job. You will have many questions for the applicants, but you should also _______

15. (A) be
    (B) do
    (C) have
    (D) will be

ready for questions from them. In addition to understanding the job duties, they may want to know about _______ offered by your company such as vacations and health care.

16. (A) beneficiaries
    (B) beneficial
    (C) beneficent
    (D) benefits

Getting a promotion is a great honor. It means your company __________ your merits.

17. (A) recruits
    (B) contributes
    (C) recognizes
    (D) dedicates

When you are promoted to the position of supervisor, your work life changes. You are now in a position of responsibility. It is important to set a good example because your staff looks __________ you. If you carry out your job responsibilities __________, you will

18. (A) for
    (B) up to
    (C) down on
    (D) forward to

19. (A) confident
    (B) confidence
    (C) confidently
    (D) confidential

gain their respect. This is the key to success in your new position.

Lesson 16: Shopping

WORDS TO LEARN

- bargain
- bear
- behavior
- checkout
- comfort
- expand
- explore
- item
- mandatory
- merchandise
- strictly
- trend

Study the following definitions and examples.

1. **bargain** v., to negotiate; n., an advantageous purchase
   a. She bargained for over an hour, finally reducing the price by half.
   b. Lois compared the sweaters carefully to determine which was a better bargain.
2. **bear** v., to have tolerance for; to endure
   a. Moya can't bear crowded stores so she does most of her shopping online.
   b. If you can bear with me, I'd like to stop in one more store.
3. **behavior** n., the manner of one's actions
   a. Annu is conducting a survey on whether consumer behavior differs between men and women.
   b. Suspicious behavior in a department store will draw the attention of the security guards.
4. **checkout** n., the act, time, or place of checking out, as at a hotel, library, or supermarket
   a. The line at this checkout is too long, so let's look for another.
   b. This store has plenty of cashiers and checkout takes no time at all.
5. **comfort** v., to calm somebody; n., a condition or feeling of pleasurable ease, well-being, and contentment
   a. Some people use shopping as a way to comfort themselves after a stressful day.
   b. I like to dress for comfort if I'm spending the day shopping.
6. **expand** v., to increase the size, volume, quantity, or scope of; to enlarge
   a. The new manager has significantly expanded the store's inventory.
   b. The shoe store is out of room, so the owners are expanding into the adjacent vacant building.
7. **explore** v., to investigate systematically
   a. The collector likes to explore antique shops looking for bargains.
   b. If you explore the Internet, you'll probably find the item you're looking for at a good price.
8. **item** n., a single article or unit
   a. The grocery store has a special checkout line for people who are purchasing fewer than ten items.
   b. Do you think I can get all these items into one bag?
9. **mandatory** adj., required or commanded; obligatory
   a. The jewelry store has a mandatory policy of showing customers only one item at a time.
   b. There is a mandatory limit of nine items for use of this checkout line.
10. **merchandise** n., items available in stores
    a. I am very impressed with the quality of the merchandise on this website.
    b. Helen made sure that the store had a wide variety of merchandise before buying a gift certificate.
11. **strictly** adv., rigidly, without flexibility
    a. Our store strictly enforces its return policy.
    b. Their high turnover rate is no surprise, considering how strictly the manager deals with them.
12. **trend** n., the current style; the general direction in which something develops
    a. The clothing store tries to stay on top of all the new trends.
    b. Mioshi followed market trends closely before she bought a clothing franchise.

WORD FAMILIES

noun	comfort	This car is designed with plush seats for your comfort and air bags for your safety.
adjective	comfortable	I prefer this sweater because it's more comfortable.
adverb	comfortably	I'd suggest buying the larger table, which comfortably seats six.

verb	expand	The bookstore expanded its selection by offering books in several foreign languages.
noun	expansion	The expansion of our sales territory into a new region will mean more stock will have to be ordered.
adjective	expanded	The expanded inventory is great, but it's hard to find room to store it.

verb	explore	I like to explore the stores in the mall, and I sometimes find interesting items for sale.
noun	exploration	The store designer's exploration of the art of different cultures gave the store an exotic look.
adjective	exploratory	We took an exploratory trip downtown to look for a site for our new store.

verb	mandate	Store policy mandates that all customers be greeted at the door.
noun	mandate	One of the company mandates is to treat all customers with respect.
adjective	mandatory	A credit card is mandatory for shopping online.

verb	merchandise	The purpose of this website is to merchandise a wide selection of office supplies at the lowest possible price.
noun	merchandise	Many stores make their merchandise available online as well as in the store itself.
noun	merchant	The merchants in this neighborhood organize a special sale every year during the holidays.

noun	strictness	Ms. Judd was appalled by the strictness of the store's policy not to renew her gift certificate after it had expired.
adjective	strict	Our store has a strict policy of no returns.
adverb	strictly	The no-food-or-drinks rule is strictly enforced in the bookstore.

WORDS IN CONTEXT

Read the following passage and write the words in the blanks below.

bargains	checkout	exploring	merchandise
bear	comfort	items	strictly
behavior	expand	mandatory	trend

Some people love to shop. Others can't (1) _______________ shopping and only go when their clothes are completely worn out or their shelves are empty. No one can get away from shopping—unless you can do without eating! Consumption and consumer (2) _______________ affects everything we do.

Some purchases are absolutely (3) _______________. Everyone needs to eat, wear clothing, and sit on furniture. Other purchases are (4) _______________ for luxury (5) _______________. The vast majority of what most of us buy is somewhere in between essential items and frivolous items.

Some people enjoy visiting stores in their free time. It's fun to (6) _______________ the number of places you shop in by (7) _______________ new stores—even if you don't make a purchase.

Many shoppers are looking for (8) _______________. Some people even check out all the aisles looking to see if the items they normally use have been marked down. Everyone loves finding that their favorite items are discounted to a lower price. A sale makes going to the (9) _______________ counter a happier event.

The current (10) _______________ is towards shopping from home. Instead of taking the time to go to stores, many people select (11) _______________ from catalogs or websites. You can get almost everything, from books to clothing, without leaving the (12) _______________ of your home.

WORD PRACTICE

Listening Comprehension

Track 17

PART 1 PHOTO

Look at the picture and listen to the sentences. Choose the sentence that best describes the picture.

1. Ⓐ Ⓑ Ⓒ Ⓓ

PART 2 QUESTION–RESPONSE

Listen to the question and the three responses. Choose the response that best answers the question.

2. Ⓐ Ⓑ Ⓒ 3. Ⓐ Ⓑ Ⓒ

PART 3 CONVERSATION

Listen to the dialogue. Then read each question and choose the best response.

4. What class is the man taking?
   (A) Psychology
   (B) Sociology
   (C) Economics
   (D) Marketing

5. How much time did he spend watching consumers?
   (A) Two weeks
   (B) Three weeks
   (C) Four weeks
   (D) Five weeks

6. What did he learn about consumers' shopping habits?
   (A) They hunt for bargains.
   (B) They buy more during sales.
   (C) Color is a key motivator in clothing selections.
   (D) They feel comfortable with the brands they know.

PART 4 TALK

Listen to the talk. Then read each question and choose the best answer.

7. What items are reduced in price?
   (A) Scarves
   (B) Boots
   (C) Hats
   (D) Coats

8. What kind of merchandise does the store carry?
   (A) Winter sports equipment
   (B) Gift items
   (C) Clothing
   (D) Work uniforms

9. How many store visits are required to get a gift?
   (A) Three
   (B) Four
   (C) Nine
   (D) Ten

Reading

PART 5 INCOMPLETE SENTENCES

Choose the word that best completes the sentence.

10. It's hard to tell if these shoes will be _____ because the leather is so stiff.

(A) comfort
(B) comfortably
(C) comfortable
(D) comforting

11. Due to the store's success, the owners began to plan an _____ into a larger location.

(A) expansion
(B) expand
(C) expanse
(D) expanded

12. We _____ the entire store but still couldn't find the item we needed.

(A) exploratory
(B) exploration
(C) explorer
(D) explored

13. According to store policy, it is _____ to show photo identification when making a purchase with a credit card.

(A) mandatory
(B) exploratory
(C) expanded
(D) trendy

14. I generally find the _____ in this store to be of such good quality that I don't mind paying the high prices.

(A) trends
(B) bargains
(C) merchandise
(D) checkout

15. We _____ adhere to the store's policy of only specially ordering products that have been paid for in advance.

(A) strictness
(B) strict
(C) strictly
(D) strictest

Attention Bargain Hunters!

Greene's Department Store is having its biggest sale ever. Every single item in the store is on sale at unbelievable prices. That's right—all merchandise, including clothes, shoes, toys, sports equipment, home furnishing, music, and music equipment, is 25 to 75 percent off the usual price.

* Have you always wanted ____ (16.) the underwater world? We have diving equipment on sale at 50 percent off.
* Would you like to sleep in a more ____ (17.) bed? The prices of beds, mattresses, and bedroom furniture have been reduced by 35 percent.
* Are you planning ____ (18.) your garden? Now it is more affordable than ever. All garden plants and gardening equipment are on sale at discounts from 20 to 50 percent off the usual price.

____ (19.). Sale ends Sunday.

16. (A) explore
    (B) explores
    (C) to explore
    (D) exploring

17. (A) comfort
    (B) comforter
    (C) comfortable
    (D) comfortably

18. (A) to merchandise
    (B) to mandate
    (C) to bear
    (D) to expand

19. (A) Sorry, but we can no longer accept personal checks as payment for merchandise.
    (B) You won't find better bargains than these at any other store.
    (C) Interest in gardening as a hobby is a growing trend.
    (D) Greene's is the largest store in the city.

PART 7 READING COMPREHENSION

Questions 20–24 refer to the following article.

DESIGNING RETAIL SPACE TAKES CAREFUL PLANNING. ATTENTION SHOULD BE PAID TO WHAT RESEARCH TELLS US ABOUT CONSUMER BEHAVIOR. STORES MUST BE DESIGNED WITH THE COMFORT OF SHOPPERS IN MIND. THE AISLES SHOULD BE WIDE ENOUGH TO ALLOW SHOPPERS TO MOVE THROUGH THEM COMFORTABLY. ITEMS SHOULD BE PLACED WHERE THEY CAN BE EASILY SEEN BY SHOPPERS. NOTHING SHOULD BE PUT ON HIGH SHELVES WHERE IT CANNOT BE REACHED. PLEASANT LIGHTING AND MUSIC ALSO CONTRIBUTE TO THE COMFORT AND GOOD FEELING OF SHOPPERS. SHOPPERS WHO FEEL HAPPY AND RELAXED WILL MAKE MORE PURCHASES.

WHEN ORGANIZING THE MERCHANDISE IN A STORE, THE TRENDS OF EACH SEASON SHOULD BE KEPT IN MIND. PICNIC AND BEACH EQUIPMENT SHOULD BE PROMINENTLY DISPLAYED IN THE SUMMER, FOR EXAMPLE, WHILE WARM CLOTHING SHOULD BE FEATURED IN THE WINTER. THEN, SHOPPERS WILL RETURN TO THE STORE BECAUSE THEY WILL SEE IT AS A PLACE THAT PROVIDES WHAT THEY NEED.

THERE SHOULD BE PLENTY OF CHECKOUT AISLES SO THAT LONG LINES ARE AVOIDED. MANY PEOPLE CANNOT BEAR LONG WAITS, AND LONG CHECKOUT LINES SCARE SHOPPERS AWAY FROM STORES. MANY STORES ARE NOW USING SELF-SERVICE CHECKOUT AISLES, ALTHOUGH THEY HAVE NOT YET BEEN COMPLETELY ACCEPTED BY SHOPPERS. THEY ARE OFTEN CONFUSING TO USE, AND MANY SHOPPERS FIND THEM IMPERSONAL. THE OLD-FASHIONED HUMAN CASHIER IS STILL POPULAR IN MOST RETAIL OUTLETS. THEREFORE, IT IS STILL CONSIDERED MANDATORY FOR STORES TO HAVE AT LEAST SOME FULL-SERVICE CHECKOUT LINES MANNED BY CASHIERS.

WHEN A STORE IS PROPERLY DESIGNED, SHOPPERS HAVE A PLEASANT EXPERIENCE AND WILL WANT TO RETURN. THIS HELPS THE BOTTOM LINE OF THE STORE OWNER, WHICH IS, OF COURSE, INCREASED SALES.

20. According to the article, which shoppers buy more?
    (A) Those who have more money
    (B) Those who can reach high shelves
    (C) Those who feel comfortable in the store
    (D) Those who shop in the summer

21. What does the article say about self-service checkout aisles?
    (A) They are popular everywhere.
    (B) They aren't always easy to use.
    (C) They are personal.
    (D) They are mandatory.

22. According to the article, what is the most important thing for a store owner?
    (A) More sales
    (B) Lighting and music
    (C) Pleasant cashiers
    (D) Wide aisles

23. The word *behavior* in line 2 is closest in meaning to
    (A) questions.
    (B) desires.
    (C) interests.
    (D) actions.

24. The word *bear* in paragraph 3, line 2 closest in meaning to
    (A) tolerate.
    (B) understand.
    (C) refuse.
    (D) decrease.

Lesson 17: Ordering Supplies

WORDS TO LEARN

- consistent
- diversify
- enterprise
- essentially
- function
- maintain
- obtain
- prerequisite
- quality
- smooth
- source
- stationery

Study the following definitions and examples.

1. **consistent** adj., steady; regular; dependable
   a. If we order new paper and ink at the beginning of every month, we will have a consistent supply of these necessary items.
   b. We order from that supplier because of the consistent quality of their merchandise.
2. **diversify** v., to broaden; to make more varied
   a. The stationery department plans to diversify its offering of paper products.
   b. The consultant that we hired recommends that we don't diversify at this time.
3. **enterprise** n., a business; a large project
   a. The new enterprise quickly established an account with the office supply store.
   b. This enterprise has become unmanageable and is beginning to lose money.
4. **essentially** adv., necessarily, basically, finally
   a. Essentially, she wants to win the contract and put the competition out of business.
   b. After distributing all of the cartridges that were ordered, we were essentially left with none.
5. **function** v., to perform tasks; n., a purpose
   a. This room will function as the supply closet while the office is being painted.
   b. What is the function of this device?
6. **maintain** v., to continue; to support; to sustain
   a. I've been maintaining a list of office supplies that are in greatest demand.
   b. Trying to maintain two different stockrooms is too much work.
7. **obtain** v., to acquire
   a. I've been trying to obtain a list of supplies from the administrator for three weeks now.
   b. We can obtain all the supplies we need online.
8. **prerequisite** n., something that is required or necessary as a prior condition
   a. A prerequisite for ordering supplies is getting the approval of the office manager.
   b. Here are the prerequisites that you need to purchase before coming to class.
9. **quality** n., a distinguishing characteristic; a degree of excellence
   a. The most important qualities we look for in a supplier are reliability and quick response.
   b. I don't recommend ordering supplies from that website since the quality of their merchandise is usually poor.
10. **smooth** adj., without difficulties; deliberately polite and agreeable in order to win favor
    a. Thanks to our smooth transition to the new supplier, there was no interruption in shipments.
    b. Her smooth manner won her the appreciation of the manager but not her colleagues.
11. **source** n., the origin
    a. This website is a good source for paper and other office supplies.
    b. The source of this rare pottery that we are selling in our shop is a small village in India.
12. **stationery** n., writing paper and envelopes
    a. We do not have enough stationery, so please order some more.
    b. The new stationery featured the company's logo in blue ink at the top of the page.

WORD FAMILIES

noun	consistence	That store messes up our order with a consistence that is amazing.
adjective	consistent	The office manager is consistent about ordering supplies at the end of every month.
adverb	consistently	The office manager consistently orders supplies that we don't really need.

verb	diversify	That supplier has diversified its product line and is offering computer accessories as well as computers.
noun	diversity	We order from a website that offers a diversity of office and shipping supplies.
adjective	diverse	The wholesaler offered a more diverse range of computer accessories than I expected.

noun	essence	The essence of the problem lies in the lack of money allocated for supplies.
adjective	essential	Make sure we don't run out of essential supplies such as ink and paper.
adverb	essentially	His title is office manager, but he is essentially the supply clerk.

verb	function	She will function as office manager until a replacement is found.
noun	function	As assistant office manager you have two important functions: keep the supply closet stocked and maintain the office calendar.
adjective	functional	This machine isn't functional so I suggest buying a new one.

verb	maintain	If we maintain the organization of the supply closet, we will know what we have on hand and what we need to order.
noun	maintenance	The maintenance of this photocopier is costing us a great deal of money.
adjective	maintainable	We want to purchase equipment that is easily maintainable.

noun	smoothness	The smoothness of the ordering process encourages me to continue buying supplies from that website.
adjective	smooth	The vendor was so smooth on the phone that he had no difficulty in obtaining an appointment with the office manager.
adverb	smoothly	The meeting went smoothly, and we left with a lot of free samples to try out at the office.

WORDS IN CONTEXT

Read the following passage and write the words in the blanks below.

consistent	essential	obtain	smooth
diverse	functioning	prerequisite	source
enterprise	maintaining	quality	stationery

All businesses, large and small, must maintain an inventory of supplies. It is important to keep a (1) ________________ supply of certain basic items that are used every day so that they are always on hand when needed. These include items such as (2) ________________, printer ink and paper, pens, and staples. They are easy to (3) ________________ from office supply stores, and can also be found online.

Some businesses require a more (4) ________________ range of supplies. For example, businesses that ship their products usually need to keep cartons, Styrofoam peanuts, package tape, and shipping labels on hand at all times. These items can also be found at stores and websites that sell office and shipping supplies.

No matter what the type of business, the office administrator is in charge of ordering supplies and (5) ________________ an inventory. Having the (6) ________________ supplies on hand at all times is a (7) ________________ for the (8) ____________________ and efficient (9) __________________ of the (10) ____________________. The administrator should try to locate the cheapest (11) __________________ of the supplies required, but also pay attention to the (12) ________________ of the goods.

WORD PRACTICE

Listening Comprehension

Track 18

PART 1 PHOTO

Look at the picture and listen to the sentences. Choose the sentence that best describes the picture.

1. Ⓐ Ⓑ Ⓒ Ⓓ

PART 2 QUESTION–RESPONSE

Listen to the question and the three responses. Choose the response that best answers the question.

2. Ⓐ Ⓑ Ⓒ 3. 

PART 3 CONVERSATION

Listen to the dialogue. Then read each question and choose the best response.

4. What is the man looking for?
   (A) A diverse range of applicants
   (B) A glassware merchant
   (C) A pair of eyeglasses
   (D) A warehouse

5. How will he obtain more information about what he needs?
   (A) He'll write a letter.
   (B) He'll make a phone call.
   (C) The woman will tell him.
   (D) He'll visit a website.

6. When does the woman want to speak to the man again?
   (A) Today
   (B) Tuesday
   (C) Next week
   (D) On the weekend

PART 4 TALK

Listen to the talk. Then read each question and choose the best answer.

7. Who is listening to this talk?
   (A) Upper management at a stationery supplier
   (B) Employees at a stationery supplier
   (C) Upper management at Margatel
   (D) Employees at Margatel

8. What is the problem?
   (A) There was an order with a mistake.
   (B) The company lost a $50,000 client.
   (C) Employees got locked out of the office.
   (D) A worker slipped and fell.

9. When did Carla take the order?
   (A) January 14
   (B) January 19
   (C) January 21
   (D) January 30

Reading

PART 5 INCOMPLETE SENTENCES

Choose the word that best completes the sentence.

10. Many customers find that product ______ is confusing and deceptive.
    (A) diversify
    (B) diverse
    (C) diversity
    (D) diversified

11. He is starting a new ______: selling office supplies online.
    (A) source
    (B) quality
    (C) enterprise
    (D) maintenance

12. Madeline is the only one who really understands the process, so her participation in the project is ______.
    (A) smooth
    (B) diverse
    (C) essential
    (D) consistent

13. We need to have a spare copier since the only one that is ______ is on its last leg.
    (A) functioned
    (B) functions
    (C) functional
    (D) function

14. In order to ______ our lead in the market, we'll have to find a cheaper source of industrial supplies.
    (A) maintainable
    (B) maintain
    (C) maintaining
    (D) maintainability

15. She talked so ______ that we ordered every single item that she had for sale.
    (A) smoothly
    (B) smoothness
    (C) smooth
    (D) smoothed

Memo

To: All office staff
From: Luis Mendez, Office Manager
Re: Ordering office supplies

There has been a lot of confusion recently regarding the ordering of office supplies. In order to maintain a consistent stock of ____ (16.) supplies, from now on all supply orders must go through me. ____ (17.).

I can ____ (18.) supplies for you within three days of receiving your order form if it is filled out properly.

By following this procedure, the office will function more ____ (19.), and we can be sure that we will always have quality supplies on hand when we need them.

We will also avoid the problem of ordering supplies that we already have. Thank you for your cooperation.

16. (A) essence
    (B) essential
    (C) essentials
    (D) essentially

17. (A) There are forms available that you may use to order the supplies that you need.
    (B) The function of the supply room is to ensure that we have supplies available.
    (C) Please use company stationery for company business only.
    (D) We order our supplies from several different sources.

18. (A) maintain
    (B) function
    (C) diversify
    (D) obtain

19. (A) smooth
    (B) smoothly
    (C) smoother
    (D) smoothness

PART 7 READING COMPREHENSION

Questions 20–24 refer to the following letter and memo.

April 12

Dear Business Owner,

The Supply Closet, Inc., is a new office supply store in your neighborhood. We opened last month right across the street from the post office. We are your local source for quality office supplies, including all office stationery, packing materials, folders, pens, note pads, and more. We provide you with the everyday items you need to keep your business functioning smoothly. In order to introduce ourselves to you, we are enclosing a coupon for 20 percent off your entire purchase during your first visit to the Supply Closet. Please visit us soon.

Sincerely yours,

Martha and Bill Heywood
Owners

Coupon expires June 30.

Memo

To: Gisela Freeman
From: James Riley
Re: New supply store

Please see the attached letter from the Supply Closet, Inc. I think we should try them out. I know we maintain an account with the Riverdale Supply Company, but I am not completely satisfied with them as a source for supplies. I would like to find a supplier with more diverse merchandise. I'd like you to visit the Supply Closet sometime this week and purchase some stationery. We need to do a big mailing at the beginning of May, so we'll need some manila envelopes and letter paper. You can use the coupon that came with the letter. Look at the items they have for sale and see how it compares with the Riverdale Supply Company. If it looks like they're a better source for supplies, we can start ordering from them regularly. Thank you.

20. When did the Supply Closet open?
    (A) March
    (B) April
    (C) May
    (D) June

21. What can a customer get during his first visit to the store?
    (A) A free pen
    (B) An introduction
    (C) A discount
    (D) A stamp

22. Why doesn't James Riley like the Riverdale Supply Company?
    (A) It's too near the post office.
    (B) It doesn't function smoothly.
    (C) It's far from the neighborhood.
    (D) It doesn't have a variety of merchandise.

23. The word *smoothly* in line 9 of the letter is closest in meaning to
    (A) easily.
    (B) quickly.
    (C) profitably.
    (D) carefully.

24. The word *maintain* in line 3 of the memo is closest in meaning to
    (A) open.
    (B) pay.
    (C) apply.
    (D) keep.

Lesson 18: Shipping

WORDS TO LEARN

- accurately
- carrier
- catalog
- fulfill
- integral
- inventory
- minimize
- on hand
- receive
- ship
- sufficiently
- supply

Study the following definitions and examples.

1. **accurately** adv., correctly; without errors
   a. To gauge these figures accurately, we first need to get some facts from the shipping department.
   b. The container company must balance the load accurately or there could be a disaster at sea.
2. **carrier** n., a person or business that transports passengers or goods
   a. Lou, our favorite carrier, takes extra care of our boxes marked "fragile."
   b. Mr. Lau switched carriers in order to get a price savings on deliveries out of state.
3. **catalog** n., a list or itemized display; v., to make an itemized list of
   a. The fall catalog shows a number of items that Mr. Lau has never before been able to offer.
   b. Ellen cataloged the complaints according to severity.
4. **fulfill** v., to finish completely
   a. All orders are fulfilled and ready for shipment within twenty-four hours.
   b. Her expectations were so high, we knew they would be hard to fulfill.
5. **integral** adj., necessary for completion
   a. Good customer relations are an integral component of any business.
   b. A dependable stream of inventory is integral to reliable shipping of orders.
6. **inventory** n., goods in stock; an itemized record of these goods
   a. The store closes one day a year so that the staff can take inventory of the stockroom.
   b. Their inventory has not changed much over the years.
7. **minimize** v., to reduce; to give less importance to
   a. The shipping staff minimized complaints by working overtime to deliver the packages quickly.
   b. To keep customers happy and minimize the effect of the strike, we shipped orders directly to them.
8. **on hand** adj., available
   a. We had too much stock on hand, so we had a summer sale.
   b. The new employee will be on hand if we need more help with shipping orders.
9. **receive** v., get or accept something that is given
   a. You will receive your order within one week of the shipping date.
   b. When we received the package, the box was broken and some of the contents were missing.
10. **ship** v., to transport; to send
    a. We shipped the package yesterday, so it should arrive by the end of the week.
    b. Very few customers think about how their packages will be shipped, and are seldom home when the packages arrive.
11. **sufficiently** adv., enough
    a. Customers aren't choosing express shipping because it hasn't been sufficiently advertised.
    b. We are sufficiently organized to begin transferring the pallets tomorrow.
12. **supply** n., stock; v., to make available for use; to provide
    a. By making better use of our supplies, we can avoid ordering until next month.
    b. Gerald supplied the shipping staff with enough labels to last a year.

WORD FAMILIES

noun	accuracy	His firm was well known for its accuracy in predicting how long shipping would take.
adjective	accurate	Don't forget to keep accurate records; you will need them when you have your annual inventory.
adverb	accurately	The in-depth shipping records made it possible for Max to accurately estimate when the mixing bowls would arrive in the store.

verb	fulfill	We take pride in fulfilling customers' unusual requests.
noun	fulfillment	Fulfillment of duties can be tedious, but job satisfaction demands attention to detail.

verb	integrate	The new foreman is unable to integrate information about shipping perishables.
noun	integration	His full integration into the team could take weeks.
adjective	integral	This paperwork is integral to our ability to track packages.

verb	minimize	To minimize any potential risk of injury, all workers must wear closed-toed shoes in the stockroom.
noun	minimum	The minimum is $50; orders of less will be assessed a shipping charge.
adjective	minimal	Luckily, the leak from the roof did only minimal damage to the inventory in the stockroom.

verb	ship	We ship all orders within 24 hours of your phone call.
noun	shipper	We can rely on our shipper to pack large, fragile items carefully.
noun	shipment	The shipment from the supplier was short a number of items, so we complained.

verb	suffice	Will this much Styrofoam suffice?
adjective	sufficient	The postage on that box is not sufficient to get it to its destination.
adverb	sufficiently	If you are sufficiently certain that the crate is in this room, I will check them one by one.

WORDS IN CONTEXT

Read the following passage and write the words in the blanks below.

accurate	fulfill	minimize	shipping
carrier	integral	on hand	sufficient
catalog	inventory	receive	supplies

For Mr. Park's Asian housewares store, shipping is an (1) ________________ part of the business. Many customers need to send their purchases to friends or relatives who live far away. Other customers, who do not live near one of his stores, shop by (2) ________________ and need their orders sent by mail.

(3) ________________ is, of course, the process of getting goods delivered to a customer, but it is more than just getting a box in the mail. Goods must be packaged carefully to (4) ______________ breakage and ensure that they arrive safely. Customers want to (5) ______________ their orders in good condition. Staff members must keep (6) ________________ records of the inventory shipped, and both Mr. Park and his customers need to be able to track the shipments online so that they can easily find the answers to these questions: When did a box leave the store? Who was the (7) ________________ who delivered it? When did it arrive at its destination?

The shipping process must be tied to the store's (8) ________________. When orders are taken, the shipping staff must know that there is (9) ________________ inventory of the product on hand to (10) ________________ the request. If a product is on order, the sales staff should advise the customer to expect a delay. When orders are shipped out, they must be deleted from the inventory records so Mr. Park knows exactly how many items are (11) _______________ in his warehouse. It takes a good computer program to keep track of the additions and deletions to the inventory.

Sales staff must remember to charge for shipping and appropriate taxes. Mr. Park must keep good records on the cost of the shipping and packing materials and other (12) ____________, the cost of the carriers, and staff time to assess whether he is billing enough to cover his shipping expenses.

WORD PRACTICE

Listening Comprehension

Track 19

PART 1 PHOTO

Look at the picture and listen to the sentences.
Choose the sentence that best describes the picture.

1. Ⓐ Ⓑ Ⓒ Ⓓ

PART 2 QUESTION–RESPONSE

Listen to the question and the three responses. Choose the response that best answers the question.

2. Ⓐ Ⓑ Ⓒ

3. Ⓐ Ⓑ Ⓒ

PART 3 CONVERSATION

Listen to the dialogue. Then read each question and choose the best response.

4. What is the problem?
   (A) There aren't enough boxes.
   (B) The addresses were lost.
   (C) The packages need repair.
   (D) The wrong materials were shipped.

5. Who is responsible for the problem?
   (A) The woman
   (B) The man
   (C) The packers
   (D) The suppliers

6. When should the boxes be shipped?
   (A) Today
   (B) Tomorrow
   (C) By Friday
   (D) On the weekend

PART 4 TALK

Listen to the talk. Then read each question and choose the best answer.

7. What is the topic of the talk?
   (A) Company mottos
   (B) High prices
   (C) Customer loyalty
   (D) A weak point in the catalog

8. What is the company's basic philosophy?
   (A) Unsurpassed customer service
   (B) A good catalog can sell anything
   (C) Outperform the competition
   (D) High quality at low cost

9. When will the catalog show a comparison of prices?
   (A) January
   (B) May
   (C) September
   (D) December

Reading

PART 5 INCOMPLETE SENTENCES

Choose the word that best completes the sentence.

10. To assure that your order is _____ filled, it will be checked by a two-person team.

(A) accurately (C) accurate
(B) accurateness (D) accuracy

11. The suppliers have _____ the terms of our agreement and are now our supplier of choice.

(A) fulfilling (C) fulfilled
(B) fulfillment (D) fulfill

12. Scanning the shipment number is an _____ part of tracking these containers.

(A) integral (C) integrating
(B) integrate (D) integration

13. The customer ordered three cartons of paper but _____ only two.

(A) received (C) supplied
(B) shipped (D) integrated

14. If we get one more complaint about a late delivery, we will have to look for a new _____ for our next shipment.

(A) supply (C) carrier
(B) catalog (D) inventory

15. Based on their credit check, it seems likely that they have _____ funds to cover this order.

(A) suffice (C) sufficiently
(B) sufficient (D) sufficed

PACKING GUIDELINES

In order to ____ (16.) breakage of merchandise and loss of shipments and to ensure accurate fulfillment of orders, please observe the following guidelines when preparing packages for shipment:

1) Check the order form carefully to make sure the item number matches the item number and description in the catalog.
2) Make sure that the address label has been ____ (17.) filled out, and particularly that names have been spelled correctly.
3) Each box must be ____ (18.) filled with packing material to protect the contents from damage.
4) Packages must be ready to be picked up by the carrier before 3:30 P.M. daily.

Following these guidelines is of the utmost importance. ____ (19.).

16. (A) minimum
    (B) minimize
    (C) minimal
    (D) minimally

17. (A) strictly
    (B) minimally
    (C) functionally
    (D) accurately

18. (A) sufficiently
    (B) sufficient
    (C) suffice
    (D) suffuse

19. (A) Many of our customers order from our online catalog.
    (B) Our carriers are usually able to deliver the shipments on time.
    (C) We need to make sure we have the right packing supplies on hand.
    (D) Lost and damaged shipments cost the company valuable time and money.

PART 7 READING COMPREHENSION

Questions 20–24 refer to the following letter.

April 15

Customer Service Department
Fleetwood Fashions
21986 North Featherstone Avenue
Hiawatha, MN

Dear Customer Service,

I am writing about an order I made from the Fleetwood Fashions catalog over a month ago, which I have not yet received. When I called to order two new purses and several spring shirts, the customer service representative assured me that there was sufficient inventory on hand to fulfill the order. He told me that it would be shipped before the end of the week and that I would receive it within ten days. When I still had not received the shipment after 14 days, I called the company. The customer service representative checked the ordering information on the computer, and we discovered that my address had not been accurately recorded. He promised to reship the order with my correct address and told me I would receive it within ten days. That was over two weeks ago, and I still have not received the shipment. I cannot understand this. Perhaps the carrier that you use is not reliable. In any case, I am tired of waiting for my order and would like to cancel it. I am not sure whether I will make an order from your company again. This is unfortunate since it is one of the few places that carry dresses and shoes in my size and at a reasonable price. However, this is the second time I have had a problem with an order, and I don't want this to happen again. Please cancel my order #20857631. Thank you.

Sincerely,

Lucinda Walker

20. When did Lucinda Walker make an order from Fleetwood Fashions?
    (A) Last week
    (B) Ten days ago
    (C) Fourteen days ago
    (D) Last month

21. What did she order?
    (A) Purses
    (B) Skirts
    (C) Shoes
    (D) Dresses

22. What is the problem with her order?
    (A) The price is unreasonable.
    (B) The dress size is wrong.
    (C) She hasn't received it yet.
    (D) It contained the wrong merchandise.

23. The word *fulfill* in line 4 is closest in meaning to
    (A) pay for.
    (B) complete.
    (C) send.
    (D) receive.

24. The word *carrier* in line 10 is closest in meaning to
    (A) communication.
    (B) employee.
    (C) transporter.
    (D) operator.

Lesson 19: Invoices

WORDS TO LEARN

- charge
- compile
- customer
- discount
- dispute
- efficient
- estimate
- impose
- mistake
- promptly
- rectify
- terms

Study the following definitions and examples.

1. **charge** v., to demand payment; n., an expense or a cost
   a. The customer service representative was responsible for telling all existing customers that higher prices would be charged next month.
   b. The extra charge for gift wrapping your purchase will appear on your invoice.
2. **compile** v., to gather together from several sources
   a. I have compiled a list of the most popular items for sale on our website.
   b. The clerk is responsible for compiling the orders at the end of the day.
3. **customer** n., one who purchases a commodity or service
   a. Let's make sure all invoices sent to customers are kept in alphabetical order.
   b. Our customer satisfaction plan offers a discount to customers who pay their invoices on time.
4. **discount** n., a reduction in price
   a. Customers who pay their invoices before the end of the month receive a 5 percent discount.
   b. The discount on the sale items was not very big.
5. **dispute** v., argue about; question; disagree with
   a. Customers may dispute certain charges on an invoice.
   b. A customer called the company to dispute the no returns policy.
6. **efficient** adj., acting or producing effectively with a minimum of waste or unnecessary effort
   a. The accountant was so efficient in processing the receipts that she had the job done by lunch.
   b. Electronic invoicing has helped us to be efficient.
7. **estimate** v., to approximate the amount or value of something; n., an approximation
   a. We estimated our losses this year at about five thousand dollars.
   b. The final cost of the project was not much more than the original estimate.
8. **impose** v., to establish or apply as compulsory; to force upon others
   a. The company will impose a surcharge for any items returned.
   b. We should not impose upon our staff by requiring them to work on weekends.
9. **mistake** n., an error or a fault
   a. I made a mistake in adding up your bill and we overcharged you twenty dollars.
   b. It was a mistake thinking that my boss would be reasonable when I explained my situation to him.
10. **promptly** adv., on time; punctually
    a. We always reply promptly to customers' letters.
    b. The new sales agent promptly offered a full refund for the damaged goods.
11. **rectify** v., to set right or correct
    a. He rectified the problem by giving the customer credit for the unused items that she returned.
    b. Embarrassed at his behavior, he rectified the situation by writing a letter of apology.
12. **terms** n., conditions
    a. The terms of payment were clearly listed at the bottom of the invoice.
    b. The terms of the agreement required that items be fully paid for before they would be shipped.

WORD FAMILIES

verb	discount	They discounted the price on the merchandise damaged in shipment.
noun	discount	There is a 20 percent discount on all the items for sale in the back room.
adjective	discountable	In most cases, damaged items are discountable.

verb	dispute	If a customer wants to dispute an item on an invoice, please let the manager know.
noun	dispute	It is not a good idea to get into a dispute with a customer about small charges on an invoice.
adjective	disputable	Customers tend to believe that late charges on an invoice are disputable.

noun	efficiency	The efficiency of our new billing system has resulted in almost all the invoices being paid on time.
adjective	efficient	We appreciate customers who are efficient about paying on time.
adverb	efficiently	If we work efficiently, we can get all these invoices sent out by the end of the day.

verb	impose	The government has decided to impose a larger sales tax on certain items, and this will be included on the invoice.
noun	imposition	The customer disputed the imposition of certain charges on the invoice.
adjective	imposing	The size of the amount due on the invoice was imposing.

verb	mistake	She mistook the amount on the invoice and overpaid.
noun	mistake	The manager called the supplier as soon as he saw the mistake on the invoice.
adjective	mistaken	The customer never received the invoice because of the mistaken address on the envelope.

noun	promptness	We appreciate the promptness with which you pay your bills.
adjective	prompt	I am happy to receive statements that thank me for my prompt payment.
adverb	promptly	Companies sometimes give discounts to customers who pay their bills promptly.

WORDS IN CONTEXT

Read the following passage and write the words in the blanks below.

charges	discount	estimated	promptly
compiled	dispute	imposed	rectified
customer	efficient	mistake	terms

Companies that sell items online through catalogs need to have an (1) ________________ process for invoicing and billing customers. When a customer places an order, a list of items must be (2) ________________ and an invoice generated. The invoice will list the items purchased, along with the cost of each item, and the quantity desired. (3) ________________ that will be incurred in shipping the items to the (4) ________________ are also added to the invoice. Sometimes shipping charges are simply (5) ________________ based on the weight or value of the items ordered.

The invoice also shows the (6) ________________ of payment. Payment is usually due within 30 days. Extra charges are often (7) ________________ on overdue accounts. Customers are not always happy to see these extra charges and may (8) ________________ them with the company. Many companies also offer a small (9) ________________ if invoices are paid promptly.

Sometimes items get damaged or lost in transit, or customers discover that the wrong items have been shipped by (10) ________________. They will usually contact the company to have the problem (11) ________________. Such complaints should be dealt with (12) ________________. If an item is missing, a replacement will be sent, usually at no additional charge to the customer.

WORD PRACTICE

Listening Comprehension

Track 20

PART 1 PHOTO

Look at the picture and listen to the sentences. Choose the sentence that best describes the picture.

1. Ⓐ Ⓑ Ⓒ Ⓓ

PART 2 QUESTION–RESPONSE

Listen to the question and the three responses. Choose the response that best answers the question.

2. Ⓐ Ⓑ Ⓒ 3. Ⓐ Ⓑ Ⓒ

PART 3 CONVERSATION

Listen to the dialogue. Then read each question and choose the best response.

4. What do they need to order?
   (A) Computers
   (B) Temporary workers
   (C) Order forms
   (D) Office supplies

5. What does the man ask the woman to do?
   (A) Compile a list
   (B) Clean the supply closet
   (C) Read the invoice carefully
   (D) Write a check

6. When will the woman place the order?
   (A) Before noon
   (B) Tonight
   (C) Tomorrow
   (D) Tuesday

PART 4 TALK

Listen to the talk. Then read each question and choose the best answer.

7. What is the topic of the talk?
   (A) Late payments
   (B) Billing customers
   (C) Immediate payment
   (D) Discounts

8. How does immediate payment benefit the company?
   (A) The company doesn't have to use collections agencies.
   (B) The company doesn't have to charge late fees.
   (C) The company gains customers.
   (D) The company doesn't have to send a bill to the customer.

9. How much do immediate payments save per project?
   (A) 4 percent
   (B) 14 percent
   (C) 15 percent
   (D) 50 percent

Reading

PART 5 INCOMPLETE SENTENCES

Choose the word that best completes the sentence.

10. After we have ______ all of the necessary documents, we will begin our analysis of the data.
    (A) compile
    (B) compiled
    (C) compiling
    (D) compilation

11. Though he worked very ______ with machines and figures, he was slow and awkward with customers and coworkers.
    (A) efficient
    (B) efficiently
    (C) efficiency
    (D) efficacy

12. Although ______ expenses works well when applying for a contract, clients appreciate itemization on their invoices.
    (A) estimate
    (B) estimator
    (C) estimating
    (D) estimation

13. The customers usually pay their invoices promptly in order to avoid the ______ of late charges.
    (A) efficiency
    (B) mistake
    (C) estimate
    (D) imposition

14. Fortunately, we realized that the charges on the invoice were too high and were able to correct the ______ before billing the customer.
    (A) mistakes
    (B) disputes
    (C) discounts
    (D) terms

15. The client would appreciate it if the invoice could be sent ______ so he can pay it before the end of the fiscal year.
    (A) promptly
    (B) promptness
    (C) prompted
    (D) prompt

____. Without invoices, after all, a business would not receive payment for services
16.

rendered. The ____ of the invoice must be stated clearly, that is, the customer
17.

needs to know exactly what he is being charged for and when the payment is due. If a customer discovers a mistake on the invoice, it should be rectified as soon as possible. If a final charge is much greater than the original estimate, the reason for this should be explained as clearly and simply as possible on the invoice. Some businesses ____
18.

a late fee on late payments. In such cases, this must also be made clear on the invoice. Finally, the invoice must be sent to the customer ____ in order to encourage timely
19.

payment.

16. (A) Invoices may be sent electronically or through the postal service.
    (B) Invoices may list charges for items purchased or for services rendered.
    (C) Invoices usually include the date by which payment must be received.
    (D) Invoices are an essential part of any business and should be given their due attention.

17. (A) terms
    (B) orders
    (C) discounts
    (D) compilations

18. (A) imposition
    (B) imposing
    (C) imposter
    (D) impose

19. (A) prompt
    (B) prompter
    (C) promptly
    (D) promptness

PART 7 READING COMPREHENSION

Questions 20–24 refer to the following invoice and letter.

CLARY CLOSETS

"Making your world more organized."

Invoice

To: Millicent Pensky
752 Montrose Avenue
Proctorville, VT

Date: November 10, 20—

Initial consultation fee	$ 75
Organizing four closets	$ 800
Supplies	$ 225
Total due	$1100

Thank you for doing business with us.

Please pay by November 30. A 10 percent late fee will be imposed on late payments.

November 15, 20—

Clary Closets
18 North Main Street
Chester, VT

Dear Ms. Clary,

I am writing to dispute the charges on the invoice I recently received from your company. The invoice contained several mistakes. First, I was told that I would not be charged an initial consultation fee if I decided to use your services. Since I did go ahead and hire you to organize my closets, I should not have to pay this fee. Second, the final charge for organizing my four closets was $250 higher than the original estimate. I think this is too much and that I should be charged no more than the original estimate. Finally, I was charged for supplies that you ordered without my authorization. I could have obtained these same supplies myself at a lower price. Since I did not authorize this charge, I think I should pay a lower price for the supplies.

I chose Clary Closets to organize my closets because several of my friends and business associates have been satisfied customers of yours. However, I find it difficult to believe that an organizing business can be so inefficient when it comes to invoices. Please rectify these mistakes and send me a corrected invoice promptly.

Sincerely,

Millicent Pensky

20. What did Ms. Pensky hire Ms. Clary to do?
    (A) Write invoices
    (B) Collect fees
    (C) Organize closets
    (D) Buy supplies

21. According to the terms of the invoice, how much will Ms. Pensky owe if she pays on December 1?
    (A) $110
    (B) $1100
    (C) $1110
    (D) $1210

22. How much was the original estimate?
    (A) $250
    (B) $550
    (C) $800
    (D) $850

23. The word *dispute* in line 1 of the letter is closest in meaning to
    (A) disagree with.
    (B) add to.
    (C) pay for.
    (D) ask for.

24. The word *rectify* in line 18 of the letter is closest in meaning to
    (A) explain.
    (B) calculate.
    (C) fix.
    (D) see.

Lesson 20: Inventory

WORDS TO LEARN

- adjustment
- automatically
- crucial
- discrepancy
- disturb
- install
- reflect
- run
- scan
- subtract
- tedious
- verify

Study the following definitions and examples.

1. **adjustment** n., a change in order to match
   a. With the adjustments to the numbers of screws, we are close to having an accurate count.
   b. An adjustment to the number of damaged items would help us align our figures.
2. **automatically** adv., independently, without outside prompting
   a. The computer automatically updates the inventory files when a sale is made.
   b. This door opens automatically so it's easier to carry large boxes out of the stockroom.
3. **crucial** adj., extremely significant or important
   a. Knowing how many products we have in stock is crucial to our shipping procedures.
   b. Inventory is a crucial process and must be taken seriously by all staff.
4. **discrepancy** n., a divergence or disagreement
   a. We easily explained the discrepancy between the two counts.
   b. Unless you catch the error immediately, the discrepancy gets entered into the computer and becomes very difficult to correct.
5. **disturb** v., to interfere with; to interrupt
   a. Let's see how many products we can count in advance of inventory so we disturb fewer customers.
   b. Sorry to disturb you, but I need to ask you to move so I can record the products behind you.
6. **install** v., put equipment into place
   a. Since we installed the new software, taking inventory has become a lot easier.
   b. We'll need to get the new computers installed before we can take inventory.
7. **reflect** v., show; indicate
   a. The numbers on the computer log should accurately reflect the actual numbers in the warehouse.
   b. The way you handled the problems with the inventory reflects your professional attitude.
8. **run** v., to operate
   a. As long as the computer is running, you can keep adding new data.
   b. The new cash registers look complicated but they are actually quite easy to run.
9. **scan** v., to look over quickly; to automatically record data with a scanner
   a. Jasmine quickly scanned the list to see if any information was missing.
   b. When we take inventory, we have to scan each item number into the computer.
10. **subtract** v., to take away; to deduct
    a. Once you ring up an item, the computer automatically subtracts it from the inventory log.
    b. Whoever did the inventory forgot to subtract the damaged items.
11. **tedious** adj., tiresome by reason of length, slowness, or dullness; boring
    a. This is tedious work, but you will be glad the inventory is accurate when you hit the holiday season.
    b. Counting merchandise all weekend is the most tedious job I can imagine.
12. **verify** v., to prove the truth of
    a. I can't verify the accuracy of these numbers, since I was not present for inventory weekend.
    b. The inventory process verifies that all the items are accounted for.

WORD FAMILIES

verb	adjust	After you've verified the quantities in the stockroom, I'll adjust the numbers in the database.
noun	adjustment	While the adjustments are being made to the computer inventory, the computer will be off-line and unavailable for use.
adjective	adjustable	The height of the shelves is adjustable, which makes it easier to reach and count the merchandise.

noun	automation	Computers have brought a heightened level of automation into the retail industry.
adjective	automatic	The automatic updating of the inventory is convenient, but always a day behind.
adverb	automatically	After every cash register transaction, the computer automatically updates the inventory record.

verb	disturb	Count as many of the items on the salesroom floor as you can without disturbing the customers.
noun	disturbance	After considering all the options, Ellen decided that closing the store a day to do the annual inventory would cause the least amount of disturbance for customers.
adverb	disturbingly	The computer count and the physical count were disturbingly incongruous, which distressed the store manager.

verb	scan	Scan the aisles and see if you find the missing carton.
noun	scanner	We will install a scanner at two of the computer terminals.

verb	subtract	Subtract 50 from the total—I just found an unusable box.
noun	subtraction	If you feel confident doing basic addition and subtraction in your head, you don't have to carry the calculator with you.

noun	tedium	I can't bear the tedium of taking inventory.
adjective	tedious	Entering all the information about the inventory into the computer is a tedious job, but it has to be done.
adverb	tediously	We worked tediously on the inventory for the entire weekend.

WORDS IN CONTEXT

Read the following passage and write the words in the blanks below.

adjusted	discrepancies	reflect	subtracts
automatically	disturbances	running	tedious
crucial	installed	scanning	verifies

In a retail business, inventory has multiple meanings. Inventory means all the goods that a company has on hand or available to it in a warehouse. Inventory also means the process by which the business (1) ________________ the number of goods. An accurate account of the inventory available is (2) ________________.

Most retail businesses have (3) ________________ cash registers that help keep count of inventory. (4) ________________ these registers is easy, and they do an important job. When a customer makes a purchase, the computer system tied to the register (5) ________________ the purchase from the inventory records. If a customer makes a return or an exchange, the inventory numbers will be (6) ________________ by the computer (7) ________________. That's why (8) ________________ the bar code is so important in stores. If merchandise is broken or damaged in the stockroom or on the sales floor, the manager will ask the sales and stock help to change the stock holdings to (9) ________________ the loss.

As good as the computer records may be, they are just an estimate. At least once a year, most businesses do an actual physical count of the inventory. This process can be (10) ________________, but it is necessary as there are always (11) ________________ between what the computer says you own and what your physical count says. Often stores close for a day, or at least close early, so that staff can perform the inventory without (12) ________________.

WORD PRACTICE

Listening Comprehension

Track 21

PART 1 PHOTO

Look at the picture and listen to the sentences. Choose the sentence that best describes the picture.

1. Ⓐ Ⓑ Ⓒ Ⓓ

PART 2 QUESTION–RESPONSE

Listen to the question and the three responses. Choose the response that best answers the question.

2. Ⓐ Ⓑ Ⓒ   3. Ⓐ Ⓑ Ⓒ

PART 3 CONVERSATION

Listen to the dialogue. Then read each question and choose the best response.

4. What information does the man want to verify?
   (A) The size of the bedspreads
   (B) The number of bedspreads on hand
   (C) The reason for the discrepancy
   (D) The number of bedspreads the customer needs

5. According to the computer, how many bed-spreads are there?
   (A) Three
   (B) Five
   (C) Seven
   (D) Eleven

6. Where are the bedspreads?
   (A) In a box
   (B) On a shelf
   (C) On the bed
   (D) In the stockroom

PART 4 TALK

Listen to the talk. Then read each question and choose the best answer.

7. What happens every year in January?
   (A) They adjust the file drawers.
   (B) They record the audio portion.
   (C) They delete unnecessary computer files.
   (D) They do a physical count.

8. What is one problem with their work?
   (A) It consumes too much time.
   (B) Nobody appreciates it.
   (C) The hourly rate is low.
   (D) It's boring.

9. How many days does it take to complete the work?
   (A) Two
   (B) Three
   (C) Four
   (D) Eight

Reading

PART 5 INCOMPLETE SENTENCES

Choose the word that best completes the sentence.

10. The computer's inventory figures will be considered inaccurate until the store manager enters the data from the physical count and _____ the figures.
    (A) adjustment
    (B) adjusts
    (C) adjustable
    (D) adjusted

11. Inventory control cannot be performed _____, but must be done by physically counting the merchandise.
    (A) automatically
    (B) automatic
    (C) automation
    (D) automated

12. Do not _____ the staff when they are counting the items; they need to concentrate.
    (A) disturb
    (B) install
    (C) reflect
    (D) run

13. We need to take a physical count to _____ the numbers in the computer.
    (A) very
    (B) verifiable
    (C) verification
    (D) verify

14. Don't just _____ the list of tasks; look it over carefully and make sure every job on it has been completed.
    (A) automate
    (B) adjust
    (C) install
    (D) scan

15. If we _____ the damaged merchandise from the inventory, our figures will accurately reflect what we have on hand.
    (A) subtract
    (B) subtracting
    (C) subtracted
    (D) subtraction

Notice

Our new cash registers will be installed over the weekend so that we can start using them next week. The main reason we have bought these new machines is that they will make it easier to keep track of our inventory. When you ____ (16.) a customer's purchase into the machine, it will automatically record the purchase in the inventory files of our computer. ____ (17.). It will save us the ____ (18.) work of manually entering data into the computer and ensure that our numbers are accurate. All staff members are required to attend a training session on Friday afternoon during which you will learn how ____ (19.) the new cash registers. See you there.

16. (A) scan
    (B) will scan
    (C) scanned
    (D) are going to scan

17. (A) We may have to make some adjustments to the machines to ensure that they run properly.
    (B) Your work will not be disturbed as the machines will be installed when the store is closed.
    (C) We expect that our checkout lines will move more smoothly and quickly.
    (D) This will help us track sales and reorder items promptly.

18. (A) tedious
    (B) crucial
    (C) automatic
    (D) adjustable

19. (A) running
    (B) to run
    (C) runs
    (D) run

PART 7 READING COMPREHENSION

Questions 20–24 refer to the following memo.

To: All store staff
From: Bill Jones, Manager
Re: Next week

This is a reminder that we will be closing the store for two days at the end of next week, Friday and Saturday, for inventory. This is a long and tedious job, and we will need the assistance of each and every one of you to get it done. Therefore, no vacation days will be granted during that time. During the inventory process, we will verify the numbers in our computer files, clear up any discrepancies we may find, and adjust our records as necessary. We need to make sure that our records accurately reflect the stock that we actually have on hand. When you report to work on Thursday, your supervisor will give you your assignment. Some of you will be required to work in the stockroom taking a physical count, and others will be asked to work in the office entering data on the computers. We won't reopen the store until the following Tuesday since Monday is a national holiday. I hope that will give you a chance to rest up a bit after the big job. Thank you in advance for your assistance with this crucial work.

20. Why will the store close next week?
    (A) Everyone will be on vacation.
    (B) They need to count their stock.
    (C) The staff members need a rest.
    (D) There will be a computer training session.

21. Who will give the assignments?
    (A) The manager
    (B) The assistants
    (C) The supervisors
    (D) The record keeper

22. When will the store open again?
    (A) Monday
    (B) Tuesday
    (C) Thursday
    (D) Friday

23. The word *adjust* in line 10 is closest in meaning to
    (A) enter.
    (B) write.
    (C) change.
    (D) create.

24. The word *crucial* in line 23 is closest in meaning to
    (A) important.
    (B) boring.
    (C) difficult.
    (D) lengthy.

WORD REVIEW #4
LESSONS 16–20 PURCHASING

Choose the word that best completes the sentence.

1. Several local merchants are working together to _________ their businesses and are looking for ways to attract more customers.
   (A) expand
   (B) impose
   (C) compile
   (D) integrate

2. All fashion _________ have a limited life span.
   (A) trend
   (B) trends
   (C) trendy
   (D) trending

3. It is a poorly run office that does not _________ adequate office supplies.
   (A) maintain
   (B) maintained
   (C) maintaining
   (D) maintenance

4. Sometimes office policy doesn't allow the company to _________ less expensive supplies when they are available from someone other than a preferred provider.
   (A) obtain
   (B) obtained
   (C) obtaining
   (D) obtainable

5. A supplier who has chronic trouble _________ his obligations to a customer will quickly lose customers.
   (A) fulfill
   (B) fulfills
   (C) fulfilling
   (D) fulfillment

6. To _________ disruption, buyers should order well ahead of need.
   (A) minimum
   (B) minimal
   (C) minimize
   (D) minimally

7. It is wise to begin by _________ an inventory of equipment on hand.
   (A) compile
   (B) compiling
   (C) compiler
   (D) compilation

8. If the provider does not meet his client's demand, he should _________ the problem as soon as possible.
   (A) rectify
   (B) rectifier
   (C) rectifiable
   (D) rectification

9. If some supplies show a steady rise in consumption, the office manager should make an appropriate _________ in his standard order.
   (A) adjust
   (B) adjuster
   (C) adjusting
   (D) adjustment

10. Every time you remove an item from the shelves, you should _________ it from the inventory list.
   (A) compile
   (B) subtract
   (C) adjust
   (D) expand

Choose the one word or phrase that best completes each sentence.

Memo

To: Floor Managers
From: Head Manager
Re: Spring Sale

Our large Spring Sale begins next week. Before the store opens on Monday, all sale items should be placed on racks near the _________ area. This ensures that customers will see them right before

11. (A) catalog
    (B) merchandise
    (C) carrier
    (D) checkout

they pay for their purchases. We expect large crowds in the store during the sale, so it will be important to _________ order. This means picking up any items that fall on the floor or end

12. (A) disturb
    (B) maintain
    (C) estimate
    (D) compile

up on the wrong shelf, and making sure that all items are clearly marked with the correct price. Remember, a neat and organized store _________ more business.

13. (A) receives
    (B) receiving
    (C) received
    (D) has received

To: Betsy Barnes
From: Lighting Limited Customer Service
Subject: Your order

Dear Betsy Barnes,

We have received your message about your recent order of a desk lamp with a glass shade. You state that the_________ arrived in damaged condition. We will be happy to replace the damaged merchandise at

14. (A) ship
    (B) shipping
    (C) shipment
    (D) shippable

no extra _________ to you. You will not have to pay anything. Simply place the damaged item back in

15. (A) term
    (B) supply
    (C) carrier
    (D) charge

the box and affix the "postage paid" sticker to the outside. As soon as we receive it, a replacement lamp will be _________ sent to you. We are sorry for any inconvenience this may have caused.

16. (A) prompt
    (B) promptly
    (C) prompter
    (D) promptness

Manuel Gozanlez
Lighting Limited Customer Service Associate

To: Joanne Simmons
From: Bill Smithers
Subject: Supplies

Joanne,

It's time to order some supplies. We need several boxes of _______________, including large

17. (A) stationery
(B) invoice
(C) bargain
(D) inventory

and small envelopes as well as letter paper. Don't order this from XYZ Printers. I was not satisfied with the _______________ of the paper in our last order. It tore very easily.

18. (A) subtraction
(B) efficiency
(C) quality
(D) quantity

Zippo Printers on Elm Street might be a better source. Let's try them this time. It might be a good idea to get some ink cartridges, too. Why don't you check to see how many we have _______________ hand? If we have just one or two boxes left, you should order more.

19. (A) by
(B) to
(C) up
(D) on

Thanks.
Bill

Lesson 21: Banking

WORDS TO LEARN

- accept
- balance
- borrow
- cautiously
- deduct
- dividend
- down payment
- mortgage
- restricted
- signature
- take out
- transaction

Study the following definitions and examples.

1. **accept** v., to receive; to respond favorably
   a. He could not manage his bank account online because the website would not accept his password.
   b. Without hesitating, she accepted the job of teller.
2. **balance** n., the remainder; v., to compute the difference between credits and debits of an account
   a. His healthy bank balance showed a long habit of savings.
   b. It took him over an hour to balance his checkbook.
3. **borrow** v., to use temporarily
   a. Myra borrowed a pen so that she could sign the check.
   b. The couple borrowed money from the bank to buy a home.
4. **cautiously** adv., carefully; warily
   a. The bank manager spoke cautiously when giving out information to people she did not know.
   b. Act cautiously when signing contracts and read them thoroughly first.
5. **deduct** v., to take away from a total; to subtract
   a. If you choose, the bank will deduct regular charges, such as electric bills, from your account.
   b. By deducting the monthly fee from her checking account, Yi was able to make her account balance.
6. **dividend** n., a share in a distribution
   a. The stockholders were outraged when their quarterly dividends were so small.
   b. The dividend was calculated and distributed to the group.
7. **down payment** n., an initial partial payment
   a. Mary bought her car with an initial down payment in cash and then made her monthly payments online.
   b. Karl was disappointed when the real estate agent told him he needed a larger down payment on the house.
8. **mortgage** n., the amount due on a property; v., to borrow money with your house as collateral
   a. Due to low interest rates, Sheila moved quickly to find a good deal on a mortgage.
   b. Hiram mortgaged his home to get extra money to invest in his business.
9. **restricted** adj., limited
   a. The number of free withdrawals a customer can make each month is restricted to five.
   b. Access to the safe deposit box vault is restricted to key holders.
10. **signature** n., the name of a person written by the person
    a. Once we have your signature, the contract will be complete.
    b. The customer's signature was kept on file for identification purposes.
11. **take out** v., withdraw; remove
    a. My checking account allows me to take out money at any bank branch without a fee.
    b. They took out the chairs in the bank lobby so now there is no place to sit.
12. **transaction** n., a business deal
    a. Banking transactions will appear on your monthly statement.
    b. The most common transactions can be made from your personal computer.

WORD FAMILIES

verb	accept	The bank will not accept a student ID as a valid form of identification.
noun	acceptance	The bank's acceptance of checks allows extra time for out-of-state checks to clear before they are credited to your account.
adjective	acceptable	Shorter banking hours are acceptable to customers because they can do their bank transactions at any hour online.

verb	caution	Our friends cautioned us against putting our money into an account that pays such a low interest rate.
adjective	cautious	The bank officer was cautious about approving Chen's loan because of his unfavorable credit history.
adverb	cautiously	We spent our money cautiously because we were not sure we would be able to borrow more.

verb	deduct	Remember to deduct the monthly bank fee from your statement.
noun	deductible	Taxes and health insurance payments are called deductibles because they are deducted from your paycheck.
noun	deduction	Deductions are made electronically every month and will appear on your statement.

verb	restrict	The bank's policies restrict the number of deductions you can make from your account without a penalty.
noun	restriction	The restrictions on who was eligible for a mortgage made it impossible for many low-income families to borrow money.
adjective	restricted	You can feel confident that your personal banking information is completely safe because of the restricted access to our website.

verb	sign	Once you have signed the mortgage contract, the bank will make a check payable to you.
noun	signature	Your signature can be electronically recorded to be verified later.

verb	transact	Our company transacts all its financial business at this bank.
noun	transaction	All parties concerned were pleased with the results of the business transactions.

WORDS IN CONTEXT

Read the following passage and write the words in the blanks below.

accept	cautious	down payment	signature
balance	deductions	mortgages	take out
borrow	dividends	restrict	transact

Banks are not only places in which to save money or to (1) ______________ your financial business, but they are also institutions from which people can (2) ______________ money. Every day, people look to banks for loans, such as (3) ______________ for new homes. A loan is essentially a contract that binds the lender to a schedule of payments, so both parties should be (4) ______________ and not enter into the arrangement without thinking. Banks will look at such factors as how much people have saved toward a (5) ______________ in determining whether to make a loan.

Banks have different kinds of accounts. Some pay high quarterly (6) ______________. Some accounts even severely (7) ______________ the number of times, if any, that you can access your account, or the amount of cash you can (8) ______________.

Today, electronic banking can be used to check the (9) ______________ on an account, or to see if automatic (10) ______________ have been made. This can all be done from your home or office computer. When you go to the bank, be sure to bring identification. Usually a bank will only (11) ______________ a photo ID; a (12) ______________ is not a valid ID.

WORD PRACTICE

Listening Comprehension

Track 22

PART 1 PHOTO

Look at the picture and listen to the sentences. Choose the sentence that best describes the picture.

1. Ⓐ Ⓑ Ⓒ Ⓓ

PART 2 QUESTION–RESPONSE

Listen to the question and the three responses. Choose the response that best answers the question.

2. Ⓐ Ⓑ Ⓒ

3. Ⓐ Ⓑ Ⓒ

PART 3 CONVERSATION

Listen to the dialogue. Then read each question and choose the best response.

4. What does the man want to do?
   (A) Open a bank account
   (B) Get a new driver's license
   (C) Put his signature on file
   (D) Cash a check

5. According to the woman, what is required?
   (A) A photo ID
   (B) An order form
   (C) A large deposit
   (D) A signed check

6. When will the man's check clear?
   (A) In seven days
   (B) In eight days
   (C) In ten days
   (D) In eleven days

PART 4 TALK

Listen to the talk. Then read each question and choose the best answer.

7. Who is this talk for?
   (A) People who are looking for a job
   (B) People who want to borrow money
   (C) People who work in a bank
   (D) People who want to open a bank account

8. How big a down payment is required?
   (A) 10 percent
   (B) 3 percent
   (C) 1 percent
   (D) 4 percent

9. What is a requirement?
   (A) A new job
   (B) An important address
   (C) Money in the bank
   (D) An accountant

Reading

PART 5 INCOMPLETE SENTENCES

Choose the word that best completes the sentence.

10. I'm going to call the bank manager ahead of time to make certain that she will _____ a personal check to start a new account.

    (A) accept (C) acceptance
    (B) accepted (D) acceptable

11. We have enough money to make a _____ on the car and will borrow the rest from the bank.

    (A) mortgage (C) balance
    (B) down payment (D) dividend

12. Every month my automatic car loan payment shows up as a _____ on my monthly statement.

    (A) mortgage (C) dividend
    (B) deduction (D) restriction

13. The number of free withdrawals from your savings account is _____ to three; after that there will be a charge for each withdrawal.

    (A) deducted (C) borrowed
    (B) restricted (D) accepted

14. There is a counter in the bank lobby where customers can _____ their documents.

    (A) signing (C) sign
    (B) signed (D) signature

15. Many customers enjoy the convenience of carrying out their bank _____ online.

    (A) transacts (C) transacted
    (B) transacting (D) transactions

PART 6 TEXT COMPLETION

Dear Customer,

Our records show that you qualify for our new automatic mortgage payment plan. Under this plan, your monthly mortgage payments ____ (16.) from your savings account automatically. Now you no longer have to worry about making your payments on time! ____ (17.). You must maintain a sufficient ____ (18.) in your account to cover the monthly payments. If you are interested in participating in this plan, simply complete the enclosed form. Certain ____ (19.) apply to this plan, so read the explanation on the back of the form carefully. You may return the form in the enclosed envelope. Don't forget to sign it at the bottom. Your automatic deductions could begin as early as next month.

16. (A) deduct
    (B) deducted
    (C) are deducted
    (D) are deducting

17. (A) There is a penalty for overdue payments.
    (B) We complete this monthly transaction for you.
    (C) You are paying back borrowed money with monthly payments.
    (D) The larger your down payment, the smaller your monthly payments will be.

18. (A) dividend
    (B) balance
    (C) transaction
    (D) down payment

19. (A) restrictions
    (B) restrictive
    (C) restricted
    (D) restricts

PART 7 READING COMPREHENSION

Questions 20–24 refer to the following two e-mail messages.

From: Marvin Gardner
To: Customer Service Bank of Augusta
Subject: service charge question

Dear Customer Service Office,

I am a new customer at your bank. I opened an account with you last month, and I have recently received my first monthly statement. I find that there is a service charge on three of the checks that I wrote. I understood that this account had free checking, so I was surprised to see this charge. Perhaps it is a mistake. I am attaching a copy of the statement. Please clarify this matter for me. Thank you.

Sincerely,

Marvin Gardner

From: Customer Service Bank of Augusta
To: Marvin Gardner
Subject: re: service charge question

Dear Mr. Gardner,

Thank you for your message regarding charges to your account. While it is true that your account has free checking, some restrictions apply. You may write five checks a month free of charge. After that, you must maintain a minimum average balance of $600 in your account in order to continue with free checking. Since your average account balance last month was only $435, you were entitled to only five free checks. A service charge was applied to the checks you wrote beyond that minimum. I hope this explanation is satisfactory to you.

Let me take this opportunity to make sure that you are aware of other services you can get with your account. You can arrange to have your monthly utility bills deducted from your account. You are also eligible to borrow small amounts of money from the bank at a low interest rate. If you are interested in these or any other services, please visit us at the bank, and an officer will be happy to explain all the details to you. Thank you for being a National Bank of Augusta customer.

Sincerely,

Eloise Lockwood
Customer Service Officer

20. Why did Mr. Gardner write this e-mail?
    (A) To pay his monthly utility bills
    (B) To find out about borrowing money
    (C) To ask a question about his monthly statement
    (D) To order some free checks

21. When did he open an account at the National Bank of Augusta?
    (A) May
    (B) June
    (C) July
    (D) August

22. How many checks did he write last month?
    (A) Three
    (B) Five
    (C) Six
    (D) Eight

23. The word *restrictions* in line 3 of the second letter is closest in meaning to
    (A) limitations.
    (B) fees.
    (C) customers.
    (D) numbers.

24. The word *deducted* in line 13 of the second letter is closest in meaning to
    (A) borrowed.
    (B) attached.
    (C) subtracted.
    (D) added.

Lesson 22: Accounting

WORDS TO LEARN

- accounting
- accumulate
- asset
- audit
- budget
- build up
- client
- debt
- outstanding
- profitably
- reconcile
- turnover

Study the following definitions and examples.

1. **accounting** n., the recording and gathering of financial information for a company
   a. Good accounting is needed in all businesses.
   b. There are a number of good software programs to help with both personal and business accounting.
2. **accumulate** v., to gather; to collect
   a. They have accumulated more than enough information.
   b. The bills started to accumulate after the secretary quit.
3. **asset** n., something of value
   a. The company's assets are worth millions of dollars.
   b. A sophisticated accounting system is an asset to a company.
4. **audit** n., a formal examination of financial records; v., to examine the financial records of a company
   a. No one looks forward to an audit by the government.
   b. The independent accountants audited the company's books.
5. **budget** n., a list of probable expenses and income for a given period; v., to plan for expenses
   a. The department head was pleased that she received a 10 percent increase in her budget.
   b. The company will have to budget more money for this department next year.
6. **build up** v., to increase over time
   a. The firm has built up a solid reputation for itself.
   b. Be careful. Your inventory of parts is building up.
7. **client** n., a customer
   a. The accountant attracted many new clients through her website.
   b. Maintaining close contact with clients keeps the account managers aware of changing needs.
8. **debt** n., something owed, as in money or goods
   a. The company has been very careful and is slowly digging itself out of debt.
   b. The banks are worried about your increasing debt.
9. **outstanding** adj., still due; not paid or settled
   a. That client still has several outstanding bills.
   b. Clients with outstanding bills will not receive further service until the bills are paid.
10. **profitably** adv., advantageously
   a. The company used its accountant's advice profitably.
   b. We invested in the stock market profitably.
11. **reconcile** v., to make consistent
   a. The client uses his bank statements to reconcile his accounts.
   b. The accountant found the error when she reconciled the account.
12. **turnover** n., the number of times a product is sold and replaced or an employee leaves and another employee is hired
   a. We have had a low turnover of inventory this month and didn't bring in much money.
   b. Because of our high employee turnover we actually spend less money on salaries.

WORD FAMILIES

noun	accountant	The accountant was precise and hardworking.
noun	accounting	Accounting is a popular field of study.
noun	account	The client closed his bank account and withdrew all of his money.

verb	accumulate	The owner's goal was to accumulate as much wealth as possible.
noun	accumulation	The accumulation of goods may lead to an inventory problem.
adjective	accumulated	The sum of all your accumulated resources equals your total assets.

verb	audit	Some bookkeeping inconsistencies showed up when our records were audited.
noun	audit	If you keep your financial records carefully, you will always be ready for audit.
noun	auditor	The auditor will ask to see your recent spreadsheets.

verb	budget	There was no travel expense budgeted for the editorial department.
noun	budget	The boss asked for input on next year's budget.
adjective	budgetary	Due to budgetary constraints, we cannot hire additional staff at this time.

verb	build up	Over the years, our office has built up a solid list of clients.
noun	buildup	A buildup of debt will weaken the company's finances.

verb	profit	Our business has really profited from hiring an expert accountant.
noun	profit	After you enter your income and expenses, the spreadsheet will show your profit.
adjective	profitable	The accountant was able to show us where our business was profitable and where we were losing money.

WORDS IN CONTEXT

Read the following passage and write the words in the blanks below.

accounting	audited	clients	profitable
accumulated	budget	debt	reconcile
assets	building up	outstanding	turnover

Accounting information is pulled together or (1) ______________ to help someone make decisions. A manager must come up with a (2) ______________ to help control expenses. A retail store owner realizes that her (3) ______________ have (4) ______________ bills. A restaurant owner wants to know if it is (5) ______________ to serve lunch. A nonprofit organization is being (6) ______________ by the government. All of these people and organizations could use the services of an accountant.

Accountants and (7) ______________ systems help a company stay on track. They raise flags when expenses are (8) ______________ and keep an eye on the (9) ______________ of inventory. They (10) ______________ their clients' accounts to ensure that their clients' records are correct. Good accounting systems allow managers to come up with ways to improve their business.

The accountant prepares information for both internal and external use. Financial statements provide a quick look into the life of a business. They show how much (11) ______________ the company is carrying and how much its (12) ______________ are worth. The outside world uses this information to judge the health of the company.

WORD PRACTICE

Listening Comprehension

Track 23

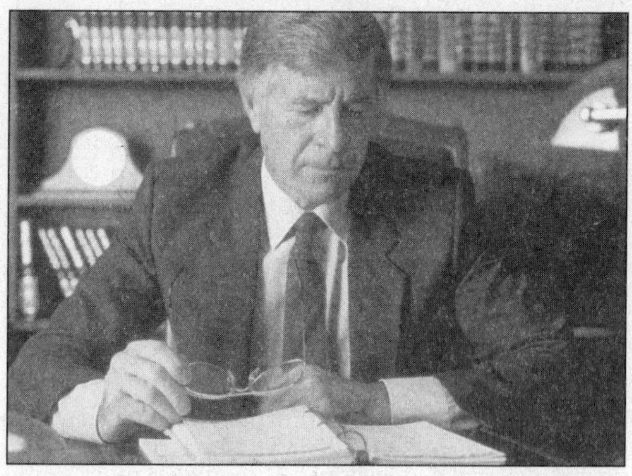

PART 1 PHOTO

Look at the picture and listen to the sentences. Choose the sentence that best describes the picture.

1. Ⓐ Ⓑ Ⓒ Ⓓ

PART 2 QUESTION–RESPONSE

Listen to the question and the three responses. Choose the response that best answers the question.

2. Ⓐ Ⓑ Ⓒ   3. Ⓐ Ⓑ Ⓒ

PART 3 CONVERSATION

Listen to the dialogue. Then read each question and choose the best response.

4. What time does the woman expect to return to the office?
   - (A) By 1:00
   - (B) By 2:00
   - (C) By 4:00
   - (D) By 5:00

5. What is the client's problem?
   - (A) He doesn't understand his accountant.
   - (B) He won't be in his office today.
   - (C) He has a lot of debt.
   - (D) He doesn't have a savings account.

6. What does the woman plan to do with the client today?
   - (A) Show him a new budget
   - (B) Give him a present
   - (C) Ask him for more work
   - (D) Make a business deal with him

PART 4 TALK

Listen to the talk. Then read each question and choose the best answer.

7. What is the topic of this talk?
   - (A) How to start an accounting firm
   - (B) How to avoid client turnover
   - (C) How to have a profitable accounting firm
   - (D) How to get clients

8. How can an accounting firm make more money?
   - (A) By charging higher fees
   - (B) By getting recommendations from their clients
   - (C) By hiring new accountants
   - (D) By making a new list of clients

9. According to the speaker, what is a firm's most valuable asset?
   - (A) The staff
   - (B) Money
   - (C) Office space
   - (D) Equipment

Reading

PART 5 INCOMPLETE SENTENCES

Choose the word that best completes the sentence.

10. The firm's _____ studied finance and business administration.
    (A) account (C) accounted
    (B) accounting (D) accountant

11. Mr. Smith knows how to manage his money and has been able to _____ a great deal of wealth in a relatively short period of time.
    (A) accumulate (C) reconcile
    (B) account (D) audit

12. We went over our records carefully in order to prepare for the meeting with the _____.
    (A) audit (C) auditing
    (B) auditor (D) audited

13. At the end of next week, all the division heads will meet to present one consolidated _____.
    (A) budgeting (C) budgeted
    (B) budget (D) budgets

14. I _____ some savings in my bank account before I made any investments in business.
    (A) building up (C) built up
    (B) buildup (D) build up

15. The company's real estate _____ include several valuable properties in the downtown business district.
    (A) profits (C) assets
    (B) clients (D) budgets

PART 6 TEXT COMPLETION

Wilson and Jones, Ltd.
Accountants
We specialize in small businesses.

Are you having trouble reconciling your accounts?
Do you need to improve your tax situation?
Do you want to get out of debt and make your business ____ ?
16.

Wilson & Jones, Ltd., is a full-service accounting firm that can help small business owners like you with all aspects of your accounts. Our budget planning service will help you pay off ____ debts so that you
17.

can start accumulating savings. Our tax service provides tax planning assistance, tax return preparation, and preparation for audits. Our bookkeeping service guarantees that your accounts are always up to date. ____ So contact us today. You'll be out of the red and free of ____ tomorrow.
18. 19.

16. (A) profiting
    (B) profitable
    (C) profitably
    (D) profiteer

17. (A) client
    (B) budget
    (C) turnover
    (D) outstanding

18. (A) A good financial plan is your best asset.
    (B) We have several tax specialists on our team
    (C) The first appointment is free for new clients.
    (D) Many small businesses fail because of poor budgeting.

19. (A) debate
    (B) doubt
    (C) debit
    (D) debt

PART 7 READING COMPREHENSION

Questions 20–24 refer to the following letter.

January 17, 20—

Buzzi Accountants
128 Waterford Drive
New Hanover, VA

Dear Ms. Buzzi,

I have just found out that my tax records will be audited by the government. I would like to hire someone from your firm to help me prepare for this. I run a small editing business that I started five years ago. I initially took out a loan from the bank to get my business started. My business has always been profitable, and I was able to repay the loan quickly. As of now, my business has no outstanding debts. My staff is quite small. I started out with one assistant, who is still with me. As I built up my client list, I hired a second assistant, who is also still working for me. Thus, I have not had a problem with staff turnover. In short, you can see that my business and financial situation are quite stable.

I have always prepared my taxes carefully, and I keep thorough records. I imagine that this audit will be fairly routine. However, I want to be sure that I am correctly prepared for it, and I feel that hiring an accountant is the best route to take. Please call me so that we can discuss the matter. I can be reached at my office Mondays, Wednesdays, and Fridays. One of my assistants is also usually in the office on Tuesdays and Thursdays and the occasional Saturday and will take messages for me.

I look forward to speaking with you.

Sincerely,

Jonathan Stein

20. Why does Mr. Stein want to hire an accountant?
    (A) To prepare his taxes
    (B) To help with an audit
    (C) To get him out of debt
    (D) To help him stabilize his finances

21. How many people work for Mr. Stein?
    (A) One
    (B) Two
    (C) Three
    (D) Four

22. When is Mr. Stein in his office?
    (A) Monday through Friday
    (B) Tuesday and Thursday
    (C) Monday, Wednesday, and Friday
    (D) On occasional Saturdays

23. The word *profitable* in the first paragraph, line 4, is closest in meaning to
    (A) large.
    (B) in debt.
    (C) interesting.
    (D) earning money.

24. The words *built up* in the first paragraph, line 5, are closest in meaning to
    (A) constructed.
    (B) increased.
    (C) employed.
    (D) served.

Lesson 23: Investments

WORDS TO LEARN

- aggressively
- attitude
- commit
- conservative
- fund
- invest
- long-term
- portfolio
- pull out
- resource
- return
- wisely

Study the following definitions and examples.

1. **aggressively** adv., competitively; assertively
   a. Some people are risk takers and prefer to invest aggressively.
   b. His ideas were not well received because he spoke so aggressively.
2. **attitude** n., a feeling about something or someone
   a. The new fund manager's attitude changed quickly after the first big downturn in the market.
   b. Each investor should assess his or her own attitude toward investment.
3. **commit** v., to consign for future use; to promise
   a. It is a good idea to commit a certain percentage of your income to investments.
   b. The stockbroker committed herself to finding the best investments for each client.
4. **conservative** adj., cautious; restrained
   a. Her conservative strategy paid off over the years.
   b. Generally, older people should be more conservative in their investing than younger people.
5. **fund** n., an amount of money; an organization that manages money for a particular purpose
   a. If you have extra funds, talk to your stockbroker about the best place to put them.
   b. My stockbroker recommended investing in this fund.
6. **invest** v., to put money into a business or activity in order to make more money; to put effort into something
   a. The chief financial officer invested in the stock at a very good time.
   b. Don't invest all of your time in just one project.
7. **long-term** adj., involving or extending over a long period
   a. The CEO's long-term goal was to increase the return on investment.
   b. Long-term investments are not really affected by the daily ups and downs of the stock market.
8. **portfolio** n., a list of investments
   a. Investors are advised to have diverse portfolios.
   b. The investor's portfolio consisted of blue chip company stocks and government bonds.
9. **pull out** v., to withdraw; to stop participating
   a. A lot of people pulled out their money when it became clear that the bank was in trouble.
   b. He pulled out of the company and took all of his money with him.
10. **resource** n., assets; valuable things
    a. I would like to invest more in the stock market but I don't have the resources at the moment.
    b. The company's most valuable resource was its staff.
11. **return** n., the amount of money gained as profit
    a. The 44 percent return on the new stock was far more than the stockbroker had anticipated.
    b. Some investors are satisfied with a 5% return, while others want a much larger return.
12. **wisely** adj., knowledgeably; smartly
    a. If you invest wisely, you will be able to retire early.
    b. Mary wisely followed her stockbroker's advice and took her money out of some bad investments.

WORD FAMILIES

noun	aggression	The act of aggression against our country caused a fear of war and had a negative effect on the stock market.
adjective	aggressive	The director's aggressive position on investing was frowned upon by the Board of Directors.
adverb	aggressively	I chose this stockbroker because he invests my money aggressively.

verb	commit	I've committed to donating a portion of my salary to charitable causes.
noun	commitment	The employee's commitment to working hard and saving her money was commendable.
adjective	noncommittal	I had hoped that the discussion would yield a definite answer from them, but they were noncommittal.

verb	conserve	Conserve your money now so you will be able to invest when the stock market gets better.
adjective	conservative	Some people are conservative investors and take few risks with their money.
adverb	conservatively	If you invest too conservatively, you may lose some chances for making money.

verb	fund	Private investors will fund the new business.
noun	fund	The stockbroker suggested investing funds in foreign companies.
noun	funder	We are looking for funders who can commit at least $50,000 each.

verb	invest	The company has been successful because it has invested wisely in its resources.
noun	investment	Some people like to manage their investments online by themselves, while others prefer to work with a stockbroker.
noun	investor	The fall in the stock market shook up the investors.

noun	wisdom	Common wisdom is to place your money in a variety of investments.
adjective	wise	The wise investor does her homework before parting with her money.
adverb	wisely	She planned her retirement wisely and was able to retire to her summer house.

WORDS IN CONTEXT

Read the following passage and write the words in the blanks below.

aggressive	conservative	long-term	resources
attitude	fund	portfolio	return
committed	invest	pull out	wise

Investment is a common, everyday occurrence. Companies (1) ____________ time and money in finding and training their employees. Employees invest in their own training and education. Financial investment takes place at a corporate level and at an individual level. Whether an individual or a company, a decision must be made on the percentage of (2) ____________ to have invested and the percentage to have in cash.

To avoid making stupid decisions, many people use financial advisors. Financial advisors help individuals and corporations make (3) ____________ investment decisions. What kind of portfolio should be maintained? What should be in this (4) ____________? At what point should an investor pull back or (5) ____________ of the market? What kind of (6) ____________ should the investor realistically expect? How much risk can an investor take (both emotionally and financially)? Investors who are (7) ____________ to (8) ____________ investments can more easily weather the ups and downs of a market. As one analyst commented, "If you're staying awake at night thinking about the stock market, you probably have too much invested."

Many employees have retirement plans at work. They decide what level of contribution to make to a certain (9) ____________. These decisions and large company decisions depend to a large degree on (10) ____________. Is the decision maker (11) ____________ or (12) ____________? That attitude often depends on the age of the investor or on the stage and the needs of the business.

WORD PRACTICE

Listening Comprehension

Track 24

PART 1 PHOTO

Look at the picture and listen to the sentences. Choose the sentence that best describes the picture.

1. Ⓐ Ⓑ Ⓒ Ⓓ

PART 2 QUESTION–RESPONSE

Listen to the question and the three responses. Choose the response that best answers the question.

2. Ⓐ Ⓑ Ⓒ 3. Ⓐ Ⓑ Ⓒ

PART 3 CONVERSATION

Listen to the dialogue. Then read each question and choose the best response.

4. What does the man recommend?
   (A) Investing mainly in natural resources
   (B) Investing in various industries
   (C) Investing aggressively
   (D) Investing in the basket industry

5. How much money has the man made through his investments?
   (A) One million dollars
   (B) Two million dollars
   (C) Five million dollars
   (D) Ten million dollars

6. What will the woman do?
   (A) Take her money out of the stock market
   (B) Hire an investment advisor
   (C) Start a marketing business
   (D) Follow the man's investment strategy

PART 4 TALK

Listen to the talk. Then read each question and choose the best answer.

7. What is this talk about?
   (A) How to invest in the stock market
   (B) How to choose a good college
   (C) How to choose investments
   (D) How to save money for college

8. When should parents start saving money for college?
   (A) Two or three years from now
   (B) When their children are small
   (C) After they have had two or three children
   (D) When their children are in high school

9. How often should parents put money in the stock market?
   (A) Every month
   (B) Every two or three months
   (C) Every year
   (D) Every two or three years

Reading

PART 5 INCOMPLETE SENTENCES

Choose the word that best completes the sentence.

10. The stockbroker recommended investing some money more _______.

    (A) aggressive (C) aggressively
    (B) aggression (D) aggressor

11. All employees are encouraged to _______ a percentage of their earnings to the retirement fund.

    (A) committed (C) commitment
    (B) commit (D) committing

12. Because he had made such _______ investments, he lost very little money when the stock market went down.

    (A) conservative (C) conservatively
    (B) conserved (D) conserve

13. After months of study and research, the _______ decided to put his money into new facilities and materials.

    (A) investor (C) investing
    (B) investment (D) invested

14. The goal of investing is to make a profit; therefore, people look for those investments that will generate the highest _______.

    (A) attitudes (C) returns
    (B) resources (D) commitments

15. Is it _______ to consider funding a new project when we haven't even seen the returns from the last one?

    (A) wisdom (C) wisely
    (B) wisest (D) wise

Many people try to save money by acting as their own investment advisors. This is not usually considered to be a wise choice. ____. A professional investment advisor understands
16.

investment options more thoroughly than the layperson ever could. A good investment advisor becomes familiar with her clients' ____ toward investing and
17.

gives advice accordingly. The advisor makes certain recommendations to clients who are conservative investors and makes different recommendations to clients who prefer to invest more ____. The best way to create a strong investment ____ that matches your needs and
18. 19.

preferred investing strategy is to work with a professional investment advisor.

16. (A) Make a decision about the amount of your income that you are willing to commit to investments.
    (B) It can actually end up costing the investor more money because of poor investment decisions.
    (C) The amount you invest depends on the funds you have available.
    (D) Obviously, people want a good return on their investments.

17. (A) funds
    (B) returns
    (C) attitudes
    (D) resources

18. (A) aggressor
    (B) aggression
    (C) aggressive
    (D) aggressively

19. (A) portage
    (B) portrait
    (C) portfolio
    (D) portmanteau

PART 7 READING COMPREHENSION

Questions 20–24 refer to the following two e-mail messages.

To: Amelia Waddell
From: Peter Simpkins
Subject: Investment

Hi Amelia,

I wondered if you would give me the name of your investment advisor. My business is doing very well this year. In fact, I am now making a lot more money than I did when I had a job with a salary. I would prefer to invest my profits in the stock market as I'm sure I would earn more money that way than just letting it earn interest in a bank account. Of course, I want to invest wisely, so I am looking for professional advice. You know I tend to have a conservative attitude toward money, and I hope your advisor can help me make some safe investments. Please get back to me soon as I'd like to get started on this before the end of the month. Thanks.

Peter

To: Peter Simpkins
From: Amelia Waddell
Subject: Re: Investment

Hi Peter,

I would be happy to help you out. As a matter of fact, I just talked with my investment advisor this morning, and she mentioned that she is looking for more clients. Her name is Susannah Oliveros. I have been working with her for several years and have always been satisfied. I have gotten good returns on the investments I have made with her. I will call you this afternoon, and we can discuss all the details then. I will also give you her phone number so you can call her tomorrow. I know you will like her.

Amelia

20. Why did Peter write the e-mail message?
    (A) He is looking for a job.
    (B) He needs some investment advice.
    (C) He lent some money to Amelia.
    (D) He is looking for new clients.

21. Why does Peter have extra money to invest?
    (A) He earned a lot of interest in his bank account.
    (B) He has a high salary.
    (C) His business is very profitable.
    (D) He made money in the stock market last year.

22. When will Amelia call Peter?
    (A) This morning
    (B) This afternoon
    (C) Tomorrow
    (D) Before the end of the month

23. The word *wisely* in line 9 of the first e-mail is closest in meaning to
    (A) smartly.
    (B) carefully.
    (C) quickly.
    (D) easily.

24. The word *returns* in line 8 of the second e-mail is closest in meaning to
    (A) goes back.
    (B) gives back.
    (C) suggestions.
    (D) profits.

Lesson 24: Taxes

WORDS TO LEARN

- calculation
- deadline
- file
- fill out
- give up
- joint
- owe
- penalty
- preparation
- refund
- spouse
- withhold

Study the following definitions and examples.

1. **calculation** n., computation; estimate
   a. It took my accountant some time to complete the calculations on my income tax.
   b. According to my calculations, I'll owe less money on my income taxes this year.
2. **deadline** n., a time by which something must be finished
   a. The deadline for paying this year's taxes is just two weeks away.
   b. My best work is done with strict deadlines.
3. **file** v., to enter into public record
   a. If you file your taxes late, you will have to pay a fine.
   b. If you believe the tax preparer gave you incorrect information, you should file a complaint.
4. **fill out** v., to complete
   a. I usually ask someone to help me fill out my tax form.
   b. Don't forget to sign the tax form after you have filled it out.
5. **give up** v., to quit; to stop
   a. Bruce gave up paying an accountant to prepare his tax return and now does it himself.
   b. Ms. Gomez gave up hope that she would ever receive a large tax refund.
6. **joint** adj., together; shared
   a. We opened a joint bank account five years ago.
   b. The couple no longer files joint tax returns.
7. **owe** v., to have a debt; to be obligated to pay
   a. People are surprised to discover that they owe money in income taxes at the end of the year.
   b. As the business grew, the owner paid back loans and owed less money.
8. **penalty** n., a punishment; a consequence
   a. Anyone who pays less than they should in taxes will face a penalty.
   b. Penalties are imposed to discourage underpayment of taxes.
9. **preparation** n., the act of making something ready
   a. Income tax preparation can take a long time.
   b. You should do some preparation on your own before hiring an accountant to work on your taxes.
10. **refund** n., the amount paid back; v., to give back
    a. With the tax refund, we bought two plane tickets.
    b. The government will refund any money that you overpaid.
11. **spouse** n., a husband or wife
    a. You can claim your spouse as a dependent on your tax return if he doesn't earn an income.
    b. My spouse prepares the tax return for both of us.
12. **withhold** v., to keep from; to refrain from
    a. My employer withholds money from each paycheck to apply toward my income taxes.
    b. Do not withhold information from your accountant, or he won't be able to prepare your taxes correctly.

WORD FAMILIES

verb	calculate	The tax software calculates your taxes for you.
noun	calculation	The calculation is no more difficult than high school math.
noun	calculator	In order to avoid making addition and subtraction errors, I suggest you use a calculator.

verb	file	Don't wait until the last minute to file your taxes.
noun	file	I keep all my tax information in one file.

adjective	joint	My husband and I filed a joint tax return.
adverb	jointly	Even though you are separated right now, you will save money if you and your wife file your taxes jointly.

verb	penalize	The government will penalize taxpayers who try to evade paying their fair share of taxes.
noun	penalty	For every dollar you owe in overdue taxes, a 10 percent penalty is imposed.
adjective	penal	Tax evasion is a penal offense.

verb	prepare	Most people wait until the last minute to prepare their tax returns.
noun	preparation	If you are organized, income tax preparation takes only a few hours.
adjective	preparatory	The preparatory work for doing my taxes is more time-consuming than filling out the forms.

verb	refund	The government should refund your overpaid taxes within a few weeks of filing your tax return.
noun	refund	If you have overpaid your income taxes, you will get a refund at the end of the year.
adjective	refundable	Sales tax that tourists pay in a foreign country may be refundable when they leave the country.

WORDS IN CONTEXT

Read the following passage and write the words in the blanks below.

calculated	fill out	owe	refund
deadline	gave up	penalized	spouse
filed	joint	prepares	withhold

Every year, my wife gathers all of our pay stubs and expense reports and (1) _____________ to fill out our tax forms. She tries to finish them in March, well before the April 15th (2) _____________. It's a time-consuming process. There are receipts to find, records to organize, and forms to (3) _____________. When we first got married, we (4) _____________ separate returns. But now she marks me as her (5) _____________ and files the (6) _____________ return. It saves us money and saves me time!

My wife is very proud of her accuracy. The government has never sent the forms back with corrections. For several years now, we have received a (7) _____________. But this year, she (8) _____________ the numbers over and over again and found we had not paid enough taxes throughout the year. She didn't want to (9) _____________ any money. Finally, she (10) _____________ and sent in our check. Actually, it was my fault. I had changed jobs and didn't ask my employer to (11) _____________ enough money from my paychecks. I'm just glad we found and corrected the mistake before we got (12) _____________.

WORD PRACTICE

Listening Comprehension

Track 25

PART 1 PHOTO

Look at the picture and listen to the sentences.
Choose the sentence that best describes the picture.

1. Ⓐ Ⓑ Ⓒ Ⓓ

PART 2 QUESTION–RESPONSE

Listen to the question and the three responses. Choose the response that best answers the question.

2. Ⓐ Ⓑ Ⓒ 3. Ⓐ Ⓑ Ⓒ

PART 3 CONVERSATION

Listen to the dialogue. Then read each question and choose the best response.

4. Who usually prepares the man's taxes?
   - (A) The man
   - (B) His wife
   - (C) The man and his wife together
   - (D) An accountant

5. When did the man file his taxes last year?
   - (A) One month before the deadline
   - (B) Two months before the deadline
   - (C) One month after the deadline
   - (D) Two months after the deadline

6. What is the penalty for missing the deadline?
   - (A) 1 percent
   - (B) 2 percent
   - (C) 9 percent
   - (D) 10 percent

PART 4 TALK

Listen to the talk. Then read each question and choose the best answer.

7. Who is the speaker?
   - (A) A tax preparer
   - (B) A government tax agent
   - (C) A tax filer
   - (D) An employer

8. When can the refund check be expected?
   - (A) In eighteen weeks
   - (B) Before six weeks
   - (C) In four weeks
   - (D) In ten weeks at the latest

9. What does the speaker offer to do?
   - (A) Calculate the amount to withhold from the paycheck
   - (B) Make an arrangement with the employer
   - (C) Show the listener a fee schedule
   - (D) Send in the tax payment

Reading

PART 5 INCOMPLETE SENTENCES

Choose the word that best completes the sentence.

10. According to my ______, we owe a lot of money in taxes this year.

    (A) calculations (C) calculators
    (B) calculated (D) calculate

11. Those ______ on my desk contain all the information we'll need for preparing our taxes.

    (A) filed (C) file
    (B) files (D) filing

12. It is usually advantageous for spouses to file their income taxes ______.

    (A) joints (C) joint
    (B) jointly (D) jointed

13. We didn't know we had to claim the interest from our savings account as part of our income, and we were ______ for the error.

    (A) owed (C) refunded
    (B) withheld (D) penalized

14. The ______ of the forms took much less time than we expected.

    (A) preparatory (C) prepared
    (B) preparation (D) prepares

15. I didn't overpay my taxes this year, so I didn't get a ______.

    (A) calculation (C) refund
    (B) deadline (D) file

Smith & Johnson
Tax Preparation

We take away the headaches of tax time.

____ your own taxes can be frustrating and often leads to costly
16.

errors in calculations. Are you ready to give up trying to fill ____ your
17.

tax forms on your own? Smith & Johnson Tax Preparation can help you! People who use professional tax preparers get larger refunds and avoid ____ for underpayment and missed deadlines.
18.

____. So don't wait. Call us today.
19.

16. (A) Prepare
    (B) Prepares
    (C) Preparing
    (D) Preparation

17. (A) in
    (B) up
    (C) out
    (D) through

18. (A) debts
    (B) penalties
    (C) preparations
    (D) calculations

19. (A) We will bill you later for the amount you owe us for our services.
    (B) Many people engage the services of a professional tax preparer.
    (C) You and your spouse may choose to file jointly or individually.
    (D) Our deadline for taking on new clients is March 7.

PART 7 READING COMPREHENSION

Questions 20–24 refer to the following letter.

April 1, 20—

Mr. Roger Earnshaw
2943 Northern Boulevard
New Orange, NH

Dear Mr. Earnshaw,

Enclosed are your completed tax forms, which I have prepared for you at your request. I am sorry to report that you will not receive the $500 refund that you expected. Instead, my calculations show that you owe $450 in taxes, as well as an additional penalty of $45 for underpayment of taxes. The reason for this is that you and your spouse have chosen not to file your taxes jointly this year. You may want to reconsider this for the future since, as you can see, it is more costly for married couples to file separately. If you and your spouse wish to continue to file separately, you may want to ask your employer to withhold a greater amount from your paychecks so that you don't end up owing money again next year. This will be even more important if you get the salary increase that you have been hoping for.

Write out a check for the taxes that you still owe and the penalty and mail it together with your tax forms before the April 15 deadline. Please let me know if I can be of any further assistance.

Sincerely,

Kathleen O'Hara
CPA

20. Who wrote the letter?
    (A) A tax agent
    (B) A tax preparer
    (C) Mr. Earnshaw's spouse
    (D) Mr. Earnshaw's employer

21. What is the total amount that Mr. Earnshaw owes?
    (A) $45
    (B) $450
    (C) $495
    (D) $500

22. What does Ms. O'Hara recommend to Mr. Earnshaw to improve his tax situation?
    (A) Get married
    (B) File separately
    (C) Ask for a salary increase
    (D) Withhold more from his checks

23. The word *jointly* in line 5 is closest in meaning to
    (A) together.
    (B) apart.
    (C) on time.
    (D) finally.

24. The word *deadline* in line 12 is closest in meaning to
    (A) holiday.
    (B) schedule.
    (C) anniversary.
    (D) due date.

Lesson 25: Financial Statements

WORDS TO LEARN

- desire
- detail
- forecast
- level
- overall
- perspective
- project
- realistic
- target
- translation
- typically
- yield

Study the following definitions and examples.

1. **desire** v., to wish
   a. We desire to have our own home.
   b. He desires to retire when he becomes forty.
2. **detail** v., to report or relate minutely or in particulars
   a. The business planner detailed the steps we should follow to write our financial statement.
   b. Fabio created a financial statement that detailed every expected expenditure for the next quarter.
3. **forecast** n., a prediction of a future event; v., to estimate or calculate in advance
   a. The financial forecast indicates a deficit in the next quarter.
   b. Analysts forecast a strong economic outlook.
4. **level** n., a relative position or rank on a scale
   a. We have never had an accountant work at such a sophisticated level before.
   b. If you expect your business to earn at higher levels, your financial statement should show that.
5. **overall** adj., regarded as a whole; general
   a. The company's overall expectations were out of proportion.
   b. Our overall financial situation is not too bad.
6. **perspective** n., a mental view or outlook
   a. The budget statement gave us perspective on where the costs of running the business are found.
   b. Joseph's accountant gave him some perspective as well as some data on how much he could expect to earn in his first year in business.
7. **project** v., to estimate or predict
   a. We need to project our earnings and expenses in order to plan next year's budget.
   b. The director projects that the company will need to hire ten new employees this year.
8. **realistic** adj., tending to or expressing an awareness of things as they really are
   a. An accurate accounting gave Stefano a realistic idea of his business's financial direction.
   b. Realistic expectations are important when you review your financial statements.
9. **target** v., to establish as a goal; n., a goal
   a. We targeted March as the deadline for completing the financial statement.
   b. Matilde hoped to sign on five new clients last month, but she didn't reach her target.
10. **translation** n., something expressed in a different language or form
    a. The translation of the statement from Japanese into English was very helpful.
    b. The accountant provided a translation of the financial terms in a language we could all understand.
11. **typically** adv., acting in conformity to a type; characteristically
    a. Office expenses typically include such things as salaries, rent, and office supplies.
    b. Banks typically require a financial statement before they will lend money to a small business.
12. **yield** n., an amount produced; v., to produce
    a. Henry's budget gave him the desired yield: a better indication of his expected profit.
    b. The company's investment yielded high returns.

WORD FAMILIES

verb	desire	Our manager is trying to predict how many customers will desire our product over the next quarter.
noun	desire	Her desire for greater control of the business led her to discuss her need for more information with her accountant.
adjective	desirable	The category summary, while desirable, was time-consuming to prepare.

verb	detail	The statement details all of our income and expenses.
noun	detail	The budget report needs to be accurate down to the last detail.
adjective	detailed	The loan officer asked for a detailed financial statement.

verb	project	The budget summary helped us project our expenditures for the year.
noun	project	The financial project was time-consuming and challenging.
noun	projection	Maurice's projections for the upcoming fiscal year were not as helpful as we had hoped.

verb	realize	The plan helps her realize her dream of having the business turn a profit.
noun	reality	The financial statement reinforced the reality that our business is in deep trouble.
adjective	realistic	The accountant needs realistic numbers on which to base his plan.

verb	translate	We need to translate all of this information into a financial statement that shows the true condition of our business.
noun	translation	The translation of the document was provided at no charge.
adjective	translatable	The data was not translatable between programs and had to be entered by hand, which took hours.

noun	type	This type of business requires a lot of start-up money.
adjective	typical	Part of a category summary is defining the expenses that are typical of the business in question.
adverb	typically	Typically, we finish preparing the budget just in time to meet the deadline.

WORDS IN CONTEXT

Read the following passage and write the words in the blanks below.

desired	level	projected	translate
detailed	overall	realistic	typical
forecasts	perspective	target	yield

A business budget focuses on future profits and future capital requirements. A budget can help the business owner determine the amount of profit the business is expected to make, the amount of sales it will take to reach a goal, and what (1) _____________ of expenses are attached to those sales. A business establishes a (2) _____________, a goal to work toward. A business (3) _____________ the sales that will be needed to reach this target.

Projecting or planning ahead is part of (4) _____________ business planning. When creating a (5) _____________ income statement, a business owner tries to determine how to reach the (6) _____________ target. The annual profit must be sufficient to (7) _____________ the owner a return for his or her time spent operating the business, plus a return on the investment. The owner's target income is the sum of a reasonable salary for the time spent running the business and a normal return on the amount invested in the firm.

After projecting the income needed, the business owner has to (8) _____________ the target profit into a net sales figure for the forecasted period. The owner has to determine whether this sales volume is (9) _____________. One useful technique is to break down the required annual sales into a daily sales figure to get a better (10) _____________ of the sales required to yield the annual profit.

At this stage in the financial plan, the owner should create a (11) _____________ picture of the firm's expected operating expenses. Many books and business organizations give (12) _____________ operating statistics data, based on a percentage of net sales. The business's accountant can help you assign dollar values to anticipated expenses.

Developing a projected income statement is an important part of any financial plan, as the process forces the business owner to examine the firm's future profitability.

WORD PRACTICE

Listening Comprehension

Track 26

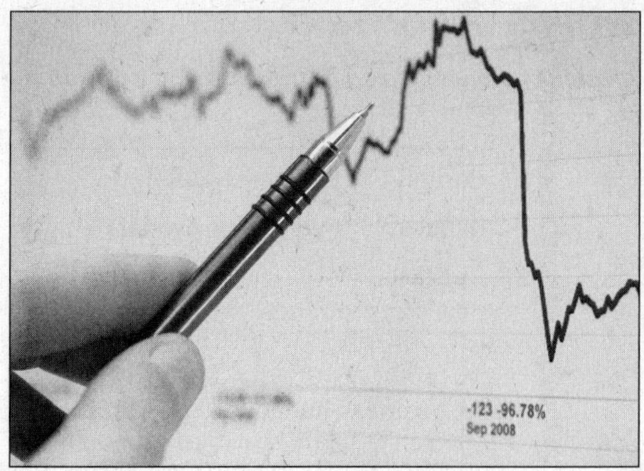

PART 1 PHOTO

Look at the picture and listen to the sentences. Choose the sentence that best describes the picture.

1. Ⓐ Ⓑ Ⓒ Ⓓ

PART 2 QUESTION–RESPONSE

Listen to the question and the three responses. Choose the response that best answers the question.

2. Ⓐ Ⓑ Ⓒ

3. Ⓐ Ⓑ Ⓒ

PART 3 CONVERSATION

Listen to the dialogue. Then read each question and choose the best response.

4. What is the woman doing?
   (A) Developing a project report
   (B) Preparing a financial statement
   (C) Making a weather forecast
   (D) Writing an expense report

5. When does she want to have this finished?
   (A) By noon
   (B) Before 8:00
   (C) By the end of the week
   (D) Before the end of the year

6. What does the man offer to do?
   (A) Write a check
   (B) Sign a statement
   (C) Solve her financial problems
   (D) Correct her calculations

PART 4 TALK

Listen to the talk. Then read each question and choose the best answer.

7. Who is this talk directed at?
   (A) Large companies
   (B) Financial advisors
   (C) Small business owners
   (D) Finance companies

8. When does a business typically become profitable?
   (A) During the first year
   (B) After five years
   (C) During the first five years
   (D) After nine years

9. According to the speaker, what is the first step to take when starting a small business?
   (A) Get an office with a key
   (B) Write a financial statement
   (C) Raise start-up funds
   (D) Hire a project manager

Reading

PART 5 INCOMPLETE SENTENCES

Choose the word that best completes the sentence.

10. Improved sales and increased profits are the most _______ outcome of our efforts to grow our business.

(A) overall (C) desirable
(B) detailed (D) cautious

11. The accountant can review all the _______ of the financial statement with you.

(A) detailed (C) details
(B) detailing (D) detail

12. We don't really have enough information yet to _______ figures for the next quarter.

(A) translate (C) desire
(B) project (D) realize

13. The projected financial statement demonstrated to Susan that her business had a _______ chance of increasing its profit over the next two quarters.

(A) realistic (C) realistically
(B) realist (D) reality

14. To create our financial strategy, our consultant took the experiences of similar businesses and _______ relevant outcomes to our situation.

(A) translatable (C) translator
(B) translation (D) translated

15. Our business experienced a _______ fall in profits during the third quarter of the year.

(A) typical (C) type
(B) typically (D) typed

PART 6 TEXT COMPLETION

Memo

To: Department Heads
From: Roy Jones, Manager
Re: Planning Meeting

As you know, our quarterly planning meeting will take place in two weeks. I want to let you know some of the topics that will be discussed, to give you a chance to prepare.

First, the overall economic situation in the country looks very good for the coming year. Economists ____ (16.) an increase in consumer spending, especially in our sector. Therefore, we should look into increasing production. ____ (17.). Second, since the company plans to increase sales overseas, we will need to hire several ____ (18.).

We will need to discuss how many we need and which languages should have priority.

These are the most important topics for the meeting. If anyone ____ (19.) to put a special item on the meeting agenda, please let me know by the beginning of next week.

16. (A) foreclose
    (B) forebode
    (C) forego
    (D) forecast

17. (A) I believe that raising it by 15 percent by the end of the year is a realistic target.
    (B) We probably do not have the resources to increase production.
    (C) Much of our production has been moved to our new factory.
    (D) The details of the report will be available soon.

18. (A) translators
    (B) translates
    (C) translations
    (D) transports

19. (A) desire
    (B) desires
    (C) will desire
    (D) have desired

PART 7 READING COMPREHENSION

Questions 20–24 refer to the following article and e-mail message.

Do you have a sound financial plan for your small business? You should. The majority of small businesses fail during the first five years, typically because they have not made realistic financial plans. A new business owner may start out with the necessary funds, a qualified staff, and office space and equipment. These things may not save the business from disaster, however, if the business owner hasn't set realistic targets and made plans to reach them. Everyone who contemplates starting a new business should sit down and write out all the details of a financial plan before doing anything else.

To: Shirley Haines
From: Matthew Rockwell
Subject: Financial planning
Attach: Financial Plans for Small Businesses

Shirley,

Have you seen the attached article on financial planning? It appeared in this week's issue of *Small Business Owner* magazine. It has given me a new perspective on things. I can't believe we have already been running our business for six months, but we still haven't sat down together to write out a financial plan. Overall, I believe our business is doing well, and we certainly have enough clients. But, I now understand that our future success depends on having a good financial plan. We need to project our earnings for the next year and set financial targets. We should get to work on this right away. Can we meet tomorrow afternoon? Three o'clock is a good time for me. Let me know soon.

Matthew

20. According to the article, why do most small businesses fail?
    - (A) Lack of financial planning
    - (B) Lack of adequate office space
    - (C) Lack of qualified staff
    - (D) Lack of adequate funds

21. Why did Matthew write the e-mail message?
    - (A) He wants to start a small business with Shirley.
    - (B) He is writing an article for a magazine.
    - (C) He wants to make a financial plan.
    - (D) He is looking for new clients.

22. When does Matthew want to meet with Shirley?
    - (A) Tomorrow
    - (B) Next week
    - (C) In six months
    - (D) Next year

23. The word *typically* in line 4 of the article is closest in meaning to
    - (A) unfortunately.
    - (B) usually.
    - (C) really.
    - (D) sadly.

24. The word *perspective* in line 4 of the e-mail is closest in meaning to
    - (A) information.
    - (B) advice.
    - (C) goal.
    - (D) view.

WORD REVIEW #5
LESSONS 21–25 FINANCING AND BUDGETING

Choose the word that best completes the sentence.

1. Most banks have special loans for people looking to __________ money to start a small business.
   (A) borrow
   (B) invest
   (C) reconcile
   (D) deduct

2. When we __________ out a loan, we got very good terms.
   (A) take
   (B) took
   (C) taken
   (D) taking

3. Most people get nervous when someone is __________ their books.
   (A) audit
   (B) audits
   (C) audited
   (D) auditing

4. Sometimes it is difficult to pull __________ of bad investments.
   (A) through
   (B) out
   (C) at
   (D) to

5. I prefer __________ in socially conscious funds.
   (A) invest
   (B) investment
   (C) investing
   (D) investor

6. When starting a new business, expect to lose money at first because it may take several years before the business becomes __________.
   (A) cautious
   (B) resourceful
   (C) profitable
   (D) outstanding

7. Sometimes it is difficult to understand how the government __________ tax liability.
   (A) calculating
   (B) calculations
   (C) calculators
   (D) calculates

8. One decision with tax returns is whether to give __________ itemizing in favor of the standard deduction.
   (A) up
   (B) in
   (C) to
   (D) out

9. The company's __________ earnings over the next six months were exciting.
   (A) project
   (B) projects
   (C) projection
   (D) projected

10. Some parts of the tax code are so confusing that they need __________.
    (A) translate
    (B) translates
    (C) translated
    (D) translation

Choose the one word or phrase that best completes each sentence.

At Grover Investment Services, we understand that you work hard to earn your money, and it is important to invest it __________. This is where we come in. We offer our __________ a full

11. (A) wise
    (B) wisely
    (C) wizened
    (D) wisdom

12. (A) accountants
    (B) officers
    (C) spouses
    (D) clients

range of investment services. Whether you are a conservative or aggressive investor, we can help you develop an investment plan that suits your needs. At Grover, we are __________ to helping you get the best possible return for your money.

13. (A) commit
    (B) committee
    (C) committed
    (D) commitment

Call us today.

First-time home buyers may feel overwhelmed by the process of applying for a mortgage. However, the process of __________ money to buy a house is not very complicated. First,

14. (A) borrow
    (B) borrows
    (C) borrowed
    (D) borrowing

you will have to fill out a form giving information about your financial situation. You need to show that you have a good income. It is also important not to have a lot of __________. If you

15. (A) funds
    (B) debt
    (C) returns
    (D) investments

already owe a lot of money, the bank may hesitate to lend you more. Then, you will have to make a __________, usually about 10 percent of the total price of the house.

16. (A) refund
    (B) target
    (C) down payment
    (D) forecast

The bank lends you the rest of the money for the purchase.

Many people use the services of an accountant to help ____________ their tax forms. They consider it

17. (A) prepare
(B) preparer
(C) preparation
(D) preparatory

well worth the money. An accountant can help you avoid ____________ for underpayment of taxes

18. (A) portfolios
(B) penalties
(C) refunds
(D) assets

and, in general, ensure that your tax form has been filled out correctly. But remember, accountants have deadlines too. Be sure to give all your tax information to your accountant early, then you can be sure that your taxes will be ready to ____________ on time. No one wants to pay a fine for sending in

19. (A) file
(B) fund
(C) budget
(D) invest

his or her tax form too late.

Lesson 26: Property and Departments

WORDS TO LEARN

- adjacent
- collaboration
- concentrate
- conducive
- disruption
- hamper
- inconsiderately
- lobby
- move up
- open to
- opt
- scrutiny

Study the following definitions and examples.

1. **adjacent** adj., next to
   a. My office is adjacent to the receptionist area on the third floor.
   b. The office manager found it very efficient to have the copier adjacent to the mail room.
2. **collaboration** n., the act of working with someone
   a. The manager had never seen such effective collaboration between two groups.
   b. We believe that it was our collaboration that enabled us to achieve such favorable results.
3. **concentrate** v., to focus; to think about
   a. In his quiet, corner office, the manager could finally concentrate and finish his work.
   b. We should concentrate our efforts on the last quarter of the year.
4. **conducive** adj., contributing to; leading to
   a. The new office is much more conducive to work than the dark space we had before.
   b. Arranging chairs so that participants can see each other easily is conducive to open communication.
5. **disruption** n., interruption; disturbance
   a. If there are no disruptions, the office renovations will be finished this week.
   b. The strike caused a disruption in production at the factory.
6. **hamper** v., to impede or interfere
   a. When the weight of the snow broke the telephone lines, the telemarketers' jobs were hampered.
   b. The lack of supplies hampered our ability to finish on schedule.
7. **inconsiderately** adv., rudely; impolitely
   a. The manager inconsiderately scheduled the meeting for late Friday afternoon.
   b. Mr. Peterson inconsiderately disrupted the meeting by asking a lot of irrelevant questions.
8. **lobby** n., an anteroom, foyer, or waiting room
   a. The salesperson waited in the busy lobby for the buyer to see him.
   b. The reception area was moved from the lobby of the building to the third floor.
9. **move up** v., to advance; improve position
   a. As the employee moved up the corporate ladder, she never forgot where she started.
   b. In order to move up in the company, employees had to demonstrate their loyalty.
10. **open to** adj., receptive to; vulnerable
    a. My previous supervisor was always open to ideas and suggestions.
    b. Since the junior executive was still on probation, he was open to much scrutiny and criticism.
11. **opt** v., to choose; to decide on
    a. The operations manager opted for the less expensive office design.
    b. If Mary opts to join that department, you will be working together.
12. **scrutiny** n., close, careful examination
    a. After a great deal of scrutiny, the manager decided that the employee's work had improved.
    b. Jim left his old job because he found it difficult to work under the close scrutiny of his boss.

WORD FAMILIES

verb	collaborate	If we collaborate on this project, you will be sure to receive credit.
noun	collaboration	Collaboration often brings about results that no one could have predicted.
adjective	collaborative	The new project is a collaborative effort among several departments.

verb	concentrate	Some people find it difficult to concentrate when there is a lot of noise and activity around them.
noun	concentration	The concentration of a large percentage of the company's funds in just a few areas left several departments underfunded.
adjective	concentrated	With some concentrated effort, we should be able to finish this work by the deadline.

verb	disrupt	Try not to disrupt the meeting being held in the sales department.
noun	disruption	I'm sorry for the disruption, but this phone call is very important.
adjective	disruptive	Having to temporarily move the offices proved to be very disruptive and sales decreased during that quarter.

noun	inconsiderateness	The inconsiderateness of many of the customers caused several employees to quit their jobs.
adjective	inconsiderate	Would it be inconsiderate to ask to use your office while you are away?
adverb	inconsiderately	John inconsiderately looked through his coworker's mail before putting it on his desk.

verb	opt	When we moved offices, I opted for the one without a window.
noun	option	Presented with several options, we chose the one that required the least amount of effort.
adjective	optional	Attendance at tomorrow's meeting is optional for the people working in this department.

verb	scrutinize	The auditor carefully scrutinized the financial records.
noun	scrutiny	Employees under constant scrutiny tend to perform worse than those employees who have more freedom.
adjective	inscrutable	You can never tell what she is thinking, since her facial expressions are inscrutable.

WORDS IN CONTEXT

Read the following passage and write the words in the blanks below.

adjacent	conducive	inconsiderate	open to
collaboration	disruptive	lobby	opting
concentrate	hampered	move up	scrutinized

The layout of any office has an important influence on the atmosphere and operations in the company. The shipping department most likely will not be located next to the customer service department. The noise would be too (1) ______________. Likewise, locating a kitchen (2) ______________ to the (3) ______________ would be (4) ______________ of office visitors and clients. The marketing department is often situated close to the sales department due to their necessary (5) ______________.

Employee productivity may be (6) ______________ or improved by the arrangement of workers and departments. Employees vie for corner offices as they (7) ______________ the corporate ladder. They want to be accessible to top management, but not so close that everything that they do is (8) ______________. At the same time, many companies are (9) ______________ for open work spaces versus traditional offices. Open spaces are more (10) ______________ to team projects, where employees interact freely. However, some employees feel that such an environment makes it difficult to (11) ______________. Employees know under which conditions they work the best. If employers are willing to listen and are (12) ______________ suggestions, they can take advantage of office space and help employees to realize their full potential.

WORD PRACTICE

Listening Comprehension

Track 27

PART 1 PHOTO

Look at the picture and listen to the sentences. Choose the sentence that best describes the picture.

1. Ⓐ Ⓑ Ⓒ Ⓓ

PART 2 QUESTION–RESPONSE

Listen to the question and the three responses. Choose the response that best answers the question.

2. Ⓐ Ⓑ Ⓒ 3. Ⓐ Ⓑ Ⓒ

PART 3 CONVERSATION

Listen to the dialogue. Then read each question and choose the best response.

4. What does the man think of the current lobby?
   (A) People conduct a lot of conversations there.
   (B) It's quite pleasant.
   (C) More people should use it.
   (D) It's not a good place for conversations.

5. What might be disruptive to the business?
   (A) Loud conversations in the lobby
   (B) Remodeling work
   (C) The need to scrutinize plans
   (D) A heavy workload

6. When will the new lobby be finished?
   (A) This afternoon
   (B) In two weeks
   (C) Next month
   (D) In four months

PART 4 TALK

Listen to the talk. Then read each question and choose the best answer.

7. What is this talk about?
   (A) How to encourage collaboration
   (B) How to increase productivity
   (C) How to concentrate
   (D) How to design an office

8. What is the problem with a large, open office?
   (A) It isn't conducive to collaboration.
   (B) It doesn't include options.
   (C) Work is easily disrupted.
   (D) It isn't adjacent to a lobby.

9. Why is it important to have a large work room?
   (A) To allow staff members to work together
   (B) To maintain a high level of activity
   (C) To increase concentration
   (D) To have a more attractive design

Reading

PART 5 INCOMPLETE SENTENCES

Choose the word that best completes the sentence.

10. I always know who is entering and leaving the office because my workspace is ______ to the reception area.

    (A) hampered (C) optional
    (B) adjacent (D) conducive

11. Some people are easily distracted and can't ______ on their work unless they are in a quiet area.

    (A) collaborate (C) disrupt
    (B) concentrate (D) move up

12. The constant flow of traffic by the researcher's desk proved to be very ______.

    (A) disruptive (C) disruption
    (B) disrupts (D) disrupted

13. The employee lounge is for everyone's enjoyment so please don't use it ______.

    (A) inconsiderate (C) inconsiderately
    (B) inconsiderateness (D) inconsideration

14. Some people always ______ for the easy way out.

    (A) opt (C) optional
    (B) option (D) options

15. After close ______ of the new offices, they decided to put the photocopier in a small room where no one would be bothered by the noise.

    (A) scrutinize (C) scrutiny
    (B) scrutinizing (D) scrutinized

NOTICE

In order to maintain a professional office environment that is ____ (16.) to work, all staff members are asked to observe the following guidelines.

- Be ____ (17.) of your coworkers. When using an open work area, do not speak in loud voices or turn on radios. ____ (18.)
- Remember that the lobby is the first place our clients see when they enter the office. Please cooperate by doing your best to keep this area clean and neat.
- Our clients are important. ____ (19.) your coworkers when they are meeting with clients.

16. (A) optional
    (B) conducive
    (C) inscrutable
    (D) collaborative

17. (A) concentrated
    (B) adjacent
    (C) considerate
    (D) hampering

18. (A) People often find it difficult to concentrate in a noisy environment.
    (B) We are open to hearing your ideas about this issue.
    (C) There is plenty of time for parties on weekends.
    (D) We encourage collaboration among coworkers.

19. (A) Not disrupt
    (B) Won't disrupt
    (C) Isn't disrupting
    (D) Don't disrupt

PART 7 READING COMPREHENSION

Questions 20–24 refer to the following memo.

Memo

To: All office staff
From: P. Windermere, Office Manager
Re: Parking situation

As you may be aware, starting next week, the parking garage will be closed for repairs to the upper level due to damage caused by the heavy rains last month. There will be no parking allowed on any level of the garage while the repairs are taking place, as parked cars may hamper the work. Cars parked in the garage will be towed at the owner's expense. While the garage is closed, you may opt to park on the street or in the lot adjacent to the building. Remember that it is a private lot and a fee will be charged. I realize that the parking options will be limited, and I am open to any suggestions for solutions to this parking situation that any of you may have. Unfortunately, the repair work will take more than a few weeks. We cannot expect the garage to open again until two months from now. In the meantime, I thank you for your cooperation.

20. Why will the garage be closed?
    (A) It needs repairs.
    (B) The fees are too high.
    (C) Its parking options are limited.
    (D) Street parking is better.

21. What will happen to cars that are parked in the garage?
    (A) They will be charged a fee.
    (B) They will be repaired.
    (C) They will be towed.
    (D) They will be used for work.

22. When will the garage reopen?
    (A) In a week
    (B) In just a few weeks
    (C) In a month
    (D) In two months

23. The word *hamper* in line 5 is closest in meaning to
    (A) allow.
    (B) interfere.
    (C) encourage.
    (D) contribute.

24. The word *adjacent* in line 7 is closest in meaning to
    (A) distant.
    (B) underneath.
    (C) next to.
    (D) across from.

Lesson 27: Board Meetings and Committees

WORDS TO LEARN

- adhere to
- agenda
- bring up
- conclude
- go ahead
- goal
- lengthy
- matter
- periodically
- priority
- progress
- waste

Study the following definitions and examples.

1. **adhere to** v., to follow; to pay attention to
   a. The chairman never adhered to his own rules.
   b. The best committee members are those who adhere to the time limits and speak only when they have something important to add.
2. **agenda** n., a list of topics to be discussed
   a. The board was able to cover fifteen items on the agenda.
   b. The agenda was sent out three weeks ago so that everyone could prepare for the meeting.
3. **bring up** v., to introduce a topic
   a. Just as the meeting was about to finish, the manager brought up a controversial issue.
   b. No one brought up the resignation of the director.
4. **conclude** v., to stop; to come to a decision
   a. The committee members concluded the meeting early so that they could finish their budgets.
   b. After long discussions, the board has concluded that the project has to be canceled.
5. **go ahead** v., to proceed with; n., permission to do something
   a. Five of the six members felt that they should go ahead with the plan.
   b. The manager was just waiting for the go-ahead from her boss before mailing the report.
6. **goal** n., objective; purpose
   a. Employees are expected to analyze and evaluate their annual goals.
   b. The director had to report to the committee that his department wouldn't reach its financial goal.
7. **lengthy** adj., long in time, duration, or distance
   a. After lengthy discussions, the chairperson was reelected for another term.
   b. The report was so lengthy that members had to take it home and read it over the weekend.
8. **matter** n., an item, issue, or topic of interest
   a. If there are no other matters to discuss, we will conclude the meeting.
   b. This is not the place to bring up personal matters.
9. **periodically** adv., from time to time
   a. The group tried to meet periodically.
   b. Periodically, new members were nominated to the committee.
10. **priority** n., something of importance; something that should be done before other things
    a. Since the remaining issues were not a priority, they moved them to the next week's agenda.
    b. The manager was ineffective because she was unable to set priorities.
11. **progress** n., a movement forward; v., to move forward on something, especially work or a project
    a. The executive committee asked each group to present a report showing their progress for the year.
    b. This project is taking a long time, but every day we progress a little more toward our goal.
12. **waste** v., to use carelessly; n., the careless use of something
    a. Without a leader, the group members wasted time and energy trying to organize themselves.
    b. The meeting wasn't a waste of time, but the members had hoped to accomplish more.

WORD FAMILIES

verb	adhere	The chairperson asked us to adhere to the items on the agenda.
noun	adherence	Your adherence to these guidelines would be appreciated.

verb	conclude	To conclude, we must all focus on the year ahead of us and the challenges that we will face.
noun	conclusion	Unfortunately, the conclusion of the meeting was that they needed to downsize their workforce.
adjective	conclusive	There is no conclusive evidence to back up the report.

verb	lengthen	Ms. Greene decided to lengthen the time allotted to the meeting to allow each person a chance to speak.
noun	length	Because of its length, we decided not to read the entire report at the meeting.
adjective	lengthy	A presentation that is too lengthy will only put the audience to sleep.

noun	period	The sales reports for the current period are excellent.
adjective	periodic	They received periodic updates from the overseas licensees.
adverb	periodically	The employee checked his messages periodically during the week-long seminar.

verb	prioritize	Once the team members learned to prioritize their work, they were much more productive.
noun	priority	The committee member has difficulties setting priorities for herself.
adjective	prior	The director did not give much attention to Ellen's proposal as he had several prior matters to attend to.

verb	progress	Everyone was surprised at how quickly the meeting had progressed.
noun	progress	The director is really pleased with the progress we have made on this project.
adjective	progressive	The discussion focused on the progressive decline of interest in these types of products.

WORDS IN CONTEXT

Read the following passage and write the words in the blanks below.

adhered to	concluded	lengthy	priority
agenda	go-ahead	matters	progress
brought up	goals	periodically	waste

Committee meetings are a frequent and necessary event at almost every company. In order for meetings to be productive and not viewed as a (1) ______________ of time, they should be run efficiently. Critical to the success of any meeting is the (2) ______________. Everyone who attends the meeting should be aware of the agenda and be prepared to discuss the (3) ______________ at hand and the (4) ______________ to be accomplished. To avoid (5) ______________ discussions, time frames should be set and (6) ______________.

The meeting is called to order by the chairperson. Attendance is taken and agenda items are (7) ______________ one by one. In general, (8) ______________ topics should be at the beginning of the agenda, to make sure that the attendees are able to discuss them fully and make timely decisions. Once the (9) ______________ is given for a plan or project, a plan of action is developed. The committee must then (10) ______________ check up on the (11) ______________ of that plan. The meeting is (12) ______________ without any outstanding issues and a date for the next meeting is set.

WORD PRACTICE

Listening Comprehension

Track 28

PART 1 PHOTO

Look at the picture and listen to the sentences. Choose the sentence that best describes the picture.

1. Ⓐ Ⓑ Ⓒ Ⓓ

PART 2 QUESTION–RESPONSE

Listen to the question and the three responses. Choose the response that best answers the question.

2. Ⓐ Ⓑ Ⓒ 3. Ⓐ Ⓑ Ⓒ

PART 3 CONVERSATION

Listen to the dialogue. Then read each question and choose the best response.

4. What do the speakers say about the meeting?
   (A) They had a good time.
   (B) A lot was accomplished.
   (C) Important matters were discussed.
   (D) It was too long.

5. How long did the meeting last?
   (A) Two hours
   (B) Three hours
   (C) Four hours
   (D) Nine hours

6. What will the speakers do the next time there is a meeting?
   (A) Look at the agenda
   (B) Accomplish more things
   (C) Avoid attending it
   (D) Plan it better

PART 4 TALK

Listen to the talk. Then read each question and choose the best answer.

7. What is this talk about?
   (A) How to have a better staff meeting
   (B) How to make speeches
   (C) How to write an agenda
   (D) How to develop guidelines

8. What are the listeners asked to do?
   (A) Make long speeches
   (B) Discuss personal matters
   (C) Bring something to the meeting
   (D) Follow the agenda

9. What will happen at 4:30?
   (A) The meeting will end.
   (B) Goals will be discussed.
   (C) Guidelines will be presented.
   (D) A new item will be introduced.

Reading

PART 5 INCOMPLETE SENTENCES

Choose the word that best completes the sentence.

10. When using these facilities, please ______ to the rules posted by the door.

    (A) adhere (C) adherence
    (B) adhering (D) adhered

11. As the chairman stood to give his ______, everyone in the room was listening.

    (A) conclusion (C) conclusive
    (B) conclude (D) concluding

12. Nobody wanted to ______ the meeting, but it was necessary in order to have enough time to cover the entire agenda.

    (A) waste (C) bring up
    (B) lengthen (D) conclude

13. Our financial ______ for this quarter is to reduce spending by 5%.

    (A) period (C) goal
    (B) agenda (D) matter

14. As her first ______, the committee chairwoman wanted to attract new, energetic members to the group.

    (A) prior (C) prioritize
    (B) priority (D) prioritized

15. Even as they ______ through the hundreds of pages of supporting material, the committee was still not convinced that the project was justified.

    (A) progression (C) progresses
    (B) progressed (D) progressive

PART 6 TEXT COMPLETION

Memo

To: Department Staff
From: Alison Roth, Department Manager
Re: Meeting

All members of the department staff are requested to attend a department meeting next Friday morning. As you know, we meet ____ (16.) to review our work of the past months and finalize plans for the coming months. The goal of this Friday's meeting is to set our priorities for the next six months. The meeting agenda is attached for your review. Let's agree to follow the agenda and not ____ (17.) other matters at this time so that we can finish the meeting in a timely manner. The most important item on the agenda is the budget. ____ (18.). We ____ (19.) too much money over the past six months. Please come up with ideas about how we can use our funds more efficiently in the future. Please arrive at the meeting on time so that we can conclude before 12:00.

16. (A) period
    (B) periodic
    (C) periodical
    (D) periodically

17. (A) set back
    (B) go ahead
    (C) bring up
    (D) adhere to

18. (A) We need to take a careful look at our spending practices.
    (B) This is a matter we discuss at each staff meeting.
    (C) Please go ahead and review the agenda now.
    (D) I hope we can adhere to the planned agenda.

19. (A) waste
    (B) have wasted
    (C) will waste
    (D) are wasting

PART 7 READING COMPREHENSION

Questions 20–24 refer to the following agenda and e-mail message.

Perruche, Inc.
Annual Meeting
May 17, 20—
1:00 P.M.

Agenda

1. Progress report on overseas expansion	Robert Fleurat
2. Reducing waste in our plants	Madeline Costello
3. Reassessing our financial goals	Jean Duprey
4. Hiring and firing policies	Cynthia Weinstein
5. Looking ahead: priorities for the next decade	Samuel Lyon

To: Cynthia Weinstein
From: Samuel Lyon
Subject: Yesterday's meeting

Hello Cynthia,

We all missed you at yesterday's meeting. We were concerned that a medical emergency prevented your attendance but are glad to know that you are all right now. The meeting went well, and we were able to adhere to the agenda for the most part. There was only one small change. Jean gave his presentation on finance right after Robert since he had to leave early. Your secretary e-mailed a copy of your report to me, and I read it in your place. There were a few questions that will be submitted to you by e-mail. The meeting was not lengthy at all. In fact, even though we had scheduled three hours for the entire meeting, we actually concluded half an hour earlier than that. You see how efficient we have become. A copy of the meeting minutes will be e-mailed to you before 5:00 today. I hope to speak with you soon.

Samuel

20. What was the second item presented at the meeting?
    (A) Progress report on overseas expansion
    (B) Reducing waste in our plants
    (C) Reassessing our financial goals
    (D) Hiring and firing policies

21. Who read the report on hiring and firing policies?
    (A) Madeline Costello
    (B) Jean Duprey
    (C) Cynthia Weinstein
    (D) Samuel Lyon

22. What time did the meeting end?
    (A) 1:00
    (B) 3:30
    (C) 4:00
    (D) 4:30

23. The word *goals* in line 3 of the agenda is closest in meaning to
    (A) objectives.
    (B) problems.
    (C) needs.
    (D) decisions.

24. The words *adhere to* in line 3 of the e-mail are closest in meaning to
    (A) study.
    (B) design.
    (C) follow.
    (D) understand.

Lesson 28: Quality Control

WORDS TO LEARN

- brand
- conform
- defect
- enhance
- garment
- inspect
- perceptive
- repel
- take back
- throw out
- uniformly
- wrinkle

Study the following definitions and examples.

1. **brand** n., an identifying mark or label; a trademark
   a. Consumers often buy highly advertised brands of athletic shoes.
   b. All brands of aspirin are the same.
2. **conform** v., to match specifications or qualities
   a. The quality control manager insisted every product leaving the plant conform to rigorous standards.
   b. Our safety standards conform to those established by the government.
3. **defect** n., an imperfection or flaw
   a. Because of a defect in stitching, the entire suit was thrown out.
   b. One way to sell a product with a defect is by labeling it as such and reducing the price.
4. **enhance** v., to make more attractive or valuable
   a. The reason behind quality control is to enhance the company's reputation for superior products.
   b. A stylish color enhances the appeal of a car.
5. **garment** n., an article of clothing
   a. Every garment must be carefully inspected for defects before it is shipped.
   b. The garment workers are accountable for production mistakes.
6. **inspect** v., to look at closely; to examine carefully or officially
   a. A quality control agent who doesn't inspect all products carefully can ruin a company's reputation.
   b. Children's car seats are thoroughly inspected and tested for safety before being put on the market.
7. **perceptive** adj., able to see or understand
   a. Dora always hires good workers because she is very perceptive about people's abilities.
   b. It takes a perceptive person to be a good manager.
8. **repel** v., to keep away; to fight against
   a. Umbrellas that do not repel water should never be passed through quality control.
   b. This product is guaranteed to repel mosquitoes for up to five hours.
9. **take back** v., to return something; to withdraw or retract
   a. Good quality control significantly limits the number of products taken back for a refund.
   b. The quality inspector took the inferior work back to the assembly line to confront the workers.
10. **throw out** v., to dispose of
    a. It is cheaper to throw out shoddy products than to lose customers.
    b. The factory decided to throw out all lightbulbs that may have been damaged, rather than lose customers.
11. **uniformly** adv., in the same way; consistently
    a. The products are checked to make sure they are uniformly packaged before they leave the factory.
    b. The food at chain restaurants is uniformly prepared, so customers will always find the same quality.
12. **wrinkle** n., a crease, ridge, or furrow, especially in skin or fabric
    a. A wrinkle that is ironed into a permanent-press product will annoy the consumer each time the garment is worn.
    b. A wrinkle in the finish can be repaired more economically before a sale than after.

WORD FAMILIES

noun	defect	Even a small defect can cause a product to fail.
adjective	defective	Good quality control employees will notice defective machinery before a serious breakdown occurs.

verb	inspect	We must inspect every product before we sell it.
noun	inspection	Each employee must conduct a careful inspection.
noun	inspector	The inspector leaves his identification number on the product to ensure accountability.

verb	perceive	The worker perceived that the stitching on the seams could not withstand normal strain.
noun	perception	Customers' perception of quality is often based on their experience with a given store or brand.
adjective	perceptive	Perceptive workers are excellent quality control inspectors.

verb	repel	A quality raincoat can repel rain and keep you dry.
noun	repellent	Testing insect repellent is never a pleasant task.
adjective	repellent	Testing stain removers can be repellent to workers because of the toxic fumes.

noun	uniform	The employees at this company are required to wear uniforms.
adjective	uniform	A successful company will ensure the uniform quality of its products.
adverb	uniformly	All of our company's products must be uniformly labeled.

verb	wrinkle	Linen is not a practical fabric because it wrinkles easily.
noun	wrinkle	Inspect garments carefully and remove any wrinkles that you find.
adjective	wrinkled	Garments become wrinkled after they have been tried on several times at the store.

WORDS IN CONTEXT

Read the following passage and write the words in the blanks below.

brand	enhance	perceive	throws out
conform	garment	repel	uniform
defects	inspect	take back	wrinkle

Alex is excited about his new job with Parapluie Rain Wear. As quality control manager, his job is to make sure that his company's goods (1) _____________ to standardized quality criteria and are free from (2) _____________. Before any (3) _____________ leaves the factory, Alex must (4) _____________ it. He knows that if he (5) _____________ a damaged garment before a customer sees it, he will (6) _____________ his company's reputation and increase the demand for its products. Alex must ensure that all products meet certain criteria: A customer who buys a raincoat that does not (7) _____________ rain will probably (8) _____________ the raincoat to the store and buy another (9) _____________. The same is true if the seams are not sewn tightly or the color is not (10) _____________. Alex knows that, in addition to keeping out rain, the product must be attractive to look at and to touch. It should not (11) _____________ easily, and it should last a long time. Alex knows that it is important for customers to (12) _____________ his company's goods as quality products so that his company will profit—and he can get a raise.

WORD PRACTICE

Listening Comprehension

Track 29

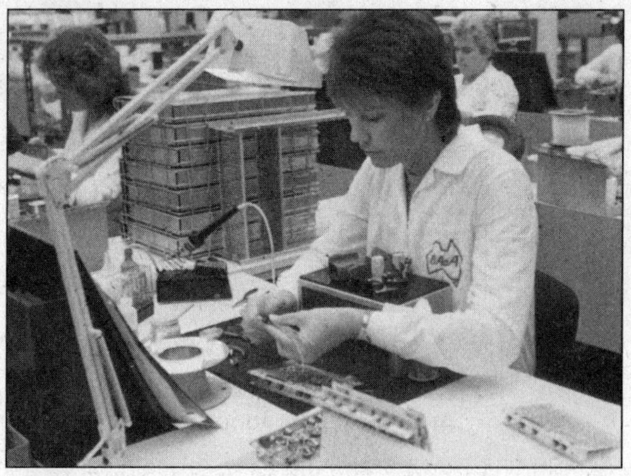

PART 1 PHOTO

Look at the picture and listen to the sentences. Choose the sentence that best describes the picture.

1. Ⓐ Ⓑ Ⓒ Ⓓ

PART 2 QUESTION–RESPONSE

Listen to the question and the three responses. Choose the response that best answers the question.

2. Ⓐ Ⓑ Ⓒ 3. Ⓐ Ⓑ Ⓒ

PART 3 CONVERSATION

Listen to the dialogue. Then read each question and choose the best response.

4. What does the company do with garments that have defects?
   (A) It exchanges them for better products.
   (B) It throws them out.
   (C) It stores them at the factory.
   (D) It sells them at a discount.

5. How many of the garments end up with defects?
   (A) 15 percent
   (B) 16 percent
   (C) 50 percent
   (D) 60 percent

6. What type of garment does the company manufacture?
   (A) Shirts
   (B) Skirts
   (C) Sweaters
   (D) Uniforms

PART 4 TALK

Listen to the talk. Then read each question and choose the best answer.

7. Who is this talk directed at?
   (A) Store employees
   (B) Factory workers
   (C) Product inspectors
   (D) Customers

8. When is a product inspected?
   (A) When it reaches the store
   (B) Before it leaves the factory
   (C) Before the customer takes it home
   (D) When the customer returns it

9. What can a customer do with a defective product?
   (A) Ask for a new product in exchange
   (B) Send it back to the factory
   (C) Show it to an inspector
   (D) Return it to the store

Reading

PART 5 INCOMPLETE SENTENCES

Choose the word that best completes the sentence.

10. Any defective item must be ______ so that it never reaches the stores.

(A) enhanced (C) thrown out
(B) repelled (D) conformed

11. Rebecca is known as ______ #321 among her quality control coworkers.

(A) inspect (C) inspector
(B) inspection (D) inspecting

12. An employee who ______ his job as important performs better than one who wants only a paycheck.

(A) perceives (C) perceptive
(B) perceived (D) perception

13. Agnes was ______ by the odor of the waterproofing.

(A) repel (C) repelled
(B) repellent (D) repelling

14. Standardized products are ______ in appearance.

(A) uniforms (C) uniform
(B) uniformly (D) unformed

15. If you package these garments correctly, you will avoid ______ and keep the items looking nice.

(A) wrinkles (C) inspectors
(B) brands (D) perceptions

PART 6 TEXT COMPLETION

Thank you for buying a Flexco product. Flexco is a top name in women's clothing, and the Flexco brand carries a reputation for excellence. Customer satisfaction is our top priority, and all Flexco garments carry the Flexco guarantee. All our products must ____ (16.) to high standards. They ____ (17.) by trained professionals before they leave the factory. ____ (18.) If your purchase is unsatisfactory in any way, you may take it ____ (19.) to the store for a complete refund.

16. (A) conform
(B) conforms
(C) conforming
(D) to conform

17. (A) inspect
(B) inspected
(C) are inspected
(D) have inspected

18. (A) Our company also contracts with individual companies to manufacture uniforms.
(B) Any defective garment is thrown out long before it reaches customers' hands.
(C) All our products are uniformly labeled with the Flexco logo.
(D) Flexco is known for creating garments in the very latest styles.

19. (A) up
(B) out
(C) off
(D) back

PART 7 READING COMPREHENSION

Questions 20–24 refer to the following product review.

Don't buy this garment

I bought this Flexco garment as a gift for my wife because Flexco has always been one of her favorite brands. She loved it at first, and it fit her perfectly. But when she wore it in a rainstorm last week, we discovered that it was not water repellent at all. My wife returned home from her walk very wet. Also, the fabric became very wrinkled in the rain. We were quite surprised by this. My wife already owns several Flexco skirts, dresses, and blouses, and we never expected to be disappointed by a Flexco product. Also, the company does not fulfill its stated guarantee. When I contacted them, they would not give me a refund but offered instead a different coat in exchange for the flawed one. After this experience, we will not purchase another Flexco product.

20. What product did the reviewer buy?
    (A) Blouse
    (B) Raincoat
    (C) Dress
    (D) Skirt

21. What does the reviewer say about the product?
    (A) It repelled water.
    (B) It did not fit well.
    (C) It cost too much.
    (D) It was defective.

22. What did the Flexco company offer to the reviewer?
    (A) A discount on a future purchase
    (B) A return of his money
    (C) A new garment
    (D) An apology

23. The word *brands* in line 2 of the review is closest in meaning to
    (A) companies.
    (B) products.
    (C) fabrics.
    (D) gifts.

24. The word *wrinkled* in line 4 of the review is closest in meaning to
    (A) destroyed.
    (B) creased.
    (C) dirty.
    (D) damp.

Lesson 29: Product Development

WORDS TO LEARN

- anxious
- ascertain
- assume
- decade
- examine
- experiment
- logical
- research
- responsibility
- solve
- supervisor
- systematically

Study the following definitions and examples.

1. **anxious** adj., worried
   a. The developers were anxious about the sales forecast for the new product.
   b. The designers looked calm during the presentation but were anxious it wouldn't be well received.
2. **ascertain** v., to discover; to find out for certain
   a. A necessary part of product development is to ascertain whether the product is safe.
   b. A customer survey will help to ascertain whether there is a market for the product.
3. **assume** v., to take upon oneself; to believe to be true
   a. The young man felt ready to assume the new responsibilities of his promotion.
   b. A company should assume nothing about the market but instead pay attention to research results.
4. **decade** n., a period of ten years
   a. After a decade of trying, the company finally developed a vastly superior product.
   b. Each decade seems to have its own fad products.
5. **examine** v., to interrogate; to scrutinize
   a. Before marketing a new product, researchers must carefully examine it from every aspect.
   b. Good researchers have to examine every possible option, including some that seem bizarre.
6. **experiment** v., to try out a new procedure or idea; n., a test or trial
   a. Product developers must conduct hundreds of experiments in their research.
   b. After designing a product, researchers continue experimenting to determine if it has other uses.
7. **logical** adj., formally valid; using orderly reasoning
   a. It is logical for a research and development team to focus on one or two products at a time.
   b. In addition to logical thinkers, a good research and development team should include a few dreamers.
8. **research** n., the act of collecting information about a particular subject.
   a. Part of the research the team does is to see if similar products are already on the market.
   b. For toy manufacturers, research can be pure fun.
9. **responsibility** n., a task or duty; something for which one is responsible
   a. The product development department has a responsibility to be sure that the product is safe.
   b. One responsibility of product development is to ensure that there is a demand for the product.
10. **solve** v., to find a solution, explanation, or answer
    a. Researchers find that every time they solve one problem, two more result.
    b. One of the biggest problems to solve is why people would want to own the new product.
11. **supervisor** n., an administrator in charge
    a. The department supervisor has to balance his department's responsibilities in order to keep the president satisfied with its progress.
    b. A good supervisor gets his team to work with him, not just for him.
12. **systematically** adv., methodically; following a system
    a. Once creative development is complete, we must work systematically to make it a reality.
    b. While creative thinking is necessary, analyzing a problem systematically is indispensable.

WORD FAMILIES

noun	anxiety	The level of anxiety was high when the experimental car underwent road tests.
adjective	anxious	If you feel anxious, sit down and try to relax.
adverb	anxiously	The stockholders anxiously awaited the release of the new drug that, if successful, would make their stocks more valuable.

verb	assume	Product developers should assume nothing that research does not support.
noun	assumption	Most consumers make the assumption that, unless they are warned otherwise, the products they buy are safe.
adjective	assumed	Luis was the assumed replacement for the retiring Director of Product Development.

verb	experiment	The product developer had experimented with improving electronic equipment since she was in the sixth grade.
noun	experiment	After many experiments, they were finally able to develop a paint that would not fade.
adjective	experimental	The new computer was experimental, so you could try it at the store, but you couldn't buy one.

noun	logic	Most problems can be easily solved by the application of logic.
adjective	logical	It was logical to put Martha in charge of the project as she had spent so much time developing the idea.
adverb	logically	I thought Mr. Lee answered the question quite logically.

noun	responsibility	Although the ultimate responsibility falls on the supervisor, every employee shares it.
adjective	responsible	The researcher responsible for passing the defective product has joined the cafeteria workers' assembly line.
adverb	responsibly	Product designers must act responsibly when they consider how a product might be misused.

verb	supervise	It's important to carefully supervise the collection of research data to ensure its accuracy.
noun	supervisor	George hopes to be promoted to supervisor of his department.
noun	supervision	Many employees do better work when they are under less supervision.

d write the words in the blanks below.

decade	logical	solve
examining	researched	supervisor
experiments	responsible	systematic

s worried about his promotion. He needn't have been ___ though. He had worked in the Product Development Division alf years, almost a (2) ______________. He knew the department however, he would be the director. As a member of the department, o what his (3) ______________ told him. As the director, he would 4) ______________ for the success of his department. Fears are not ___________; in fact, they are often illogical.

sk, he decided to conduct a (6) ______________ analysis of the steps elop new products, and to organize the tasks into a logical order. The eloping new products would be to (7) ______________ what kind of arket needed and what problems existed with the products currently

task would be to find out how best to examine these problems and at kind of research would be needed to (8) ______________ the vould be better to say, "reexamine these problems," since most of these blems had been thoroughly (9) ______________ over the years.

task would be to look at the quality and characteristics of the products. By (10) ______________ the competition's products, ow where he should improve. And the final task would be to decide her the most substantial information from the fewest number of ________. Michael smiled and sat back to read over his list. Confident a good team and a good plan, he felt ready to (12) ______________ his

WORD PRACTICE

Listening Comprehension

Track 30

PART 1 PHOTO

Look at the picture and listen to the sentences. Choose the sentence that best describes the picture.

1. Ⓐ Ⓑ Ⓒ Ⓓ

PART 2 QUESTION-RESPONSE

Listen to the question and the three responses. Choose the response that best ans

2. Ⓐ Ⓑ Ⓒ 3. Ⓐ Ⓑ Ⓒ

PART 3 CONVERSATION

Listen to the dialogue. Then read each question and choose the best response.

4. What does the woman want to do with the doll?
   (A) Make it less expensive
   (B) Examine it
   (C) Change it's color
   (D) Add a noisemaker

5. How much does the woman think that sales will increase?
   (A) 13 percent
   (B) 15 percent
   (C) 30 percent
   (D) 40 percent

6. What does the man s
   (A) Search for a bigge
   (B) Research prices a
   (C) Give the doll a ne
   (D) Hire more salespe

PART 4 TALK

Listen to the talk. Then read each question and choose the best answer.

7. Why is the product popular?
   (A) It has a low price.
   (B) People are familiar with it.
   (C) It is available everywhere.
   (D) Nobody is sure of the reason.

8. How long has the product been on the market?
   (A) Exactly two years
   (B) Exactly twenty years
   (C) More than twenty years
   (D) About ten years

9. Who buys the product?
   (A) Children
   (B) Teenagers
   (C) Men and women
   (D) People of all ages

PART 7 READING COMPREHENSION

Questions 20–24 refer to the following two e-mail messages.

From: Dean Ayers
To: Kathleen Hollinger
Subject: Product Development opening

Dear Ms. Hollinger,

I understand that the company has an opening in the Product Development Department. I am interested in applying for this position. I have been working for New Age Systems for close to a decade. Currently I am a research assistant in the Marketing Department. During my time at New Age Systems, I have worked in several departments at the company and have had the opportunity to learn a great deal about its work. I feel that I am now ready to assume the responsibilities of a higher level position. I am anxious to speak with you about working in the Product Development Department. Thank you for your attention. I look forward to hearing from you.

Sincerely,

Dean Ayers

From: Kathleen Hollinger
To: Dean Ayers
Subject: re: Product Development opening

Dear Mr. Ayers,

Thank you for your message expressing interest in applying for the position in the Product Development Department. Unfortunately, the position you are interested in has already been filled. However, I have communicated with your supervisor, and he speaks very highly of you. I have also examined your work record. It is clear that you would be a good asset to our department. I expect that we will have another opening before the end of this year. As soon as I have ascertained the availability of that position, I will be in contact with you. I look forward to meeting with you in the near future.

Sincerely,

Kathleen Hollinger
Manager, Product Development Department

20. How long has Mr. Ayers worked for New Age Systems, Inc.?
    (A) Almost ten years
    (B) Exactly ten years
    (C) Almost twenty years
    (D) More than twenty years

21. What job does Mr. Ayers have now?
    (A) Product developer
    (B) Department head
    (C) Marketing manager
    (D) Research assistant

22. What will Ms. Hollinger do?
    (A) Hire Mr. Ayers right away
    (B) Ask Mr. Ayers to supervise a project
    (C) Tell Mr. Ayers when a position becomes available
    (D) Send Mr. Ayers a copy of his work record

23. The word *assume* in line 10 of the first letter is closest in meaning to
    (A) teach.
    (B) study.
    (C) decide.
    (D) accept.

24. The word *examined* in line 7 of the second letter is closest in meaning to
    (A) looked at.
    (B) brought up.
    (C) taken back.
    (D) given up.

Lesson 30: Renting and Leasing

WORDS TO LEARN

- apprehensive
- circumstance
- condition
- due to
- fluctuate
- get out of
- indicator
- lease
- lock into
- occupy
- subject
- tenant

Study the following definitions and examples.

1. **apprehensive** adj., anxious about the future
   a. Most new home buyers are apprehensive about their decision.
   b. The mortgage lender was apprehensive about the company's ability to pay.
2. **circumstance** n., a condition; a situation
   a. Under the current economic circumstances, they will not be able to purchase the property.
   b. If the circumstances change in the near future and we have new properties, we will be sure to call you.
3. **condition** n., the state of something; a requirement
   a. Except for some minor repairs, the building is in very good condition.
   b. There are certain conditions that are unique to leasing a property.
4. **due to** prep., because of
   a. Due to the low interest rates, good office space is difficult to find.
   b. He didn't believe that the low prices were due only to the neighborhood.
5. **fluctuate** v., to go up and down; to change
   a. No one is very comfortable investing in real estate while property prices are fluctuating so much.
   b. Prime business areas fluctuate with local economies, crime rates, and cost of living indices.
6. **get out of** v., to escape; to exit
   a. The agent wasn't sure if the executives could get out of their prior real estate arrangement.
   b. The company wanted to get out of the area before property values declined even further.
7. **indicator** n., a sign; a signal
   a. If the economy is an accurate indicator, rental prices will increase rapidly in the next six months.
   b. The results of the elections were seen as an important indicator of the stability in the area.
8. **lease** n., a contract to pay to use property for an amount of time; v., to make a contract to use property
   a. With the lease expiring next year, they need to start looking for a new location.
   b. They decided to lease the property rather than buy it.
9. **lock into** v., to commit; to be unable to change
   a. The company locked itself into a ten-year lease that they didn't want.
   b. Before you lock yourself into something, check all your options.
10. **occupy** v., to dwell or reside in
    a. Tenants are usually allowed to occupy their space beginning on the first day of the month.
    b. Our company has occupied this office for more than five years.
11. **subject** adj., under legal power; dependent
    a. This contract is subject to all the laws and regulations of the state.
    b. The go-ahead to buy is subject to the president's approval.
12. **tenant** n., a person who rents property
    a. Property owners want tenants who are respectful of their neighbors and pay their rent on time.
    b. The new tenant wants to move in before the first of the month.

WORD FAMILIES

noun	apprehension	The air was thick with apprehension as the landlord met with the tenants.
adjective	apprehensive	The tenants were apprehensive about the conditions of their rental agreement.

noun	circumstance	Because of our circumstances, the rental agent kindly allowed us to get out of our lease early.
adjective	circumstantial	The judge's decision that the tenant was responsible for repairing the damage was based solely on circumstantial evidence.

verb	condition	The president conditioned her acceptance on two factors that were spelled out in the letter of agreement.
noun	condition	They decided to rent the space, under the condition that the price would not be raised for the next two years.
adjective	conditional	If you give a conditional go-ahead, we will start drawing up the plans.

verb	fluctuate	As interest rates began to fluctuate, many investors became nervous and took their money out of the real estate market.
noun	fluctuation	Construction is sensitive to any fluctuations in the economy.

verb	indicate	As was indicated in the terms of the lease, any changes to the property must be approved by the owners.
noun	indicator	The state of local schools is a good indicator of the health of the economy.
noun	indication	The management team had every indication that the tenants were planning to stay for the near future.

verb	occupy	The owner must make sure that the space is in good condition before the tenant occupies it.
noun	occupant	Most of the occupants of this building are doctors and lawyers.
noun	occupancy	The occupancy rate of the building has never fallen below 85 percent.

WORDS IN CONTEXT

Read the following passage and write the words in the blanks below.

apprehensive	due to	indicator	occupancy
circumstances	fluctuations	lease	subject
condition	get out of	lock into	tenant

Starting a new business is both an exciting and frightening undertaking. Most new business owners are (1) _______________ about their ability to make all the decisions that arise during the course of opening a business. One of the first issues that will arise is whether to buy or (2) _______________ property. In order to evaluate the options, business owners research the current real estate market. (3) _______________ rates are a good (4) _______________ of the overall business climate. Too many empty properties can be a sign that the local economy is not healthy.

Economic change is part of the business climate. There are often large (5) ____________ in prices within a given city. These changes are (6) ___________ many factors like the (7) _______________ of the building, the surrounding neighborhood, access to public transportation, and business projections for the area.

Because there is so much uncertainty in starting a business, many owners do not want to (8) _______________ themselves ________ a long-term lease. Many negotiate clauses in their contracts to (9) _______________ a lease under certain (10) _______________. They want to insure the prices and conditions of a property before making a large commitment. Leases often provide more flexibility than buying a property. They like to leave their options open. They don't like to be (11) ____________ to the whims of the marketplace. Being a (12) ____________ rather than a property owner has its advantages.

WORD PRACTICE

Listening Comprehension

Track 31

PART 1 PHOTO

Look at the picture and listen to the sentences. Choose the sentence that best describes the picture.

1. Ⓐ Ⓑ Ⓒ Ⓓ

PART 2 QUESTION–RESPONSE

Listen to the question and the three responses. Choose the response that best answers the question.

2. Ⓐ Ⓑ Ⓒ 3. Ⓐ Ⓑ Ⓒ

PART 3 CONVERSATION

Listen to the dialogue. Then read each question and choose the best response.

4. What does the man want to do?
   (A) Validate his signature
   (B) Sign a contract
   (C) Become a lawyer
   (D) Get out of a lease

5. What is he afraid of?
   (A) Wearing the wrong suit
   (B) Paying too much money
   (C) Making the wrong decision
   (D) Being sued

6. When does he have to make a decision?
   (A) Before 10:00
   (B) Before the end of the month
   (C) In four months
   (D) In ten months

PART 4 TALK

Listen to the talk. Then read each question and choose the best answer.

7. Who is the audience for this talk?
   (A) Customers and clients
   (B) Landlords
   (C) Lawyers
   (D) Tenants

8. What should a business owner do before signing a lease?
   (A) Make sure her business is successful
   (B) Look at the neighborhood
   (C) Get more customers
   (D) Occupy the space

9. What length of time does the speaker recommend for a lease?
   (A) Four years
   (B) Five years
   (C) Nine years
   (D) Ten years

Reading

PART 5 INCOMPLETE SENTENCES

Choose the word that best completes the sentence.

10. The president was _______ about adding more space to the factory.

(A) apprehend (C) apprehension
(B) apprehensive (D) apprehended

11. The financial _______ of our business don't allow us to lease an office with such a high monthly rent.

(A) circumstances (C) circumstantially
(B) circumstantial (D) circumstanced

12. The landlord allowed us to keep pets in the apartment with the _______ that we pay a larger deposit.

(A) lease (C) circumstance
(B) indicator (D) condition

13. The buyer _______ with a nod of his head that he was placing a bid on the property.

(A) indicates (C) indicated
(B) indication (D) indicator

14. _______ as it does, I don't understand how anyone can depend on that country's market to provide a safe investment.

(A) Fluctuated (C) Fluctuation
(B) Fluctuating (D) Fluctuate

15. We had to wait until the end of the year to move out of our apartment because we were unable to _______ our lease sooner.

(A) occupy (C) get out of
(B) fluctuate (D) lock into

FOR RENT

Large, sunny office in prime downtown location. Current occupant must leave due ___ unforeseen circumstances. ___.
16. 17.

The new ___ will take over the six months remaining on the lease and will have
18.

the option to renew for an additional year. The office has been recently repainted and is in excellent ___. Call 567-0943 between 10:00 and 4:00 Monday
19.

through Friday to make an appointment to see the space.

16. (A) to
(B) of
(C) by
(D) on

17. (A) Therefore, we are seeking someone to take over the lease.
(B) Rental rates do not fluctuate much in this neighborhood.
(C) Economic indicators are good for downtown businesses.
(D) However, most rental properties are fully occupied at this time.

18. (A) circumstance
(B) occupancy
(C) tenant
(D) owner

19. (A) fluctuation
(B) indication
(C) apprehension
(D) condition

PART 7 READING COMPREHENSION

Questions 20–24 refer to the following e-mail message.

To: Ted Van Dorn
From: Bernadette Riley
Subject: Office space
Date: April 10

Ted,

I have found the solution to our office problems. I know that you have been wanting to get out of the neighborhood where our office is currently located, but that you have been apprehensive about the cost of renting in a better neighborhood. I have found an office downtown that I am sure we can afford. It is a bit smaller than our current space, but I think it will be big enough. The best part is, the rent is the same as we are paying now. This is due to the fact that the office is not in excellent condition. However, I think it will be easy for us to paint it and make a few small repairs. The space will be available for occupancy on the fifteenth of next month. We have the option of signing a one- or two-year lease, so we won't have to lock ourselves into a long-term contract. However, in order to get the low rent, we have to sign by the thirtieth of this month. If you are interested in this, I can arrange for you to see the space this weekend. Let me know as soon as possible.

Bern

20. Why doesn't Ted like his current office?
    (A) It is in a bad location.
    (B) It is too expensive.
    (C) It isn't big enough.
    (D) It isn't in good condition.

21. When can Ted and Bernadette move into the new office?
    (A) April 10
    (B) April 15
    (C) May 10
    (D) May 15

22. What do they have to do before the end of this month?
    (A) Paint the office
    (B) Sign the lease
    (C) Change the locks
    (D) Leave their old office

23. The word *apprehensive* in line 3 is closest in meaning to
    (A) certain.
    (B) relaxed.
    (C) anxious.
    (D) delighted.

24. The word *condition* in line 7 is closest in meaning to
    (A) state.
    (B) price.
    (C) location.
    (D) requirement.

WORD REVIEW #6
LESSONS 26–30 MANAGEMENT ISSUES

Choose the word that best completes the sentence.

1. The owner of the new company personally ___________ every expense.
   (A) scrutiny
   (B) scrutinize
   (C) scrutinized
   (D) scrutinizing

2. Several employees will ___________ on designing the office for efficiency.
   (A) collaborate
   (B) collaborated
   (C) collaborating
   (D) collaboration

3. When there is a problem with company policy, it should be ___________ before the board of directors.
   (A) thrown out
   (B) moved over
   (C) brought up
   (D) taken back

4. The quality control department felt it was making good ___________ when the number of defects declined.
   (A) progress
   (B) progressed
   (C) progressing
   (D) progressive

5. ___________ goods can ruin the future of a new company.
   (A) Defect
   (B) Defects
   (C) Defective
   (D) Defection

6. The public's ___________ of a company depends on how solidly the company stands behind its products.
   (A) perceive
   (B) perceptive
   (C) perceived
   (D) perception

7. We can finish the meeting by 3:00 if we ___________ to the agenda and avoid introducing new topics.
   (A) examine
   (B) perceive
   (C) assume
   (D) adhere

8. Determining the safeness of a particular appliance requires a ___________ investigation of the electrical components.
   (A) system
   (B) systems
   (C) systematic
   (D) systematize

9. When ___________ office space, it is wise to insist upon an option to renew.
   (A) lease
   (B) leasing
   (C) leased
   (D) lessor

10. Getting ___________ a lease requires legal advice and could end up being quite expensive.
    (A) in
    (B) on
    (C) off of
    (D) out of

Choose the one word or phrase that best completes each sentence.

To: m_schwartz@donner.com
From: j_holmes@blitzen.com
Subject: board meeting

Mary,

We all missed you at yesterday's meeting, but you will be happy to know it went well. We were able to adhere __________ the agenda and cover all topics in the allotted

11. (A) to
    (B) at
    (C) of
    (D) in

time. Wilbur gave a __________ explanation of the budget, and now I feel we all

12. (A) length
    (B) lengthy
    (C) lengthen
    (D) lengthily

understand it quite thoroughly. He plans to e-mail you a copy of his notes. The meeting __________ on time, at 5:00. The next meeting is scheduled for June 16.

13. (A) solved
    (B) progressed
    (C) concluded
    (D) indicated

John

Our job here in the Quality Control Department is to make sure that no garment leaves the factory in less than perfect condition. This means that each garment __________

14. (A) inspects
    (B) is inspected
    (C) is inspecting
    (D) has inspected

carefully by a trained garment inspector. We throw out all __________ garments. It is

15. (A) defect
    (B) defects
    (C) detective
    (D) defective

important to protect our __________ and make sure that the name of our company is

16. (A) lobby
    (B) research
    (C) brand
    (D) wrinkle

always associated with top-quality products.

Dear Mr. Wilcox,

Your lease for the office you __________ at 121 North Main Street will expire next month. I will be

17. (A) occupy
    (B) occupied
    (C) occupant
    (D) occupancy

very happy to have you renew the lease if you desire. You have occupied that space for a __________,

18. (A) month
    (B) semester
    (C) decade
    (D) century

and during those ten years you have always been a reliable tenant. Unfortunately, __________ to

19. (A) because
    (B) up
    (C) ought
    (D) due

rising costs everywhere, I will have to raise the rent on that space by 20 percent. I hope this won't cause you any hardship. Please let me know if you are still interested in renewing the lease, and I will have my assistant send one over to you.

Sincerely,

Amanda Brightwood

Lesson 31: Selecting a Restaurant

WORDS TO LEARN

- appeal
- compromise
- daringly
- delicious
- familiar
- guide
- majority
- mix
- rely
- secure
- subjective
- suggestion

Study the following definitions and examples.

1. **appeal** n., the ability to attract
   a. A restaurant with good food and reasonable prices has a lot of appeal.
   b. The pleasing decor and friendly waiters are what give that restaurant its appeal.
2. **compromise** n., a settlement of differences; v., to settle differences
   a. The couple made a compromise and ordered food to take out.
   b. John doesn't like sweet dishes so I compromised by adding just a small amount of sugar.
3. **daringly** adv., bravely
   a. We daringly ordered the raw squid.
   b. Bob daringly asked to see the menu in French.
4. **delicious** adj., tasty; good to eat
   a. This restaurant is famous for its delicious soups.
   b. The fish stew wasn't as delicious as we had expected it to be.
5. **familiar** adj., often encountered or seen; common
   a. It's nice to see some familiar items on the menu.
   b. The chef blends the familiar tastes with the unusual.
6. **guide** n., one who leads, directs, or gives advice; a guidebook
   a. The guide led our tour group to a small restaurant only known to the locals.
   b. I don't know where to go, so why don't we consult the guide.
7. **majority** n., the greater number or part
   a. The majority of the group wanted to try the new Chinese restaurant.
   b. Claude was in the majority, so he was very pleased with the decision.
8. **mix** v., to combine or blend into one mass; n., a combination
   a. The daring chef mixed two uncommon ingredients.
   b. The mix of bright colors on the plate was very pleasing.
9. **rely** v., to have confidence in; to depend on
   a. You can rely on that website to give accurate restaurant reviews.
   b. I seldom rely on restaurant reviews when choosing a restaurant.
10. **secure** v., to get possession of; to obtain
    a. Despite the popularity of the restaurant, Max was able to secure reservations for this evening.
    b. The hostess secured us another chair, so we could eat together.
11. **subjective** adj., particular to a given person; highly personal; not objective
    a. Food preferences are subjective and not everyone agrees on what tastes good.
    b. The reviews on this website are highly subjective but fun to read.
12. **suggestion** n., a proposal; advice
    a. Can I make a suggestion about what to order?
    b. We followed the waiter's suggestion and ordered one of the specials.

WORD FAMILIES

verb	appeal	On a beautiful spring day, a sidewalk café appeals to many people.
noun	appeal	That restaurant has been around for a long time but it hasn't lost its appeal.
adjective	appealing	An ice-cold drink seems very appealing on a hot day.

verb	dare	I prefer familiar things and don't usually dare to try new restaurants.
adjective	daring	Kobi had more daring tastes than the rest of his family.
adverb	daringly	Jane daringly refused a fork and attempted to eat her entire meal with chopsticks.

noun	deliciousness	The deliciousness of the desserts is hard to resist.
adjective	delicious	All the comments on that blog agree that this restaurant serves the most delicious food in the city.
adverb	deliciously	The stew smells deliciously good.

verb	guide	The hostess guided us to our table.
noun	guidance	Li asked the waiter for guidance in selecting the wine.
noun	guide	I couldn't find any reviews for this restaurant in the online restaurant guide.

verb	mix	The chef never mixes sweet ingredients with salty foods.
noun	mixture	The texture of the vegetable mixture was too lumpy for my taste.
adjective	mixable	Oil and water are not mixable.

verb	rely	We will rely on the hostess's recommendations.
noun	reliability	The reliability of deliveries became a problem for the manager.
adjective	reliable	Hiring a reliable staff is the first priority for every restaurant manager.

verb	suggest	Can I suggest a good wine to go with the entrée?
noun	suggestion	Clark asked his boss for a suggestion of a good place to eat.
adjective	suggestible	The patrons were in a suggestible mood, and were easily convinced to have dessert.

WORDS IN CONTEXT

Read the following passage and write the words in the blanks below.

appeal	delicious	majority	secure
compromise	familiar	mix	subjective
daring	guidance	relies	suggestion

When Atul is trying to impress business contacts who are potential new clients, he takes them to the best restaurant in town. He hopes this will help (1) ___________ a new contract for his telecommunications business.

It's hard to determine which restaurants are best. Atul (2) ___________ on reviews that he finds on the Internet. He also asks his friends and colleagues for (3) ___________. They are happy to make a (4) ___________.

Food tastes are (5)___________. Although Atul likes to be (6) ___________ and take risks, he knows that the food should (7) ___________ to a variety of palates. He realizes that a dish that he enjoys may not taste (8) ___________ to someone else. He wants the (9) ___________ of his guests to be happy. He usually decides to (10) ___________ on a restaurant that offers a menu with a (11) ___________ of (12) ___________ standards and some exciting specials.

WORD PRACTICE

Listening Comprehension

Track 32

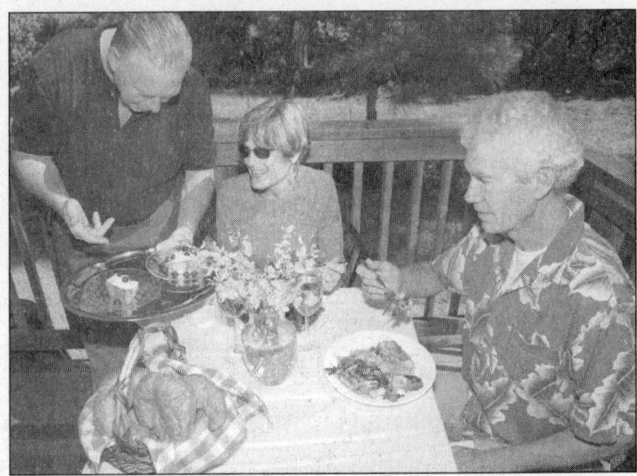

PART 1 PHOTO

Look at the picture and listen to the sentences. Choose the sentence that best describes the picture.

1. Ⓐ Ⓑ Ⓒ Ⓓ

PART 2 QUESTION–RESPONSE

Listen to the question and the three responses. Choose the response that best answers the question.

2. Ⓐ Ⓑ Ⓒ 3. Ⓐ Ⓑ Ⓒ

PART 3 CONVERSATION

Listen to the dialogue. Then read each question and choose the best response.

4. How often do restaurant reviews appear in the local newspaper?
   (A) Every day
   (B) Every week
   (C) Every month
   (D) Every year

5. What is the man's opinion of restaurant reviews?
   (A) They are appealing.
   (B) They are usually helpful.
   (C) They are very subjective.
   (D) They are mean.

6. Who recommends restaurants to the man?
   (A) His friends
   (B) His mother
   (C) His brother
   (D) His coworkers

PART 4 TALK

Listen to the talk. Then read each question and choose the best answer.

7. Where is the listener now?
   (A) At home
   (B) In the bar
   (C) At the restaurant
   (D) In the parking lot

8. What does the speaker suggest?
   (A) Driving to the restaurant
   (B) Arriving early for drinks
   (C) Making a reservation
   (D) Bringing a big appetite

9. What time is the reservation for?
   (A) 7:30
   (B) 8:00
   (C) 8:30
   (D) 11:00

Reading

PART 5 INCOMPLETE SENTENCES

Choose the word that best completes the sentence.

10. The colorful vegetables made the dish look _______.

(A) appealed (C) appeals
(B) appealing (D) appealingly

11. Even though the restaurant looked expensive, Pat _______ to order her meal without asking about the prices.

(A) daring (C) dared
(B) daringly (D) dares

12. If you need some _______ on what to order, be sure to consult your server.

(A) guide (C) guided
(B) guides (D) guidance

13. The _______ of sweet and spicy flavors in this dish is unusual but really delicious.

(A) compromise (C) appeal
(B) majority (D) mix

14. This website accepts reviews from anybody, so I would question their _______.

(A) rely (C) reliability
(B) reliance (D) relying

15. I wasn't sure where to take my clients for dinner, but my friend Lola _______ several nice restaurants.

(A) suggested (C) relied
(B) secured (D) dared

ARE YOU LOOKING FOR A DELICIOUS LUNCH EXPERIENCE THAT WON'T EMPTY YOUR WALLET?

TRY THE BLUE SHUTTERS CAFÉ.

OUR VARIED MENU ____ TO ALL TASTES.
16.

WE'RE FAMOUS FOR OUR HOMEMADE SOUPS, GARDEN-FRESH SALADS, AND FRESHLY BAKED BREADS AND PASTRIES.

TRY OUR HOMEMADE PIES IN ALL FLAVORS FROM ____ FAVORITES LIKE
17.
APPLE PIE TO EXOTIC CHOICES SUCH AS LOGANBERRY AND CHESTNUT MERINGUE.
BUT ____ ON OUR WORD ALONE. COME ON DOWN AND TRY FOR YOURSELF.
18.

WE'RE OPEN MONDAY THROUGH SATURDAY FROM 11:00 A.M. UNTIL 2:30 P.M.

____. VISIT THE ONLINE GUIDE TO LOCAL RESTAURANTS AT
19.
WWW.RESTAURANTSOFRIVERDALE.COM TO READ THEIR OPINIONS OF THE BLUE SHUTTERS CAFÉ AND OTHER LOCAL FAVORITES.

16. (A) appeal
    (B) appeals
    (C) appealed
    (D) are appealing

17. (A) famously
    (B) famished
    (C) familiar
    (D) family

18. (A) no rely
    (B) not rely
    (C) not to rely
    (D) don't rely

19. (A) You can review our lunch and dinner menus and order meals to go online.
    (B) Interested in what the professional reviewers have to say?
    (C) Our wait staff can suggest dishes to suit your preferences.
    (D) We offer a mix of regional and international cuisine.

PART 7 READING COMPREHENSION

Questions 20–24 refer to the following restaurant review and e-mail message.

The Mountain View Restaurant is a charming dinner location that just opened up in Falls Village. The menu provides an interesting mix of both meat and vegetarian entrées. The chef, who trained in Paris, has introduced some exotic dishes such as Octopus Soufflé and Three Tuber Salad. For the less daring diner, the menu also abounds in such familiar choices as Baked Chicken and Pepper Crusted Steak. Whether you choose to rely on a familiar dish or decide to experiment with something exotic, you are sure to be delighted with your meal. All the selections I tasted were delicious, and the prices are quite reasonable. Don't forget to leave room for dessert. I especially suggest the chocolate cake. It's the best in town. Unfortunately, the charm of the menu selections is not matched by the charm of the décor. It is rather drab and uninspiring. If you visit the inn on a weekend evening, arrive by 6:00 since the restaurant does not take reservations, and it is difficult to get a table after 7:00 unless you are willing to wait half an hour or more.

To: Margaret Smithers
From: Anna Simpson
Subject: Dinner out

Hi Margaret,

Did you read the review of the Mountain View Inn in this Sunday's Falls Village Times? It sounds great. I usually read the restaurant reviews in that paper, and the majority of them are quite accurate. I rely on those reviews a great deal more than the ones in our local restaurant guide. I think we should try the inn. Are you free Saturday night? I think we should arrive at the time suggested in the paper. Then we can have a relaxed meal and still have time to go to an 8:30 movie afterward. Can you do it? Let me know before you leave work today.

Anna

20. What is the reviewer's opinion of the restaurant?
    (A) The prices are too high.
    (B) The food is very good.
    (C) The décor is exotic.
    (D) The menu is boring.

21. What does the reviewer recommend ordering?
    (A) Octopus soufflé
    (B) Tuber salad
    (C) Baked chicken
    (D) Chocolate cake

22. When does Anna want to arrive at the restaurant?
    (A) Before 6:00
    (B) After 7:00
    (C) At 8:00
    (D) By 8:30

23. The word *mix* in line 4 of the restaurant review is closest in meaning to
    (A) style.
    (B) combination.
    (C) number.
    (D) course.

24. The word *majority* in line 5 of the e-mail is closest in meaning to
    (A) few.
    (B) some.
    (C) most.
    (D) several.

Lesson 32: Eating Out

WORDS TO LEARN

- appetite
- complete
- excite
- flavor
- foreign
- ingredient
- judge
- mix-up
- patron
- predict
- randomly
- remind

Study the following definitions and examples.

1. **appetite** n., desire to eat
   a. The delicious smells coming from the restaurant kitchen increased my appetite.
   b. People generally have a good appetite after a long day of work.
2. **complete** v., to finish or make whole
   a. We ordered some dessert to complete our meal.
   b. Some restaurants want to hear their customers' opinions and ask them to complete a survey.
3. **excite** v., to arouse an emotion
   a. Exotic flavors always excite me.
   b. The new Asian restaurant has excited the interest of many people.
4. **flavor** n., a distinctive taste
   a. Fusion cooking is distinguished by an interesting mix of flavors.
   b. The cook changed the flavor of the soup with a unique blend of herbs.
5. **foreign** adj., of another country; unfamiliar
   a. It's fun to try the local food when traveling in a foreign country.
   b. The ingredients in this dish are foreign to me; I have never tried any of them before.
6. **ingredient** n., an element in a mixture
   a. The chef went to the farmer's market to select the freshest ingredients for tonight's menu.
   b. I was unfamiliar with some of the ingredients in the dish.
7. **judge** v., to form an opinion
   a. I was not familiar with Asian cooking, so I couldn't judge if the noodles were cooked correctly.
   b. The restaurant review harshly judged the quality of the service.
8. **mix-up** n., a confusion
   a. There was a mix-up in the kitchen so your order will be delayed.
   b. There was a mix-up about the ingredients and the dish was ruined.
9. **patron** n., a customer, especially a regular customer
   a. Once the word was out about the new chef, patrons lined up to get into the restaurant.
   b. This restaurant has many loyal patrons.
10. **predict** v., to state, tell about, or make known in advance
    a. I predicted this restaurant would become popular and I was right.
    b. Kona was unable to predict what time Andy, who is always late, would show up at the restaurant.
11. **randomly** adv., without any specific pattern
    a. We randomly made our selections from the menu.
    b. That chef chooses his spices randomly, but his dishes always taste great.
12. **remind** v., to cause to remember
    a. Ms. Smith was annoyed at having to remind the waitress to bring the check.
    b. I reminded the client that we are meeting for dinner tomorrow.

WORD FAMILIES

noun	appetite	I don't have much of an appetite tonight so I think I'll just order a salad.
noun	appetizer	We can order some appetizers to enjoy while we're waiting for the main course.
adjective	appetizing	All the dishes on the menu look so appetizing that it's hard to know which one to choose.

verb	complete	The meal could not be completed without dessert.
noun	completion	The coffee was the last item ordered and brought the meal to completion.
adverb	completely	The chef forgot that the dessert was in the oven and completely ruined it.

verb	excite	The chef knows how to excite his patrons.
noun	excitement	You can feel the excitement in the air.
adjective	excited	I am really excited about trying out this new restaurant.

verb	flavor	I like a chef who uses exotic spices to flavor the food.
noun	flavor	Some people don't like Mexican food because the flavors are too spicy.
adjective	flavorful	The special ingredients made the dish very flavorful.

verb	mix up	An inexperienced waiter can easily mix up orders.
noun	mix-up	We had a big mix-up in our plans and I ended up waiting for my friends at the wrong restaurant.
adjective	mixed up	Bob always gets mixed up when he tries to order food at a foreign restaurant.

verb	predict	I predict that this restaurant will be a success.
noun	prediction	The manager's prediction came true, and the chef was named to the "Top 100" list.
adverb	predictably	Predictably, because the waiter neglected to write down the order, he forgot some necessary items.

WORDS IN CONTEXT

Read the following passage and write the words in the blanks below.

appetites	flavor	judged	predict
complete	foreign	mix up	randomly
excite	ingredients	patrons	remind

The key to a happy meal is that everyone should enjoy eating what they ordered. Before the waiter takes your order, you can ask him for a recommendation or you can select (1) ______________ from the menu. It's a good idea to ask the waiter for suggestions when eating at a (2) ______________ restaurant as you might not be familiar with the food.

Good service is part of the overall enjoyment of the meal. The waiter should make the (3) ______________ feel welcome and comfortable. Good waiters can (4) ______________ what you need, like more water, without having to be asked for it. It's easy for a waiter to forget things, but you should not have to (5) ______________ a waiter more than once to bring you something. Nor do you want the waiter to (6) ______________ the food orders. You should get what you ordered, and your order should be (7) ______________.

The quality of the food is the primary way restaurants are (8) ______________. The food should taste and look wonderful. Your plate of food should (9) ______________ all your senses and be fragrant and colorful. A chef can bring out a distinct (10) ______________ in a dish, depending on the (11) ______________ he or she uses. Well-prepared food can satisfy even the hungriest patrons with the biggest (12) ______________.

WORD PRACTICE

Listening Comprehension

Track 33

PART 1 PHOTO

Look at the picture and listen to the sentences.
Choose the sentence that best describes the picture.

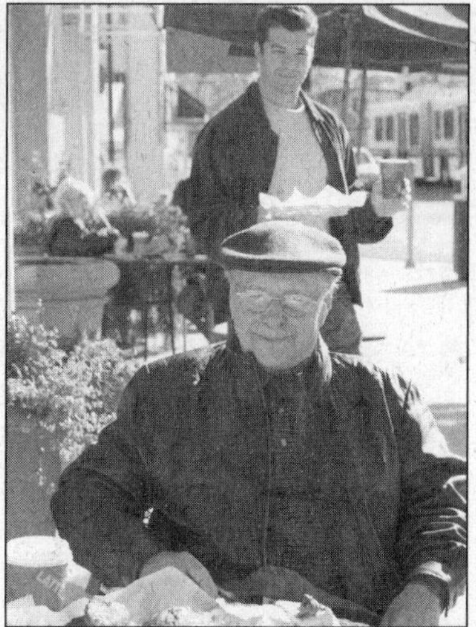

1. Ⓐ Ⓑ Ⓒ Ⓓ

PART 2 QUESTION–RESPONSE

Listen to the question and the three responses. Choose the response that best answers the question.

2. Ⓐ Ⓑ Ⓒ   3. Ⓐ Ⓑ Ⓒ

PART 3 CONVERSATION

Listen to the dialogue. Then read each question and choose the best response.

4. What are the speakers discussing?
   (A) The flavor of the food
   (B) Their last vacation
   (C) The restaurant décor
   (D) The serving dishes

5. What does the man want to do?
   (A) Take a rest
   (B) Return to the restaurant
   (C) Forget about the restaurant
   (D) Get a new set of dishes

6. What does the woman predict?
   (A) The restaurant will close soon.
   (B) The flavor of the dishes will improve.
   (C) The waiter will be very patient.
   (D) The restaurant will become popular.

PART 4 TALK

Listen to the talk. Then read each question and choose the best answer.

7. Who is speaking?
   (A) The kitchen assistant
   (B) The head chef
   (C) A patron
   (D) A waitress

8. What does the speaker offer?
   (A) To cook the meal
   (B) To take the order
   (C) To bring some free food
   (D) To serve water

9. When will the food be ready?
   (A) In 2 minutes
   (B) In 8 minutes
   (C) In 15 minutes
   (D) In 50 minutes

Reading

PART 5 INCOMPLETE SENTENCES

Choose the word that best completes the sentence.

10. Would you like to _______ your meal with an after-dinner drink?

    (A) complete (C) completely
    (B) completed (D) completion

11. I've had enough _______ for the day.

    (A) excite (C) excitement
    (B) exciting (D) excites

12. I can't figure out which ingredients the chef used to _______ this dish.

    (A) flavored (C) flavors
    (B) flavorful (D) flavor

13. I enjoy eating at _______ restaurants because I like to try food from different countries.

    (A) predicted (C) foreign
    (B) appetizing (D) exciting

14. Unfortunately, on the day the restaurant opened there was a huge _______ in the kitchen.

    (A) mix-up (C) mix up
    (B) mixed up (D) mixing up

15. No one could have _______ how successful the restaurant would become.

    (A) reminded (C) completed
    (B) excited (D) predicted

____. Travelers should always make a point of eating the local dishes. It is exciting to try out
16.

dishes made with unfamiliar ingredients and unusual ____. Daring travelers can order ____
17. 18.

from the menu. Or, they can look at the dishes that other patrons are eating and order one that looks appealing. A traveler who doesn't speak the local language well can order by pointing to the dishes he wishes to order. That is the easiest way to avoid a mix-____.
19.

Finally, dessert should not be forgotten. A sweet treat at the end of the meal will complete the experience of enjoying foreign cooking.

16. (A) People may not like the ingredients in some foreign dishes.
    (B) Customers may get mixed up when trying to order from an unfamiliar menu.
    (C) It can be difficult to know which are the best restaurants when visiting an unfamiliar city.
    (D) One of the joys of visiting a foreign country is taking the opportunity to try out different kinds of food.

17. (A) favors
    (B) flavors
    (C) fivers
    (D) fevers

18. (A) random
    (B) randomly
    (C) randomize
    (D) randomness

19. (A) up
    (B) in
    (C) of
    (D) out

PART 7 READING COMPREHENSION

Questions 20–24 refer to the following advertisement.

> *Don't miss the Yorktown Festival of Food. This exciting annual event will take place May 10–16 at the Yorktown Fairgrounds.* Over 100 local restaurants will participate. Which are the best restaurants in town? You be the judge! The price of admission includes:*
>
> - *Samples of food from all participating restaurants*
> - *Cooking demonstrations by local chefs*
> - *Copies of recipes of some of Yorktown's favorite dishes, including ingredients lists and preparation instructions*
> - *A free Festival of Food chef's hat and apron*
>
> *Fifty festival ticket holders will be randomly selected to enjoy a meal especially prepared for the festival by world-renowned chef Jean Pierre de la Farge, director of the Paris School of Cuisine. You could be one of them! Get your tickets today. An unforgettable experience is guaranteed.*
>
> *Tickets are available at all participating restaurants and at the Yorktown Office of Tourism. Ticket prices are $15/day or $50 for the entire week.*
>
> **If rain is predicted, the event will take place in the Yorktown Sports Arena.*

20. How often does the festival take place?
    (A) Once a day
    (B) Once a week
    (C) Once a month
    (D) Once a year

21. What can people do at the festival?
    (A) Try different kinds of food
    (B) Cook a meal
    (C) Judge a contest
    (D) Buy hats and aprons

22. What will fifty people win?
    (A) A ticket
    (B) A cooking lesson
    (C) A free meal
    (D) A trip to Paris

23. The word *randomly* in line 11 is closest in meaning to
    (A) quickly.
    (B) by chance.
    (C) beforehand.
    (D) with determination.

24. The word *predicted* in line 19 is closest in meaning to
    (A) heavy.
    (B) expected.
    (C) falling.
    (D) problematic.

Lesson 33: Ordering Lunch

WORDS TO LEARN

- burden
- commonly
- delivery
- elegance
- fall to
- impress
- individual
- multiple
- narrow
- pick up
- reasonable
- settle

Study the following definitions and examples.

1. **burden** n., a responsibility; something that is carried
   a. The secretary usually takes on the burden of ordering lunch for business meetings.
   b. The deliveryman's back ached from the heavy burden he carried.
2. **commonly** adv., usually; habitually
   a. Employees who work in this building commonly order lunch from the deli on the first floor.
   b. The restaurants in this area commonly serve office workers and are only open during the week.
3. **delivery** n., the act of conveying or delivering
   a. The caterer hired a courier to make the delivery.
   b. The restaurant is reluctant to make deliveries, but makes an exception for our office.
4. **elegance** n., refinement; beauty; grace
   a. The elegance of the restaurant made it a pleasant place to eat.
   b. A sandwich may lack elegance, but it makes a convenient and inexpensive lunch.
5. **fall to** v., to become one's responsibility
   a. The task of preparing the meal fell to the assistant chef when the chief chef was ill.
   b. The menu was in French, so ordering for us fell to Monique, who spoke French.
6. **impress** v., to affect strongly, often favorably
   a. I was impressed with how quickly they delivered our lunch.
   b. If you want to impress the new staff member, order her a nice lunch.
7. **individual** adj., by or for one person; special; particular
   a. We had the delivery man mark the contents of each individual order.
   b. The jaunty whistle of the delivery woman marked her individual style.
8. **multiple** adj., having, relating to, or consisting of more than one part
   a. The delivery person was not able to keep track of the multiple order, causing a food mix-up.
   b. We had to repeat the order multiple times before the server understood it correctly.
9. **narrow** v., to limit or restrict
   a. Etseko narrowed the restaurant possibilities down to three.
   b. This restaurant delivers only pizza and sandwiches, so that certainly narrows down the choices.
10. **pick up** v., to take on passengers or freight
    a. The delivery man picks up lunch orders on his motor scooter.
    b. If you ask me nicely, I will pick up the order on my way home.
11. **reasonable** adj., fairly priced; fair in quality
    a. I usually have lunch in the cafeteria because of the location and the reasonable prices.
    b. The lunches at this place are not top quality, but they're reasonable.
12. **settle** v., to make compensation for; to pay; to choose
    a. We settled the bill with the cashier.
    b. After much debate, we finally settled on the bistro on the corner.

WORD FAMILIES

verb	burden	The frequently complicated lunch orders unfairly burdened Jacques.
noun	burden	In addition to all her other responsibilities, Marie had the burden of picking up the daily lunch order.
adjective	burdensome	Keeping track of everybody's lunch orders can be a burdensome task.

verb	deliver	That restaurant delivers food at no extra charge.
noun	delivery	We all got very hungry waiting for the delivery to arrive.

noun	elegance	The elegance of the surroundings was accentuated by the wonderful meal the caterers delivered.
adjective	elegant	Delores set an elegant table that was sure to impress.
adverb	elegantly	The tasty appetizers were elegantly served from silver platters.

verb	impress	I am favorably impressed by how quickly the pizza was delivered.
noun	impression	She gave the impression that the food would be delivered within the hour.
adjective	impressionable	I have an impressionable child, so I don't like him to see deliverymen running red traffic lights.

verb	individualize	The take-out shop does not allow you to individualize your order by asking for substitutions.
noun	individual	The portions are large enough to feed two individuals.
adverb	individually	The individually marked boxes made it easy for us to claim our orders.

noun	reasonableness	Although the food is not fantastic, we eat here often because of the reasonableness of the prices.
adjective	reasonable	You can get a good meal for a reasonable cost at this café.
adverb	reasonably	They prepare Japanese dishes reasonably well at that restaurant.

WORDS IN CONTEXT

Read the following passage and write the words in the blanks below.

burdensome	elegant	individual	pick up
commonly	falls to	multiple	reasonably
delivered	impress	narrow	settled

As the office manager, it usually (1) _____________ Lucia to order the food for a working lunch or an office party. Lucia finds ordering food for a working lunch to be especially (2) _____________. First, in order to avoid placing (3) _____________ small orders from different food establishments, she must (4) _____________ down the choice to one kind of food. It's best to keep the ordering as simple as possible since each (5) _____________ has his or her own tastes. The lunches that she orders most (6) _____________ consist of sandwiches and pizza.

Once she has (7) _____________ on a good choice, she calls a restaurant on her approved list. Usually she needs the food (8) _____________ so she does not have to leave the office and (9) _____________ the order herself.

In case of a more formal lunch, where her boss is trying to (10) _____________ new clients, for example, Lucia will call a catering service that can provide a more (11) _____________ meal. Even though the meal is a fancy one, it still must be (12) _____________ priced to fit the company's entertainment budget.

WORD PRACTICE

Listening Comprehension

Track 34

PART 1 PHOTO

Look at the picture and listen to the sentences. Choose the sentence that best describes the picture.

1. Ⓐ Ⓑ Ⓒ Ⓓ

PART 2 QUESTION–RESPONSE

Listen to the question and the three responses. Choose the response that best answers the question.

2. Ⓐ Ⓑ Ⓒ
3. Ⓐ Ⓑ Ⓒ

PART 3 CONVERSATION

Listen to the dialogue. Then read each question and choose the best response.

4. Why does the man want to have lunch at the office?
   (A) It is burdensome to leave the office.
   (B) He has a bad impression of the restaurant.
   (C) The office is more elegant than the restaurant.
   (D) He wants to show slides during lunch.

5. Who will the man have lunch with?
   (A) The woman
   (B) The sales staff
   (C) The regional manager
   (D) The conference attendees

6. What time will lunch be delivered?
   (A) Noon
   (B) 1:00
   (C) 1:30
   (D) 2:00

PART 4 TALK

Listen to the talk. Then read each question and choose the best answer.

7. What takes 10 minutes?
   (A) Delivering the order
   (B) Selecting a meal from the list
   (C) Getting the food ready to be picked up
   (D) Making a group order.

8. How much does a delivery cost?
   (A) 15 percent
   (B) 50 cents
   (C) It's free
   (D) 50 percent

9. What kind of food can be ordered from the Parkside Café?
   (A) Rice
   (B) Meat
   (C) Sandwiches
   (D) Ice cream

Reading

PART 5 INCOMPLETE SENTENCES

Choose the word that best completes the sentence.

10. George no longer wants to be in charge of lunch orders because he finds that job too ______.

(A) burdens
(B) burdened
(C) burden
(D) burdensome

11. We ______ meet the delivery person in the lobby to pick up our orders.

(A) common
(B) comment
(C) commonly
(D) commonness

12. The ______ from that restaurant always arrive late.

(A) delivers
(B) deliveries
(C) delivered
(D) delivering

13. The table was beautifully decorated and, despite being served in disposable containers, the meal had ______ feel.

(A) an elegant
(B) a common
(C) a multiple
(D) an individual

14. Our office manager was so ______ by the speed of the delivery, she decided to order from them again.

(A) impressive
(B) impressed
(C) impression
(D) impressionable

15. Let's order ______ so we can all get what we want for lunch.

(A) individualize
(B) individualist
(C) individually
(D) individual

MEMO

To: All department staff
From: J. Holtzman, Manager
Re: Ordering Lunch

It has long been the practice in this department to order lunch to be served during department meetings. While this is a custom we all enjoy, it has become a ____ (16.) on our budget.

Therefore, I have developed the following guidelines for ordering meeting lunches.

- We cannot afford to constantly order elegant lunches. Please limit your orders to common, everyday lunch choices such as sandwiches and salads.
- There are many restaurants in the area that offer take-out lunches. I will ____ (17.) the choices down to three or four places that have reasonable prices, then let you know which they are. Please order only from the restaurants on the approved list.
- ____ (18.). Therefore, all lunch orders must be ____ (19.) up in person.

Thank you in advance for your cooperation.

16. (A) burden
    (B) delivery
    (C) reason
    (D) settlement

17. (A) select
    (B) allow
    (C) enlarge
    (D) narrow

18. (A) We will no longer pay for delivery.
    (B) Individuals are responsible for providing their own lunch.
    (C) Please settle on your lunch choices before calling the restaurant.
    (D) Many of the restaurants in this area offer delivery at a reasonable price.

19. (A) stood
    (B) taken
    (C) looked
    (D) picked

PART 7 READING COMPREHENSION

Questions 20–24 refer to the following advertisement and e-mail message.

NOW OPEN

The Broad Street Eatery
1001 Broad Street
Phone: 298-0943

Serving breakfast and lunch
Monday–Saturday 6:30 A.M. – 2:30 P.M.

Don't settle for lunch choices that are commonly found anywhere.

At the Broad Street Eatery, we offer a tempting range of soups, sandwiches, and salads for the discerning eater.

We specialize in take-out orders. Call ahead for pick up.

We also offer free delivery on all orders over $30.
(There is a 10 percent delivery charge on smaller orders.)

To: Molly Anderson
From: Jerry Pinsky
Subject: New restaurant

Hi Molly,

Have you heard about the Broad Street Eatery? It's that new place that opened up last month just around the corner. I think we should order the lunch for this Friday's meeting from there. Some of the menu choices look quite elegant and I'm sure will impress our clients. Best of all, the prices are quite reasonable. I'll send you a list later of what I want you to order. Since the order will be large, I think you should call it in the day before the meeting. I'm sure we'll qualify for the free delivery, so you won't have to worry about picking it up. That will lighten your burden a bit. Thanks for your help with this.

Jerry

20. When should Molly place the lunch order?
    (A) Monday
    (B) Thursday
    (C) Friday
    (D) Saturday

21. If the order costs $45, how much will the delivery charge be?
    (A) $0
    (B) $3
    (C) $450
    (D) $30

22. What is Jerry's opinion of the restaurant?
    (A) It's too far away.
    (B) The prices are very high.
    (C) It should be open later.
    (D) The food looks good.

23. The word *commonly* in line 8 of the advertisement is closest in meaning to
    (A) usually.
    (B) rarely.
    (C) tastily.
    (D) differently.

24. The word *elegant* in line 7 of the e-mail is closest in meaning to
    (A) ordinary.
    (B) expensive.
    (C) pleasing.
    (D) large.

Lesson 34: Cooking as a Career

WORDS TO LEARN

- accustom
- apprentice
- culinary
- demand
- draw
- incorporate
- influx
- method
- outlet
- profession
- relinquish
- theme

Study the following definitions and examples.

1. **accustom** v., to become familiar with; to become used to
   a. Chefs must accustom themselves to working long hours.
   b. It can be hard to accustom oneself to eating new types of food.
2. **apprentice** n., a student worker in a chosen field
   a. Instead of attending cooking school, Raul chose to work as an apprentice to a chef.
   b. The cooking school has an apprentice program that places students in restaurants to gain experience.
3. **culinary** adj., relating to the kitchen or cooking
   a. The chef was widely known for his culinary artistry.
   b. His interest in culinary arts drew him to a commercial foods program.
4. **demand** v., to require
   a. Theodore was always exhausted because his new job at the restaurant demanded so much of him.
   b. This style of cooking demands many exotic ingredients and a lot of preparation time.
5. **draw** v., to cause to come by attracting
   a. We hope the new restaurant will draw other business to the area.
   b. Matthew was drawn to a career in cooking.
6. **incorporate** v., to unite one thing with something else already in existence
   a. Coca incorporated the patron's suggestions into her new menu.
   b. Here are the fresh greens for you to incorporate into a salad.
7. **influx** n., a flowing in
   a. An influx of new chefs is constantly needed to fill open jobs.
   b. Due to the recent interest in cooking, cooking schools report an influx of applications.
8. **method** n., a procedure
   a. Gloria perfected a simple method for making croissants.
   b. Many chefs borrow cooking methods from other cultures and use them in their cooking style.
9. **outlet** n., a means of release or gratification, as for energies, drives, or desires
   a. Even before he became a professional baker, Jacob used baking as an outlet for frustration.
   b. Many people find cooking to be a hands-on outlet for their creativity.
10. **profession** n., an occupation requiring considerable training and specialized study
    a. Cooking is considered as much a profession as is law or medicine.
    b. Lulu took up cooking as her profession and is very happy with her decision.
11. **relinquish** v., to let go; to surrender
    a. People find it hard to relinquish their accustomed food preferences and try something new.
    b. After Claude married, he had to relinquish his hold on the kitchen and share the joys of cooking.
12. **theme** n., an implicit or recurrent idea; a motif
    a. The caterers prepared food for a party with a tropical island theme.
    b. The restaurant's food and decor demonstrated its southwestern theme.

WORD FAMILIES

verb	accustom	Shirley could not accustom herself to the fast pace of the restaurant kitchen.
noun	custom	It is the custom at this restaurant to offer free meals to patrons on their birthdays.
adjective	accustomed	Janet has become accustomed to cooking with a variety of spices.

verb	apprentice	Instead of attending cooking school, Michael decided to apprentice to a master chef.
noun	apprentice	The new group of apprentices will start working any day now.
noun	apprenticeship	The apprenticeship was a grueling period, but George learned a lot.

verb	demand	The head chef demands a lot from his assistants.
noun	demand	Pierre could not keep up with the many demands of the customers.
adjective	demanding	Working as a chef is a very demanding job.

verb	incorporate	Take these items and incorporate them into a stew.
noun	incorporation	The restaurant was the incorporation of every good idea the chef had thought of in his career.

noun	method	The chef discovered a more efficient method of peeling boiled eggs.
noun	methodology	Even the order of adding ingredients is an unappreciated aspect of cooking methodology.
adjective	methodical	The head cook was not so artistic as methodical in preparing standard dishes.

noun	profession	The number of people choosing cooking as a profession has risen over the past decade.
adjective	professional	She was professional in her approach to dealing with the problem of late deliveries.
adverb	professionally	Although the customer was rude and loud, the waiter handled the situation very professionally.

WORDS IN CONTEXT

Read the following passage and write the words in the blanks below.

accustomed	demanding	influx	profession
apprenticeship	drawn	methods	relinquish
culinary	incorporate	outlet	themes

When people start thinking about careers, they may be looking for an (1) ______________ for their creativity. Many people are (2) ______________ to cooking as a career and see it as a (3) ______________, not merely a trade. The restaurant business is (4) ______________ and needs a constant (5) ______________ of new talent.

Chefs (6) ______________ ingredients and (7) ______________ of cooking from around the world into successful menus. Most chefs offer meals that are variations on standard (8) ______________. They will try to stretch their patrons' range of food tastes by taking food that is still recognized as traditional and infusing it with something new, like a rare spice or seasoning. People (9) ______________ to certain tastes and textures aren't going to (10) ______________ their preferences immediately.

Chefs attend (11) ______________ school or train in restaurants with experienced chefs, in an (12) ______________. For those of you who like hands-on creativity, being a chef might be a good choice.

WORD PRACTICE

Listening Comprehension

Track 35

PART 1 PHOTO

Look at the picture and listen to the sentences.
Choose the sentence that best describes the picture.

1. Ⓐ Ⓑ Ⓒ Ⓓ

PART 2 QUESTION–RESPONSE

Listen to the question and the three responses. Choose the response that best answers the question.

2. Ⓐ Ⓑ Ⓒ   3. Ⓐ Ⓑ Ⓒ

PART 3 CONVERSATION

Listen to the dialogue. Then read each question and choose the best response.

4. According to the conversation, what do good chefs do?
   (A) Demand a lot from their assistants
   (B) Manage their restaurants well
   (C) Attract customers
   (D) Influence new chefs

5. What does the woman think of cooking as a career?
   (A) It pays well.
   (B) It's hard to manage.
   (C) It's not worth the effort.
   (D) It's very demanding.

6. What does the man plan to do?
   (A) Take more rests
   (B) Eat at restaurants more often
   (C) Become a chef
   (D) Practice cooking

PART 4 TALK

Listen to the talk. Then read each question and choose the best answer.

7. Who is this talk for?
   (A) Cooking instructors
   (B) People who work in the culinary arts
   (C) People looking for a profession
   (D) Career counselors

8. What kind of people are attracted to the cooking profession?
   (A) Bored
   (B) Demanding
   (C) Exciting
   (D) Creative

9. What does the speaker recommend to become a professional chef?
   (A) Becoming an apprentice
   (B) Reading cookbooks
   (C) Visiting restaurants around the world
   (D) Attending a culinary school

Reading

PART 5 INCOMPLETE SENTENCES

Choose the word that best completes the sentence.

10. Susannah is having a hard time becoming accustomed _______ the long hours of her job at the restaurant.
(A) with (C) of
(B) at (D) to

11. The student accepted a six-month _______ with a famous chef.
(A) apprentice (C) apprenticing
(B) apprenticed (D) apprenticeship

12. The patrons at this restaurant are often _______, but they make up for it by tipping well.
(A) accustomed (C) demanding
(B) drawn (D) culinary

13. I love this chef's cooking style, which _______ so many different tastes.
(A) incorporation (C) incorporating
(B) incorporates (D) incorporator

14. The experienced chef was _______ about the way he prepared his award-winning dish.
(A) method (C) methodically
(B) methodical (D) methodology

15. The chef is only interested in working with _______ kitchen staff and will not hire anyone without training and experience.
(A) professional (C) culinary
(B) demanding (D) thematic

PART 6 TEXT COMPLETION

More and more people are choosing to become professional chefs. The number of students enrolled in culinary schools is growing every year. People choose this career for different reasons. Some ____ (16.) to a cooking career because of a love of food. Others find that cooking is the perfect ____ (17.) for their creativity. People traditionally think of Paris as the city where professional chefs are trained. ____ (18.). The ____ (19.) of a cooking career are great, but there are also many rewards.

16. (A) draw
(B) are drawn
(C) have drawn
(D) are drawing

17. (A) apprentice
(B) demand
(C) influx
(D) outlet

18. (A) It's important to become accustomed to a chef's working schedule.
(B) In addition, it's a good idea to learn different methods of cooking.
(C) However, fine culinary schools can be found all over the world.
(D) That's why they choose cooking as a career.

19. (A) demand
(B) demands
(C) demanders
(D) demanding

PART 7 READING COMPREHENSION

Questions 20–24 refer to the following article.

Welcome to the National Institute of the Culinary Arts. You have chosen to enter a highly rewarding profession. People are drawn to this career for many different reasons, but you all have something in common—an appreciation of fine food. At the institute you will have the opportunity to study with some of the most highly skilled chefs in the world. In order to take the best advantage of this opportunity, you need to approach it with an open mind. Be ready to relinquish your old ideas about cooking and take in new ideas about the most artistic methods of preparing food. While at the institute, you will become accustomed to long hours, hard work, and also wonderful results. By the time you have finished with your coursework and are ready to start your apprenticeship, you will feel that you have accomplished much more than you ever expected to here at the institute. Please take the time to look over the following pages carefully as they contain all the information you need about course requirements, textbooks, apprenticeship opportunities, and the instructors at the institute.

20. Who is the audience for this article?
    (A) Students
    (B) Instructors
    (C) Working chefs
    (D) Restaurant patrons

21. What kind of place is the institute?
    (A) A restaurant
    (B) A bookstore
    (C) An art school
    (D) A cooking school

22. What does the writer ask the readers to do?
    (A) Start cooking
    (B) Order more courses
    (C) Keep reading
    (D) Enjoy fine food

23. The word *relinquish* in line 9 is closest in meaning to
    (A) let go.
    (B) add to.
    (C) share.
    (D) discuss.

24. The word *accustomed* in line 12 is closest in meaning to
    (A) interested in.
    (B) tired from.
    (C) bored by.
    (D) used to.

Lesson 35: Events

WORDS TO LEARN

- assist
- coordinate
- dimension
- event
- exact
- general
- ideally
- lead time
- proximity
- regulate
- site
- stage

Study the following definitions and examples.

1. **assist** v., to give help or support to
   a. Bonnie hired a secretary to assist her with the many details of the event.
   b. The hotel manager was able to assist us with some last-minute advice.
2. **coordinate** v., to adjust or arrange parts to work together
   a. Benet tried to coordinate all departments to make sure the event ran smoothly.
   b. The colors of the flowers were ordered to coordinate with the colors in the corporate logo.
3. **dimension** n., a measure of width, height, or length
   a. What are the dimensions of the ballroom?
   b. We need the dimensions of the room before we can determine how many chairs it will hold.
4. **event** n., an organized occasion
   a. The spring conference is our biggest yearly event.
   b. This hotel is a popular place for events because of its beautiful location.
5. **exact** adj., characterized by accurate measurements or inferences
   a. We will need an exact head count by noon tomorrow.
   b. The exact measurements of the room are unknown, but we can guess.
6. **general** adj., involving only the main features rather than precise details
   a. We have a general idea of how many guests will attend.
   b. In general, about half the guests will bring their spouses.
7. **ideally** adv., perfectly; conforming to an ideal
   a. Ideally, the location for the concert would have plenty of parking.
   b. Ideally, Lucy would like her wedding to be on the beach, but she realizes it is difficult to arrange.
8. **lead time** n., the time between the initial stage of a project and the appearance of results
   a. The lead time for reservations is unrealistic.
   b. We will need to give the caterer enough lead time to cut the cake.
9. **proximity** n., the state, quality, sense, or fact of being near or next to; closeness
   a. The fans were worried by the proximity of the storm clouds.
   b. An important factor in selecting the site was its close proximity to a parking garage.
10. **regulate** v., to control
    a. The state strictly regulates the preparation of food for public consumption.
    b. The site staff closely regulates how many cars can be brought on the grounds.
11. **site** n., a place or setting
    a. Once we saw the site, we knew it would be perfect for the event.
    b. The manager of the site was most helpful.
12. **stage** v., to exhibit or present
    a. The gazebo outside was the perfect location from which to stage the cutting of the cake.
    b. A historic house can be the perfect site to stage a small reception.

WORD FAMILIES

verb	assist	Let me assist you with planning your next event.
noun	assistance	Dennis's idea of assistance is to call a professional firm for advice.
noun	assistant	In light of the number of events she had to run this year, Annu asked her boss for an assistant.

verb	coordinate	Ralph had a hard time coordinating the schedules of everybody involved in planning the event.
noun	coordination	Edna is a very good organizer, and coordination of events is one of her specialties.
noun	coordinator	The staff chose Marcel to be the coordinator for the company picnic.

noun	exactness	Exactness in all details is important when planning a large event.
adjective	exact	Everything went according to schedule so we were able to begin the speeches at the exact time that had been planned.
adverb	exactly	It is impossible to know ahead of time exactly how many people will attend an event.

verb	generalize	When we generalize, we must be aware of the many exceptions.
adjective	general	I need a general idea of what you want before I can provide specific answers.
adverb	generally	Although I cannot speak for every case, generally it is less expensive to buy in quantity.

verb	idealize	Rhoda idealized the location until she could no longer see any flaws in it.
adjective	ideal	A hotel with a large garden would be the ideal site for the reception.
adverb	ideally	Ideally, the site would be within our budget and have an outdoor area.

verb	regulate	The state will regulate the food-handling precautions.
noun	regulation	Please obey the state regulations regarding serving alcohol to minors.
adjective	regulatory	Even though it is private, the country club's kitchen is subject to the rules of regulatory agencies.

WORDS IN CONTEXT

Read the following passage and write the words in the blanks below.

assist	event	ideally	regulations
coordinated	exact	lead time	site
dimensions	general	proximity	stage

Planning an (1) ______________ is not simple. There are hundreds of details that have to be (2) ______________, whether it is a wedding or a business conference. Early in the planning process, you need to decide on the (3) ______________. If you know where you want to (4) ______________ the event, you should contact the site representative for an (5) ______________ description of the facility. The staff will provide you with information about room (6) ______________; food and beverage arrangements, including whether there are local (7) ______________ or restrictions for serving alcoholic beverages; and required (8) ______________ for reserving the site.

If you decide that the first site is not (9) ______________ suited for your specific requirements, a guidebook will (10) ______________ you in finding an alternative setting. In considering location, you should also think about its (11) ______________ to public transportation.

With a (12) ______________ idea of how many people will attend, and how much money you can spend, you can narrow down the available sites to the ones that best accommodate the needs of your group.

WORD PRACTICE

Listening Comprehension

Track 36

PART 1 PHOTO

Look at the picture and listen to the sentences. Choose the sentence that best describes the picture.

1. Ⓐ Ⓑ Ⓒ Ⓓ

PART 2 QUESTION–RESPONSE

Listen to the question and the three responses. Choose the response that best answers the question.

2. Ⓐ Ⓑ Ⓒ   3. Ⓐ Ⓑ Ⓒ

PART 3 CONVERSATION

Listen to the dialogue. Then read each question and choose the best response.

4. What are the speakers discussing?
   (A) The wedding coordinator
   (B) The place for the wedding reception
   (C) The decorations for the reception
   (D) The wedding date

5. Where does the man want to hold the wedding reception?
   (A) At a hotel
   (B) In a park
   (C) At a club
   (D) In his backyard

6. When do they have to sign the contract?
   (A) Right now
   (B) Later today
   (C) This week
   (D) In four weeks

PART 4 TALK

Listen to the talk. Then read each question and choose the best answer.

7. What event is being planned?
   (A) A meeting
   (B) An awards ceremony
   (C) A formal dance
   (D) An office party

8. When will the event take place?
   (A) Next week
   (B) Next month
   (C) In the afternoon
   (D) Next weekend

9. What kind of site are they looking for?
   (A) One that is near the office
   (B) A small one
   (C) One that has a stage
   (D) An inexpensive one

Reading

PART 5 INCOMPLETE SENTENCES

Choose the word that best completes the sentence.

10. Do you need our _______ with any of the evening's details?
    (A) assist
    (B) assisting
    (C) assistance
    (D) assistant

11. The event did not go off well because the _______ did a poor job of organizing it.
    (A) coordinator
    (B) coordination
    (C) coordinated
    (D) coordinates

12. _______ speaking, the event was poorly organized.
    (A) General
    (B) Generally
    (C) Generality
    (D) Generalizations

13. When the event planner saw the hotel ballroom, she knew that the size wasn't _______, but the price was right.
    (A) ideal
    (B) ideally
    (C) idealize
    (D) idealist

14. It was difficult to plan a tight schedule because we didn't know _______ when the guest speaker would arrive.
    (A) exact
    (B) exactor
    (C) exactly
    (D) exactness

15. Because of the hotel's _______ to the subway station, guests coming to our event will not have to drive their cars.
    (A) regulation
    (B) proximity
    (C) ideal
    (D) site

PART 6 TEXT COMPLETION

The most important part of planning an event is to give yourself plenty of ____.
16.

You don't want to leave important details until the last minute. Ideally, you should give yourself several weeks to plan your event, or several months if it will be a large affair. The first step is to find a suitable ____ for your event. You want a place that is pleasant
17.
and convenient. You also need a place that is the right size. If you have even a general idea of the number of guests you can expect to attend, it will be easy to calculate the ____ of the room that you will need. Many places that rent rooms for events can also
18.
provide food and entertainment. ____.
19.

16. (A) assistants
    (B) guest list
    (C) coordinators
    (D) lead time

17. (A) site
    (B) stage
    (C) assistant
    (D) regulation

18. (A) exactness
    (B) coordination
    (C) dimensions
    (D) generalities

19. (A) Finally, you can hire an events coordinator who will take care of all these details for you.
    (B) Additionally, you need to know the exact number of guests before finalizing your plans.
    (C) Food is an important part of an event, so be sure to budget enough money for it.
    (D) You can ask someone to assist you in choosing the entertainment.

PART 7 READING COMPREHENSION

Questions 20–24 refer to the following advertisement and e-mail message.

Hold your next event at the

Starlight Hotel

The grandest hotel in Weston

Are you planning a party, banquet, reception, or conference? We have the ideal location for you. We can accommodate groups of all sizes. Choose from any of our elegant event rooms:

The Garden View Room—holds up to 100 people
The Starlight Room—holds up to 200 people
The Banquet Hall—holds up to 250 people
The Stardust Ballroom—holds up to 350 people

We are ready to assist you with planning food, entertainment, invitations, and decorations.

We are conveniently located in the heart of the downtown entertainment district, in proximity to major bus and subway lines.

Contact Prisca Haines, Site Coordinator
phone: 953-9172
e-mail: p_haines@starlight.com

To: Prisca Haines
From: Peter Richards
Subject: Event room
Date: September 22

Dear Ms. Haines,

I saw the ad for event rooms at the Starlight Hotel in the Weston Daily News of September 20th. I am coordinating our company's annual awards banquet, which will be held on the 18th of next month. We would like to stage a simple but elegant affair. We don't expect more than about 75–85 guests. We would like to have a dinner followed by speeches and presentations of awards. Other than that, we don't plan to have any special entertainment. I would like to discuss the menu with you. Ideally, we would like to provide our guests with a choice of a meat entrée and a vegetarian entrée. I would like to know if your hotel kitchen can provide that, and which dishes you would specifically recommend.

Please call me before the weekend to discuss planning this event. I can be reached at 953-0955. Thank you.

Peter Richards

---

20. When will the company banquet take place?
    (A) This weekend
    (B) September 20
    (C) September 22
    (D) October 18

21. Which room will Ms. Haines probably recommend for the banquet?
    (A) The Garden View Room
    (B) The Starlight Room
    (C) The Banquet Hall
    (D) The Stardust Ballroom

22. What will Mr. Richards need assistance with?
    (A) The entertainment
    (B) The decorations
    (C) The invitations
    (D) The food

23. The word *ideal* in line 5 of the advertisement is closest in meaning to
    (A) large.
    (B) perfect.
    (C) beautiful.
    (D) convenient.

24. The word *coordinating* in line 3 of the e-mail is closest in meaning to
    (A) hosting.
    (B) presenting.
    (C) arranging.
    (D) discussing.

WORD REVIEW #7
LESSONS 31–35 RESTAURANTS AND EVENTS

Choose the word that best completes the sentence.

1. The aroma coming from the restaurant was so __________ that the tourists did not hesitate before entering.
   (A) random
   (B) subjective
   (C) appealing
   (D) reasonable

2. Because the menu was not in his native language, the visitor asked the waiter for __________.
   (A) guide
   (B) guided
   (C) guiding
   (D) guidance

3. The waiter __________ that the customer would enjoy the duck.
   (A) predict
   (B) predicted
   (C) predicting
   (D) prediction

4. Food critics are also expected to __________ a restaurant's service and atmosphere.
   (A) judge
   (B) judges
   (C) judging
   (D) judgment

5. My assistant usually picks __________ our lunch order before noon.
   (A) over
   (B) on
   (C) off
   (D) up

6. Sometimes when several friends dine together, they each want to pay for their own meal, so they request __________ checks.
   (A) ideal
   (B) common
   (C) individual
   (D) accustomed

7. The most __________ customers seem to be the worst tippers.
   (A) demand
   (B) demanded
   (C) demanding
   (D) demandingly

8. Food preparation is not just frying hamburgers; it is a respected __________.
   (A) profess
   (B) professing
   (C) profession
   (D) professional

9. An event planner must __________ the entire affair, not just choose the menu.
   (A) coordinated
   (B) coordinating
   (C) coordinator
   (D) coordinate

10. The planner must also ensure that participants observe all local __________.
    (A) regulated
    (B) regulations
    (C) regulating
    (D) regulate

Choose the one word or phrase that best completes each sentence.

To: Robert Hughes
From: Betsy Wyman
Subject: re: places to eat

Hi Rob,

I got your message asking for ideas about places to take your clients to dinner. I have a great ___________ for

11. (A) suggest
    (B) suggesting
    (C) suggestion
    (D) suggestible

you. The Waterfall Room is a fantastic restaurant that just opened on Maple Avenue. The atmosphere is pleasant and the food is very good. The menu features dishes from different countries, so it's a good place to eat if you like ___________ food. They also have a dinner special that includes three courses and only costs $30. I really think

12. (A) foreign
    (B) appealing
    (C) random
    (D) exciting

this is the best place in town to enjoy an ___________ meal at a reasonable price. Let me know how you like it.

13. (A) elegantly
    (B) elegance
    (C) elegies
    (D) elegant

Betsy

To: Sue Evans
From: Ron Smith
Subject: lunch tomorrow

Sue,

George will be out of the office all week, so it will ___________ you to

14. (A) pick up
    (B) fall to
    (C) rely on
    (D) mix up

order the lunch for tomorrow's staff meeting. We always order from Sam's Deli. We'll need enough for 15 people. Look at their list of sandwiches and order three or four different kinds. ___________ them to send a

15. (A) Reminding
    (B) To remind
    (C) Reminder
    (D) Remind

variety of desserts, too. People always like a sweet treat with their meal. Please make sure that the food ___________ by noon tomorrow. Thanks.

16. (A) delivers
    (B) is delivered
    (C) is delivering
    (D) will deliver

Ron

Do you have what it takes to become a professional chef? The first requirement, of course, is an interest in the ___________ arts. There is no point in becoming a chef if you don't love fine

17. (A) fine
    (B) visual
    (C) culinary
    (D) performing

food. You will also need to be willing to work long hours because this is a very ___________

18. (A) narrow
    (B) regulated
    (C) reasonable
    (D) demanding

profession. In addition, you will need leadership qualities. A working chef has ___________

19. (A) to coordinate
    (B) coordinating
    (C) coordinates
    (D) coordinate

the work of everyone in the kitchen.

Lesson 36: General Travel

WORDS TO LEARN

- agent
- announcement
- beverage
- board
- claim
- delay
- depart
- embarkation
- itinerary
- luggage
- prohibit
- valid

Study the following definitions and examples.

1. **agent** n., a representative of a company
   a. The gate agent will make an announcement when it is time to board the plane.
   b. You can buy your ticket from the ticket agent at the train station right before you get on the train.
2. **announcement** n., a public notification
   a. Did you hear an announcement about our new departure time?
   b. I expect an announcement any time now about a snow emergency at the airport.
3. **beverage** n., a drink other than plain water
   a. The flight attendant offered all passengers a cold beverage during the flight.
   b. Hot and cold beverages as well as snacks are for sale in the train's café car.
4. **board** v., to enter a boat, plane, or train
   a. For security reasons, visitors are not allowed in the area of the airport where passengers board the planes.
   b. We will board the train for New York in ten minutes.
5. **claim** v., to take as rightful; to retrieve
   a. Please proceed directly to the baggage arrival area to claim your luggage.
   b. Lost luggage can be claimed at the airline office.
6. **delay** v., to postpone until a later time
   a. The bus was delayed due to inclement weather.
   b. The heavy traffic delayed our arrival at the train station.
7. **depart** v., to go away or leave; to vary from a regular course of action
   a. After the wedding, the married couple departed for their honeymoon in Morocco.
   b. We're going to depart from our usual policy and allow you to leave work early one day a week.
8. **embarkation** n., the process of getting on a plane or ship
   a. Cruise passengers are given a pass for embarkation when they check in at the dock.
   b. The flight crew must check the passengers' documents before embarkation.
9. **itinerary** n., a proposed route for a journey, showing dates and means of travel
   a. He planned his itinerary after visiting several travel websites.
   b. I had to change my itinerary when I decided to add two more countries to my vacation.
10. **luggage** n., suitcases; baggage
    a. Airlines often limit the amount of luggage each person is allowed to carry.
    b. Traveling is a lot easier if you bring less luggage with you.
11. **prohibit** v., to forbid by authority or to prevent
    a. The bus company prohibits people without tickets from boarding the bus.
    b. Airline regulations prohibit the passengers from having beverages open during takeoff and landing.
12. **valid** adj., having legal efficacy or correctness
    a. I need to make certain that my passport is valid if we plan to go overseas this December.
    b. These tickets are no longer valid after the date printed on the back.

WORD FAMILIES

verb	announce	The captain announced that the flight would be landing in approximately 15 minutes.
noun	announcement	The flight attendant made an announcement reminding the passengers that this was a no-smoking flight.
noun	announcer	The announcer gave the instructions for boarding, in three languages.

verb	claim	International passengers must proceed to customs as soon as they claim their baggage.
noun	claim	If the airline has lost your luggage, you can file a claim with the insurance company.
noun	claimant	There was a long line of claimants waiting at the lost luggage office.

verb	delay	Please don't delay me; I need to get to my gate immediately.
noun	delay	The delay in takeoff times was caused by a bad storm.

verb	depart	The flight will depart from Gate 25.
noun	departure	The pilot always reminds the flight attendants to make sure that all passengers are ready for departure.
adjective	departed	The house felt empty without the departed guests.

verb	prohibit	Bus company regulations prohibit passengers from talking with the driver while the bus is moving.
noun	prohibition	The prohibition of many common items on airplanes can make it difficult for airplane travelers to pack their luggage.
adjective	prohibited	A passenger who carries a prohibited item onto an airplane may end up in the hands of security officers.

verb	validate	You can get your parking ticket validated at the concierge desk.
noun	validity	The agent will check the validity of your passport before you board the plane.
adjective	valid	Your ticket is no longer valid because it was issued over a year ago.

WORDS IN CONTEXT

Read the following passage and write the words in the blanks below.

agent	board	depart	luggage
announcements	claims	embarkation	prohibited
beverage	delayed	itinerary	valid

When Ms. Tan is planning a business trip, she prefers to act as her own travel (1) ______________. If she is traveling to another country, first she checks her passport to make sure it is still (2) ______________. Then she goes online and checks several travel websites to find out about airline flights and hotels. She likes to plan her own (3) ______________, to choose when she will arrive at each place, how she will get there, and which hotels she will stay at. On the day her trip begins, she looks at the airline's website to make sure that her flight is on time and not (4) ______________.

At the airport, Ms. Tan checks her suitcases at the check-in counter since she is (5) ____________ from taking more than one piece of carry-on (6) ____________ with her onto the plane. At the same time, she receives her boarding pass for (7) ______________.

She will present this at the gate when it is time to (8) ______________ her flight. She is told to be at the gate 15 minutes before the flight is to (9) ______________. During the flight, the attendant may offer her a (10) ______________, and a snack or meal. The captain will make (11) ______________ during the flight to let the passengers know at what altitude they are flying, and when they may expect to arrive at their destination.

Once the flight has landed, Ms. Tan disembarks and must go through customs after she (12) ____________ her baggage. After this, she will take a cab to the hotel where she is staying, so she can rest and prepare for her meeting the next day. She will also reconfirm her return flight a day or two before she leaves to return home.

WORD PRACTICE

Listening Comprehension

Track 37

PART 1 PHOTO

Look at the picture and listen to the sentences. Choose the sentence that best describes the picture.

1. Ⓐ Ⓑ Ⓒ Ⓓ

PART 2 QUESTION–RESPONSE

Listen to the question and the three responses. Choose the response that best answers the question.

2. Ⓐ Ⓑ Ⓒ　　3. Ⓐ Ⓑ Ⓒ

PART 3 CONVERSATION

Listen to the dialogue. Then read each question and choose the best response.

4. Whom is the man speaking with?
   (A) A pilot
   (B) A waitress
   (C) A travel agent
   (D) A flight attendant

5. What does the woman offer the man?
   (A) Something to eat
   (B) Something to read
   (C) Something to drink
   (D) Something to listen to

6. When will they arrive?
   (A) In one hour
   (B) In two hours
   (C) In three hours
   (D) In four hours

PART 4 TALK

Listen to the talk. Then read each question and choose the best answer.

7. What do passengers have to show the flight attendant?
   (A) An embarkation card
   (B) A passport
   (C) A trip itinerary
   (D) A boarding pass

8. When will the flight leave?
   (A) At 1:15
   (B) In twenty minutes
   (C) At nine o'clock
   (D) In five minutes

9. What is not allowed before takeoff?
   (A) Talking on the phone
   (B) Selling things
   (C) Drinking
   (D) Dining

Reading

PART 5 INCOMPLETE SENTENCES

Choose the word that best completes the sentence.

10. The gate number for your flight will be _______ about an hour before the scheduled departure time.

    (A) embarked (C) boarded
    (B) delayed (D) announced

11. When it's time to _______ the flight, an announcement will be made.

    (A) boarded (C) board
    (B) boarding (D) boarder

12. As soon as John _______ his luggage, he went outside to look for a taxi.

    (A) boarded (C) departed
    (B) claimed (D) prohibited

13. The man had to _______ his travel plans because an emergency came up at work.

    (A) delay (C) delayed
    (B) delaying (D) delays

14. The train's _______ was delayed because of a problem on the track.

    (A) departed (C) departs
    (B) departure (D) depart

15. The airport applied a blanket rule that all passengers must be in possession of _______ tickets in order to enter the waiting area.

    (A) valid (C) validate
    (B) validity (D) validation

PART 6 TEXT COMPLETION

Information for Travelers

* We make every effort to leave on time. To avoid ____ (16.), please plan to arrive at least one hour before your scheduled departure time. This is especially important because all passengers must pass through security control.
* Scissors, nail clippers, and other sharp instruments ____ (17.) on board. Leave these items at home or surrender them to the security officer in charge.
* Each passenger is allowed two small carry-on bags. ____ (18.). You can claim it at the end of your trip.
* We request that passengers remain in the waiting area until the attendant ____ (19.) the embarkation time. Please don't attempt to board ahead of time.
* Your comfort is our priority. Snack service is available on board. Please ask the attendant for pillows and blankets if you require them.

Thank you for traveling with us. Have a safe and happy trip.

16. (A) delays
    (B) claims
    (C) departures
    (D) prohibitions

17. (A) prohibit
    (B) prohibits
    (C) are prohibited
    (D) are prohibiting

18. (A) If your bags are heavy, you can rent an airport luggage cart.
    (B) Bags should be stowed in the overhead compartment.
    (C) Check your excess luggage with the attendant.
    (D) Many travelers carry larger bags.

19. (A) announce
    (B) announces
    (C) will announce
    (D) does announce

PART 7 READING COMPREHENSION

Questions 20–24 refer to the following travel itinerary.

BREEZEWAY, INC.

Itinerary for: Edward Rochester

April 15	Depart New York City — 10:30 P.M. *Solar Airlines flight 133 Arrive Seattle, WA — 12:15 P.M.
	Hotel: Puget Inn 1764 Capital Street Seattle, WA
April 18	Depart Seattle — 8:05 A.M. **Train # 10 ***Arrive Vancouver, Canada 11:20 A.M.
	Hotel: Gas Town Hotel 375 Alaska Avenue Vancouver, Canada
April 20	Depart Vancouver — 11:30 P.M. *Solar Airlines flight 136
April 21	Arrive New York City — 8:10 A.M.

* Please arrive at airport at least two hours ahead of scheduled departure time. Plane will begin boarding 20 minutes ahead of scheduled departure time. It is prohibited to bring firearms, explosive devices, or sharp instruments on board any Solar Airlines flight. There is no meal service on board any Solar Airlines flight. Beverages will be available for sale.

** Please arrive at train station 30 minutes before scheduled departure time.

*** A valid passport is required for entry into Canada.

20. How many nights will Mr. Rochester stay at the Puget Inn?
    (A) One
    (B) Two
    (C) Three
    (D) Four

21. What time can he board the plane on the return flight to New York City?
    (A) 10:30
    (B) 11:10
    (C) 11:30
    (D) 5:10

22. What can he buy during the flight?
    (A) A meal
    (B) A drink
    (C) A passport
    (D) A train ticket

23. The word *itinerary* in line 2 is closest in meaning to
    (A) bill.
    (B) ticket.
    (C) advice.
    (D) schedule.

24. The word *prohibited* in line 19 is closest in meaning to
    (A) not encouraged.
    (B) uncommon.
    (C) permitted.
    (D) not allowed.

Lesson 37: Airlines

WORDS TO LEARN

- deal with
- destination
- distinguish
- economize
- equivalent
- excursion
- expense
- extend
- prospective
- scenery
- situation
- substantially

Study the following definitions and examples.

1. **deal with** v. phrase, to attend to; to manage; to see to
   a. Ticket agents must deal courteously with irate customers.
   b. Sick passengers and frightened children are just a few things cabin attendants have to deal with.
2. **destination** n., the place to which one is going or directed
   a. The Great Barrier Reef is a popular tourist destination this year.
   b. Once you have determined your desired destination, we can work toward getting the best airfare.
3. **distinguish** v., to perceive a difference; to make noticeable or different
   a. Suki was able to distinguish between the different types of jets on the runway.
   b. This airline has distinguished itself as one of the most reliable in the business.
4. **economize** v., to be careful about spending money
   a. I like to economize when I travel, so I always do a thorough search for the best ticket prices.
   b. We decided to economize and take our vacation during the off season, when prices are lower.
5. **equivalent** adj., equal
   a. Carlos used the Internet to search for hotels of equivalent dollar value to the one recommended.
   b. The food the airline serves in coach class is equivalent to that served in first class.
6. **excursion** n., a pleasure trip; a trip at a reduced fare
   a. With some time between meetings in London, I enjoyed an excursion to Stonehenge.
   b. The finance officer was pleased to find an excursion for the entire consulting team.
7. **expense** n., something requiring payment
   a. A luxury vacation involves many expenses.
   b. If we keep our expenses down, we might have enough money to take a longer trip.
8. **extend** v., to make longer
   a. The delayed flight extended our wait in the airport.
   b. We enjoyed the beach so much that we extended our stay another day.
9. **prospective** adj., likely to become or be
   a. Airlines advertise on travel websites in order to attract prospective customers.
   b. I narrowed my list of prospective destinations to my three top choices.
10. **scenery** n., a view of the surrounding area; a landscape
   a. It is difficult to appreciate the natural scenery from an airplane seat.
   b. Many travelers visit this area because of the beautiful scenery.
11. **situation** n., the combination of circumstances at a given moment
   a. The airline said to check with the State Department about the political situation in the country I'm flying to.
   b. The vast number of different airfares available makes for a complicated situation.
12. **substantially** adv., significantly
   a. The airline I work for has a substantially higher service rating than our competitors.
   b. The airfares charged by different airlines are not substantially different.

WORD FAMILIES

verb	distinguish	I can't distinguish any difference in the two airlines, since their fares are the same.
adjective	distinguishable	The airline's planes were easily distinguishable by the bright logo on the planes' tails.
adverb	distinguishably	Even though that city looks farther away on the map, the flight there is not distinguishably longer.

verb	economize	We no longer fly first class, since our company is trying to economize.
adjective	economical	Without hesitation, we chose the more economical of the two airline tickets.
adverb	economically	The best way to plan a trip economically is to compare prices on the Internet.

noun	expense	To stay within our travel budget, we must keep all our expenses as low as possible.
adjective	expensive	Only the most expensive fares were still available.
adverb	expensively	The first-class seats are for those who travel expensively and with great style.

verb	extend	When people travel to an interesting destination for business, they often extend their trip by a few days in order to enjoy the place as a tourist.
noun	extent	Larry has traveled to Japan many times and the extent of his knowledge of that country is impressive.
adjective	extensive	Pamela is taking six months off from work in order to take an extensive tour of South America.

noun	prospect	The prospects of getting a seat on this evening's flight are not good.
adjective	prospective	Once you know the prospective dates for your trip, you can look on the Internet to see what flights are available.

noun	substance	The advantages of traveling first class made up the substance of our conversation.
adjective	substantial	Ms. Qin found there was a substantial difference in the price quoted for the plane ticket, depending on which day she flew.
adverb	substantially	There is substantially no difference in the quality of food served in first class and in economy class.

WORDS IN CONTEXT

Read the following passage and write the words in the blanks below.

deal with	economical	expensive	scenery
destination	equivalent	extending	situation
distinguishable	excursion	prospective	substantial

If you travel, you most likely will have to (1) _______________ flying. Flying is the quickest, most convenient means of travel between countries, and often between different parts of one country. Flying is (2) _______________, but when all costs are taken into account for traveling any (3) _______________ distance, air travel usually costs less than driving by car. It is also the most (4) _______________ way to go in terms of time. You won't be able to enjoy the (5) _______________ en route, as you would in a car, but you'll have more time to enjoy your surroundings when you arrive at your vacation (6) _______________.

Airlines sell seats at a variety of prices through a system of requirements and restrictions. Full-fare tickets are the most expensive, but give you the most flexibility in terms of making changes. A (7) _______________ traveler can buy a ticket up to takeoff time as long as a seat is available.

Fares change rapidly, and even travel experts find it difficult to keep up. The changing (8) _______________ is due to many factors, including increased competition. As a general rule, the less you pay for the ticket, the more restrictions you can expect. If you are trying to save money, look for (9) _______________ fares. These are (10) _______________ to a special sale. Most excursion fares are for round-trip travel and have strict regulations and a minimum and maximum length of stay, so don't count on (11) _______________ your vacation or staying less time than required. However, once you are on the plane, you are not (12) _______________ from passengers who paid higher fares.

WORD PRACTICE

Listening Comprehension

Track 38

PART 1 PHOTO

Look at the picture and listen to the sentences. Choose the sentence that best describes the picture.

1. Ⓐ Ⓑ Ⓒ Ⓓ

PART 2 QUESTION–RESPONSE

Listen to the question and the three responses. Choose the response that best answers the question.

2. Ⓐ Ⓑ Ⓒ 3. Ⓐ Ⓑ Ⓒ

PART 3 CONVERSATION

Listen to the dialogue. Then read each question and choose the best response.

4. What are the speakers discussing?
   (A) The length of the trip
   (B) The schedule of the airline
   (C) The cost of the ticket
   (D) The quality of the airline

5. How can the woman get a lower airfare?
   (A) By staying for just two days
   (B) By flying to a different city
   (C) By charging it as a work expense
   (D) By changing the day of her arrival

6. When does the woman want to arrive?
   (A) Sunday
   (B) Monday
   (C) Tuesday
   (D) Wednesday

PART 4 TALK

Listen to the talk. Then read each question and choose the best answer.

7. What kind of business is Fun Time Vacations?
   (A) Vacation resort
   (B) Tour company
   (C) Cruise company
   (D) Restaurant chain

8. What is indicated about Fun Time Vacations?
   (A) Its prices are low.
   (B) It's very popular.
   (C) It's a new business.
   (D) It's not well known.

9. What are listeners asked to do?
   (A) Make a phone call
   (B) Go to a website
   (C) Choose a destination
   (D) Visit the company's office

Reading

PART 5 INCOMPLETE SENTENCES

Choose the word that best completes the sentence.

10. Let me point out the features of our service that _______ our airline from our competitors.
    (A) distinguishably (C) distinguishing
    (B) distinguishable (D) distinguish

11. Let's shop around until we find a more _______ airfare.
    (A) economical (C) economy
    (B) economize (D) economically

12. We need to watch our _______, so we'll have to look for better prices on those airline tickets.
    (A) destinations (C) expenses
    (B) prospects (D) extents

13. I would have _______ my stay in Los Angeles if I hadn't had to return home for a business meeting.
    (A) extended (C) economized
    (B) situated (D) distinguished

14. If you wait until the last minute, the _______ of getting an airline ticket on a holiday weekend are not good.
    (A) prospective (C) prospectors
    (B) prospectively (D) prospects

15. Unless the airfares differ _______, you should book seats on the airline with which you have frequent flyer miles.
    (A) substance (C) substantial
    (B) substantially (D) substantiality

Renovated City Airport Now Open

Frequent flyers will be happy to know that the renovations at City Airport are finally finished. ____ (16.). However, the construction team fell behind schedule and ____ (17.) the deadlines twice. Now the work is completed, and travelers no longer have to deal ____ (18.) the noise, dust, and inconvenience of construction work. Passengers can move more easily and comfortably through the airport, and everything is easier to find. One of the biggest improvements in the renovated airport is the signs indicating the location of the various airlines' check-in counters. The new signs are much ____ (19.) than the old ones, and it is easier for passengers to find the airlines they are looking for. In general, now that the work at the airport is finally over, the situation there has substantially improved.

16. (A) The scenery at the airport was greatly improved.
    (B) Construction work often takes longer than expected.
    (C) Airport users can now get to their destinations more conveniently.
    (D) The renovations were scheduled for completion at the end of last year.

17. (A) extend
    (B) extended
    (C) have extended
    (D) had extended

18. (A) to
    (B) for
    (C) with
    (D) from

19. (A) distinguishable
    (B) more distinguishable
    (C) most distinguishable
    (D) the most distinguishable

PART 7 READING COMPREHENSION

Questions 20–24 refer to the following two e-mail messages.

To: Belinda Tuttle
From: Mark Wallaby
Subject: Re: Amazon Tours

Dear Ms. Tuttle,

In response to your request for information on guided tours in the Amazon region, I have found two excursions that may interest you. Both are led by reputable companies that are known for organizing interesting and educational trips at reasonable expense. One led by Jungle Tours, Inc. goes to all the destinations you are interested in visiting and lasts two weeks, the length of time you requested. However, it leaves on November 10th, a week earlier than the date you mentioned. I don't know whether or not you would be able to leave this early. There is a tour leaving on your designated date, run by Paradise Adventures. It doesn't, however, go to all the destinations you are interested in, and it lasts three weeks, not two, so you wouldn't return until December 8th. I don't know whether or not you would be able to extend the length of your vacation. If either of these two prospects interests you, let me know. Otherwise I will keep looking for a tour that will suit you.

Mark Wallaby
Southern Travel

To: Mark Wallaby
From: Belinda Tuttle
Subject Re: Amazon Tours

Dear Mr. Wallaby,

Thank you for the information on trips to the Amazon. Unfortunately, I cannot change the dates of my vacation because of my work situation. The end of the year is a very busy time for accountants, and I will have a lot of work to deal with as soon as I return from my trip. On the other hand, I don't really need to economize, so I am flexible about the expense. The exact destinations don't really matter either. I will be happy just to visit that part of the world and get a chance to see the Amazon scenery I have heard so much about. So please keep looking and let me know what you find. Thank you for your efforts.

Belinda Tuttle

20. What is Mark Wallaby's job?
    (A) Tour guide
    (B) Educator
    (C) Accountant
    (D) Travel agent

21. When does Ms. Tuttle want to begin her vacation?
    (A) November 10
    (B) November 17
    (C) December 1
    (D) December 8

22. Why doesn't Ms. Tuttle like the tours suggested by Mr. Wallaby?
    (A) They are too expensive.
    (B) The companies have a bad reputation.
    (C) They go to the wrong destinations.
    (D) The dates don't fit her vacation time.

23. The word *situation* in line 4 of the second e-mail is closest in meaning to
    (A) circumstances.
    (B) responsibilities.
    (C) requirements.
    (D) location.

24. The word *scenery* in line 14 of the second e-mail is closest in meaning to
    (A) culture.
    (B) climate.
    (C) landscape.
    (D) vegetation.

Lesson 38: Trains

WORDS TO LEARN

- comprehensive
- deluxe
- directory
- duration
- entitle
- fare
- offset
- operate
- punctually
- relatively
- remainder
- remote

Study the following definitions and examples.

1. **comprehensive** adj., covering broadly; inclusive
   a. The conductor has a comprehensive knowledge of rail systems from all over the world.
   b. You can get a comprehensive travel package, if you visit the travel company's website.
2. **deluxe** adj., noticeably luxurious
   a. My parents decided to splurge on deluxe accommodations for their trip.
   b. The train station is not near any of the deluxe hotels, so we will have to take a taxi.
3. **directory** n., a book or collection of information or directions
   a. We consulted the directory to see where the train station was located.
   b. Mr. Scannel found the telephone number for the local train station in the telephone directory.
4. **duration** n., the time during which something lasts
   a. Mother lent me her spare jacket for the duration of the trip.
   b. Despite our differences, my roommate and I agreed to be pleasant for the duration of the train ride.
5. **entitle** v., to allow or qualify
   a. During the holiday rush, a train ticket entitled the passenger to a ride, but not necessarily a seat.
   b. The mess the train line made of Pedro's sleeping room reservations entitled him to a free upgrade.
6. **fare** n., the money paid for transportation
   a. The train fare has increased since I rode last.
   b. Pay your fare at the ticket office and you will get a ticket to board the train.
7. **offset** v., to counterbalance
   a. The high cost of the hotel room offset the savings we made by taking the train instead of the plane.
   b. By reducing her transportation costs once in the U.S., Mrs. Sato offset the cost of getting here.
8. **operate** v., to perform a function
   a. The train operates on a punctual schedule.
   b. The train only operates in this area at the height of the tourist season.
9. **punctually** adv., promptly; on time
   a. Please be on time; the train leaves punctually at noon.
   b. The train usually arrives punctually; I can't imagine what is delaying it today.
10. **relatively** adv., somewhat
    a. The train is relatively empty for this time of day.
    b. The train station has been relatively busy for a weekday.
11. **remainder** n., the part that is left; leftover
    a. The Alaskan frontier has train service in the summer, but for the remainder of the year the tracks are impassable.
    b. Please move me to a less expensive room and credit the remainder of the cost to my charge card.
12. **remote** adj., far away; not close to populated areas
    a. I was surprised to find train service to such a remote location.
    b. We took the train out of the city and found a remote hotel in the country for the weekend.

WORD FAMILIES

noun	comprehensiveness	Due to the comprehensiveness of the train system, the complete timetable was a thick document.
adjective	comprehensive	Due to the comprehensive reach of the rail system, the train can take you to every major city and many smaller ones.
adverb	comprehensively	The surveyors comprehensively studied the terrain before planning the site for the new train tracks.

verb	direct	We were unfamiliar with the city, so the hotel manager directed us to the train station.
noun	direction	The ticket agent at the train station gave us directions to the nearest restaurant.
noun	directory	On the Tourist Office website, you'll find a link to a thorough directory to local museums, parks, and other places of interest to visitors.

verb	operate	Trains don't operate in this town after the summer tourism season is over.
noun	operation	The train system is a massive operation with thousands of large and small stations across the country.
adjective	operational	As the operational costs of the train system rose, the managers were forced to either cut services or raise prices.

noun	punctuality	The Swiss trains are legendary for their punctuality.
adjective	punctual	For a transportation service to have any credibility, it must be punctual.
adverb	punctually	The conductor arrived punctually at the train station.

verb	remain	It is safer for all passengers to remain in their seats until the train comes to a complete stop.
noun	remains	The waiter cleared off the remains of our meal after we left the dining car.
noun	remainder	After our exciting stay in New York, the remainder of the trip seemed dull.

noun	remoteness	The remoteness of the state park was part of its attraction, but since it's not served by a train line, I couldn't get to it.
adjective	remote	The remote cabin in the woods can only be reached by car; the nearest train station or airport is more than 100 miles away.
adverb	remotely	I wasn't remotely interested in taking a cross-country trip by train since I can't stand to be confined for a long time.

WORDS IN CONTEXT

Read the following passage and write the words in the blanks below.

comprehensive	duration	offset	relatively
deluxe	entitle	operate	remainder
directories	fares	punctual	remote

Trains are among the best ways to see a lot of a country in a (1) _______________ short amount of time. In addition to the consideration of time, traveling by train allows you to really see the country you are passing through. You need only get to the station on time; after that, you can relax and watch from the window.

Most trains are on time and run on a (2) _______________ schedule. Routes, schedules, and (3) _______________ are listed in a timetable available at a train station, in many travel (4) _______________, or posted on the Internet. Directories that are (5) _______________ list all the trains, the cities they serve, the stations they depart from, and the class of services available. A few (6) _______________ travel destinations are accessible only during the peak tourist season; the train does not (7) _______________ there the (8) _______________ of the year.

The fare is based on how far you travel and the quality of your accommodations. The basic fare buys you a seat for the (9) __________________ of the trip. To be more precise, an unreserved seat guarantees a passenger transportation only; seats are allocated on a first-come, first-served basis. On busy holidays, it is possible that you could stand for at least some of your trip. For long trips, you will want to reserve a seat.

If you are traveling overnight, the cost of your room accommodation will depend on how (10) _______________ your room is. Although taking the train is less expensive than flying, the savings may be (11) _______________ by the cost of booking a sleeping room.

Travelers coming to the United States can take advantage of special rates not available in the United States. These passes (12) _______________ the bearer to unlimited coach travel on trains for a fixed period of days, usually a month.

WORD PRACTICE

Listening Comprehension

Track 39

PART 1 PHOTO

Look at the picture and listen to the sentences.
Choose the sentence that best describes the picture.

1. Ⓐ Ⓑ Ⓒ Ⓓ

PART 2 QUESTION–RESPONSE

Listen to the question and the three responses. Choose the response that best answers the question.

2. Ⓐ Ⓑ Ⓒ 3. Ⓐ Ⓑ Ⓒ

PART 3 CONVERSATION

Listen to the dialogue. Then read each question and choose the best response.

4. What are the speakers discussing?
   (A) The operator of the train
   (B) The comfort of the train ride
   (C) The directions to the train station
   (D) The time the train leaves

5. How long will their train ride be?
   (A) Three and a half hours
   (B) Five hours
   (C) Ten hours
   (D) Thirty hours

6. What will they do now?
   (A) Eat some snacks
   (B) Buy their train tickets
   (C) Get on the train
   (D) Buy something to read

PART 4 TALK

Listen to the talk. Then read each question and choose the best answer.

7. What is an advantage of riding a high-speed train?
   (A) It is always on time.
   (B) It goes to many cities.
   (C) You can get off anytime you want.
   (D) It is cheaper than a plane.

8. What is true about a high-speed train?
   (A) It operates in most cities.
   (B) It is almost as slow as a traditional train.
   (C) It is almost as fast as a plane in some cases.
   (D) It is just as fast as a traditional train.

9. What is included in the cost of a high-speed train ticket?
   (A) A comfortable seat
   (B) A movie
   (C) A class
   (D) A free meal

Reading

PART 5 INCOMPLETE SENTENCES

Choose the word that best completes the sentence.

10. Do you have a _______ map that shows all the station stops west of the Mississippi?
    (A) comprehension
    (B) comprehensively
    (C) comprehensive
    (D) comprehensiveness

11. We got lost in the train station and had to ask for _______ to the gate that our train was leaving from.
    (A) directions
    (B) directed
    (C) directory
    (D) directs

12. The train has stopped because of a malfunction, but we expect it to be _______ again within minutes.
    (A) operational
    (B) operate
    (C) operation
    (D) operationally

13. John never arrives _______, so I am always anxious when we travel together for fear of missing a train.
    (A) relatively
    (B) punctually
    (C) remotely
    (D) fairly

14. Sylvia's family _______ with her in the station until she was ready to board the train.
    (A) remains
    (B) remainder
    (C) remained
    (D) remaining

15. With this traffic, there isn't even a _______ chance that we will get to the train station on time.
    (A) remotely
    (B) remote
    (C) remoteness
    (D) remotest

PART 6 TEXT COMPLETION

Dear Henry,

I have made your train reservations for you. The tickets are enclosed. Your train leaves Sunday morning at 11:15. All trains leave punctually. ____.
16.

All the first-class tickets were sold out, so I wasn't able to get you deluxe accommodations. The tourist-class ticket I got you is considerably cheaper than a first-class ticket, so I hope the lower ____ offsets your
17.

disappointment in not getting to ride first-class. I don't think you will notice the difference since the trip is ____ short. I am sure you will be quite
18.

comfortable for the ____ of the ride. I will be waiting at the station for
19.

you when you arrive.

I look forward to seeing you.
Eliza

16. (A) Nevertheless, you could easily take a taxi to the station.
    (B) Therefore, you should be sure to arrive at the station on time.
    (C) That's why the gate number is listed on your ticket.
    (D) However, the train ride is only a few hours long.

17. (A) remainder
    (B) direction
    (C) economy
    (D) fare

18. (A) relatively
    (B) relation
    (C) relative
    (D) related

19. (A) duration
    (B) during
    (C) endure
    (D) endurance

PART 7 READING COMPREHENSION

Questions 20–24 refer to the following brochure.

Western Train Adventure

This comprehensive travel package includes round-trip train fare with sleeping car accommodations, deluxe hotel accommodations and meals at all over-night stops, and guided tours of selected cities along the way. In addition, your train ticket entitles you to three meals a day in the dining car or snack car while on board the train. We will travel through some remote areas with spectacular scenery. Every morning, a professional guide will provide information about the geology, natural history, and flora and fauna native to the areas we will travel through. You can spend the remainder of the day relaxing in your seat, chatting with your fellow passengers, or viewing movies. They will be shown twice a day in the lounge car, following lunch and dinner. An optional boat excursion to Victoria Island will be available at the western end of the trip for an extra fee. This special excursion is two days in duration and must be reserved and paid for two weeks prior to the trip departure date. The following trip departure dates are available:

June 7
June 28
July 21
August 8

Visit our website at *www.trainadventures.com* and make your reservation today!

20. Who is this information for?
    (A) Travel agents
    (B) Tour guides
    (C) Vacationers
    (D) Business travelers

21. Where can passengers watch movies?
    (A) In the dining car
    (B) In the lounge car
    (C) In the sleeping car
    (D) In the snack car

22. What is not included in the price of the travel package?
    (A) Hotel accommodations
    (B) Meals
    (C) Guided tours
    (D) A trip to an island

23. The word *comprehensive* in line 2 is closest in meaning to
    (A) inclusive.
    (B) selected.
    (C) reserved.
    (D) popular.

24. The word *entitles* in line 5 is closest in meaning to
    (A) suggest.
    (B) reminds.
    (C) expects.
    (D) qualifies.

Lesson 39: Hotels

WORDS TO LEARN

- advanced
- chain
- check in
- confirm
- expect
- housekeeper
- notify
- preclude
- quote
- rate
- reservation
- service

Study the following definitions and examples.

1. **advanced** adj., highly developed; at a higher level
   a. Since the hotel installed an advanced computer system, all operations have been functioning more smoothly.
   b. Pablo has been promoted to assistant manager and he is happy with his advanced position.
2. **chain** n., a group of enterprises under a single control
   a. Budget-priced hotel chains have made a huge impact in the industry.
   b. The hotel being built in Seoul is the newest one in the chain.
3. **check in** v., to register at a hotel; to report one's presence
   a. Patrons check in at the hotel immediately upon their arrival.
   b. We ask conference participants to check in at the registration desk so that we know they have arrived.
4. **confirm** v., to make definite
   a. Jorge contacted the hotel to confirm his room reservation.
   b. We automatically send an e-mail to let you know that your travel dates have been confirmed.
5. **expect** v., to consider probable or reasonable
   a. You can expect a clean room when you check in at a hotel.
   b. Mr. Kim expected that the bed linens would be changed daily.
6. **housekeeper** n., someone employed to do domestic work
   a. Eloise's first job at the hotel was as a housekeeper and now she is the manager.
   b. The desk clerk has asked the housekeeper to bring more towels to your room.
7. **notify** v., to report
   a. They notified the hotel that they had been delayed in traffic and would be arriving late.
   b. Lydia notified the hotel in writing that she was canceling her reservation.
8. **preclude** v., to make impossible; to rule out
   a. The horrible rainstorm precluded us from traveling any farther.
   b. The unexpected cost of the room precluded a gourmet dinner for the travelers.
9. **quote** v., to give exact information on; n., a quotation
   a. We were quoted a price of $89 for the room for one night.
   b. Call ahead and get a price quote for a week-long stay.
10. **rate** n., the payment or price according to a standard
    a. The rate for the hotel room is too high considering how few services are available on-site.
    b. The sign in the lobby lists the seasonal rates.
11. **reservation** n., an arrangement to set something aside
    a. I know I made a reservation for tonight, but the hotel staff has no record of it in the system.
    b. It is difficult, if not impossible, to get reservations at this hotel at the height of the summer season.
12. **service** n., useful functions
    a. The hotel has a number of luxury services like the on-site gym, sauna, pool, and beauty salon.
    b. Mr. Rockmont called room service to order a late-night snack.

WORD FAMILIES

verb	advance	We are advancing steadily toward our goal of improving customer service at every hotel in the chain.
noun	advance	Clarissa booked the bridal suite in advance of the hotel's official opening.
adjective	advanced	All hotel employees who do well at their jobs will be given the opportunity to move up to an advanced position.

verb	confirm	It is wise to confirm your reservation before you leave for your trip.
noun	confirmation	The confirmation code given to Suzanne when she booked her room made it easy for her to resolve her problem.
adjective	confirmed	If you don't have a confirmed reservation, you may end up without a hotel room.

verb	expect	We expect to reach our destination by dinner.
noun	expectation	The guest's expectations were not met, so he complained to the manager.
adjective	expectant	The expectant travelers, loaded with luggage, left the hotel for their scheduled flight.

verb	notify	Please notify the front desk clerk if there are any problems with your room.
noun	notification	Written notification is required for any changes in reservations.

verb	quote	When customers ask for the room rate, just quote them the prices listed on this sheet.
noun	quote	The quote given to me didn't make sense, so I called again to verify it.
adjective	quotable	Our manager instructed us that the current room rates would be quotable only until the end of the month, when a rate increase would go into effect.

verb	reserve	We reserved a room well in advance.
noun	reservation	Seeing the crowds on the highway, I decided to pull over and telephone the hotel to make a reservation.
noun	in reserve	Like many other businesses, a hotel must keep some cash in reserve to pay for emergencies.

WORDS IN CONTEXT

Read the following passage and write the words in the blanks below.

advance	confirm	notify	rates
chains	expect	preclude	reservations
check in	housekeeper	quoted	service

People stay in hotels for business and personal travel. But with room rates being so high, many travelers are staying home. Since high costs can (1) _______________ travel, smart travelers know they can save money and get the best (2) _____________ for a room by making (3) _______________ well in (4) _______________ of the beginning of their trip. When you make a reservation, the hotel staff will ask you to (5) _______________ them as soon as there is any change in your travel plans. To avoid any surprises, it's a good idea to call and (6) _______________ the availability of your room and the rate you were (7) _______________.

In selecting a hotel, first think about the kinds of (8) _______________ you will need or like to have. You will naturally (9) _______________ a comfortable, well-lit room and that a (10) _______________ will make the bed and clean things up daily, even in the smallest hotels. Large hotel (11) _______________ offer the most services, such as a pool, health club, or money exchange. The front desk clerks will tell you about such services when you (12) _______________ at the hotel.

WORD PRACTICE

Listening Comprehension

Track 40

PART 1 PHOTO

Look at the picture and listen to the sentences. Choose the sentence that best describes the picture.

1. Ⓐ Ⓑ Ⓒ Ⓓ

PART 2 QUESTION–RESPONSE

Listen to the question and the three responses. Choose the response that best answers the question.

2. Ⓐ Ⓑ Ⓒ   3. Ⓐ Ⓑ Ⓒ

PART 3 CONVERSATION

Listen to the dialogue. Then read each question and choose the best response.

4. When must a customer notify the hotel?
   (A) When he wants to leave a deposit
   (B) When he will check in early
   (C) When he expects to return to the hotel
   (D) When he wants to cancel a reservation

5. How much in advance should the customer notify the hotel?
   (A) Two to four hours
   (B) Four hours
   (C) Twenty-four hours
   (D) Forty-four hours

6. What does the man tell the woman to do?
   (A) Telephone the customer
   (B) Send the customer a bill
   (C) Charge the customer extra
   (D) Get the customer's credit card number

PART 4 TALK

Listen to the talk. Then read each question and choose the best answer.

7. Who is the speaker addressing?
   (A) New hotel employees
   (B) Regular hotel customers
   (C) Experienced hotel managers
   (D) Hotel chain owners

8. What is the goal of the hotel chain?
   (A) To get more customers
   (B) To provide the best service
   (C) To charge higher rates
   (D) To hire more employees

9. Where will the speaker take the listeners?
   (A) To the front door
   (B) To the service entrance
   (C) To the tour office
   (D) To the dining room

Reading

PART 5 INCOMPLETE SENTENCES

Choose the word that best completes the sentence.

10. We paid a lot of money for this room and we expect an _______ level of service.
    (A) advance (C) advanced
    (B) advances (D) advancing

11. Gladys _______ her reservation by calling in advance.
    (A) confirmation (C) confirming
    (B) confirmed (D) confirmative

12. The Chamber of Commerce had high _______ for the amount of business the new hotel would bring to the town.
    (A) expectancy (C) expect
    (B) expected (D) expectations

13. Since we _______ the hotel of our early arrival well ahead of time, they were able to have everything ready for us.
    (A) checked in (C) notified
    (B) reserved (D) quoted

14. I expect the rate that I was _______ over the phone and I will not accept any changes.
    (A) quoted (C) quotable
    (B) quotation (D) quotes

15. The hotel offers lower _______ on weekends hoping that more guests will be attracted by the decreased prices.
    (A) chains (C) services
    (B) rates (D) reservations

Welcome to the Springflower Radford Hotel.
We are part of the Radford Hotel Group, one of the top hotel chains in the world.

Your comfort is important to us. When you check ____ (16.), please let us know if you will need any special services during your stay.

A ____ (17.) will clean your room daily and supply you with fresh linens. Please notify her if you need any extra supplies for your room.

The exercise room and pool are available for the use of all guests. Exercise classes are offered daily. Registration is required in ____ (18.).

You can book city tours through us at very reasonable rates. ____ (19.). If you have already made a reservation for a city tour, we can confirm it for you.

Thank you for choosing a Radford Hotel. Have a pleasant stay.

16. (A) in
    (B) out
    (C) up
    (D) for

17. (A) manager
    (B) server
    (C) housekeeper
    (D) janitor

18. (A) advancement
    (B) advanced
    (C) advancer
    (D) advance

19. (A) You can expect most tourist sites to be open seven days a week.
    (B) Many tourists enjoy visiting our city throughout the year.
    (C) Some people prefer walking tours to bus tours.
    (D) See the front desk clerk for a quote.

PART 7 READING COMPREHENSION

Questions 20–24 refer to the following two letters.

June 10, 20—

Gisela Fried
Springflower Radford Hotel
2857 King Street
Hartsdale, WI

Dear Ms. Fried,

I am writing to let you know of the excellent service I received from your staff during my recent stay at the Springflower Radford Hotel. Although I had made an advance reservation for my stay, I had forgotten to confirm it. Thus, when I checked in at the hotel, there were no rooms available of the type I had wanted. Your kind and professional staff immediately found another, more luxurious, room for me. Although it was more expensive than the room I had reserved, they charged me the rate I had originally been quoted.

The excellent service continued throughout my stay and, indeed, exceeded my expectations. For example, the housekeeper cheerfully arrived to clean my room at 10:00 one evening after I had had problems with the bathtub overflowing. The staff at the front desk were always ready to answer my questions and were very helpful in assisting me to find my way around the city. All in all, my stay at the hotel was a very pleasant experience. I will certainly recommend this hotel to any of my friends who plan a visit to Hartsdale in the future.

Sincerely,

Andrew Wyatt

June 17, 20–

Andrew Wyatt
23 North Cuttersville Road
Creek Lake, MI

Dear Mr. Wyatt,

Thank you very much for your letter of June 10 notifying me of the fine service you received during your stay at the Springflower Radford Hotel. I am pleased to know that you had such a good experience as our guest. We at the Radford Hotel chain pride ourselves on the high quality of our service. As the hotel manager, I sometimes hear complaints about my staff, but it is just as important for me to hear about the fine work that they do.

I am enclosing a coupon for the hotel restaurant so that the next time you stay with us, you can enjoy a meal free of charge at the Springflower Restaurant.

Sincerely,

Gisela Fried

20. Why did Mr. Wyatt write the letter?
    (A) To complain about the hotel
    (B) To ask for a rate quote
    (C) To reserve a room
    (D) To praise the hotel staff

21. Who is Ms. Fried?
    (A) A hotel guest
    (B) The hotel manager
    (C) A housekeeper
    (D) The front desk clerk

22. What does Ms. Fried offer Mr. Wyatt?
    (A) A free meal
    (B) A less expensive room
    (C) A recommendation
    (D) A job

23. The word *rate* in the first letter, first paragraph, line 10, is closest in meaning to
    (A) time.
    (B) place.
    (C) price.
    (D) speed.

24. The word *notifying* in the second letter, first paragraph, line 2, is closest in meaning to
    (A) advertising.
    (B) complaining.
    (C) informing.
    (D) scolding.

Lesson 40: Car Rentals

WORDS TO LEARN

- coincide
- confusion
- contact
- disappoint
- guarantee
- intend
- license
- nervously
- request
- tempt
- thrill
- tier

Study the following definitions and examples.

1. **coincide** v., to happen at the same time
   a. The wedding coincided with a long weekend, so it was a good time to rent a car and go for a drive.
   b. Sean hoped that the days for the discount on car rentals would coincide with his vacation, but they didn't.
2. **confusion** n., a lack of clarity, order, or understanding
   a. There was some confusion about which discount coupons applied to which car rental agency.
   b. To avoid any confusion about renting the car, Yolanda asked her travel agent to make the arrangements on her behalf.
3. **contact** v., to get in touch with
   a. Manuel contacted at least a dozen car rental agencies to get the best deal.
   b. Last night I was contacted by my travel agent who said he had found a better price on a car rental.
4. **disappoint** v., to fail to satisfy the hope, desire, or expectation of
   a. Leila was disappointed that no rental cars were available the weekend she wished to travel.
   b. I hate to disappoint you, but I can't allow you to rent a car unless you have a major credit card.
5. **guarantee** v., promise
   a. The rental agency guarantees that all their cars are in good working order.
   b. By reserving a car ahead of time, you will be guaranteed the make and model of car that you want.
6. **intend** v., to have in mind
   a. I never intended to drive to Los Angeles until my brother suggested we do it together.
   b. Do you intend to return the car to this location or to another location?
7. **license** n., the legal permission to do or own a specified thing
   a. First, I'll need to see your driver's license and a major credit card.
   b. You will need a license in order to run this business.
8. **nervously** adv., in a distressed or uneasy manner
   a. In the city, Lonnie started driving nervously, so I volunteered to drive that part of the trip.
   b. I looked around nervously the entire time I was in the dark parking garage.
9. **request** v., ask for something politely or formally
   a. When Sonia reserved her rental car, she requested a luxury model.
   b. Most rental agencies request that you return the car with a full tank of gasoline.
10. **tempt** v., to be inviting or attractive to
    a. I am tempted by the idea of driving across the country instead of flying.
    b. Gina is tempted to rent the smaller car to save a few dollars.
11. **thrill** n., the source or cause of excitement or emotion
    a. The thought of renting a sports car gave John a thrill.
    b. Just taking a vacation is thrill enough, even if we are driving instead of flying.
12. **tier** n., a rank or class
    a. The car rental company had a few tiers of cars, each one costing more than the previous tier.
    b. If you are on a budget, I suggest you think about renting a car from our lowest tier.

WORD FAMILIES

verb	confuse	These long car rental contracts always confuse me.
noun	confusion	The crowds at the car rental office resulted in a lot of confusion.
adjective	confusing	Driving in an unfamiliar city can be quite confusing.

verb	coincide	This year, my vacation coincides with a national holiday, which will make renting a car more expensive.
noun	coincidence	By coincidence, I ran into an old friend in line waiting to rent a car.
adverb	coincidentally	Coincidentally, we are offering a special discount if you are over age 65.

verb	disappoint	The service at that car rental agency always disappoints me, so next time I plan to use a different agency.
noun	disappointment	The poor condition of the car we rented was an unexpected disappointment.
adjective	disappointing	The weather during our trip was so disappointing that we came home early.

noun	intention	I have every intention of paying by cash even though I reserved the car with my credit card.
adjective	intent	Intent on avoiding an accident, Zola drove cautiously through the rush hour traffic.
adverb	intently	The tourist intently studied the road map.

noun	nervousness	I hope my nervousness did not show when I was filling out the forms.
adjective	nervous	This was Jane's first time renting a car, so she was somewhat nervous.
adverb	nervously	Mr. Lane nervously parallel parked the rental car between two others in the parking garage.

verb	tempt	Can I tempt you to rent a larger car with a special discount?
noun	temptation	The temptation to drive the sports car fast was too great for Karl to resist.
adjective	tempting	As tempting as it sounds to drive to Florida, I think I'd rather fly.

WORDS IN CONTEXT

Read the following passage and write the words in the blanks below.

coincided	disappointment	license	tempted
confusing	guaranteed	nervous	thrill
contacted	intended	request	tier

When Yoko was planning her vacation, she went online to reserve a rental car at her vacation destination. Although she was (1) _______________ to book a car once she arrived at her destination, Yoko was (2) _______________ about not having a reservation. Her vacation (3) _______________ with a holiday, so she knew many other people would also be renting cars. Yoko wanted to avoid the (4) _______________ of finding that a car was not available at this time. By making a reservation ahead of time, she was (5) _______________ to have a car available when she arrived at her destination.

There are a lot of car rental firms, so Yoko (6) _______________ several of them to compare rates and requirements. While each company had different rates, they all had the same requirements: a valid driver's (7) _______________ and a major credit card.

Yoko found the many different rates for renting cars (8) _____________. Some companies offered substantial discounts provided that the car was reserved for a certain number of days. One company offered her a great daily rate, but it was based on a three-day rental. Since she only (9) _______________ to rent the car for two days, the discount did not apply to her.

Another factor influencing the rate was the type of car. Rentals are based on a (10) _______________ price system. The more luxurious or sporty, or the larger the car, the higher the daily rate. Since Yoko planned to (11) _______________ only a small, basic car, she found a reasonable rate—although she would have liked the (12) _______________ of driving a convertible.

WORD PRACTICE

Listening Comprehension

Track 41

PART 1 PHOTO

Look at the picture and listen to the sentences. Choose the sentence that best describes the picture.

1. Ⓐ Ⓑ Ⓒ Ⓓ

PART 2 QUESTION–RESPONSE

Listen to the question and the three responses. Choose the response that best answers the question.

2. Ⓐ Ⓑ Ⓒ   3. Ⓐ Ⓑ Ⓒ

PART 3 CONVERSATION

Listen to the dialogue. Then read each question and choose the best response.

4. Whom is the man speaking with?
   (A) An insurance agent
   (B) A police officer
   (C) Another customer
   (D) A car rental agent

5. How much does insurance cost?
   (A) $4
   (B) $9
   (C) $13
   (D) $30

6. How will the man pay?
   (A) Cash
   (B) Check
   (C) Credit card
   (D) Money order

PART 4 TALK

Listen to the talk. Then read each question and choose the best answer.

7. Who is the audience for this talk?
   (A) People who work in travel agencies
   (B) People who rent cars locally
   (C) People who work in car rental agencies
   (D) People who travel to other countries

8. When should a traveler get an international driver's license?
   (A) After arriving in another country
   (B) After contacting a local rental agency
   (C) Before leaving on a trip
   (D) When signing a car rental contract

9. What should a traveler do when picking up a rental car?
   (A) Look for damage
   (B) Sign a check
   (C) Drive it right away
   (D) Make an appointment

Reading

PART 5 INCOMPLETE SENTENCES

Choose the word that best completes the sentence.

10. If you have any questions about our rental policy, you can _____ the manager, and she will be happy to explain it to you.

    (A) guarantee
    (B) request
    (C) confuse
    (D) contact

11. My trip to Seattle coincides _____ a holiday, so it may be difficult to find a good price on a rental car.

    (A) with
    (B) on
    (C) at
    (D) from

12. It was _____ to discover that the rental agency only had compact cars available, as we needed to rent a larger vehicle.

    (A) disappointing
    (B) confusing
    (C) tempting
    (D) thrilling

13. Our _____ is to rent a comfortable car and spend several weeks driving through the mountains.

    (A) intent
    (B) intently
    (C) intention
    (D) intend

14. Tito _____ drove the rental car through the crowded garage following the signs to the car rental return location.

    (A) nerve
    (B) nervousness
    (C) nervous
    (D) nervously

15. The new car rental company _____ me to try them by offering a discount coupon toward my next rental.

    (A) tempted
    (B) tempting
    (C) temptation
    (D) temptress

PART 6 TEXT COMPLETION

Are you looking for a reliable rental car? Look no more.

Riverton Rent-a-Car offers the most reliable and economical rental cars in town.

We ____ (16.) that you will find the car you want at **Riverton Rent-a-Car**. ____ (17.).

Our rates start at $19.99 daily for a compact car, with several options available including two-door and four-door sedans and hatchbacks.

Have you always wanted to experience the ____ (18.) of driving a luxury sports car?

Live your dream by renting a sports car from **Riverton Rent-a-Car**. Daily and weekly rates are available. Contact us to find out more.

Rent a car from ***Riverton Rent-a-Car****. You won't be* ____ (19.).

16. (A) guarantees
    (B) guarantee
    (C) to guarantee
    (D) guaranteeing

17. (A) A valid driver's license is required.
    (B) All our cars are thoroughly cleaned between rentals.
    (C) We have several tiers of cars, from budget to luxury.
    (D) We have been in the car rental business for over 50 years.

18. (A) thrill
    (B) thriller
    (C) thrilled
    (D) thrilling

19. (A) contacted
    (B) disappointed
    (C) intended
    (D) tempted

PART 7 READING COMPREHENSION

Questions 20–24 refer to the following article.

> Will your next trip involve a rental car? With a little careful planning, you can prevent some common headaches. If your travel plans coincide with a holiday, you need to plan well ahead of time. Car rental agencies are very busy at such times, and you won't be guaranteed a car unless you make your reservation well in advance. Contact the car rental agency and specify the kind of car you want and the dates you will need it. It's a good idea to call the agency again shortly before you begin your trip to confirm your reservation. This is the best way to avoid disappointment.
>
> Another common problem that car renters face is extra charges. Some agencies add charges for options without letting the renter know about them. Sometimes renters aren't aware of this until they receive their credit card bill. Read the contract carefully before you sign it to make sure that you are paying only for what you requested. And don't be tempted to pay for things you don't need. It might be fun to drive a large, luxury car, but if you are traveling alone and are on a budget, it probably isn't worth paying for such a car.

20. Who is the audience for this article?
    (A) Car rental agents
    (B) Travel agents
    (C) Car renters
    (D) Car owners

21. What is a problem for holiday travelers?
    (A) Businesses are closed.
    (B) Rental agencies are very busy.
    (C) Rental rates go up.
    (D) People get headaches.

22. How can a car renter avoid paying extra charges?
    (A) Read the contract
    (B) Confirm reservations
    (C) Pay with a credit card
    (D) Make a budget

23. The word *disappointment* in the first paragraph, line 11, is closest in meaning to
    (A) expense.
    (B) disagreement.
    (C) cancellation.
    (D) unhappiness.

24. The word *requested* in the second paragraph, line 7, is closest in meaning to
    (A) tuned in.
    (B) asked for.
    (C) looked at.
    (D) read about.

WORD REVIEW #8
LESSONS 36–40 TRAVEL

Choose the word that best completes the sentence.

1. When ________ your luggage, be sure to check the name on the tag.

   (A) claim
   (B) claimed
   (C) claimant
   (D) claiming

2. The plane's ________ was delayed until the wings were defrosted.

   (A) depart
   (B) departed
   (C) departure
   (D) departing

3. Many airlines ________ courtesy discounts to senior citizens.

   (A) extend
   (B) extending
   (C) extension
   (D) extensive

4. It is easier to deal ________ making reservations if you are specific about your requirements.

   (A) in
   (B) from
   (C) out
   (D) with

5. Trains are generally more ________ than airlines.

   (A) punctuality
   (B) punctually
   (C) punctual
   (D) punctuate

6. Some travel agencies ________ on a very tight budget.

   (A) operating
   (B) operation
   (C) operates
   (D) operate

7. Even if you pay cash, you will have to show your credit card when you ________ to the hotel.

   (A) check in
   (B) fill out
   (C) pick up
   (D) pull out

8. Sometimes when you arrive, there is no room for you, even with a ________ reservation.

   (A) confirm
   (B) confirms
   (C) confirmed
   (D) confirmation

9. Without a reservation, renting a car could be a big ________.

   (A) disappoint
   (B) disappointed
   (C) disappointing
   (D) disappointment

10. Mary felt very ________ as she drove through the city because she wasn't accustomed to driving in such heavy traffic.

    (A) remote
    (B) nervous
    (C) expectant
    (D) prospective

Choose the one word or phrase that best completes each sentence.

DO YOU NEED TO ________? TRAINS ARE A GREAT WAY TO SAVE MONEY WHEN IT COMES TO

11. (A) economy
    (B) economize
    (C) economist
    (D) economical

TRAVEL. TRAIN FARE COSTS CONSIDERABLY LESS THAN PLANE FARE IN MOST CASES. ON THE OTHER HAND, IF COMFORT IS MORE IMPORTANT TO YOU THAN SAVING MONEY, YOU WILL BE HAPPY TO KNOW THAT MOST TRAINS OFFER ________ ACCOMMODATIONS. WHEN YOU

12. (A) deluxe
    (B) valid
    (C) remote
    (D) punctual

________ YOUR TICKET, SIMPLY NOTIFY THE AGENT THAT YOU WANT A FIRST-CLASS SEAT.

13. (A) will reserve
    (B) reserving
    (C) reserved
    (D) reserve

To: Margaret Berdan
From: Spring Flower Hotel Management
Subject: Your reservation

Dear Ms. Berdan,

Thank you for making a reservation at the Spring Flower Hotel for the nights of May 11–14. We suggest that you call the hotel ________ your reservation 24 hours in advance. Payment

14. (A) confirm
    (B) confirming
    (C) to confirm
    (D) did confirm

in full is required at the time you check ________, before we can give you your room key.

15. (A) in
    (B) up
    (C) out
    (D) through

Remember, your status as a guest at the Spring Flower Hotel ________ you to unlimited use

16. (A) tempts
    (B) entitles
    (C) intends
    (D) requests

of the hotel fitness room and swimming pool. We look forward to seeing you.

Sincerely,

The Spring Flower Hotel Management Office

If you plan to pick up a rental car at the airport, it's best to reserve a car ahead of time. This is easy to do online or by phone. When you pick up your car, you will have to show a valid __________ that proves you have legal permission to drive. Read the contract carefully

17. (A) passport
    (B) ticket
    (C) itinerary
    (D) license

and make sure that the __________ it states is the same one you were originally quoted. You

18. (A) rate
    (B) fare
    (C) remainder
    (D) destination

don't want to have to pay more than you expected. Also remember that certain features, such as GPS navigation systems or DVD players, are optional. You must __________ them if you want them.

19. (A) recount
    (B) request
    (C) require
    (D) record

Lesson 41: Movies

WORDS TO LEARN

- attainment
- combine
- continue
- description
- disperse
- entertainment
- influence
- range
- release
- representation
- separately
- successive

Study the following definitions and examples.

1. **attainment** n., achievement
   a. The actress received a lot of attention for her many professional attainments.
   b. The attainment of an Academy Award validates a performer's career.
2. **combine** v., to come together
   a. The director combined two previously separate visual techniques.
   b. The new production company combines the talents of three of Hollywood's best known teams.
3. **continue** v., to maintain without interruption
   a. The film continues the story set out in an earlier film.
   b. The search for a star will continue until one is found.
4. **description** n., a representation in words or pictures
   a. The description of the film did not match what we saw on screen.
   b. The critic's description of the film made it sound very appealing.
5. **disperse** v., to spread widely; to scatter
   a. The reporters dispersed after the press agent canceled the interview with the film director.
   b. The crowd outside the movie premiere would not disperse until they had seen the movie stars.
6. **entertainment** n., a diverting performance or activity
   a. The movie was provided for our entertainment.
   b. There was no entertainment for children of guests at the hotel.
7. **influence** v., to alter or affect
   a. The editor's style influenced a generation of film editors.
   b. The producer was able to influence the town council to allow her to film in the park.
8. **range** n., the scope
   a. The range of the director's vision is impressive.
   b. We wanted to go to the movie premiere, but the tickets were out of our price range.
9. **release** v., to make available to the public; to give permission for performance
   a. The film was finally released to movie theaters after many delays.
   b. The producers of the film are hoping to release it in time for the holidays.
10. **representation** n., exemplification; symbolization
    a. The actor's representation of his character did not seem authentic.
    b. The film's representation of world poverty through the character of the hungry child was quite moving.
11. **separately** adv., apart
    a. Each scene of the movie was filmed separately from the others.
    b. The theater was very crowded so we had to sit separately.
12. **successive** adj., following in order
    a. The script went through successive rewrites.
    b. Somehow the successive images were interrupted and had to be edited again.

WORD FAMILIES

verb	attain	The film quickly attained a reputation as a "must-see" movie.
noun	attainment	The technical attainments in the movie's special effects were impressive.
adjective	attainable	The director's goal of having an unlimited budget was not attainable.

verb	continue	Continue giving out movie passes until I tell you to stop.
noun	continuation	The continuation of the film will be shown after the intermission.
adjective	continual	The actors' continual demands slowed down the pace of production.

verb	describe	Please describe the new movie theater to me.
noun	description	The description of Africa in the film was not as I remembered it.
adjective	descriptive	The writer's descriptive account of the war is shocking and saddening.

verb	entertain	The comedian worked hard to entertain the children in the hospital.
noun	entertainment	Movies are one of the most popular forms of entertainment.
adjective	entertaining	The light comedy was entertaining, if not memorable.

verb	represent	The actor represented the ideals of the culture.
noun	representation	We felt that the movie's representation of the effects of war was very realistic.
noun	representative	The actress couldn't attend the awards ceremony so she had a representative accept the award for her.

verb	separate	Some movie fans can't separate fantasy from reality and confuse an actor with the character he plays.
adjective	separate	Moviemaking combines several separate processes.
adverb	separately	The actors rehearsed their lines separately before filming the scene together.

WORDS IN CONTEXT

Read the following passage and write the words in the blanks below.

attain	descriptions	influence	represent
combines	disperse	range	separate
continues	entertaining	released	successive

The popularity of the movies began early in the 20th century and (1) _______________ today. People of all ages find movies (2) _______________. Movies are a worldwide phenomenon, as the internationalism of movie distribution has helped to (3) _______________ ideas around the globe. One movie can quickly (4) _______________ other movies. But why are movies so popular?

Movies are a kind of storytelling. They try to describe an idea or record an observation about our culture. These (5) _______________ are recorded using moving visual images. Some movies portray the situation accurately and realistically, whereas other movies find visual symbols to (6) _______________ those situations.

On the most simple level, movies are a succession of moving images. These (7) _______________ images are captured on film. Directors film a wide (8) _______________ of shots—long, medium, and close up—to create a visual composition. The visual images, along with plot, characterization, and sound, produce the desired narrative. The shots are joined together in any number of combinations in a process called editing.

Making a film is a massive, complex, and expensive task that (9) _______________ art and business. It involves the talents of hundreds, and sometimes thousands, of artists, producers, and business people. It can take months, even years, for a film to be (10) _______________ into a movie theater.

Like a novel, a movie is not just a story, but a story told a certain way. A film director may want to make a movie that tells a meaningful story or one that is primarily entertaining, and will use different filming techniques to (11) _______________ that goal. It is impossible to (12) _______________ what is told in a movie from how it is told. A director's artistic vision can range from improvised to carefully controlled. Think about the complexity of a movie the next time you see one.

WORD PRACTICE

Listening Comprehension

Track 42

PART 1 PHOTO

Look at the picture and listen to the sentences. Choose the sentence that best describes the picture.

1. Ⓐ Ⓑ Ⓒ Ⓓ

PART 2 QUESTION–RESPONSE

Listen to the question and the three responses. Choose the response that best answers the question.

2. Ⓐ Ⓑ Ⓒ   3. Ⓐ Ⓑ Ⓒ

PART 3 CONVERSATION

Listen to the dialogue. Then read each question and choose the best response.

4. What are the speakers discussing?
   (A) The lighting in the theater
   (B) The price of entertainment
   (C) Shows on television
   (D) An actor's acting style

5. What type of movie does the woman prefer?
   (A) Comedy
   (B) Drama
   (C) Mystery
   (D) Documentary

6. How many movies has the actor made this year?
   (A) One
   (B) Two
   (C) Three
   (D) Ten

PART 4 TALK

Listen to the talk. Then read each question and choose the best answer.

7. Who is Ms. Moreno?
   (A) A director
   (B) An actress
   (C) A movie producer
   (D) A movie reviewer

8. What will Ms. Moreno do next week?
   (A) She will attend a performance.
   (B) She will start a trip around the world.
   (C) She will be interviewed.
   (D) She will start a new career.

9. When will the movie be released?
   (A) Next month
   (B) In several weeks
   (C) Next year
   (D) In several years

Reading

PART 5 INCOMPLETE SENTENCES

Choose the word that best completes the sentence.

10. Do you think this actor will _______ the heights of his famous father?

(A) attain
(B) attaining
(C) attainable
(D) attainment

11. A sequel is a _______ of a story set in motion by a previous film.

(A) range
(B) release
(C) continuation
(D) combination

12. After hearing a description _______ the film, I decided I had to see it as soon as possible.

(A) of
(B) to
(C) from
(D) over

13. _______ is one of the fastest growing sectors of the economy.

(A) Entertained
(B) Entertainment
(C) Entertain
(D) Entertainingly

14. We were impressed by the director's _______ of the conflict between good and evil.

(A) representative
(B) represented
(C) represents
(D) representation

15. The actors left the hotel _______ in order to avoid attracting a lot of attention.

(A) separate
(B) separately
(C) separation
(D) separating

The Silver Screen Movie House is a new entertainment option in the downtown area. The Silver Screen is not your typical movie house. It combines a movie theater with a coffeehouse, so that patrons can relax with coffee and snacks while they enjoy the show. In addition to a menu of delicious homemade sandwiches and tempting pastries, the Silver Screen offers a ____ (16.) of movies to suit all tastes. Everything from comedy to drama to action is on their schedule, and it's easy to choose movies you want to see. ____ (17.). Prices are reasonable, and frequent customers can take advantage of the ticket special. A booklet of five tickets for the price of four is available, or individual tickets can be bought ____ (18.) for each show. The place tends to fill up for the evening show, but if you like quiet, you can stay later. The crowds ____ (19.) when the last movie is over, but the café stays open until 1:00 A.M., so night owls can enjoy a quiet cup of coffee into the wee hours. We predict that the Silver Screen will soon attain the status of one of the most popular entertainment venues in the city.

16. (A) separation
    (B) dispersal
    (C) release
    (D) range

17. (A) Movie descriptions and reviews are posted on the Silver Screen website.
    (B) Some people prefer to stay home and stream movies from the Internet.
    (C) Movie reviewers influence people's opinions about movies.
    (D) New movies are often released in the summer.

18. (A) separate
    (B) separator
    (C) separately
    (D) separation

19. (A) remain
    (B) settle
    (C) converge
    (D) disperse

PART 7 READING COMPREHENSION

Questions 20–24 refer to the following movie review and e-mail message.

The newly released romantic comedy, ***West Wind***, opens this week at the State Street Cinema. The combination of a great script with superb acting talent results in a movie that you won't soon forget. The show is entertaining from start to finish, and you'll still be laughing when you leave the theater. If you've been bored to tears by movies recently, don't give up on the cinema yet. Give ***West Wind*** a try. You're sure to love it.

West Wind continues at the State Street Cinema through next week with shows at 5:15, 7:00, and 9:15 nightly.

To: Madeline Wrightwood
From: Dan Green
Subject: Let's go to the movies

Hi Maddy,

Have you seen the reviews of *West Wind*? I think it's a movie worth seeing. I don't usually go for romances, but you know how I love comedies, and the description of this one sounds really good. There's also an action movie playing next door, but I know you don't like that kind of movie, and I don't really, either.

I can't leave work before 5:15, so we should go to the second show. I'd like to invite you to have dinner afterward. I can make reservations at that restaurant you like for 9:00. We should make it there by then easily. Since we'll each be coming from work, we'll have to arrive at the theater separately. If you get there first, would you mind getting the tickets? Thanks. See you tonight.

Dan

20. What is the reviewer's opinion of the movie?
    (A) It's sad.
    (B) It's boring.
    (C) It's funny.
    (D) It's forgettable.

21. What kind of movie does Dan like?
    (A) Action
    (B) Comedy
    (C) Romance
    (D) Drama

22. What time does Dan want to go to the movies?
    (A) 5:15
    (B) 7:00
    (C) 9:00
    (D) 9:15

23. The word *entertaining* in line 5 of the movie review is closest in meaning to
    (A) enjoyable.
    (B) educational.
    (C) lengthy.
    (D) describing.

24. The word *separately* in the e-mail, second paragraph, line 7, is closest in meaning to
    (A) connected.
    (B) jointly.
    (C) slowly.
    (D) alone.

Lesson 42: Theater

WORDS TO LEARN

- action
- approach
- audience
- creative
- dialogue
- element
- experience
- occur
- perform
- rehearse
- review
- sell out

Study the following definitions and examples.

1. **action** n., the series of events that form the plot of a story or play
   a. The director decided that the second act needed more action and asked the playwright to review the work.
   b. The action on stage was spellbinding.
2. **approach** v., to go near; to move toward
   a. The performance approaches perfection.
   b. The director approached the play from an unusual angle.
3. **audience** n., the spectators at a performance
   a. The audience cheered the actors as they walked off the stage.
   b. The playwright expanded his audience by writing for film as well as for stage.
4. **creative** adj., imaginative or artistic
   a. The writer's creative representation of the Seven Deadly Sins was astounding.
   b. There are a number of creative people writing for the theater these days.
5. **dialogue** n., a conversation between two or more persons
   a. The actors performed the dialogue without using scripts.
   b. The written dialogue seemed great, but was hard to perform.
6. **element** n., fundamental or essential constituent
   a. The audience is an essential element of live theater.
   b. By putting together all the elements of theater into one play, he overwhelmed the critics.
7. **experience** n., an event or a series of events participated in or lived through
   a. The experience of live theater is very thrilling.
   b. Going to the theater was not part of Claude's experience growing up.
8. **occur** v., to take place; to enter one's mind
   a. The murder in the play occurs in the second act.
   b. It never occurred to me that the wife whom the character referred to was imaginary.
9. **perform** v., to act before an audience; to give a public presentation of
   a. The theater group performed a three-act play.
   b. Juan performed the role without forgetting any lines.
10. **rehearse** v., to practice in preparation for a public performance; to direct in rehearsal
    a. The players rehearsed for only three weeks before the show opened.
    b. The director rehearses with the actors ten hours each day.
11. **review** n., a critical estimate of a work or performance; v., writing a criticism of a performance
    a. The critic's influential review of the play was so negative that it sank the entire production.
    b. The newspaper sent a rank amateur to review the play.
12. **sell out** v., to sell all the tickets
    a. The Broadway opening sold out months in advance.
    b. We expect that this play will be a smash and sell out quickly.

WORD FAMILIES

verb	act	Roger's dream is to act in a Broadway play.
noun	action	There isn't much action in the play, but it is captivating nonetheless.
noun	actor	There are quite a few well-known actors in the cast.

verb	approach	The actress approached me with the idea for a new play.
noun	approach	The informal approach to the play was unconventional.
adjective	approachable	Despite his great fame, the director was friendly and approachable.

verb	create	The playwright created a realistic town and townspeople with the scenery and dialogue.
noun	creation	The creation of the elaborate costumes took months.
adjective	creative	The director is one of the most creative people I know.

verb	experience	The actor experienced great self-doubt before he became famous.
noun	experience	Directors bring their experience of the world onto the stage.
adjective	experienced	The experienced make-up artist transformed Maxine into an old woman in a matter of minutes.

verb	perform	The popular actress was hired to perform Shakespeare on a world tour.
noun	performance	I booked tickets for the performance the day they went on sale.
noun	performer	The performers each had three costume changes.

verb	rehearse	The cast had to rehearse the scene over and over again until the director was finally satisfied.
noun	rehearsal	The actors spent several months in rehearsal before they performed the play.
adjective	rehearsed	Lydia's acceptance speech for her award sounded more rehearsed than natural.

WORDS IN CONTEXT

Read the following passage and write the words in the blanks below.

action	created	experiences	rehearsal
approach	dialogue	occurs	reviews
audience	elements	performance	sell out

Many people find nothing as exciting as an evening of live theater. The theater combines great works of literature written for the stage, the talents of great actors, and the efforts of hundreds of skilled artisans who work to create a mood. This mood, (1) ________________ by the actors, director, and playwright with the supporting (2) ________________ of sets, lighting, and costumes, is what makes a theatrical (3) ________________ magical. When the curtain goes up, this magic (4) ________________ right before your eyes.

The director of a play will (5) ________________ the work from his or her own artistic perspective. Each director has a different vision and this shapes how he or she directs the movement or (6) ________________ between the characters. Directors use not only their theatrical training, but real-life experiences to create a meaningful, realistic evening. Actors also bring their own artistic and personal (7) ________________ to their work. This is why every staging of a play is unique.

Plays construct another world before your eyes. Ordinary words turn into meaningful (8) ________________. Costumes and sets can be realistic or symbolic. Everything in a play looks easy, but it takes many weeks of (9) ________________ to get everything in place.

Watching a play from the (10) ________________ is great fun. To find out if a play is good, read (11) ________________ or ask friends for their opinions. When plays are really popular, the available seats can fill up quickly and the play will (12) ________________.

WORD PRACTICE

Listening Comprehension

Track 43

PART 1 PHOTO

Look at the picture and listen to the sentences. Choose the sentence that best describes the picture.

1. Ⓐ Ⓑ Ⓒ Ⓓ

PART 2 QUESTION–RESPONSE

Listen to the question and the three responses. Choose the response that best answers the question.

2. Ⓐ Ⓑ Ⓒ   3. Ⓐ Ⓑ Ⓒ

PART 3 CONVERSATION

Listen to the dialogue. Then read each question and choose the best response.

4. When did the review appear in the newspaper?
   (A) Today
   (B) Yesterday
   (C) Four weeks ago
   (D) Five weeks ago

5. What does the woman say about the play?
   (A) She has heard that it is funny.
   (B) Tickets are still on sale.
   (C) It got a bad review.
   (D) The dialogue is hard to understand.

6. What did the woman do last Friday?
   (A) She wrote a review.
   (B) She won a prize.
   (C) She saw a performance.
   (D) She bought tickets.

PART 4 TALK

Listen to the talk. Then read each question and choose the best answer.

7. When can a performance of *Romeo and Juliet* be seen?
   (A) Today
   (B) On Thursday afternoon
   (C) On Sunday morning
   (D) On Thursday evening

8. How can you get tickets to the play?
   (A) Call the Shakespeare Organization
   (B) Call 656-9025
   (C) Write to the theater
   (D) Order them by e-mail

9. Where can reviews of the play be read?
   (A) In a newspaper
   (B) On a website
   (C) In a magazine
   (D) At the theater

Reading

PART 5 INCOMPLETE SENTENCES

Choose the word that best completes the sentence.

10. The director's creativity showed in everything from her _______ to the literary quality of the play to the costumes and sets.

(A) approaching (C) approachable
(B) approach (D) approachability

11. Edward is a very talented _______ although he can't sing or dance well at all.

(A) actor (C) action
(B) acts (D) acting

12. As your director, I call upon you to bring your life _______ into your role.

(A) experienced (C) experiential
(B) experiencing (D) experience

13. I am not _______ enough to work in the theater, but I certainly enjoy attending it.

(A) create (C) creative
(B) creativeness (D) creativity

14. The _______ last night was quite small, and there were a number of empty seats in the theater.

(A) audience (C) review
(B) performance (D) action

15. There isn't much time left to _______ before the play opens.

(A) rehearsals (C) rehearsing
(B) rehearse (D) rehearsed

To: Jack Sprague
From: Sabrina Clark
Subject: Play

Hi Jack,

I just saw that play that opened recently at the City Theater. You really ought to see it, too. I know you would enjoy the experience. The play combines ____ (16.) from both comedy and drama, so it's funny, but it also has an important message. Some people say this play is boring because there isn't a lot of action, but I think the ____ (17.) is very creative. The actors say some really funny lines. You can tell that the actors rehearsed a long time before the play opened. ____ (18.). You should call the theater today to get a ticket because they will probably sell ____ (19.) soon. Let me know how you like the play.

Sabrina

16. (A) elements
    (B) elemental
    (C) elementally
    (D) elementary

17. (A) audience
    (B) rehearsal
    (C) dialogue
    (D) element

18. (A) Their costumes are very interesting.
    (B) Their performances are excellent.
    (C) There were several theater reviewers in the audience.
    (D) Acting can be an exciting experience.

19. (A) up
    (B) out
    (C) from
    (D) down

PART 7 READING COMPREHENSION

Questions 20–24 refer to the following theater review.

Audiences have waited a long time for the opening of the play *Dusk to Dawn* at the City Theater. Unfortunately, the long wait only adds to the disappointment of seeing a mediocre play. It is an uncomfortable experience from start to finish. The action is slow and the dialogue boring. The performance by most of the cast is awkward and, on the night I attended at least, many of the actors forgot their lines. They obviously did not rehearse enough before opening night. The plot is trite. Theatergoers had been told to expect a fresh approach to the age-old boy-meets-girl romance story. Instead, we get a story that is dull enough to drive one to tears. Although the play is relatively short—under two hours—the performance is so tedious it seems to drag on for three or four hours. The audience made an audible sigh of relief when the final curtain dropped. Rather than the predicted sold-out performances, I expect that the play will close very shortly. Unfortunately, the producers invested a lot of money in this play, which they are not likely to get back. My advice to would-be theatergoers: spend the weekend at the movies instead.

20. What is the reviewer's opinion of the play?
    (A) It's very sad.
    (B) It's boring.
    (C) It's too short.
    (D) It's romantic.

21. How long is the play?
    (A) Less than two hours
    (B) Exactly two hours
    (C) Three hours
    (D) Four hours

22. What does the reviewer predict about the play?
    (A) The performances will be sold out.
    (B) The producers will make a lot of money.
    (C) The play will be made into a movie.
    (D) The play will close in a short time.

23. The word *experience* in line 3 is closest in meaning to
    (A) act.
    (B) wait.
    (C) event.
    (D) seat.

24. The word *rehearse* in line 6 is closest in meaning to
    (A) plan.
    (B) sleep.
    (C) memorize.
    (D) practice.

Lesson 43: Music

WORDS TO LEARN

- available
- broaden
- category
- disparate
- divide
- favor
- instinct
- lively
- reason
- relaxation
- taste
- urge

Study the following definitions and examples.

1. **available** adj., ready for use; willing to serve
   a. In order to understand the words to the opera, Sue kept an Italian dictionary available at all times.
   b. The website has an amazing variety of music available for downloading.
2. **broaden** v., to make wider
   a. Dominique wants to broaden her knowledge of opera history.
   b. You will appreciate music more if you broaden your tastes and listen to several types of music.
3. **category** n., a division in a system of classification; a general class of ideas
   a. Jazz is one of many categories of music.
   b. The works of Mozart are in a category by themselves.
4. **disparate** adj., fundamentally distinct or different
   a. In the song, the disparate voices hauntingly join a blended chorus.
   b. Religious songs cut across disparate categories of music.
5. **divide** v., to separate into parts
   a. The class was evenly divided between those who liked country music and those who didn't.
   b. The broad topic of music can be divided into parts, such as themes, styles, or centuries.
6. **favor** v., to be partial to
   a. Sam enjoys the works of several composers, but he tends to favor Mozart.
   b. I'd favor an evening at a jazz concert over an evening at the opera any time.
7. **instinct** n., an inborn pattern that is a powerful motivation
   a. The student's ability to play the cello was so natural, it seemed an instinct.
   b. The music lover followed his instincts and collected only music that he enjoyed.
8. **lively** adj., full of energy
   a. Some people enjoy lively music, whereas others tend to prefer slower types of music.
   b. The lively dance was fun but very tiring.
9. **reason** n., the basis or motive for an action; an underlying fact or cause
   a. We'll never understand the reason why some music is popular and some is not.
   b. There is every reason to believe that Beethoven will still be popular in the next century.
10. **relaxation** n., the act of relaxing or the state of being relaxed; refreshment of body or mind
    a. Listening to soothing music before bedtime provides good relaxation.
    b. He played the piano for relaxation and pleasure.
11. **taste** n., the ability to discern what is excellent or appropriate
    a. Ella had the taste required to select a musical program for the visiting dignitaries.
    b. This music does not appeal to my tastes; but I'm old-fashioned.
12. **urge** v., to advocate earnestly
    a. His mother urged him to study the piano; the rest is musical history.
    b. Despite my reluctance, my friends urged me to attend an opera.

WORD FAMILIES

verb	broaden	Connie listens to all different types of music because she is trying to broaden her musical tastes.
adjective	broad	We'll cover a broad range of music in the music appreciation class.
adverb	broadly	The orchestra director travels broadly in search of new musical talent.

verb	categorize	Some singers have a broad range of styles and are difficult to categorize.
noun	category	Most of the music Sam listens to falls into the category of classical music.

verb	divide	Louise can divide her musical tastes into two broad categories: rock and jazz.
noun	division	There are a lot of different styles of rock music, but the divisions between them aren't always distinct.
noun	divider	The room divider didn't effectively block sound and we could clearly hear the piano students as they practiced.

verb	favor	The music critic clearly favors some musicians over others.
adjective	favorite	The teenager had an extensive colleciton of music by all her favorite groups.
adjective	favorable	The favorable reviews of the group's new album helped to push the album up the sales charts.

verb	relax	After a long concert tour, the singer liked to relax by the pool.
noun	relaxation	Listening to music is an enduring form of relaxation.
adjective	relaxing	There is nothing more relaxing than listening to music.

verb	urge	My music teacher urged me not to give up the violin even though I was having such a hard time with it.
noun	urge	Richard gets the urge to play the guitar every time he passes a music store window.
adjective	urgent	My friend sent an urgent text message asking me to order the concert tickets as soon as possible because they will sell out quickly.

WORDS IN CONTEXT

Read the following passage and write the words in the blanks below.

available	disparate	instinctive	relax
broad	divided	lively	taste
category	favorite	reason	urge

Everyone loves music, it seems. And there's little (1) ______________ to wonder why. There is so much music (2) ______________ from which to choose, and there is a (3) ______________ of music to appeal to every (4) ______________. The major groups of music are (5) ______________ broadly into classical, popular, and jazz. Within these (6) ______________ groups are many other subcategories. For example, such (7) ______________ types of music as movie sound tracks, rhythm and blues, rock, and rap all fit within the category of popular music.

The (8) ______________ to make and enjoy music may be (9) ______________. Even small children enjoy music. Since they tend to be active, children often prefer (10) ______________ music that they can move and dance to.

Another reason that music is so popular is the variety of settings in which one can enjoy his or her (11) ______________ kind of music. You can go to a church to hear great religious music, or to a concert hall to hear a well-known classical symphony. On another night, you might go to a small club to listen to an up-and-coming jazz group while you enjoy a drink. A few nights later, you might go with some friends to join thousands of other people in a stadium to hear your favorite rock band play in your city on a world tour. And, back at your house or apartment, you can (12) ______________ while listening to your favorite artists on your preferred devicc.

WORD PRACTICE

Listening Comprehension

Track 44

PART 1 PHOTO

Look at the picture and listen to the sentences. Choose the sentence that best describes the picture.

1. Ⓐ Ⓑ Ⓒ Ⓓ

PART 2 QUESTION–RESPONSE

Listen to the question and the three responses. Choose the response that best answers the question.

2. Ⓐ Ⓑ Ⓒ 3. Ⓐ Ⓑ Ⓒ

PART 3 CONVERSATION

Listen to the dialogue. Then read each question and choose the best response.

4. What does the man say about the website that the woman recommended?
   (A) It matches his taste.
   (B) It is boring.
   (C) It has good music.
   (D) It is interesting.

5. Why is the man looking for music?
   (A) For relaxation
   (B) For a music class
   (C) For a dance party
   (D) For a present

6. What does the woman suggest that the man do?
   (A) Ask another friend for help
   (B) Go to a store
   (C) Read a book
   (D) Change his musical tastes

PART 4 TALK

Listen to the talk. Then read each question and choose the best answer.

7. What is the class about?
   (A) The history of music
   (B) Playing musical instruments
   (C) Music appreciation
   (D) Reading music

8. What does the speaker urge the listeners to do?
   (A) Buy the text right away
   (B) Try a musical instrument
   (C) Take a test
   (D) Start listening to music every day

9. How much will students pay for concert tickets?
   (A) $3
   (B) $13
   (C) $25
   (D) $30

Reading

PART 5 INCOMPLETE SENTENCES

Choose the word that best completes the sentence.

10. My friends have urged me to ______ my tastes to include more classical music.

    (A) divide
    (B) favor
    (C) broaden
    (D) categorize

11. I have no musical talent at all and have never felt the ______ to learn to play an instrument.

    (A) urge
    (B) taste
    (C) favor
    (D) category

12. The string quartet received a ______ comparison to the best of the genre.

    (A) favor
    (B) favoritism
    (C) favorably
    (D) favorable

13. The piano teacher ______ his classes into beginning, intermediate, and advanced levels.

    (A) divide
    (B) divides
    (C) have divided
    (D) are dividing

14. After a hard day at work, we like to ______ to soothing music.

    (A) relaxation
    (B) relaxes
    (C) relaxing
    (D) relax

15. They have such ______ tastes in music that it's hard to choose something they both would enjoy listening to.

    (A) favorite
    (B) disparate
    (C) lively
    (D) broad

PART 6 TEXT COMPLETION

Music Lover's Guide

These days, it's easy to hear the music you like anytime you want. Almost any piece of music you can think of is ____ (16.) on the Internet. You can listen to your ____ (17.) songs and artists over and over again, or you can explore styles of music that are unfamiliar to you. Just reach for your computer or smartphone and discover the world of music that awaits you. ____ (18.). Whether you feel like listening to ____ (19.) songs, romantic ballads, or have the urge to dance, the music you want is right there at your fingertips.

16. (A) agreeable
    (B) affordable
    (C) available
    (D) avoidable

17. (A) favors
    (B) favoring
    (C) favorable
    (D) favorite

18. (A) The cost of streaming music over the Internet depends on the service you use.
    (B) Whatever categories of music you prefer, you can find them online.
    (C) Or, you can ask your friends to suggest music that you might like.
    (D) People all over the world enjoy listening to many types of music.

19. (A) lively
    (B) liven
    (C) livelier
    (D) liveliness

PART 7 READING COMPREHENSION

Questions 20–24 refer to the following review and e-mail message.

We were fortunate to have internationally acclaimed violinist Maria Rogoff play at Symphony Hall last Saturday night. Ms. Rogoff appears to have been born with a musical instinct. She played her violin quite naturally, as if it were an old friend. The selection of pieces she played was superb. She favored lively, interesting pieces that kept the audience enthralled during the entire performance. All in all, it was a thoroughly enjoyable and relaxing evening. Music lovers everywhere are urged to hear Ms. Rogoff play anytime there is an opportunity.

To: Polly Andrews
From: Gus Hall
Subject: Concert

Hi Polly,

Did you see the review of Maria Rogoff's concert in the Sunday paper? Can you believe they gave her such a good review? I didn't agree at all with what the reviewer said about her selection of pieces. In fact, I thought quite the opposite. And she made several mistakes in her playing. Did you notice? Oh, well. I prefer cello music anyhow. It is much more to my taste. Maybe that's the real reason I didn't enjoy the concert. By the way, there is another concert this Friday. A pianist will be playing at Symphony Hall. Do you want to go? I am pretty sure there are still tickets available. I think there is a performance on Thursday, too, but I have a meeting that night. Let me know if you can make it, and I'll order the tickets.

Gus

20. When was Maria Rogoff's concert?
    (A) Thursday
    (B) Friday
    (C) Saturday
    (D) Sunday

21. What is Gus's opinion of the music at the concert?
    (A) It was lively.
    (B) It was boring.
    (C) It was relaxing.
    (D) It was enthralling.

22. What instrument does Gus prefer?
    (A) Viola
    (B) Cello
    (C) Violin
    (D) Piano

23. The word *instinct* in line 5 of the review is closest in meaning to
    (A) preference.
    (B) knowledge.
    (C) parentage.
    (D) nature.

24. The word *relaxing* in line 11 of the review is closest in meaning to
    (A) fun.
    (B) exciting.
    (C) peaceful.
    (D) educational.

Lesson 44: Museums

WORDS TO LEARN

- acquire
- admire
- collection
- criticism
- express
- fashion
- leisure
- respond
- schedule
- significant
- specialize
- spectrum

Study the following definitions and examples.

1. **acquire** v., to gain possession of; to get by one's own efforts
   a. The museum acquired a van Gogh during heavy bidding.
   b. The sculptor acquired metalworking skills after much practice.
2. **admire** v., to regard with pleasure; to have esteem or respect for
   a. Raisa, admiring the famous smile, stood before the Mona Lisa for hours.
   b. I admire all the effort the museum put into organizing this wonderful exhibit.
3. **collection** n., a group of objects or works to be seen, studied, or kept together
   a. The museum's collection contained many works donated by famous collectors.
   b. The museum's collection kept two full-time curators busy.
4. **criticism** n., an evaluation, especially of literary or other artistic works
   a. According to the criticism of the Victorian era, the painting was a masterpiece; now it is considered merely a minor work.
   b. The revered artist's criticism of the piece was particularly insightful.
5. **express** v., to give an opinion or depict emotion
   a. The sculptor was able to express his feelings better through the use of clay rather than words.
   b. The photograph expresses a range of emotions.
6. **fashion** n., the prevailing style or custom
   a. According to the fashion of the day, the languid pose of the sculpture was high art.
   b. The museum's classical architecture has never gone out of fashion.
7. **leisure** n., freedom from time-consuming duties; free time
   a. The woman took up painting in her retirement, when she had more time for leisure.
   b. Spending a day at an art museum is a form of leisure that many people enjoy.
8. **respond** v., to make a reply; to react
   a. You should respond to the invitation to attend the museum gala.
   b. The visitors who viewed those poignant photographs responded emotionally.
9. **schedule** v., to enter in a planner or diary
   a. We didn't schedule enough time to see all the exhibits that we were interested in.
   b. The museum is scheduling a collection of works by Japanese masters.
10. **significant** adj., meaningful; having a major effect; important
   a. The use of lambs to symbolize innocence is significant in Western art.
   b. The rash of new acquisitions represented a significant change in the museum's policies.
11. **specialize** v., to concentrate on a particular activity
   a. The art historian specialized in Navajo rugs.
   b. The museum shop specializes in Ming vases.
12. **spectrum** n., a range of related qualities, ideas, or activities
   a. The painting crosses the spectrum from symbolic to realistic representation.
   b. The whole spectrum of artistic expression was represented in the exhibit.

WORD FAMILIES

verb	admire	People from all around the world visit the museum to admire the great works of art on display.
noun	admiration	I have great admiration for anyone who can create art.
adjective	admirable	Her dedication to improving her artistic skills is admirable.

verb	collect	The enthusiast began to collect Shaker furniture in the 1960s.
noun	collection	The collection at the museum is small, but it includes several significant pieces.
noun	collector	The avid collector spent weekends at estate sales looking for rare art objects.

verb	criticize	The sculptor was criticized for his lack of perspective.
noun	critic	The art critic gave the show a poor review, which saddened the exhibition team.
noun	criticism	The writer's elegant essays on the use of light in Flemish painting were landmarks in art criticism.

verb	respond	When Mr. Hon did not respond to the invitation to the opening, we assumed he was not able to attend.
noun	response	The response to the request for assistance was overwhelming.
adjective	responsive	The director was not responsive to any of the staff's suggestions, which made them both annoyed and anxious.

verb	schedule	The museum has scheduled a lecture series to accompany the special exhibit.
noun	schedule	Several local artists are featured on the gallery's winter schedule.
adjective	scheduled	There are several scheduled events at the museum this weekend.

verb	specialize	The art student decided to specialize in French and English paintings of the 1860s.
noun	specialist	The curator is a specialist in native Caribbean art.
adjective	specialized	The museum hired specialized personnel to adjust the humidity and light for the display of ancient books.

WORDS IN CONTEXT

Read the following passage and write the words in the blanks below.

acquire	criticism	leisure	significant
admire	expressing	responded	specialize
collected	fashion	schedule	spectrum

Museums are places to view and (1) _______________ the great works of art. All large cities, and even many small cities, have good art museums in which you will find a wide (2) _______________ of paintings, sculptures, drawings, and prints.

Museums attempt to collect and display a broad range of examples of how, throughout time, men and women have (3) _______________ to what they have seen, thought, and felt by (4) _______________ themselves through materials like stone, clay, and paint, or ink and paper. The artist imposes an order on these materials that is (5) _______________. Some styles of art or particular objects are in (6) _______________ for only a while, and others earn positive (7) _______________ over time and are seen as enduring classics. Museums collect the best of these works for the public to see.

When you go to a museum, be sure to (8) _______________ plenty of time to see the art without feeling rushed. If you are lucky enough to live near a museum, you can come back again at your (9) _______________. Some museums show a broad collection of art from different times and cultures, often (10) _______________ and donated by their generous patrons. Other museums (11) _______________ in displaying art from a certain period, say from the ancient world, or by a certain group or nationality of people, such as Native Americans.

The operations of many museums are paid for by the government, and these museums are often free to the public; other museums must charge each person upon entry. These fees help the museum operate and (12) _______________ more works.

WORD PRACTICE

Listening Comprehension

Track 45

PART 1 PHOTO

Look at the picture and listen to the sentences. Choose the sentence that best describes the picture.

1. Ⓐ Ⓑ Ⓒ Ⓓ

PART 2 QUESTION–RESPONSE

Listen to the question and the three responses. Choose the response that best answers the question.

2. Ⓐ Ⓑ Ⓒ　　3. Ⓐ Ⓑ Ⓒ

PART 3 CONVERSATION

Listen to the dialogue. Then read each question and choose the best response.

4. What are the speakers discussing?
   (A) A drawing
   (B) A sculpture
   (C) A painting
   (D) A photograph

5. What does the man like about it?
   (A) The size
   (B) The color
   (C) The style
   (D) The subject

6. What does the woman say about the museum?
   (A) The admission fee is too expensive.
   (B) They should acquire more works.
   (C) It's not very interesting.
   (D) The collection is varied.

PART 4 TALK

Listen to the talk. Then read each question and choose the best answer.

7. When does the lecture series at the museum begin?
   (A) Next month
   (B) Next week
   (C) This month
   (D) This week

8. How can you find out the schedule of guided tours?
   (A) Visit the main gallery
   (B) Press two
   (C) Go online
   (D) Speak with an operator

9. What is the topic of the print exhibit?
   (A) Fashion
   (B) Sculpture
   (C) African art
   (D) Nineteenth-century art

Reading

PART 5 INCOMPLETE SENTENCES

Choose the word that best completes the sentence.

10. The museum ________ these paintings as a gift from a local art collector.

(A) admired (C) acquired
(B) criticized (D) expressed

11. Mimi owns some beautiful pottery and is always looking for new pieces to add to her ________.

(A) leisure (C) collection
(B) spectrum (D) schedule

12. The curator's ________ of the museum's fund-raising plan seemed shortsighted.

(A) criticism (C) critical
(B) critic (D) criticize

13. We have been asked to respond ________ the proposal by the end of the month.

(A) on (C) to
(B) at (D) of

14. Tickets for the museum's ________ tours are available at the front desk.

(A) scheduling (C) schedules
(B) schedule (D) scheduled

15. After becoming a ________ in Egyptian tomb painting, the art historian lost her interest in other kinds of art.

(A) specialize (C) specially
(B) specialist (D) special

PART 6 TEXT COMPLETION

Thank you for visiting the Museum of History. This brochure has been developed to provide you with information to make your visit more enjoyable.

Viewing the Exhibits

Our main exhibits are located on the first and second floors of the museum. They cover all aspects of local history up to the present and are organized in chronological order. You are invited to join one of our regular guided tours at no extra charge, or you can visit the exhibits on your own and view them at your ____.
16.

Group Tours

School groups and other groups that wish to visit the museum may ____ special group tours.
17.

Please contact the Museum Tour Office for more information.

Museum Bookstore

The Museum Bookstore is located on the first floor next to the cafeteria. ____. Gift items are also for sale.
18.

In ____ to the requests of many of our visitors, the bookstore hours have been extended. It is now open daily
19.

from 10:00 A.M. until 6:00 P.M.

16. (A) fashion
    (B) response
    (C) collection
    (D) leisure

17. (A) schedule
    (B) scheduling
    (C) to schedule
    (D) have schedule

18. (A) This store specializes in books about local history.
    (B) Museum visitors are often book lovers as well.
    (C) It is a source of revenue for the museum.
    (D) Most museums offer souvenirs for sale.

19. (A) responsible
    (B) responsive
    (C) response
    (D) respond

PART 7 READING COMPREHENSION

Questions 20–24 refer to the following brochure.

Most visitors to our city spend time visiting some of the many museums that we are famous for. The City Art Museum, Museum of History, National University Museum of Scientific Research, and the Hall of Presidents are among the most popular destinations for museumgoers. The National Transportation Museum, currently undergoing renovations, is scheduled to reopen next year with a larger number of exhibits and extended hours.

Visitors to the City Art Museum can admire the collection of paintings by local artists as well as famous works of art from around the world. The museum's collection covers a wide spectrum of artists and styles, and critics have called it one of the most significant in the world. Art classes offered at the museum provide both the serious and the casual student of art with opportunities to explore the world of artistic expression. The Museum of History features rotating exhibits focusing on various aspects of our nation's history, and a permanent collection of portraits of our nation's presidents. This summer's special exhibit focuses on the history of fashion. The National University Museum of Scientific Research specializes in exhibits on research undertaken at the university. It also features a special hands-on exhibit for children.

All museums have the same entrance price: $10 for adults and $5 for children. A special $35 weekly pass, available at any museum, allows the holder entrance to all city museums for a week. This pass is especially recommended to visitors from out of town as it provides the opportunity to visit all the museums at their leisure.

20. Who is this brochure for?
    (A) Museum employees
    (B) Historians
    (C) Students
    (D) Tourists

21. Where can portraits of presidents be seen?
    (A) City Art Museum
    (B) Museum of History
    (C) National University Museum
    (D) Hall of Presidents

22. What is the price of a one-day museum ticket for an adult?
    (A) $350
    (B) $5
    (C) $10
    (D) $35

23. The word *admire* in the second paragraph, line 1, is closest in meaning to
    (A) look at.
    (B) look to.
    (C) look up.
    (D) look for.

24. The word *significant* in the second paragraph, line 4, is closest in meaning to
    (A) large.
    (B) varied.
    (C) interesting.
    (D) important.

Lesson 45: Media

WORDS TO LEARN

- assignment
- constantly
- constitute
- decision
- disseminate
- impact
- in-depth
- investigate
- link
- politician
- subscribe
- thorough

Study the following definitions and examples.

1. **assignment** n., something, such as a task, that is assigned
   a. This assignment has to be turned in before midnight.
   b. When the reporter is on assignment, research piles up on her desk.
2. **constantly** adv., continually
   a. An advantage of online news reports is that they can be constantly updated.
   b. People constantly look to the news to keep up to date on what is going on in the world.
3. **constitute** v., to be the elements or parts of
   a. All the different news sources constitute the media industry.
   b. A talented staff, adequate printing facilities, and sufficient distribution points constitute a successful newspaper.
4. **decision** n., judgment or choice
   a. The court made the decision to allow the newspaper to print the controversial story.
   b. Newspaper editors often have to make quick decisions about which stories to publish.
5. **disseminate** v., to scatter widely; to distribute
   a. The Internet disseminates news more quickly than newspapers, TV, or the radio can.
   b. The computer virus was disseminated through the newsroom by reporters sharing terminals.
6. **impact** n., a strong, immediate impression
   a. The story of the presidential scandal had a huge impact on the public.
   b. The impact of the news coverage is yet to be known.
7. **in-depth** adj., in complete detail; thorough
   a. The newspaper gave in-depth coverage of the tragic bombing.
   b. Ivan's in-depth story on the spread of the disease received praise from many of his colleagues.
8. **investigate** v., to uncover and report hidden information
   a. Reporters need to thoroughly investigate the facts before publishing their stories.
   b. Michelle's editor sent her to the capital to investigate the story behind the government scandal.
9. **link** n., an association; a relationship
   a. The computer links will take you to today's headlines.
   b. The father-daughter team of reporters is just one example of many family links at this newspaper.
10. **politician** n., a person involved in government activities
    a. The news media cover the activities of all the major politicians.
    b. The politician refused to talk to reporters about her private life.
11. **subscribe** v., to receive a periodical regularly on order
    a. Jill subscribes to a gardening magazine.
    b. Many people have stopped subscribing to newspapers because they prefer to read the news online.
12. **thorough** adj., exhaustively complete
    a. The reporters were thorough in their coverage of the event.
    b. The story was the result of thorough research.

WORD FAMILIES

noun	constancy	The reporter's constancy in writing thorough news reports earned her a loyal following of readers.
adjective	constant	The constant ringing of the telephone distracted Susan from writing her report.
adverb	constantly	The editor constantly asks the reporters to recheck their facts.

verb	decide	The editor decided not to publish the story because the facts were unreliable.
noun	decision	The decision to lay off several reporters was made for financial reasons alone.
adjective	decisive	Newspaper editors must be decisive when determining which stories go on the front page.

verb	investigate	Alban was excited about his first chance to investigate a story.
noun	investigation	The investigation into the president's past was covered by the media worldwide.
adjective	investigative	After turning up details in the crime that even the police had missed, Helen became well-known as an investigative reporter.

noun	politician	You can get basic information about a politician's background and experience on her website.
noun	politics	Anyone who chooses a career in politics has to learn how to speak with news reporters.
adjective	political	Many blogs focus on political news and opinions.

verb	subscribe	I subscribe to the local newspaper to stay current.
noun	subscription	Buying a subscription to the magazine was much less expensive than buying individual issues.
noun	subscribers	The magazine went out of business because it did not have enough subscribers.

noun	thoroughness	A newspaper cannot survive long without a reputation for thoroughness.
adjective	thorough	Toshi is famous for her thorough and fair reporting of the issues.
adverb	thoroughly	The reporter thoroughly checked all his facts to avoid any potential embarrassment.

WORDS IN CONTEXT

Read the following passage and write the words in the blanks below.

assignments	decisions	in-depth	political
constant	disseminated	investigative	subscribes
constitutes	impact	links	thoroughly

Chen likes to go online to read the news. Lemma turns on the television to find out what's going on in the world. Eve (1) _______________ to several newspapers, which arrive at her house daily. Kobi, who is especially interested in (2) _______________ news, listens to radio talk shows that (3) _______________ cover government issues. All these people are touched by the media.

What is the media? What (4) _______________ the media? The media consists of all the ways that news and information is (5) _______________ to a mass audience. The media covers everything from hard news, which is (6) _______________ reporting, to stories that are purely entertaining, such as whether your favorite movie star was on the "Best Dressed/Worst Dressed" list. Whether in print or broadcast on TV, the stories are the product of the reporting of many journalists who write the stories, and editors who give out the (7) _______________, assess the quality of the writing and research, and make the (8) _______________ about where and when the stories run.

The news has an immediate (9) _______________. The Internet puts global news onto the personal computer on your desk. Almost all browsers have (10) _______________ to up-to-the-minute news stories from various news services. You can get (11) _______________ news updates from a variety of sources via your smartphone, providing you with the most up-to-date and (12) _______________ coverage.

WORD PRACTICE

Listening Comprehension

Track 46

PART 1 PHOTO

Look at the picture and listen to the sentences. Choose the sentence that best describes the picture.

1. Ⓐ Ⓑ Ⓒ Ⓓ

PART 2 QUESTION–RESPONSE

Listen to the question and the three responses. Choose the response that best answers the question.

2. Ⓐ Ⓑ Ⓒ   3. Ⓐ Ⓑ Ⓒ

PART 3 CONVERSATION

Listen to the dialogue. Then read each question and choose the best response.

4. According to the woman, why are newspapers better than TV news shows?
   (A) Newspaper editors are decisive.
   (B) Newspaper coverage is more thorough.
   (C) Newspaper stories are more interesting.
   (D) Newspapers cover better stories.

5. How long has the woman worked as a newspaper reporter?
   (A) Four years
   (B) Thirteen years
   (C) Fourteen years
   (D) Thirty years

6. What is the man's job?
   (A) Investigative reporter
   (B) TV news reader
   (C) Journalism teacher
   (D) Journalism student

PART 4 TALK

Listen to the talk. Then read each question and choose the best answer.

7. What is the topic of the news report?
   (A) A speech made by the country's president
   (B) The state of the national economy
   (C) Fraud committed by a company president
   (D) An industry report

8. At what time can this news report be heard?
   (A) 5:00
   (B) 12:00
   (C) 6:00
   (D) 10:00

9. Why won't Mary Milo report the news tonight?
   (A) She is sick.
   (B) She got a new job.
   (C) She is away on vacation.
   (D) She has another assignment.

Reading

PART 5 INCOMPLETE SENTENCES

Choose the word that best completes the sentence.

10. It is very easy to find the latest _______ news online.

    (A) politics (C) political
    (B) politician (D) polite

11. The actor was annoyed by the _______ questions about his personal life and finally decided to stop giving interviews.

    (A) political (C) linked
    (B) decisive (D) constant

12. Georgette _______ to stop subscribing to the newspaper because she felt the quality of the reporting had deteriorated.

    (A) decision (C) decides
    (B) decided (D) decisive

13. The reporters followed the official _______ by interviewing all the witnesses to the crime.

    (A) investigate (C) investigative
    (B) investigation (D) investigational

14. Myrtle is very interested in the political scene in her city and subscribes _______ all the local newspapers.

    (A) for (C) in
    (B) to (D) with

15. The editor was impressed with how _______ the reporter was in getting the details from his sources.

    (A) thorough (C) thoroughly
    (B) thoroughness (D) thoroughbred

PART 6 TEXT COMPLETION

> Stay on top of what's happening in today's world by ____ to *News Story Weekly*,
> 16.
> the weekly news magazine that is read by politicians, corporate executives, and ordinary citizens like you.
>
> *News Story Weekly* provides you with ____ coverage of the week's most important news,
> 17.
> both national and international. *News Story Weekly* thoroughly investigates worldwide events that have an impact on your life and delivers this news to your mailbox every week. People who care about what's happening in the world read *News Story Weekly*. Shouldn't you be one of them? *News Story Weekly* is ____ throughout the country to readers
> 18.
> from all walks of life.
>
> Subscribing to *News Story Weekly* is easy! ____.
> 19.

16. (A) subscribe
    (B) to subscribe
    (C) subscribing
    (D) should subscribe

17. (A) depth
    (B) in-depth
    (C) deepen
    (D) deepened

18. (A) assigned
    (B) constituted
    (C) investigated
    (D) disseminated

19. (A) Simply visit our website and sign up today.
    (B) Our reporters are top-notch investigators.
    (C) Print copies are available at most newsstands.
    (D) The articles are interesting and a pleasure to read.

PART 7 READING COMPREHENSION

Questions 20–24 refer to the following two e-mail messages.

From: Mark Conway
To: Michelle Richards
Subject: journalist available

Dear Ms. Richards,

I am a journalist and an avid reader of *News Story Weekly*. It has long been my dream to write for your magazine. I graduated from National University a year ago with a degree in journalism. For the past six months I have been working as an investigative reporter for the *Bluefield Daily*, my hometown newspaper. This newspaper is disseminated throughout the state. I work on assignments involving local politics.

In my opinion, *News Story Weekly* is the top news magazine in the country. It has had a great impact on my life. I started reading it at an early age, and it inspired me to pursue a career as a reporter. If there is a position available for a reporter at *News Story Weekly*, I would be interested in applying for it. I believe that my educational background and work experience qualify me for such a position. I am including links below my signature to several of my articles for the *Bluefield Daily*. I have letters of reference available if you need them. I look forward to hearing from you.

Sincerely,

Mark Conway

From: Michelle Richards
To: Mark Conway
Subject: re: journalist available

Dear Mr. Conway,

Thank you for your message of April 12 inquiring about a position as a reporter. We are constantly looking for reporters to work for our magazine, and we currently have an opening for a reporter to cover regional news. You seem to be well-qualified, and we would welcome your application. I would need to see your reference letters as well as a résumé. The closing date for this position is May 15. We will make our choice after that date and let you know what we decide by the first of June. Thank you for your interest in *News Story Weekly*.

Sincerely,

Michelle Richards

20. Why did Mark Conway write the e-mail?
    (A) To express an opinion about the news
    (B) To get a subscription to *News Story Weekly*
    (C) To offer Ms. Richards an assignment
    (D) To apply for a job as a reporter

21. What did Mark Conway include in his message?
    (A) Links to newspaper articles
    (B) A copy of his résumé
    (C) Letters of reference
    (D) His university diploma

22. When will Mark Conway know Michelle Richards's decision?
    (A) April 12
    (B) April 15
    (C) May 15
    (D) June 1

23. The word *impact* in the first letter, second paragraph, line 2, is closest in meaning to
    (A) interest.
    (B) influence.
    (C) difference.
    (D) education.

24. The word *constantly* in the second letter, line 3, is closest in meaning to
    (A) always.
    (B) sometimes.
    (C) rarely.
    (D) infrequently.

WORD REVIEW #9
LESSONS 41–45 ENTERTAINMENT

Choose the word that best completes the sentence.

1. Movies are probably the most popular form of __________ in the United States.
   (A) category
   (B) experience
   (C) admiration
   (D) entertainment

2. Television has seriously __________ society.
   (A) influence
   (B) influenced
   (C) influencing
   (D) influential

3. Actors can spend too much time __________ as well as too little.
   (A) rehearse
   (B) rehearsed
   (C) rehearsing
   (D) rehearsal

4. Even when a show is sold __________, it is sometimes possible to get a ticket.
   (A) up
   (B) to
   (C) off
   (D) out

5. Orchestra music is wonderfully conducive to __________.
   (A) relaxation
   (B) relaxed
   (C) relaxes
   (D) relax

6. Some people do not have a __________ for rock and roll music, while other people love it.
   (A) taste
   (B) favor
   (C) reason
   (D) spectrum

7. New __________ are one of the most exciting aspects of museum work.
   (A) acquire
   (B) acquisitions
   (C) acquires
   (D) acquisitive

8. Sometimes I look at a famous painting and wonder why it is considered more __________ than the ones on either side of it.
   (A) signify
   (B) signified
   (C) significant
   (D) significantly

9. The Internet __________ information faster than any other medium.
   (A) disseminate
   (B) disseminates
   (C) dissemination
   (D) disseminating

10. In any news medium, the only news is what the editor __________ is news.
    (A) decide
    (B) decides
    (C) decision
    (D) decisions

Choose the one word or phrase that best completes each sentence.

Because of DVD players, cable TV, and Internet streaming, it is no longer necessary to leave home in search of __________. Families can watch movies in the comfort of their own living rooms.

11. (A) entertain
    (B) entertained
    (C) entertaining
    (D) entertainment

Nevertheless, going out to the movies is still a popular way to spend a weekend evening. Many people enjoy going to movie theaters because they like to see new movies as soon as they __________. They may also prefer to spend an evening out in the __________ atmosphere

12. (A) release
    (B) released
    (C) are released
    (D) will be released

13. (A) lively
    (B) urgent
    (C) thorough
    (D) constant

of a public place rather than quietly at home.

If you are looking for an activity that the whole family can enjoy, consider visiting one of our city's fine museums. It is the perfect way to __________ fun with education. Depending on your family's

14. (A) separate
    (B) combine
    (C) rehearse
    (D) subscribe

interests, you might __________ to visit a science, history, or art museum. If your children are older,

15. (A) subscribe
    (B) divide
    (C) decide
    (D) entertain

they will want to visit exhibits that particularly interest them and take the time to give each one a __________ look. Younger children have a shorter attention span. Museums with interactive exhibits

16. (A) thorough
    (B) through
    (C) thought
    (D) though

are best for them.

The new play, *Sunflower Sunset*, opened at the Westwood Playhouse last night. A lot of effort went into this production. The actors ___________

17. (A) rehearse
    (B) rehearsed
    (C) will rehearse
    (D) are rehearsing

for months, and an elaborate set was constructed. Unfortunately, this effort could not save the dull dialogue. It was easy to see that the ___________ was bored—snoring was heard throughout the theater,

18. (A) director
    (B) performer
    (C) audience
    (D) entertainment

and many people left before the end of the play. The actors made a fine effort with their ___________, but the best acting in the world cannot

19. (A) perform
    (B) performer
    (C) performable
    (D) performance

save a poorly written play.

Lesson 46: Doctor's Office

WORDS TO LEARN

- annually
- appointment
- assess
- diagnose
- effective
- instrument
- manage
- prevent
- recommendation
- record
- refer
- serious

Study the following definitions and examples.

1. **annually** adv., once a year
   a. Everyone should get a physical exam annually.
   b. A number of tests are provided annually by my insurance plan.
2. **appointment** n., arrangements for a meeting; a position in a profession
   a. To get the most out of your appointment, keep a log of your symptoms and concerns.
   b. The doctor holds an academic appointment at the university hospital and has a private practice.
3. **assess** v., to judge or evaluate
   a. It is a good idea to have a doctor assess your health every one or two years.
   b. The physical therapist assessed the amount of mobility Ms. Crowl had lost after her accident.
4. **diagnose** v., to recognize a disease; to analyze the nature of something
   a. After looking at the patient's test results, the doctor diagnosed the lump as benign.
   b. She diagnosed the problem as a failure to follow the directions for taking the medication.
5. **effective** adj., producing the desired result; in force
   a. Howard was pleased to find that the diet recommended by his doctor was quite effective.
   b. The new policies, effective the beginning of the year, change the cost to see the physician.
6. **instrument** n., a tool for precise work
   a. The pediatrician tried not to frighten the children with her strange-looking instruments.
   b. The senior physician carried his instruments in a black leather bag.
7. **manage** v., to handle; to deal with; to guide
   a. The head nurse's ability to manage her staff through a difficult time caught the hospital administrator's attention.
   b. By carefully managing their resources, the couple found the money for the elective surgery.
8. **prevent** v., to keep from happening; to hinder
   a. By encouraging teenagers not to smoke, doctors are hoping to prevent many cases of cancer.
   b. His full caseload prevented the doctor from taking on new patients.
9. **recommendation** n., advice; endorsement
   a. It is important to follow the doctor's recommendations if you want to improve your health.
   b. The professor gave her student a recommendation when he applied for a job at the hospital.
10. **record** n., an official copy of documents
    a. Ms. Han submitted a written request for her medical records.
    b. The records kept in the city archives showed that a high number of babies are born in the summer.
11. **refer** v., to direct for treatment or information; to mention
    a. I was referred to this specialist by the family practice nurse.
    b. As soon as Agnes referred to the failed treatment, everyone's mood soured.
12. **serious** adj., very bad or very important; not funny
    a. Sara's illness is serious, but the doctors say they can treat it.
    b. The patient felt nervous when he saw the serious expression on the doctor's face.

WORD FAMILIES

verb	assess	He was able to assess her health problems with the help of her detailed medical history.
noun	assessment	The specialist's assessment of the patient's condition was consistent with the general practitioner's.
adjective	assessable	That medical condition is not assessable by this laboratory test.

verb	diagnose	Her symptoms are overlapping, making it difficult to diagnose the exact cause of her chest pain.
noun	diagnosis	After hearing the doctor's diagnosis, Phil decided to get a second opinion.
adjective	diagnostic	The new X-ray suite has all the latest diagnostic equipment.

verb	prevent	By stopping smoking now, you may be able to prevent lung cancer.
noun	prevention	He made a career of disease prevention through mass vaccinations.
adjective	preventive	Eloise took preventive steps against gum disease by more thorough toothbrushing.

verb	recommend	I recommend that you have this test annually starting at age 40.
noun	recommendation	Against my doctor's recommendation, I decided to purchase the generic brand of medication.
adjective	recommendable	There is nothing particularly recommendable about this therapy over the other therapy I mentioned.

verb	record	The doctor records the patient's description of her symptoms in the patient's medical chart.
noun	record	When you apply for health insurance, the insurance company will probably want to look at your medical records.
adjective	recorded	After office hours there is a recorded message on the doctor's answering machine that gives an emergency telephone number.

noun	seriousness	Martha's doctor tried to make her understand the seriousness of her condition.
adjective	serious	Mr. Kim was relieved to find out that his disease was not serious.
adverb	seriously	The doctor spoke seriously with Arthur about the need to lose weight.

WORDS IN CONTEXT

Read the following passage and write the words in the blanks below.

annually	diagnosing	manage	record
appointment	effective	preventing	refer
assessment	instruments	recommend	serious

Sooner or later, everyone needs to go to the doctor's office. In fact, it's in your best interest to see your doctor at least (1) ____________. The better he or she knows you and your health, the more (2) _______________ your doctor can be. Most people need help in (3) _______________ routine medical problems they are experiencing, such as symptoms of colds and the flu, allergies, rashes, and earaches. Other times, people visit a doctor for help in (4) ___________ health problems from ever occurring, such as lowering their risk of heart attack or stroke by dieting or exercising.

When you arrive for your (5) _______________, the doctor's office staff will have ready a (6) _______________ of all your visits, so that the doctor has a complete reference of your health. The visit will begin with an (7) _______________ of your general health and a discussion of any problems that concern you.

The doctors may use a variety of (8) _______________ to get a closer look at you. The doctor will (9) _______________ your problem and (10) _______________ a treatment plan. The doctor may prescribe medication, (11) _______________ you to a specialist more experienced in treating your condition, or order tests to gain more information. In (12) _______________ cases, he or she may send you to the hospital for care.

WORD PRACTICE

Listening Comprehension

Track 47

PART 1 PHOTO

Look at the picture and listen to the sentences. Choose the sentence that best describes the picture.

1. Ⓐ Ⓑ Ⓒ Ⓓ

PART 2 QUESTION–RESPONSE

Listen to the question and the three responses. Choose the response that best answers the question.

2. Ⓐ Ⓑ Ⓒ   3. Ⓐ Ⓑ Ⓒ

PART 3 CONVERSATION

Listen to the dialogue. Then read each question and choose the best response.

4. What does the doctor recommend that the man do?
   - (A) Research diagnostic methods
   - (B) Visit patients
   - (C) See a specialist
   - (D) Check into the best hospital

5. When does the doctor say that the man should do this?
   - (A) This afternoon
   - (B) Before 10:00
   - (C) This month
   - (D) In ten months

6. What does the man ask the doctor to give him?
   - (A) An appointment
   - (B) A new diagnosis
   - (C) A special treatment
   - (D) A copy of his record

PART 4 TALK

Listen to the talk. Then read each question and choose the best answer.

7. What kind of job is being advertised?
   - (A) Doctor
   - (B) Office manager
   - (C) Director
   - (D) Office assistant

8. How can someone apply for this job?
   - (A) Send in a résumé
   - (B) Make an appointment
   - (C) Telephone the office
   - (D) Submit records

9. What is a benefit of the job?
   - (A) An annual doctor's appointment
   - (B) Three weeks of vacation a year
   - (C) A yearly salary raise
   - (D) Health insurance

Reading

PART 5 INCOMPLETE SENTENCES

Choose the word that best completes the sentence.

10. Luckily, the test results show no _______ damage from the accident.

    (A) assess
    (B) assessment
    (C) assessing
    (D) assessable

11. After seeing the test results, the doctor changed her original _______ of Roger's illness.

    (A) diagnosis
    (B) prevention
    (C) appointment
    (D) referral

12. The most effective way to treat illness is to _______ it from occurring in the first place.

    (A) refer
    (B) assess
    (C) manage
    (D) prevent

13. Gabriela did not consistently follow her doctor's _______ and her condition did not improve.

    (A) recommendations
    (B) recommendable
    (C) recommended
    (D) recommending

14. Jane's doctor asked her to _______ everything she ate for a week.

    (A) records
    (B) record
    (C) recording
    (D) recorded

15. Public health officials are just now realizing the _______ of this disease.

    (A) seriousness
    (B) serious
    (C) seriously
    (D) series

Welcome to the office of Dr. Shaw. The following office policies are in effect.

- Please check in with the receptionist when you arrive. If you were given a referral, please tell the receptionist the name of the doctor who ____ you.
  16.
- If you are a new patient, please have your former doctor forward your medical records to us. ____.
  17.
- We recognize that sometimes unexpected situations occur and you must cancel your ____. Cancellations must be made 24 hours ahead of time or you will be
  18.
  charged a fee.
- Please don't call us to find out the results of ____ tests. We will call
  19.
  you when the results are ready.
- Effective January 1, all bills must be paid in full at the time of your visit. We accept all major credit cards.

16. (A) will refer
    (B) did refer
    (C) referred
    (D) refers

17. (A) It is important for us to know your medical history.
    (B) We are acquainted with most of the doctors practicing in this city.
    (C) When making appointments, we generally give priority to current patients.
    (D) This is because we need to record your name, address, and emergency contact information.

18. (A) record
    (B) assessment
    (C) appointment
    (D) recommendation

19. (A) diagnose
    (B) diagnosis
    (C) diagnosed
    (D) diagnostic

PART 7 READING COMPREHENSION

Questions 20–24 refer to the following article.

Caring for Your Health

Your health is one of your most valuable assets, so caring for it properly is very important. Regular visits to the doctor can help prevent any health problems from becoming serious. You should visit your doctor annually if you are in good health. If you have certain health conditions or if your doctor recommends it, you may need more frequent appointments.

It is important to have a doctor you can trust. The best way to find one is to get a recommendation from a trustworthy person such as a friend or relative. Call to make an appointment several weeks or even a month ahead of time. When you call, you can also ask a few questions about the doctor's background, such as which university he got his degree from and how long he has been practicing in the area. You will also want to find out which hospital the doctor is affiliated with. When you arrive for your appointment, make sure you bring a copy of your medical records with you.

When you meet with the doctor, you will want to ask him what his approach to treatment is and what diagnostic tools he uses. This way you can find out something about his skills, as well as whether or not he is a person you can talk to and feel comfortable with. Also, take a look around the office. Is it comfortable and organized? Do the instruments look clean and well-maintained?

If your appointment goes well and you feel comfortable with the doctor, then don't forget to make an appointment for your next physical before you leave the office. If you have any doubts, look around for another doctor. Having a good doctor is an essential part of your health care plan.

20. Who is this article for?
    (A) Patients
    (B) Doctors
    (C) Hospital staff
    (D) Medical equipment salespeople

21. How often should a healthy person visit the doctor?
    (A) Once a month
    (B) Twice a month
    (C) Once a year
    (D) Twice a year

22. What is the best way to find a good doctor?
    (A) Look in the phone book
    (B) Call the hospital
    (C) Go to a university
    (D) Ask a friend

23. The word *records* in the second paragraph, line 7, is closest in meaning to
    (A) plans.
    (B) documents.
    (C) descriptions.
    (D) instructions.

24. The word *instruments* in the third paragraph, line 5, is closest in meaning to
    (A) equipment.
    (B) furniture.
    (C) environment.
    (D) clothing.

Lesson 47: Dentist's Office

WORDS TO LEARN

- aware
- catch up
- distraction
- encouragement
- evident
- habit
- illuminate
- irritate
- overview
- position
- regularly
- restore

Study the following definitions and examples.

1. **aware** adj., having knowledge
   a. I was not aware that flossing my teeth could prevent a buildup of plaque.
   b. My dentist made me aware that I should have an appointment twice a year.
2. **catch up** v., to bring up to date
   a. My dentist likes to take time to catch up before she starts the examination.
   b. The dental assistant caught up on her paperwork in between patients.
3. **distraction** n., the act of being turned away from the focus
   a. To provide a distraction from the noise, Luisa's dentist offered her a pair of earphones.
   b. My dentist provides distractions like television, which take my mind off the procedure.
4. **encouragement** n., inspiration or support
   a. The perfect checkup was certainly encouragement to keep up my good dental hygiene.
   b. Let me offer you some encouragement about your crooked teeth.
5. **evident** adj., easily seen or understood; obvious
   a. The presence of a wisdom tooth was not evident until the dentist started to examine the patient.
   b. Unfortunately, his poor dental hygiene is evident from a distance.
6. **habit** n., a customary manner or practice
   a. The toddler's father stressed the importance of toothbrushing in hopes of establishing a good habit.
   b. The patient had a habit of grinding his teeth during his sleep.
7. **illuminate** v., to provide or brighten with light
   a. The dark recesses of the mouth can only be seen clearly when illuminated with a lamp.
   b. Let me turn on more lights to properly illuminate the back teeth.
8. **irritate** v., to chafe or inflame; to bother
   a. The broken tooth rubbed against my tongue, irritating it.
   b. Hannah's gums are irritated by foods that are very cold or very hot.
9. **overview** n., a summary; a survey; a quick look
   a. I did a quick overview of your teeth and they look in good shape.
   b. An overview of your dental records shows a history of problems.
10. **position** n., the place where something is; the way in which something is placed or arranged
    a. Let me tilt your head to a more comfortable position for you.
    b. The position of the chair can be adjusted to a range of heights.
11. **regularly** adv., occurring at fixed intervals
    a. She brushes regularly after every meal.
    b. I have to remind my son regularly to brush his teeth.
12. **restore** v., to bring back to an original condition
    a. The cleaning restored the whiteness of my teeth.
    b. I will talk to my dentist about any procedure to restore the parts of my teeth that I have ground away.

WORD FAMILIES

verb	distract	The child is frightened by the instruments. Try to distract his attention while I get ready.
noun	distraction	The soothing background music was a pleasant distraction from the drilling sounds at the dentist's office.
adjective	distracted	The distracted patient left the office without paying her bill.

verb	encourage	My dentist has been encouraging me to see a specialist about my gum problem.
noun	encouragement	Although the cleaning routine recommended by the dentist was tedious, with some encouragement, Richard was able to follow it regularly.
adjective	encouraging	It was encouraging to find out that I had no serious problems at my last dental checkup.

noun	evidence	The dentist found evidence of decay on my wisdom tooth.
adjective	evident	My lack of dental hygiene was evident even without a checkup.
adverb	evidently	Proper flossing evidently worked, since my gums are now in good health.

noun	habit	I'm trying to start the habit of flossing at least once a day.
adjective	habitual	His habitual coffee drinking stained his teeth.
adverb	habitually	Jack is habitually late for his appointments, which forced the receptionist to scold him.

verb	irritate	My dentist was late for my appointment, which irritated me, especially since he did not apologize.
noun	irritation	I have an irritation on the inside of my mouth that won't heal.
adjective	irritating	Matthew decided to visit the dentist because of an irritating gum problem.

noun	regularity	Visiting the dentist with regularity is an important part of maintaining good dental health.
adjective	regular	Many dental problems can be avoided by following a regular cleaning routine.
adverb	regularly	I haven't been visiting the dentist regularly.

WORDS IN CONTEXT

Read the following passage and write the words in the blanks below.

aware	encourage	illuminates	position
catch up	evident	irritates	regularly
distraction	habit	overview	restores

At least twice a year, Toshiro makes an appointment with his dentist. He's (1) ______________ that taking good care of his teeth and seeing a dentist can help prevent the buildup of tartar and plaque that could cause serious problems later.

The dentist starts the appointment by looking over Toshiro's chart, which details all the work that has been done on his teeth, as a way to (2) ______________ on Toshiro's dental health. Toshiro brushes (3) ______________, but is not consistent about flossing. His dentist is trying to (4) ______________ a better flossing (5) ______________ by demonstrating some easy-to-use techniques.

When the dentist is ready to look into Toshiro's mouth, she adjusts the height and (6) ______________ of the chair to make sure she can see all of Toshiro's teeth. A bright light (7) ______________ Toshiro's eyes, but (8) ______________ the dark places in the back of his mouth. The dentist does a quick (9) ______________ of Toshiro's mouth, looking for any obvious problems, such as a cavity or a broken tooth. The dentist asks if Toshiro has been having any problems, like tooth pain, bleeding, or soreness.

Sometimes, problems in the mouth are quite (10) ______________ and can be seen by the dentist's trained eye. But other times, the dentist will take X-rays to make certain there are no problems in areas she cannot see, such as under the gum line or inside a tooth.

The dentist then goes to work, repairing any damage. She then (11) ______________ the natural color to his teeth with a thorough cleaning. The noise of the drills and cleaners can upset some patients, so Toshiro's dentist is kind enough to supply earphones to provide a (12) ______________.

WORD PRACTICE

Listening Comprehension

Track 48

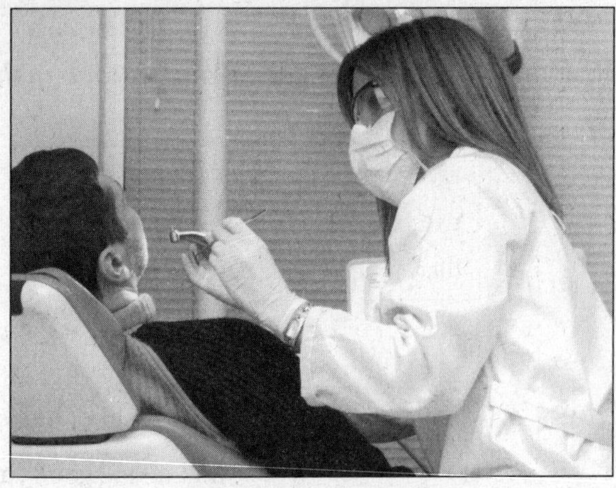

PART 1 PHOTO

Look at the picture and listen to the sentences.
Choose the sentence that best describes the picture.

1. Ⓐ Ⓑ Ⓒ Ⓓ

PART 2 QUESTION–RESPONSE

Listen to the question and the three responses. Choose the response that best answers the question.

2. Ⓐ Ⓑ Ⓒ

3. Ⓐ Ⓑ Ⓒ

PART 3 CONVERSATION

Listen to the dialogue. Then read each question and choose the best response.

4. What does the dentist recommend that the patient do?
   (A) Visit her office more regularly
   (B) Shop at a certain store
   (C) Review his records
   (D) Talk about his concerns

5. What does the patient want?
   (A) Shinier teeth
   (B) A cup of coffee
   (C) A copy of his records
   (D) Fillings in his cavities

6. When does the patient want an appointment?
   (A) This afternoon
   (B) Tonight
   (C) Next week
   (D) Next month

PART 4 TALK

Listen to the talk. Then read each question and choose the best answer.

7. What product is advertised?
   (A) False teeth
   (B) A tooth whitener
   (C) Chewing gum
   (D) A toothbrush

8. What are the customers asked to do?
   (A) Use the product for just two days
   (B) Change their cleaning habits
   (C) Use the product every night
   (D) Visit the dentist

9. Where can the product be bought?
   (A) At a store
   (B) At the dentist's office
   (C) From a sales representative
   (D) Online

Reading

PART 5 INCOMPLETE SENTENCES

Choose the word that best completes the sentence.

10. The dentist tells jokes while he is working in order to _______ patients from their fears.

    (A) encourage
    (C) restore
    (B) illuminate
    (D) distract

11. My dentist always _______ me to floss more regularly.

    (A) encouraging
    (C) encourages
    (B) encouragement
    (D) encourage

12. It was _______ from the X-rays that I needed dental work.

    (A) evident
    (C) evidence
    (B) evidently
    (D) evidential

13. Knowing his _______ tidiness, I'm not surprised to learn that David flosses three times a day.

    (A) habit
    (C) habitually
    (B) habitual
    (D) habitualness

14. Dr. Jones regularly reads dental journals so that he can catch up _______ the latest developments in dental care.

    (A) from
    (C) on
    (B) for
    (D) in

15. _______ visits to the dentist are necessary for maintaining good dental health.

    (A) Regularly
    (C) Regulate
    (B) Regular
    (D) Regulates

PART 6 TEXT COMPLETION

The state of dental health in our nation is a cause for concern according to Dr. James Hibbard, president of the National Society of Dentists. Dr. Hibbard expressed his concerns in an article appearing this week in *Our Dental Health* magazine, which is distributed among dentists and other health care workers throughout the country. "Most people don't have good dental ____,"
16.
he says. ____, When people aren't careful about keeping their teeth clean, Dr. Hibbard
17.
warns, the result is ____ gums, cavities, and even tooth loss. "Dentists should be firmer
18.
about ____ their patients to maintain their dental health. Dentists need to do more
19.
education with their patients, and patients need to follow their dentists' advice," recommends Dr. Hibbard.

16. (A) positions
    (B) habits
    (C) overviews
    (D) distractions

17. (A) Many people are aware of the recommendation to visit their dentist twice a year.
    (B) A good dentist can help patients overcome their fear of dental work.
    (C) The cost of dental work can be prohibitively high.
    (D) People need to brush their teeth regularly.

18. (A) irritate
    (B) irritant
    (C) irritated
    (D) irritation

19. (A) encourage
    (B) encourages
    (C) encouraging
    (D) to encourage

PART 7 READING COMPREHENSION

Questions 20–24 refer to the following advertisement and e-mail message.

ATTENTION DENTISTS!

You know how important it is to have the best equipment for your office. So why settle for less? Evidence shows that outdated, under-functioning equipment can reduce a dentist's efficiency by 50 percent or more. The Acme Dental Supply Company offers state-of-the-art dental equipment at affordable rates.

- Our special lighted dental mirrors illuminate all tooth surfaces better than any other light on the market. These mirrors are on sale this week at just $150 per set of three. That's 25 percent off the usual price.
- Our automated patient chairs automatically adjust their positions so that you can always work comfortably, without back or shoulder strain. Available in several models and colors.
- Our Dental Office Systems computer software streamlines record keeping so that you will never fall behind with your paperwork. Full version available at $500. Upgrade is $175.
- Our special edition Dental Office CD set provides hours of soothing music that will keep your patients relaxed. You can focus on your work without being distracted by patient anxiety. Choose from String Quartet, Contemporary Jazz, or Sounds of Nature. $35 per boxed set.

To: pdaly@dentaloffice.com
From: drbarb@dentaloffice.com
Subject: office equipment
attach: Acme Dental Supply

Peter,

Take a look at the attached ad. I think we should order a few things. I like the lighted mirrors and probably could use five or six sets, but let's spend no more than $300 on them for now, so I can see how well they work first. We probably need the upgrade for the record keeping software, too. It will help you stay caught up with the patient records. I think we could do without those CDs, though, don't you? We do better with the radio. You might as well go ahead and order paper, envelopes, and anything else you need for the front office at the same time.

Thanks,

Barbara

Barbara Hendricks, DDS

20. Who is Peter Daly?
    (A) A dentist
    (B) A dental equipment salesman
    (C) A dental patient
    (D) A dentist's office manager

21. How many sets of mirrors will Dr. Hendricks order now?
    (A) Two
    (B) Three
    (C) Five
    (D) Six

22. Which Acme product is sold to relax patients?
    (A) Computer games
    (B) Automated chairs
    (C) Special lights
    (D) CD sets

23. The word *illuminate* in the first letter, second paragraph, line 1, is closest in meaning to
    (A) smooth.
    (B) light.
    (C) clean.
    (D) repair.

24. The word *distracted* in the first letter, fifth paragraph, line 4, is closest in meaning to
    (A) interested.
    (B) entertained.
    (C) bothered.
    (D) introduced.

Lesson 48: Health Insurance

WORDS TO LEARN

- alternative
- aspect
- concern
- emphasize
- incur
- personnel
- policy
- portion
- regardless
- reimburse
- suit
- treatment

Study the following definitions and examples.

1. **alternative** adj., allowing a choice; other
   a. To lower the cost of health insurance, my employer chose an alternative method of insuring us.
   b. I'd like to discuss alternative treatments before I agree to anything.
2. **aspect** n., a feature element; an appearance
   a. The right to choose their own doctor is an important aspect of health coverage for many people.
   b. The aspect of private insurance that most people dislike is the large amount of paperwork.
3. **concern** n., anxiety; worry
   a. Whenever I have health concerns, I call my doctor.
   b. The rising cost of health care is of great concern to many people.
4. **emphasize** v., to stress
   a. The nurse emphasized the importance of eating a balanced diet.
   b. The new insurance plan emphasizes wellness by providing reimbursement for health club memberships.
5. **incur** v., to become subject to
   a. I incurred substantial expenses that my health plan does not cover.
   b. Dominic incurs the cost of a co-payment at each doctor's visit.
6. **personnel** n., a group of employees or workers
   a. The office manager insisted that she needed more personnel to finish the project on time.
   b. The employee went to see the director of personnel about taking an extended leave of absence.
7. **policy** n., a set of rules and regulations
   a. Company policy did not provide for overtime pay.
   b. The company's insurance policy did not cover cosmetic surgery.
8. **portion** n., a section or quantity within a larger thing; a part of a whole
   a. My health insurance covers only a portion of my health care costs.
   b. I am keeping a record of the portion of my income I spend on health care.
9. **regardless** adv., in spite of
   a. Regardless of the cost, we all need health insurance.
   b. I keep going to the same doctor, regardless of the fact that she does not take my pain seriously.
10. **reimburse** v., pay back money spent for a specific purpose
    a. The insurance company may not reimburse you for the entire cost of your medical care.
    b. The insurance company reimbursed Donald for the cost of his trip to the emergency room.
11. **suit** v., to be appropriate; to satisfy
    a. This insurance plan doesn't suit our family as it doesn't cover well-baby care.
    b. I have finally found a health plan that suits my needs.
12. **treatment** n., care provided for a medical condition
    a. Karl's health greatly improved under his new doctor's treatment.
    b. The treatment that the doctor recommended was expensive and not really effective.

WORD FAMILIES

noun	alternative	This medication causes headaches, so I'd like to find an alternative.
adjective	alternative	I could not meet with the insurance agent on that day, so I suggested an alternative date.
adverb	alternatively	We could continue paying the high rates charged by this insurance company. Alternatively, we could look for a new insurer.

verb	concern	It concerns me that we haven't been able to find a suitable health insurance plan.
noun	concern	A good doctor will pay attention to any and all concerns the patient expresses about his or her health.
adjective	concerned	I am concerned about the limited benefits this insurance plan offers.

verb	emphasize	The plan representative emphasized the need for a second medical opinion.
noun	emphasis	The emphasis of the health plan is on staying well.
adjective	emphatic	Hassan made an emphatic appeal to the medical insurance director.

verb	reimburse	The insurance company should reimburse you within one month.
noun	reimbursement	Paula was disappointed with the small reimbursement she received from her insurance company.
adjective	reimbursable	Before you pay for an expensive treatment, you should check with your insurance company to find out if it is reimbursable.

verb	suit	I'm dropping my health plan because it does not suit my needs.
adjective	suitable	Not every kind of health insurance is suitable for every family.
adverb	suitably	The errors on my insurance statement were caught and suitably fixed.

verb	treat	The best way to treat a cold is to stay in bed for a few days.
noun	treatment	Sam does not like to take drugs and prefers to use natural treatments.
adjective	treatable	The doctor told Marya that her condition was treatable with diet and exercise.

WORDS IN CONTEXT

Read the following passage and write the words in the blanks below.

alternatives	emphasize	policy	reimbursement
aspect	incurs	portion	suitable
concerns	personnel	regardless	treatment

The cost and availability of health insurance is one of the greatest (1) ______________ of company (2) ______________. A covered employee should be familiar with the terms and conditions of the insurance (3) ______________. Although the insured pays a (4) ______________ of the cost of his or her coverage, the employer generally covers most of the cost.

Health insurance policies vary widely. A doctor may recommend a particular (5) ______________ for a medical condition, but it is the responsibility of the patient to make sure that it is covered by his or her insurance. Also, in some cases the insurance company pays the doctor directly, whereas in others the patient pays and then receives (6) ______________ from the insurance company later.

Although the company or association negotiates the most (7) ___________ terms they can, most experts (8) _____________ that employees should be on the lookout for (9) ______________ that might better suit their needs. (10) ______________ of the cost of premiums, the most important (11) ______________ of good health insurance is that it meets the needs of the insured and (12) ______________ the least possible cost for necessary procedures.

WORD PRACTICE

Listening Comprehension

Track 49

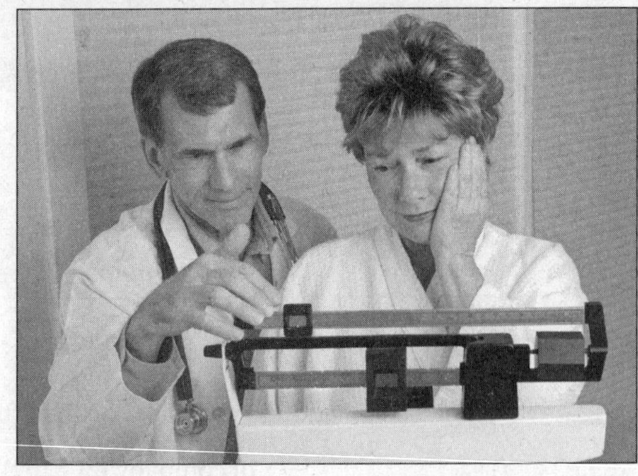

PART 1 PHOTO

Look at the picture and listen to the sentences. Choose the sentence that best describes the picture.

1. Ⓐ Ⓑ Ⓒ Ⓓ

PART 2 QUESTION–RESPONSE

Listen to the question and the three responses. Choose the response that best answers the question.

2. Ⓐ Ⓑ Ⓒ   3. Ⓐ Ⓑ Ⓒ

PART 3 CONVERSATION

Listen to the dialogue. Then read each question and choose the best response.

4. What will happen if the man sees a specialist without a referral?
   - (A) He will be dropped from his health plan.
   - (B) He will see only a portion of the bill.
   - (C) He won't be provided with good care.
   - (D) He will pay a higher percentage of the cost.

5. When can the man get an appointment with his primary care provider?
   - (A) In three days
   - (B) In ten days
   - (C) In two weeks
   - (D) In three weeks

6. What does the woman recommend to the man?
   - (A) See a specialist soon
   - (B) See his primary care provider first
   - (C) Get a treatment for his headache
   - (D) Get a special procedure

PART 4 TALK

Listen to the talk. Then read each question and choose the best answer.

7. Why has a new health plan been chosen?
   - (A) To help people save money
   - (B) Because the old plan is no longer available
   - (C) To get more benefits
   - (D) Because people are interested in alternative medicine

8. Who will the new plan be available to?
   - (A) Only people who earn a low salary
   - (B) Anyone who is interested
   - (C) Only people who have special health concerns
   - (D) Just those who have worked at the company for a long time

9. When will the new health plan be in effect?
   - (A) Today
   - (B) In two weeks
   - (C) In several months
   - (D) Next year

Reading

PART 5 INCOMPLETE SENTENCES

Choose the word that best completes the sentence.

10. The insurance company will _______ you for the cost of any treatment that is on their list.

    (A) reimburse (C) to reimburse
    (B) reimburses (D) reimbursing

11. Fortunately, a large _______ of the costs for treating my illness will be covered by my health insurance.

    (A) aspect (C) portion
    (B) treatment (D) policy

12. It _______ me that our company is not willing to look for an alternative to our current health insurance plan.

    (A) concern (C) concerns
    (B) concerned (D) concerning

13. I'm really pleased that my health plan provider is paying for my gym membership as a way to _______ its concern for my health.

    (A) emphasis (C) emphatic
    (B) emphasize (D) emphasizing

14. I am not happy with this health insurance company, but for the moment I have no other _______.

    (A) alter (C) alternatively
    (B) alternate (D) alternative

15. This insurance policy is not _______ for our family because it doesn't cover the cost of health care for our children.

    (A) treatable (C) emphatic
    (B) suitable (D) regardful

Memo

To: All personnel
From: Human Resources Office
Re: Health Insurance

Many of you have expressed an interest in certain types of health care ____ (16.) such as acupuncture and massage. In response to this, we have negotiated a new health insurance ____ (17.) with our provider, and benefits now include a discount on visits to acupuncturists, massage therapists, and naturopaths. In order to take advantage of this discount, you need only to present your insurance card on your first visit to an approved provider. Please be advised that this discount is allowed only on visits to providers from the approved list. ____ (18.). Please notify this office if you would like a copy of the list of approved ____ (19.) health care providers.

16. (A) treat
    (B) treats
    (C) treatments
    (D) treatable

17. (A) policy
    (B) concern
    (C) aspect
    (D) personnel

18. (A) If you have a concern about a particular health problem, please call your regular doctor.
    (B) Our health insurance company will not reimburse you for visits to anyone else.
    (C) Some health insurance companies do not pay for these types of treatments.
    (D) Appointments can be made to suit your convenience.

19. (A) alter
    (B) alternate
    (C) alternative
    (D) alternatively

PART 7 READING COMPREHENSION

Questions 20–24 refer to the following notice.

Workshop

Did you know that full medical coverage is available to all company employees and their families, regardless of position or salary? If you need to know more, attend the workshop that will be held in Conference Room 3 next Friday at 11:00. All aspects of our health care policy will be explained. This workshop will be particularly useful to new personnel, although all are welcome. However, you must register to attend. Please contact the Human Resources Office before 5:00 Thursday.

We will go over the various alternative plans available to company employees and discuss what criteria you need to consider in selecting the plan that best suits your needs. We will explain exactly what is covered and what is not under each alternative, and what portion of each doctor's visit or treatment that must be paid out of pocket. We will leave time at the end for a question-and-answer session to make sure that all your concerns are addressed. This workshop will last two hours.

20. What is the workshop about?
    (A) Choosing a doctor
    (B) Health insurance
    (C) Alternative medicine
    (D) Planning a medical treatment

21. Who can attend the workshop?
    (A) Anyone
    (B) New personnel only
    (C) The Human Resources staff
    (D) Only employees with families

22. What time will the workshop end?
    (A) 11:00
    (B) 1:00
    (C) 2:00
    (D) 5:00

23. The word *suits* in the second paragraph, line 3, is closest in meaning to
    (A) depends.
    (B) satisfies.
    (C) expresses.
    (D) emphasizes.

24. The word *concerns* in the second paragraph, line 7, is closest in meaning to
    (A) assignments.
    (B) answers.
    (C) benefits.
    (D) worries.

Lesson 49: Hospitals

WORDS TO LEARN

- accompany
- admit
- authorize
- designate
- escort
- identify
- mission
- pertinent
- procedure
- result
- statement
- surgery

Study the following definitions and examples.

1. **accompany** v., to go with
   a. Always have someone accompany you to a doctor's appointment when serious treatments will be discussed.
   b. Detailed instructions accompany most medications.
2. **admit** v., to permit to enter
   a. The injured patient was admitted to the unit directly from the emergency room.
   b. The staff refused to admit the patient until he had proof of insurance.
3. **authorize** v., to approve
   a. You must check with your insurance company to confirm it will authorize an extended hospital stay.
   b. We cannot share the test results with you until we have been authorized to do so by your doctor.
4. **designate** v., to indicate or specify
   a. The labels on the bags designated the type of blood they contained.
   b. On her admittance form, Grandmother designated Aunt Tessa as her chief decision-maker.
5. **escort** n., a person accompanying another to guide or protect
   a. Let's see if there is an escort available to take you to the parking garage.
   b. You cannot leave the unit on your own; you'll have to wait for an escort.
6. **identify** v., to ascertain the name or belongings of
   a. The tiny bracelets identified each baby in the nursery.
   b. Your records are all marked with your patient number to identify them in case of a mix-up.
7. **mission** n., an inner calling to pursue an activity or perform a service
   a. The hospital chaplain took as his mission to visit every patient admitted each day.
   b. The mission of the nurses in the unit was to make sure the patients got well as soon as possible.
8. **pertinent** adj., having relevance to the matter at hand
   a. You should mention any pertinent health issues to the staff before you are admitted for surgery.
   b. The patient's health record contained pertinent information, like the dates of all his inoculations.
9. **procedure** n., a series of steps taken to accomplish an end
   a. The surgical procedure can now be done in half the amount of time it took even five years ago.
   b. Call the hospital to schedule this procedure for tomorrow.
10. **result** n., an outcome
    a. Your lab results won't be ready for hours.
    b. The scientific results prove that the new procedure is not significantly safer than the traditional one.
11. **statement** n., an accounting showing an amount due; a bill
    a. The billing statement was filed with the insurance company last month.
    b. Check with your doctor's office for an original statement; we cannot process a faxed copy.
12. **surgery** n., a medical procedure that involves cutting into the body
    a. The development of medical technology has made surgery much easier on the patient.
    b. Miranda had to stay in the hospital for several days following the surgery.

WORD FAMILIES

verb	admit	The patients lined the hospital corridors waiting to be admitted.
noun	admittance	Your admittance to the hospital is dependent on your showing proof that you can pay the bills.
noun	admission	We keep careful records of all hospital admissions.

verb	authorize	Your doctor has to authorize these tests before we can proceed with them.
noun	authority	Before major surgery, it is a good idea to give decision-making authority to a close relative in case something happens to you.
noun	authorization	The nurse could not submit an authorization over the phone; it had to be done in writing.

verb	designate	The hospital administrator designated a team to create an emergency preparedness plan.
noun	designation	The designation of the hospital as one of the best in the region certainly helped its marketing efforts.
noun	designator	The national health service is the sole designator of which hospitals will get the grants.

verb	identify	If you identify your valuables, the nurse will give them back to you.
noun	identification	Please remember to bring some form of identification with you when you check in at the hospital.
adjective	identifiable	The red cross on the hospital's helicopter landing pad was identifiable from the air.

noun	pertinence	The doctor was not certain about the pertinence of many of the details in the patient's long medical history.
adjective	pertinent	The doctor will ask you for pertinent information, such as medications that you are currently taking.

noun	surgery	I have been feeling much better ever since I had surgery done on my back.
noun	surgeon	You will have an appointment with the surgeon so that she can explain the procedure to you.
adjective	surgical	It is important to keep surgical equipment absolutely clean.

WORDS IN CONTEXT

Read the following passage and write the words in the blanks below.

accompany	designated	mission	results
admission	escort	pertinent	statement
authorization	identification	procedures	surgeon

Hospitals have a (1) ______________ to provide patients with high-quality medical care. Everyone on staff will make sure that you get the best possible treatment for your condition.

When you arrive at the hospital, you should have with you all the (2) ________________ information needed to be admitted, like your insurance information and copies of X-rays and other test (3) ____________________, even if they were taken at another facility. Bring your insurance card and any referral or (4) ________________ form from your doctor. You should also have some form of (5) ______________ with a photo. You will also need to sign an agreement regarding treatment consent. Once you arrive, there is usually a concierge who will assist you with the (6) _____________ process.

Some (7) ______________ are simple and don't require an overnight stay in the hospital. You are given a while to rest and recover, and the (8) _____________ may discuss home care with you before you leave the hospital. Then an (9) ________________ takes you to the lobby and makes sure there is someone waiting for you to (10) ______________ you home. Driving yourself, even after a simple surgery, is usually not recommended. After you leave the hospital, you will receive a (11) ______________ from the hospital for the charges your insurer does not cover. Your insurance policy will outline any amount for which you may be responsible.

If you have questions about fees or payments, contact the hospital. Most hospitals have (12) ______________ staff to help with the payment process.

WORD PRACTICE

Listening Comprehension

Track 50

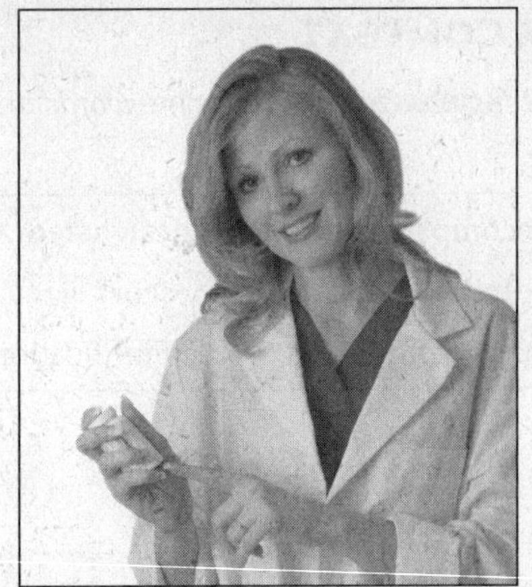

PART 1 PHOTO

Look at the picture and listen to the sentences.
Choose the sentence that best describes the picture.

1. Ⓐ Ⓑ Ⓒ Ⓓ

PART 2 QUESTION–RESPONSE

Listen to the question and the three responses. Choose the response that best answers the question.

2. Ⓐ Ⓑ Ⓒ 3. Ⓐ Ⓑ Ⓒ

PART 3 CONVERSATION

Listen to the dialogue. Then read each question and choose the best response.

4. What is the woman's complaint?
   (A) The records weren't delivered on time.
   (B) Her husband didn't get an identification card.
   (C) The computer system broke down.
   (D) Her husband's records got mixed up.

5. Who is the man?
   (A) A hospital administrator
   (B) A hospital patient
   (C) A doctor
   (D) A nurse

6. Why was the woman's husband in the hospital?
   (A) For a surgical procedure
   (B) To change his medications
   (C) For tests
   (D) To visit a friend

PART 4 TALK

Listen to the talk. Then read each question and choose the best answer.

7. Who is the speaker?
   (A) A doctor
   (B) A lab technician
   (C) A nurse
   (D) An insurance agent

8. When will the surgery take place?
   (A) In eight days
   (B) In a week
   (C) In ten days
   (D) In 23 days

9. What will the listener do with the paperwork?
   (A) Prepare it
   (B) Give it to the nurse
   (C) Take it to the lab
   (D) Submit it to the insurance company

Reading

PART 5 INCOMPLETE SENTENCES

Choose the word that best completes the sentence.

10. Before my father was _______ to the hospital, he had to undergo a series of tests.

(A) admit (C) admittance
(B) admitted (D) admissions

11. Will your insurance company _______ a visit to a specialist?

(A) authorize (C) authority
(B) authorization (D) authorizing

12. As a precaution, it's wise to _______ someone in your family to make health care decisions for you in case there is a time that you cannot.

(A) designation (C) designator
(B) designate (D) designated

13. Your X-rays will have your name and social security number printed on them, so we can easily _______ them as yours.

(A) identifiably (C) identifiable
(B) identification (D) identify

14. The inability to move my elbow was an unfortunate and unexpected _______ of the surgery I had last month.

(A) statement (C) result
(B) procedure (D) mission

15. The billing statement from the hospital _______ by a detailed explanation of what the patient owed and what the insurance company would pay.

(A) was accompanied (C) accompanied
(B) was accompanying (D) accompanies

PART 6 TEXT COMPLETION

CITY HOSPITAL ADMISSIONS PROCEDURES

—When you arrive, check in with the nurse on duty at the front desk.

—All patients must have a signed ____ (16.) from a doctor before entering the hospital. Please give the signed form to the nurse.

—The nurse will also need to see a form of identification and proof of insurance. We cannot ____ (17.) anyone to the hospital without these. There will be no exceptions.

—The nurse will complete the pertinent paperwork and assign you to a room.

—Please wait in the designated area. A hospital staff member ____ (18.) you to your room.

—Family members are not permitted to accompany patients to their rooms. ____ (19.).

A schedule of visiting hours is posted in the main lobby.

16. (A) author
    (B) authorize
    (C) authority
    (D) authorization

17. (A) identify
    (B) admit
    (C) designate
    (D) accompany

18. (A) escorts
    (B) will escort
    (C) is escorting
    (D) has escorted

19. (A) They can ask the receptionist for use of a wheelchair.
    (B) They may carry the patient's personal belongings to their room.
    (C) They must wait until the usual visiting hours to see their loved ones.
    (D) They should use the designated elevators when taking patients upstairs.

PART 7 READING COMPREHENSION

Questions 20–24 refer to the following two e-mail messages.

To: Annabelle Pope
From: Henry Rice
Subject: Surgery

Hi Annabelle,

I was wondering if you could help me out with something. My doctor has recommended that I get knee replacement surgery. I am trying to identify the best hospital for this sort of procedure. My doctor says she usually recommends City Hospital, but I have heard that Upstate Hospital specializes in this kind of surgery. You had a similar procedure last year, didn't you? I think you broke your knee, or was it your elbow? Which hospital did you go to? Were you satisfied with the results of your treatment, and were you well cared for by the staff? I would appreciate the benefit of your advice. I need to make a decision soon since my doctor thinks this should be done before another month goes by. Thanks.

Henry

To: Henry Rice
From: Annabelle Pope
Subject: Re: Surgery

Hi Henry,

I am sorry you need surgery, but I am sure you will feel it is worth it. I had my procedure done at Upstate Hospital, and I would recommend that place to anyone. The procedure I had was similar to yours, except it was my hip, not my knee. My surgeon was excellent, and I received good care from all the staff. The mission of the hospital is to provide the highest level of care possible, and the entire staff works hard to fulfill that mission. I was originally told that I would need to be in the hospital for a week, but when it became clear that I wouldn't be recovered enough by that time, the doctor didn't hesitate to keep me there for an extra three days. They wouldn't permit me to go home until they were sure I was ready. I really think Upstate is the best hospital for your surgery. Let me know when it is scheduled, and I will visit you there.

Annabelle

20. What does Henry ask Annabelle to do?
    (A) Recommend a hospital
    (B) Perform surgery
    (C) Visit him in the hospital
    (D) Talk to his doctor

21. Why was Annabelle in the hospital last year?
    (A) For a broken knee
    (B) For a broken elbow
    (C) For a hip replacement
    (D) For a knee replacement

22. How long was Annabelle in the hospital?
    (A) Three days
    (B) A week
    (C) Ten days
    (D) A month

23. The word *results* in the first e-mail, line 10, is closest in meaning to
    (A) outcome.
    (B) process.
    (C) nature.
    (D) price.

24. The word *mission* in the second e-mail, line 7, is closest in meaning to
    (A) rule.
    (B) goal.
    (C) demand.
    (D) requirement.

Lesson 50: Pharmacy

WORDS TO LEARN

- consult
- control
- convenient
- detect
- factor
- interaction
- limit
- monitor
- potential
- sample
- sense
- volunteer

Study the following definitions and examples.

1. **consult** v., to seek advice or information of
   a. The doctor consulted with a specialist before writing a new prescription.
   b. May I consult with you about a drug interaction case I have?
2. **control** v., to exercise authority or power over
   a. To control the cost of this medication, you may get the generic version.
   b. Please take your medication every day to control your high blood pressure.
3. **convenient** adj., suited or favorable to one's purpose; easy to reach
   a. Is this a convenient location for you to pick up your prescription?
   b. It is convenient to have a pharmacy right across the street from my doctor's office.
4. **detect** v., to discover or ascertain
   a. My doctor put me through some simple tests to detect if I have asthma.
   b. I have to keep track of my sleep patterns to detect how many times I get up in the night.
5. **factor** n., a contribution to an accomplishment, a result, or a process
   a. Taking medications as directed is an important factor in getting well.
   b. Could my cat be a factor contributing to my asthma?
6. **interaction** n., a mutual activity
   a. My pharmacist was concerned about the interaction of the two medications I was prescribed.
   b. The interaction between the patient and the doctor showed a high level of trust.
7. **limit** n., the point beyond which something cannot proceed
   a. My prescription has a limit of three refills.
   b. My health plan sets a limit on which health care providers I can see without their permission.
8. **monitor** v., to keep track of
   a. The nurse practitioner carefully monitors the number of medications her patients are taking.
   b. The patient had weekly appointments so that the doctor could monitor her progress.
9. **potential** adj., capable of being but not yet in existence; possible
   a. To avoid any potential side effects, be sure to tell your doctor all the drugs you are currently taking.
   b. Given the potential delay in getting reimbursed by the health plan, why don't we just fill one prescription today?
10. **sample** n., a portion, piece, or segment that is representative of a whole
    a. The pharmacist gave Myra a few free samples of the allergy medication.
    b. A sample of the people taking the medicine was surveyed to determine the side effects.
11. **sense** n., a judgment; an intellectual interpretation
    a. The doctor had a good sense about what the problem was but wanted to get a second opinion.
    b. I got the sense it would be better to get my prescription filled right away.
12. **volunteer** v., to perform a service by choice or without being asked
    a. My doctor volunteered to call the drugstore, so my medication would be waiting for me.
    b. Tom was feeling sick, so his son volunteered to pick up his prescription at the pharmacy.

WORD FAMILIES

verb	consult	Beatrice consulted her pharmacist about the number of different medications she is taking.
noun	consultation	Let me arrange a consultation with a specialist to discuss your heart problem and some possible medications.
adjective	consultative	This is a consultative process and you probably won't have a definitive answer immediately.

noun	convenience	The convenience of a 24-hour neighborhood pharmacy is not to be underestimated.
adjective	convenient	Many people shop there because of its convenient location.
adverb	conveniently	The pharmacy is conveniently located on my way home from work.

verb	detect	The laboratory test detected the presence of medication in his blood.
noun	detection	Early detection of diseases usually means that medications can be more effective.
adjective	detectable	After he took his medication faithfully for a few months and exercised more, Jack's disease was no longer detectable.

verb	limit	My health insurance company has severely limited the amount of money it will pay out for prescription medicine.
noun	limit	Even though that headache medicine does not require a prescription, there is a limit to how many times a day you should take it.
adjective	limited	The new drugstore on the corner really isn't convenient because of its limited hours of operation.

noun	potential	Be careful when taking this medication because it has the potential to make you feel sleepy.
adjective	potential	Margaret decided not to take the medicine the doctor had prescribed because of its potential side effects.
adverb	potentially	Many medications are potentially dangerous so it is important to take them exactly as prescribed by the doctor.

verb	volunteer	The pharmacist volunteers his services monthly at the free clinic for homeless people.
noun	volunteer	Volunteers bring filled prescriptions from the pharmacy to the homes of shut-ins.
adjective	voluntary	Your compliance with this new policy is completely voluntary, but we think it is in the public interest that you do so.

WORDS IN CONTEXT

Read the following passage and write the words in the blanks below.

consulting	detection	limit	samples
control	factors	monitor	sense
convenient	interactions	potential	volunteers

Yoko is having trouble with seasonal allergies this fall. After (1) ______________ with her doctor, she decides to take medication on a regular basis to (2) ______________ her symptoms. Her doctor recommends the medication he thinks will work best and offers her a handful of (3) ______________ at no charge. For her long-term needs, Yoko will need to have a prescription filled. Her doctor (4) ______________ to call the pharmacy Yoko uses to order a supply, which will (5) ______________ the time she spends waiting for the prescription to be filled.

Yoko is new in town and does not know which pharmacy she wants to use. She knows that there is a drugstore near her apartment and one near where she works, but does not remember the operating hours for either. Yoko knows that (6) ______________ hours and location are important (7) ______________ in selecting a pharmacy. Although she can fill different prescriptions at different drugstores, it makes more (8) ______________ to Yoko to fill all of her medications at one location.

Some drugs can have harmful (9) ______________ when taken together. Usually, your doctor will prevent this sort of problem before it starts. But, if you see more than one doctor, it is hard to (10) ______________ the various medications you are taking. Having all your prescriptions filled at one location increases the chances that the pharmacist will detect a (11) ______________ drug interaction problem. This timely (12) ______________ can save your life.

WORD PRACTICE

Listening Comprehension

Track 51

PART 1 PHOTO

Look at the picture and listen to the sentences.
Choose the sentence that best describes the picture.

1. Ⓐ Ⓑ Ⓒ Ⓓ

PART 2 QUESTION–RESPONSE

Listen to the question and the three responses. Choose the response that best answers the question.

2. Ⓐ Ⓑ Ⓒ 3. Ⓐ Ⓑ Ⓒ

PART 3 CONVERSATION

Listen to the dialogue. Then read each question and choose the best response.

4. Whom is the man talking to?
   (A) A doctor
   (B) A pharmacist
   (C) His wife
   (D) His friend

5. What is the man's problem?
   (A) Headache
   (B) Backache
   (C) Broken hand
   (D) Broken nose

6. When will the man fill the prescription?
   (A) Today
   (B) Within two days
   (C) On the way to work
   (D) After trying the samples

PART 4 TALK

Listen to the talk. Then read each question and choose the best answer.

7. What is a possible side effect of the medication?
   (A) Sleepiness
   (B) Stomachaches
   (C) Fatigue
   (D) Headaches

8. How often should the patient take the medication?
   (A) Once a day
   (B) Two times a day
   (C) Three times a day
   (D) Four times a day

9. Why should the patient call the doctor in a few days?
   (A) To request more days off work
   (B) To report how the medication is working
   (C) To get pills for his headaches
   (D) To ask for more samples

Reading

PART 5 INCOMPLETE SENTENCES

Choose the word that best completes the sentence.

10. Would you please schedule the patient for a medical ______ tomorrow afternoon?

    (A) consult (B) consultation (C) consulting (D) consultative

11. Your prescription will be ready in an hour, if that's ______ for you.

    (A) conveniences (B) conveniently (C) convenience (D) convenient

12. The doctor ______ a potential problem during the examination, so he wants me to consult a specialist.

    (A) detected (B) limited (C) controlled (D) monitored

13. My doctor has decided to ______ the amount of medication I am taking.

    (A) limit (B) limited (C) limiting (D) limits

14. Inform the pharmacist of any other medications you are taking to avoid any ______ drug interactions.

    (A) limited (B) potential (C) voluntary (D) convenient

15. We desperately need ______ to help at the free clinic next month.

    (A) voluntary (B) volunteer (C) volunteers (D) volunteerism

CLOVERDALE PHARMACY

The neighborhood pharmacy that you can rely on!

Cloverdale is open 24 hours a day, seven days a week. ____ . You can rely on us in
16.
an emergency at any time of day. And, our schedule makes it ____ for busy working
17.
people to fill prescriptions after work or on weekends.

You're always safe with us! When you fill a prescription at Cloverdale, we keep a careful record. This way, we can easily ____ the medications you are taking and inform you
18.
of any potentially harmful interactions.

Do you need help selecting over-the-counter medications? Our pharmacists are available to ____ with you and help you choose the medications that suit your needs.
19.

Cloverdale Pharmacy. We're here to serve you.

16. (A) Unlike other pharmacies with limited schedules, we're open all the time.
    (B) Save time by ordering your prescription refills online for store pick up.
    (C) Our pharmacists fill your prescriptions quickly and accurately.
    (D) Our hours are posted on our website.

17. (A) convenient
    (B) convenience
    (C) conveniently
    (D) convention

18. (A) are monitored
    (B) be monitored
    (C) to monitor
    (D) monitor

19. (A) limit
    (B) consult
    (C) control
    (D) volunteer

PART 7 READING COMPREHENSION

Questions 20–24 refer to the following article.

Many people don't realize that their pharmacist is an important member of their health care team. If you always fill you prescriptions at the same pharmacy, then you will have a pharmacist who is familiar with your medical issues and can detect any possible problems with your medications. In fact, it is a good idea to volunteer information about medications you are already taking when you visit a new pharmacist. Then, she can add this information to your records and have a complete file of information. She can monitor the drugs you are taking and let you know of any potential interactions or harmful side effects.

If cost is an issue for you, your pharmacist can help. Ask her if there are any less expensive brands of your medication available. Or, you can request that she fill only half the prescription, to give you a chance to try out the medication before paying for the entire amount. You can also ask your doctor for a few free samples. Once you have ascertained that the prescribed medication is working for you, you can go ahead and ask your pharmacist to fill the prescription for you. When you pick up your prescription, don't forget to ask the pharmacist to explain to you how to take it if you have any doubts. She can also supply you with written instructions.

Your pharmacist can provide you with important support, but there is a limit to what she can do. If you suspect that you have a problem that requires medical attention, you should always consult your doctor right away.

20. What is the purpose of this article?
    (A) To explain the role of a pharmacist
    (B) To help select medications
    (C) To give instructions on taking medications
    (D) To advertise a particular pharmacy

21. What can you ask your pharmacist to do?
    (A) Recommend a good doctor
    (B) Suggest different brands
    (C) Write a prescription
    (D) Give you medical attention

22. What should you ask for when you pick up your prescription?
    (A) A cheaper brand
    (B) Some free samples
    (C) Instructions
    (D) A discount

23. The word *detect* in line 3 is closest in meaning to
    (A) repair.
    (B) create.
    (C) inform.
    (D) discover.

24. The word *potential* in line 7 is closest in meaning to
    (A) common.
    (B) interesting.
    (C) dangerous.
    (D) possible.

WORD REVIEW #10
LESSONS 46–50 HEALTH

Choose the word that best completes the sentence.

1. Your doctor's ________ are as important as his prescriptions.
   (A) recommend
   (B) recommended
   (C) recommending
   (D) recommendations

2. Dentists are as concerned with your dental ________ as with the condition of your teeth.
   (A) habits
   (B) habitual
   (C) habitually
   (D) habituated

3. To avoid ________ any additional charges, you should ask to be discharged from the hospital.
   (A) incur
   (B) incurs
   (C) incurred
   (D) incurring

4. It is as fast and efficient to ________ with your pharmacist as with your physician.
   (A) consult
   (B) consulting
   (C) consulted
   (D) consultation

5. My dentist ________ me to a specialist who is better able to treat my problem.
   (A) managed
   (B) distracted
   (C) referred
   (D) admitted

6. A dentist can perform dental ________ as well as routine maintenance.
   (A) restore
   (B) restored
   (C) restoring
   (D) restoration

7. A good medical insurance policy will ________ preventive health programs as well as treatment.
   (A) emphasize
   (B) emphasis
   (C) emphasizing
   (D) emphasized

8. Joe's poor health prevents him ________ participating in many activities that he used to enjoy.
   (A) to
   (B) from
   (C) about
   (D) with

9. A pharmacist will ________ the customer's medications.
   (A) monitor
   (B) monitors
   (C) monitoring
   (D) monitored

10. I don't understand most of what I read in a hospital's billing ________.
   (A) state
   (B) stated
   (C) stating
   (D) statement

Choose the one word or phrase that best completes each sentence.

The most important part of your health care is the ___________ visit to your doctor.

11. (A) daily
    (B) monthly
    (C) annual
    (D) perennial

By visiting your doctor once a year, you can feel sure that any changes in your health will be detected. Your doctor might ___________ lifestyle changes, such as diet

12. (A) recommend
    (B) restore
    (C) detect
    (D) incur

and exercise, that you will need to make in order to maintain your health. The best way to ___________ serious disease, after all, is to maintain a healthy lifestyle.

13. (A) prevent
    (B) prevention
    (C) preventive
    (D) preventively

MEMO

To: All company staff
From: Human Resources Office
Re: Dental insurance

Dental insurance is now available to all company ___________. We can offer you a policy that

14. (A) person
    (B) personal
    (C) personify
    (D) personnel

covers all the usual dental ___________, such as cleanings and fillings. Unfortunately, surgery

15. (A) conveniences
    (B) procedures
    (C) appointments
    (D) irritations

and other complicated procedures will not be covered. If you are interested in applying for this insurance, please notify our office before the end of this month. We ___________ you to take

16. (A) are encouraged
    (B) encouraging
    (C) encouraged
    (D) encourage

advantage of this opportunity to obtain affordable dental care for yourself and your family.

Your doctor has prescribed this medication to treat your symptoms. Take it as instructed by your doctor. It is most ____________ when taken with meals. Consult

17. (A) effect
    (B) effective
    (C) effectively
    (D) effectiveness

with your doctor before taking any additional medications to avoid ____________

18. (A) suitable
    (B) habitual
    (C) potential
    (D) authorized

harmful interactions. Possible side effects of this medication include sleepiness and ____________ of the stomach.

19. (A) irritate
    (B) irritant
    (C) irritation
    (D) irritating

ANSWER SHEET
TOEIC Practice Test

LISTENING COMPREHENSION

Part 1: Photographs

1. Ⓐ Ⓑ Ⓒ Ⓓ	3. Ⓐ Ⓑ Ⓒ Ⓓ	5. Ⓐ Ⓑ Ⓒ Ⓓ
2. Ⓐ Ⓑ Ⓒ Ⓓ	4. Ⓐ Ⓑ Ⓒ Ⓓ	6. Ⓐ Ⓑ Ⓒ Ⓓ

Part 2: Question-Response

7. Ⓐ Ⓑ Ⓒ Ⓓ	14. Ⓐ Ⓑ Ⓒ Ⓓ	21. Ⓐ Ⓑ Ⓒ Ⓓ	28. Ⓐ Ⓑ Ⓒ Ⓓ
8. Ⓐ Ⓑ Ⓒ Ⓓ	15. Ⓐ Ⓑ Ⓒ Ⓓ	22. Ⓐ Ⓑ Ⓒ Ⓓ	29. Ⓐ Ⓑ Ⓒ Ⓓ
9. Ⓐ Ⓑ Ⓒ Ⓓ	16. Ⓐ Ⓑ Ⓒ Ⓓ	23. Ⓐ Ⓑ Ⓒ Ⓓ	30. Ⓐ Ⓑ Ⓒ Ⓓ
10. Ⓐ Ⓑ Ⓒ Ⓓ	17. Ⓐ Ⓑ Ⓒ Ⓓ	24. Ⓐ Ⓑ Ⓒ Ⓓ	31. Ⓐ Ⓑ Ⓒ Ⓓ
11. Ⓐ Ⓑ Ⓒ Ⓓ	18. Ⓐ Ⓑ Ⓒ Ⓓ	25. Ⓐ Ⓑ Ⓒ Ⓓ	
12. Ⓐ Ⓑ Ⓒ Ⓓ	19. Ⓐ Ⓑ Ⓒ Ⓓ	26. Ⓐ Ⓑ Ⓒ Ⓓ	
13. Ⓐ Ⓑ Ⓒ Ⓓ	20. Ⓐ Ⓑ Ⓒ Ⓓ	27. Ⓐ Ⓑ Ⓒ Ⓓ	

Part 3: Conversations

32. Ⓐ Ⓑ Ⓒ Ⓓ	42. Ⓐ Ⓑ Ⓒ Ⓓ	52. Ⓐ Ⓑ Ⓒ Ⓓ	62. Ⓐ Ⓑ Ⓒ Ⓓ
33. Ⓐ Ⓑ Ⓒ Ⓓ	43. Ⓐ Ⓑ Ⓒ Ⓓ	53. Ⓐ Ⓑ Ⓒ Ⓓ	63. Ⓐ Ⓑ Ⓒ Ⓓ
34. Ⓐ Ⓑ Ⓒ Ⓓ	44. Ⓐ Ⓑ Ⓒ Ⓓ	54. Ⓐ Ⓑ Ⓒ Ⓓ	64. Ⓐ Ⓑ Ⓒ Ⓓ
35. Ⓐ Ⓑ Ⓒ Ⓓ	45. Ⓐ Ⓑ Ⓒ Ⓓ	55. Ⓐ Ⓑ Ⓒ Ⓓ	65. Ⓐ Ⓑ Ⓒ Ⓓ
36. Ⓐ Ⓑ Ⓒ Ⓓ	46. Ⓐ Ⓑ Ⓒ Ⓓ	56. Ⓐ Ⓑ Ⓒ Ⓓ	66. Ⓐ Ⓑ Ⓒ Ⓓ
37. Ⓐ Ⓑ Ⓒ Ⓓ	47. Ⓐ Ⓑ Ⓒ Ⓓ	57. Ⓐ Ⓑ Ⓒ Ⓓ	67. Ⓐ Ⓑ Ⓒ Ⓓ
38. Ⓐ Ⓑ Ⓒ Ⓓ	48. Ⓐ Ⓑ Ⓒ Ⓓ	58. Ⓐ Ⓑ Ⓒ Ⓓ	68. Ⓐ Ⓑ Ⓒ Ⓓ
39. Ⓐ Ⓑ Ⓒ Ⓓ	49. Ⓐ Ⓑ Ⓒ Ⓓ	59. Ⓐ Ⓑ Ⓒ Ⓓ	69. Ⓐ Ⓑ Ⓒ Ⓓ
40. Ⓐ Ⓑ Ⓒ Ⓓ	50. Ⓐ Ⓑ Ⓒ Ⓓ	60. Ⓐ Ⓑ Ⓒ Ⓓ	70. Ⓐ Ⓑ Ⓒ Ⓓ
41. Ⓐ Ⓑ Ⓒ Ⓓ	51. Ⓐ Ⓑ Ⓒ Ⓓ	61. Ⓐ Ⓑ Ⓒ Ⓓ	

Part 4: Talks

71. Ⓐ Ⓑ Ⓒ Ⓓ	79. Ⓐ Ⓑ Ⓒ Ⓓ	87. Ⓐ Ⓑ Ⓒ Ⓓ	95. Ⓐ Ⓑ Ⓒ Ⓓ
72. Ⓐ Ⓑ Ⓒ Ⓓ	80. Ⓐ Ⓑ Ⓒ Ⓓ	88. Ⓐ Ⓑ Ⓒ Ⓓ	96. Ⓐ Ⓑ Ⓒ Ⓓ
73. Ⓐ Ⓑ Ⓒ Ⓓ	81. Ⓐ Ⓑ Ⓒ Ⓓ	89. Ⓐ Ⓑ Ⓒ Ⓓ	97. Ⓐ Ⓑ Ⓒ Ⓓ
74. Ⓐ Ⓑ Ⓒ Ⓓ	82. Ⓐ Ⓑ Ⓒ Ⓓ	90. Ⓐ Ⓑ Ⓒ Ⓓ	98. Ⓐ Ⓑ Ⓒ Ⓓ
75. Ⓐ Ⓑ Ⓒ Ⓓ	83. Ⓐ Ⓑ Ⓒ Ⓓ	91. Ⓐ Ⓑ Ⓒ Ⓓ	99. Ⓐ Ⓑ Ⓒ Ⓓ
76. Ⓐ Ⓑ Ⓒ Ⓓ	84. Ⓐ Ⓑ Ⓒ Ⓓ	92. Ⓐ Ⓑ Ⓒ Ⓓ	100. Ⓐ Ⓑ Ⓒ Ⓓ
77. Ⓐ Ⓑ Ⓒ Ⓓ	85. Ⓐ Ⓑ Ⓒ Ⓓ	93. Ⓐ Ⓑ Ⓒ Ⓓ	
78. Ⓐ Ⓑ Ⓒ Ⓓ	86. Ⓐ Ⓑ Ⓒ Ⓓ	94. Ⓐ Ⓑ Ⓒ Ⓓ	

ANSWER SHEET
TOEIC Practice Test

READING

Part 5: Incomplete Sentences

101. Ⓐ Ⓑ Ⓒ Ⓓ	109. Ⓐ Ⓑ Ⓒ Ⓓ	117. Ⓐ Ⓑ Ⓒ Ⓓ	125. Ⓐ Ⓑ Ⓒ Ⓓ
102. Ⓐ Ⓑ Ⓒ Ⓓ	110. Ⓐ Ⓑ Ⓒ Ⓓ	118. Ⓐ Ⓑ Ⓒ Ⓓ	126. Ⓐ Ⓑ Ⓒ Ⓓ
103. Ⓐ Ⓑ Ⓒ Ⓓ	111. Ⓐ Ⓑ Ⓒ Ⓓ	119. Ⓐ Ⓑ Ⓒ Ⓓ	127. Ⓐ Ⓑ Ⓒ Ⓓ
104. Ⓐ Ⓑ Ⓒ Ⓓ	112. Ⓐ Ⓑ Ⓒ Ⓓ	120. Ⓐ Ⓑ Ⓒ Ⓓ	128. Ⓐ Ⓑ Ⓒ Ⓓ
105. Ⓐ Ⓑ Ⓒ Ⓓ	113. Ⓐ Ⓑ Ⓒ Ⓓ	121. Ⓐ Ⓑ Ⓒ Ⓓ	129. Ⓐ Ⓑ Ⓒ Ⓓ
106. Ⓐ Ⓑ Ⓒ Ⓓ	114. Ⓐ Ⓑ Ⓒ Ⓓ	122. Ⓐ Ⓑ Ⓒ Ⓓ	130. Ⓐ Ⓑ Ⓒ Ⓓ
107. Ⓐ Ⓑ Ⓒ Ⓓ	115. Ⓐ Ⓑ Ⓒ Ⓓ	123. Ⓐ Ⓑ Ⓒ Ⓓ	
108. Ⓐ Ⓑ Ⓒ Ⓓ	116. Ⓐ Ⓑ Ⓒ Ⓓ	124. Ⓐ Ⓑ Ⓒ Ⓓ	

Part 6: Text Completion

131. Ⓐ Ⓑ Ⓒ Ⓓ	135. Ⓐ Ⓑ Ⓒ Ⓓ	139. Ⓐ Ⓑ Ⓒ Ⓓ	143. Ⓐ Ⓑ Ⓒ Ⓓ
132. Ⓐ Ⓑ Ⓒ Ⓓ	136. Ⓐ Ⓑ Ⓒ Ⓓ	140. Ⓐ Ⓑ Ⓒ Ⓓ	144. Ⓐ Ⓑ Ⓒ Ⓓ
133. Ⓐ Ⓑ Ⓒ Ⓓ	137. Ⓐ Ⓑ Ⓒ Ⓓ	141. Ⓐ Ⓑ Ⓒ Ⓓ	145. Ⓐ Ⓑ Ⓒ Ⓓ
134. Ⓐ Ⓑ Ⓒ Ⓓ	138. Ⓐ Ⓑ Ⓒ Ⓓ	142. Ⓐ Ⓑ Ⓒ Ⓓ	146. Ⓐ Ⓑ Ⓒ Ⓓ

Part 7: Reading Comprehension

147. Ⓐ Ⓑ Ⓒ Ⓓ	161. Ⓐ Ⓑ Ⓒ Ⓓ	175. Ⓐ Ⓑ Ⓒ Ⓓ	189. Ⓐ Ⓑ Ⓒ Ⓓ
148. Ⓐ Ⓑ Ⓒ Ⓓ	162. Ⓐ Ⓑ Ⓒ Ⓓ	176. Ⓐ Ⓑ Ⓒ Ⓓ	190. Ⓐ Ⓑ Ⓒ Ⓓ
149. Ⓐ Ⓑ Ⓒ Ⓓ	163. Ⓐ Ⓑ Ⓒ Ⓓ	177. Ⓐ Ⓑ Ⓒ Ⓓ	191. Ⓐ Ⓑ Ⓒ Ⓓ
150. Ⓐ Ⓑ Ⓒ Ⓓ	164. Ⓐ Ⓑ Ⓒ Ⓓ	178. Ⓐ Ⓑ Ⓒ Ⓓ	192. Ⓐ Ⓑ Ⓒ Ⓓ
151. Ⓐ Ⓑ Ⓒ Ⓓ	165. Ⓐ Ⓑ Ⓒ Ⓓ	179. Ⓐ Ⓑ Ⓒ Ⓓ	193. Ⓐ Ⓑ Ⓒ Ⓓ
152. Ⓐ Ⓑ Ⓒ Ⓓ	166. Ⓐ Ⓑ Ⓒ Ⓓ	180. Ⓐ Ⓑ Ⓒ Ⓓ	194. Ⓐ Ⓑ Ⓒ Ⓓ
153. Ⓐ Ⓑ Ⓒ Ⓓ	167. Ⓐ Ⓑ Ⓒ Ⓓ	181. Ⓐ Ⓑ Ⓒ Ⓓ	195. Ⓐ Ⓑ Ⓒ Ⓓ
154. Ⓐ Ⓑ Ⓒ Ⓓ	168. Ⓐ Ⓑ Ⓒ Ⓓ	182. Ⓐ Ⓑ Ⓒ Ⓓ	196. Ⓐ Ⓑ Ⓒ Ⓓ
155. Ⓐ Ⓑ Ⓒ Ⓓ	169. Ⓐ Ⓑ Ⓒ Ⓓ	183. Ⓐ Ⓑ Ⓒ Ⓓ	197. Ⓐ Ⓑ Ⓒ Ⓓ
156. Ⓐ Ⓑ Ⓒ Ⓓ	170. Ⓐ Ⓑ Ⓒ Ⓓ	184. Ⓐ Ⓑ Ⓒ Ⓓ	198. Ⓐ Ⓑ Ⓒ Ⓓ
157. Ⓐ Ⓑ Ⓒ Ⓓ	171. Ⓐ Ⓑ Ⓒ Ⓓ	185. Ⓐ Ⓑ Ⓒ Ⓓ	199. Ⓐ Ⓑ Ⓒ Ⓓ
158. Ⓐ Ⓑ Ⓒ Ⓓ	172. Ⓐ Ⓑ Ⓒ Ⓓ	186. Ⓐ Ⓑ Ⓒ Ⓓ	200. Ⓐ Ⓑ Ⓒ Ⓓ
159. Ⓐ Ⓑ Ⓒ Ⓓ	173. Ⓐ Ⓑ Ⓒ Ⓓ	187. Ⓐ Ⓑ Ⓒ Ⓓ	
160. Ⓐ Ⓑ Ⓒ Ⓓ	174. Ⓐ Ⓑ Ⓒ Ⓓ	188. Ⓐ Ⓑ Ⓒ Ⓓ	

TOEIC Practice Test

This model test follows the new format of the TOEIC. It contains many of the words you have studied in this book. When you take this model test, you will become familiar with the TOEIC format and also practice your new vocabulary in the context of a test.

LISTENING COMPREHENSION

In this section of the test you will have the chance to demonstrate how well you understand spoken English. There are four parts to this section, with special directions for each part. You will find an Answer Sheet on pages 427–428. Detach it from the book and use it to record your answers. Check your answers with the Answer Key on pages 467–468.

Part 1: Photographs

Track 52

Directions: You will see a photograph. You will hear four statements about the photograph. Choose the statement that most closely matches the photograph and fill in the corresponding oval on your answer sheet.

Example

Now listen to the four statements.

(A) She's getting on a plane.
(B) She's reading a magazine.
(C) She's taking a nap.
(D) She's holding a glass.

Sample Answer

Statement (B), "She's reading a magazine," best describes what you see in the picture. Therefore, you should choose answer (B).

1.

2.

3.

4.

5.

6.

Part 2: Question-Response

Track 53

Directions: You will hear a question and three possible responses. Choose the response that most closely answers the question and fill in the corresponding oval on your answer sheet.

Example

Now listen to the sample question.

You will hear:

How is the weather?

You will also hear:

(A) It's raining.
(B) He's fine, thanks.
(C) He's my boss.

The best response to the question *How is the weather?* is choice (A), *It's raining*. Therefore, you should choose answer (A).

7. Mark your answer on your answer sheet.
8. Mark your answer on your answer sheet.
9. Mark your answer on your answer sheet.
10. Mark your answer on your answer sheet.
11. Mark your answer on your answer sheet.
12. Mark your answer on your answer sheet.
13. Mark your answer on your answer sheet.
14. Mark your answer on your answer sheet.
15. Mark your answer on your answer sheet.
16. Mark your answer on your answer sheet.
17. Mark your answer on your answer sheet.
18. Mark your answer on your answer sheet.
19. Mark your answer on your answer sheet.
20. Mark your answer on your answer sheet.
21. Mark your answer on your answer sheet.
22. Mark your answer on your answer sheet.
23. Mark your answer on your answer sheet.
24. Mark your answer on your answer sheet.
25. Mark your answer on your answer sheet.
26. Mark your answer on your answer sheet.
27. Mark your answer on your answer sheet.
28. Mark your answer on your answer sheet.
29. Mark your answer on your answer sheet.
30. Mark your answer on your answer sheet.
31. Mark your answer on your answer sheet.

Part 3: Conversations

Track 54

Directions: You will hear a conversation between two or more people. You will see three questions on each conversation and four possible answers. Choose the best answer to each question and fill in the corresponding oval on your answer sheet.

32. Where does this conversation take place?

(A) In a restaurant
(B) On a train
(C) At a hotel
(D) In a store

33. What is the man going to eat?

(A) Cake
(B) Steak
(C) Fish
(D) Rice

34. How will the man pay for his meal?

(A) Cash
(B) Check
(C) Credit card
(D) Money order

35. How is the man traveling?

(A) Bus
(B) Train
(C) Plane
(D) Boat

36. What does the man say about his luggage?

(A) He wants to check it.
(B) He doesn't have any.
(C) He needs help with it.
(D) He will keep it with him.

37. What does the man ask the woman about?

(A) The location of the gate
(B) The time of departure
(C) The cost of the ticket
(D) The length of the trip

38. What is the problem?

(A) The man is tired.
(B) The woman feels sick.
(C) They have a flat tire.
(D) They confused the date.

39. What time is it now?

(A) 5:00
(B) 5:30
(C) 6:30
(D) 7:00

40. What will the woman do next?

(A) Have dinner
(B) Make a phone call
(C) Look in her briefcase
(D) Cancel her appointment

41. What is the woman doing now?

(A) Looking for her umbrella
(B) Making an appointment
(C) Folding her clothes
(D) Preparing a folder

42. What does the woman mean when she says, "You're joking, right?"

(A) She doesn't believe the man's statement.
(B) She agrees with the man's opinion.
(C) She appreciates the information.
(D) She thinks the man is funny.

43. How will she get to her appointment?

(A) Walk
(B) Train
(C) Bus
(D) Taxi

44. What is the problem with the supplies?

(A) They are the wrong size.
(B) They haven't been paid for.
(C) They haven't arrived.
(D) They are the wrong color.

45. What supplies were ordered?

(A) Paper and ink
(B) Computers
(C) Printers
(D) Pens and notebooks

46. When will the woman call the supplier again?

(A) This morning
(B) At 5:00 today
(C) Tomorrow morning
(D) On Tuesday

---

47. What will the woman do by 3:00?

(A) Go for a walk
(B) Finish her work
(C) Take a break
(D) Pay a fine

48. Where will she have lunch?

(A) At a sandwich shop
(B) At the cafeteria
(C) At her home
(D) At her desk

49. What does the man offer to do for the woman?

(A) Move her desk
(B) Drive her home
(C) Help her do her work
(D) Bring her some food

50. What do the speakers suggest about their current office?

(A) It's too small.
(B) The rent is too high.
(C) It has several rooms.
(D) The location is not good.

51. What does the woman mean when she says, "It wouldn't hurt to look?"

(A) They have time to see the office.
(B) It could be helpful to see the office.
(C) The sign about the office is easy to see.
(D) They don't have to pay to see the office.

52. What will the first man do next?

(A) Go to a health club
(B) Pay the rent
(C) Read a notice
(D) Talk to the landlord

---

53. Where does this conversation take place?

(A) At a travel agency
(B) At an art school
(C) At a museum
(D) At a map store

54. What does the woman give the man?

(A) A ticket
(B) A painting
(C) A building tour
(D) A piece of paper

55. How much does the man pay for it?

(A) $0
(B) $3
(C) $4
(D) $10

56. What day does the man have off work?
   (A) Friday
   (B) Saturday
   (C) Sunday
   (D) Monday

57. What does he want to do on his day off?
   (A) Walk in the park
   (B) Listen to music
   (C) See a movie
   (D) Take a rest

58. Why doesn't he want to eat at the restaurant?
   (A) He prefers to stay home.
   (B) He's trying to lose weight.
   (C) It's an outdoor restaurant.
   (D) It's too small and dark.

---

59. What are the tour participants doing right now?
   (A) Eating
   (B) Walking
   (C) Riding a bus
   (D) Looking at gardens

60. What will they do next?
   (A) Visit a museum
   (B) See the plaza
   (C) Walk in a park
   (D) Look at houses

61. What is in the houses?
   (A) Art
   (B) Clothes
   (C) Gardens
   (D) Architecture

62. Why does the second woman say, "You want to go there?"
   (A) She is asking where the man wants to eat.
   (B) She is surprised by the man's suggestion.
   (C) She didn't hear what the man said.
   (D) She agrees with the man's idea.

63. Why does the woman want to go to the café?
   (A) It's nearby.
   (B) It's inexpensive.
   (C) Everyone likes it.
   (D) The food is good.

64. What will the speakers do at 1:00?
   (A) Call a client
   (B) Clean the office
   (C) Look at an apartment
   (D) Participate in a meeting

---

65. Who is the man, most likely?
   (A) A doctor
   (B) A patient
   (C) A courier
   (D) A receptionist

66. What is indicated about the woman?
   (A) She has never met the doctor before.
   (B) She is an old friend of the doctor's.
   (C) She is new to the city.
   (D) She is looking for a job.

67. Look at the graphic. Where is the doctor's office?

(A) Room 1
(B) Room 3
(C) Room 4
(D) Room 5

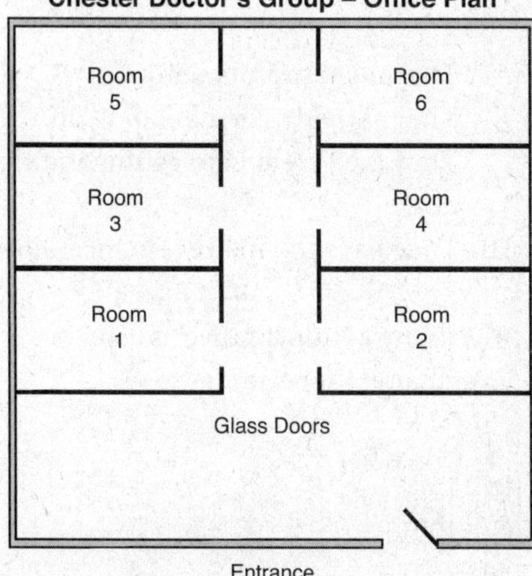

68. What kind of performance will the speakers see at the theater?

(A) A play
(B) A film
(C) A concert
(D) A lecture

69. Why can't the man drive his car?

(A) He sold it.
(B) It needs repairs.
(C) He lent it to a friend.
(D) He doesn't have a license.

70. Look at the graphic. What time will the man's bus leave?

(A) 7:55
(B) 10:00
(C) 11:15
(D) 11:45

Evening Bus Schedule

Lv. Downtown	Arr. Riverdale
6:45	7:15
7:55	8:25
9:30	10:00
11:15	11:45

Part 4: Talks

Track 55

Directions: You will hear a talk given by a single speaker. You will see three questions on each talk, each with four possible answers. Choose the best answer to each question and fill in the corresponding oval on your answer sheet.

71. What kind of business is this message about?
    (A) A store
    (B) A bank
    (C) An accountant's office
    (D) A telephone company

72. How can you hear information about your account?
    (A) By pressing 2
    (B) By entering your account number
    (C) By dialing an extension number
    (D) By staying on the line

73. What happens if you press 3?
    (A) You will speak with a customer service representative.
    (B) You can leave a message for a staff member.
    (C) You can find out an extension number.
    (D) You will hear about services offered to customers.

---

74. What is the main purpose of this report?
    (A) To tell about research results
    (B) To help supervisors become more efficient
    (C) To describe an administrative assistant's job
    (D) To explain how a typical business office works

75. What do supervisors say about their assistants?
    (A) They need to work harder.
    (B) They should take more time off.
    (C) They are essential to getting the work done.
    (D) They have too many responsibilities.

76. How many administrative assistants participated in the study?
    (A) 6
    (B) 75
    (C) 100
    (D) 250

---

77. Which of the following positions is NOT advertised?
    (A) Cook
    (B) Waiter
    (C) Manager
    (D) Dishwasher

78. What is a requirement for the jobs?
    (A) The ability to work full time
    (B) Availability on Mondays
    (C) Restaurant experience
    (D) Dependability

79. When is a good time to call to apply for a job?
    (A) Monday morning
    (B) Monday afternoon
    (C) Friday morning
    (D) Friday evening

80. What does the speaker imply when he says, "today would be a good day to stay home"?

(A) He likes to play in the snow.
(B) The weather is bad.
(C) It's the weekend.
(D) He feels tired.

81. What problem can drivers expect today?

(A) Difficulty seeing
(B) Icy roads
(C) Heavy traffic
(D) Frozen engines

82. What will happen on Sunday?

(A) There will be another storm.
(B) Temperatures will warm up.
(C) The weather will be nicer.
(D) The sun will shine.

---

83. What is suggested about River Printing Services?

(A) It has been in business for a long time.
(B) Business cards are its most popular product.
(C) It offers other services in addition to printing.
(D) The prices are lower than at other printing businesses.

84. What do consultants help customers with?

(A) Writing text for a brochure
(B) Figuring out quantities
(C) Choosing a design
(D) Creating a sample

85. Why would a customer not have to pay for an order?

(A) The customer doesn't like the design.
(B) The order isn't ready on time.
(C) It's the customer's first order.
(D) A consultant isn't available.

86. What is wrong at the station?

(A) The elevator is broken.
(B) The escalator is slow.
(C) The exits are blocked.
(D) The stairs are wet.

87. How has the problem been solved for passengers in need?

(A) They can get wheelchairs.
(B) They can take a taxi.
(C) They can take a bus.
(D) They can get a refund.

88. What does the speaker do at the end of the announcement?

(A) Warns the passengers
(B) Thanks the passengers
(C) Advises the passengers
(D) Apologizes to the passengers

---

89. Why is there a shortage of electric power?

(A) Temperatures are extremely high.
(B) The weather is colder than usual.
(C) More people are using a lot of appliances.
(D) High winds have knocked down power lines.

90. What are city residents asked to do?

(A) Avoid washing clothes
(B) Turn off household heat
(C) Postpone taking showers
(D) Keep the lights off

91. How can residents get more information?

(A) By turning on the TV
(B) By visiting a webpage
(C) By calling the electric company
(D) Keep listening to the radio

92. When will the restaurant have its grand opening?

(A) Tuesday
(B) Friday
(C) Saturday
(D) Sunday

93. What can customers get for free on opening day?

(A) A glass of soda
(B) A piece of pastry
(C) A slice of pizza
(D) A plate of spaghetti

94. Who gets a discount?

(A) Children
(B) Older adults
(C) All local citizens
(D) Lunchtime customers

---

95. Look at the graphic. Which room will the listener probably rent?

(A) Fountain Room
(B) Terrace Room
(C) Gold Room
(D) Rose Room

Party Room Schedule—April 10

	Capacity	Availability
Fountain Room	150	no
Terrace Room	125	yes
Gold Room	100	no
Rose Room	150	yes

96. What is included with the cost of the room?

(A) Decorations
(B) Tablecloths
(C) Furniture
(D) Catering

97. What does the speaker ask the listener to do?

(A) Visit the hotel
(B) Return the call
(C) Make a down payment
(D) Answer some questions

---

98. How often do the managers meet?

(A) Once a day
(B) Once a month
(C) Once a year
(D) Twice a year

99. What kind of business do they work in?

(A) Hotel
(B) Restaurant
(C) Sports store
(D) Grocery store

100. Look at the graphic. What time of day does the speaker want to discuss?

(A) Morning
(B) Noon
(C) Afternoon
(D) Evening

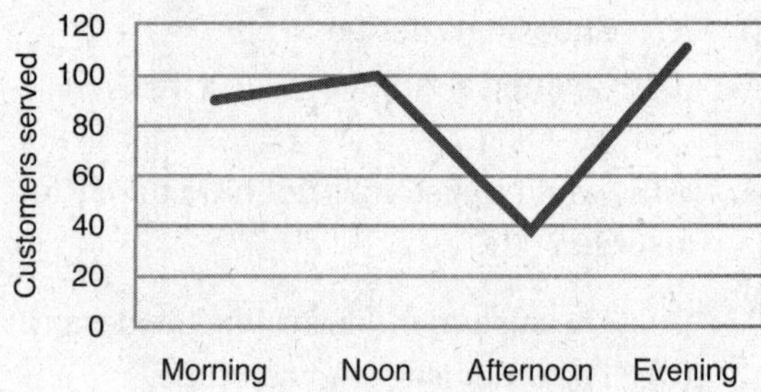

This is the end of the Listening Comprehension portion of the test. Turn to Part 5 in your test book.

READING COMPREHENSION

In this section of the test, you will have the chance to show how well you understand written English. There are three parts to this section, with special directions for each part.

YOU WILL HAVE ONE HOUR AND FIFTEEN MINUTES TO COMPLETE PARTS 5, 6, AND 7 OF THE TEST.

Part 5: Incomplete Sentences

Directions: You will see a sentence with a missing word. Four possible answers follow the sentence. Choose the best answer to the question and fill in the corresponding oval on your answer sheet.

101. We feel that the annual awards banquet is a good way to _________ the achievements of our employees.

(A) recognize
(B) dedicate
(C) reimburse
(D) indicate

102. A sound business plan is _________ to the success of any new small business.

(A) aggressive
(B) productive
(C) strict
(D) crucial

103. If you are looking for a good landscaping company, you should know that Beautiful Gardens consistently _________ excellent reviews from its customers.

(A) receive
(B) receives
(C) are receiving
(D) have received

104. After long negotiations, the two parties were _________ able to come to an agreement, and the contract was signed.

(A) commonly
(B) plainly
(C) finally
(D) strictly

105. Staff members always look forward to _________ in the annual company soccer tournament.

(A) compete
(B) competes
(C) will compete
(D) competing

106. Shirley is _________ a brilliant public speaker but also an accomplished and widely-read writer.

(A) not only
(B) only
(C) either
(D) both

107. Cress Industries is an established company that has been in the business _________ significantly more time than any of its competitors.

(A) since
(B) from
(C) for
(D) in

108. It's a good idea to order printer ink regularly because we should always have a good supply of it _________.

(A) on top
(B) on hand
(C) set up
(D) put in

109. __________ fewer than five people sign up, the workshop will be postponed until later in the year.

(A) If
(B) So
(C) While
(D) Though

110. Irving has enrolled in a music appreciation class because he is trying to __________ his knowledge of the performing arts.

(A) broad
(B) broaden
(C) broader
(D) broadly

111. Many questions __________ during the discussion but, unfortunately, there wasn't time to address them all.

(A) rose
(B) risen
(C) arose
(D) raise

112. __________ attention was paid to promoting the product, so sales remained low.

(A) Few
(B) Some
(C) Small
(D) Little

113. Every document __________ this one is ready for the lawyer to review.

(A) accept
(B) except
(C) expect
(D) accrue

114. If the price __________, then sales of that product are likely to start going up.

(A) is reduced
(B) will reduce
(C) is reducing
(D) reduces

115. The director is very strict about time and expects everyone to arrive at the meeting __________.

(A) punctual
(B) punctuate
(C) punctually
(D) punctuality

116. The report they prepared is quite __________ and covers all the required information in depth.

(A) along
(B) longed
(C) longing
(D) lengthy

117. The investment didn't seem __________ at first, but they ended up making a lot of money from it.

(A) profit
(B) profitable
(C) profitably
(D) profiteer

118. We shouldn't hire anyone without experience in a similar position __________ we are willing to provide training and support.

(A) unless
(B) since
(C) while
(D) so

119. After you fill __________ the application form, please sign it and give it to the receptionist.

(A) out
(B) up
(C) on
(D) over

120. Any employee _________ certification is about to expire should contact the personnel office immediately.

(A) who
(B) who's
(C) whose
(D) whom

121. Retail prices tend to be higher in _________ areas because of the cost of shipping goods over long distances.

(A) external
(B) remote
(C) displaced
(D) divergent

122. It is the department head's responsibility to be aware of each staff member's strengths and weaknesses and to _________ projects accordingly.

(A) signify
(B) resign
(C) assign
(D) sign

123. It is difficult to _________ the materials needed to manufacture this type of product.

(A) local
(B) location
(C) locate
(D) localize

124. We cannot comment on the details of the document _________ it has been released to the public.

(A) when
(B) until
(C) since
(D) due to

125. _________ costs is our highest priority as we make plans for the coming year.

(A) Minimizing
(B) Minimize
(C) Minimally
(D) Will minimize

126. We try to _________ meetings for the same time each month to make it easier for people to attend.

(A) time
(B) agenda
(C) calendar
(D) schedule

127. Mimi has several _________ ideas for rearranging the office to make it more comfortable and attractive.

(A) create
(B) creative
(C) creation
(D) creatively

128. The partners have all _________ to work towards expanding the company into foreign markets.

(A) agree
(B) agreed
(C) agreeing
(D) agreement

129. The article described everything that happened at the event in _________ detail.

(A) thorough
(B) thoroughly
(C) through
(D) though

130. Mr. Kim was hired because of his _________ in Internet marketing and social media.

(A) expert
(B) expertly
(C) expertise
(D) expiration

TOEIC PRACTICE TEST

Part 6: Text Completion

Directions: You will see four passages, each with four sets of blanks. Under each blank are four options. Choose the word or phrase that best completes the statement, or the sentence that best completes the passage.

Questions 131–134 refer to the following e-mail.

From: Melissa Wright, Office Manager
To: All Staff
Re: Conference room use

Please take a moment to _____ these guidelines regarding the use of the conference room.
131.

1. Any staff member may reserve the conference room for a meeting or other work-related event. My assistant, Joe Smith, is in charge of the conference room schedule. _____.
132.

   To ensure that you get the time slot you want, we suggest you contact Joe at least one week _____.
133.

2. Joe can also help you with computers, projectors, and other equipment you may need. Please let him know what equipment you will need when reserving the room.

3. The conference room is used by many groups of people throughout the week. We cannot set _____ the room for each group that uses it. Therefore, you should plan
134.

   to arrive early and make sure that all the tables and chairs are arranged for your needs.

131. (A) revise
(B) review
(C) revert
(D) reveal

132. (A) He is highly qualified for this position
(B) I hired him for this job several months ago
(C) Please contact him to reserve a time to use the room
(D) He will take messages and answer questions in my absence

133. (A) succeeding
(B) subsequent
(C) in advance
(D) in the agenda

134. (A) up
(B) in
(C) to
(D) out

Questions 135–138 refer to the following notice.

From: Theresa Schultz
To: Daniel Lee
Date: October 10
Subject: Lunch tomorrow

Hi Daniel,

The business lunch with Ms. Yu and Mr. Bao is on the calendar for tomorrow. Please call the Fountainhead Restaurant right away to make reservations for three. Any time between noon and 2:00 is fine. Please ____ (135.) a table near the fountain, if at all possible.

As soon as you have made the ____ (136.), please call Ms. Yu and Mr. Bao and let them know the time and place. The reason for the meeting is to go over the draft of the annual report, so please prepare three copies of ____ (137.) and have them on my desk by 10:00 A.M. ____ (138.).

Thank you.
Theresa

135. (A) require
(B) request
(C) requisite
(D) requite

136. (A) arranges
(B) arrangers
(C) arrangements
(D) arranging

137. (A) it
(B) me
(C) us
(D) them

138. (A) The food at that restaurant is exceptionally good
(B) I spent some time organizing my desk yesterday
(C) I expect to arrive at the office on time tomorrow
(D) That will give me time to review the report before lunch

Questions 139–142 refer to the following letter.

SHOPPERS WORLD

Returned Items Policy

We must receive returned items within 30 days of the date of purchase. Please make sure that the receipt is included and check that the price tags are still attached. ____.
139.

If the customer has lost the receipt but the tags are still attached and the item is in good ____, you may offer the customer store credit only.
140.

Items that are damaged or dirtied in any way or that have missing price tags cannot ____.
141.

If you have any questions regarding this policy or if you need help processing a return, please ____ your supervisor.
142.

139. (A) Certain items are sold at discounted prices
(B) Items may be returned for cash or store credit
(C) Most customers are satisfied with our merchandise
(D) We sell clothing and housewares for the whole family

140. (A) condition
(B) conditional
(C) conditioned
(D) conditionally

141. (A) return
(B) returns
(C) returning
(D) be returned

142. (A) invite
(B) contact
(C) impose
(D) contract

Questions 143–146 refer to the following e-mail.

Dr. I. M. Lee, world-renowned _____ (143.) on international economics, will be reading from his newest book, *Money in the New Millennium*, at the Central Bookstore on October 14. Dr. Lee has recently returned from a tour of Asia, _____ (144.) he met with leading regional economic scholars. After his reading, he will share highlights from his trip and discuss Asia's role in the new world economy. Following his talk, *Money in the New Millennium* and other titles by Dr. Lee will be on sale at special one-night only prices.

_____ (145.).

_____ (146.) to this event is free, but early arrival is recommended in order to secure a seat.

143. (A) expert
(B) exporter
(C) experience
(D) experiment

144. (A) who
(B) whom
(C) which
(D) where

145. (A) Dr. Lee plans to return to Asia before the end of the year
(B) Dr. Lee will be available to sign any books you purchase
(C) Dr. Lee speaks frequently at events around the country
(D) Dr. Lee is currently a visiting professor at a local university

146. (A) Admit
(B) Admitted
(C) Admission
(D) Admissible

Part 7: Reading Comprehension

Directions: You will see single and multiple reading passages followed by several questions. Each question has four answer choices. Choose the best answer to the question and fill in the corresponding oval on your answer sheet.

Questions 147–148 refer to the following form.

MOVING?

Fill out this card and mail it to the businesses and publications that send you mail.

For best results, mail this card at least one month before your moving date.

Your Name: John Carpenter

Old Address: 268 Monroe Highway
(Number and Street)
Salem, South Carolina 29702
(City) (State) (Zip Code)

New Address: 764 Allston Street
(Number and Street)
Columbia, South Carolina 29805
(City) (State) (Zip Code)

New address is effective: April 12

147. What is the purpose of this form?
   (A) To apply for a new address
   (B) To subscribe to a publication
   (C) To find the location of a business
   (D) To give notification of an address change

148. When should the form be sent?
   (A) By March 12
   (B) By April 12
   (C) On April 12
   (D) Before May 12

Questions 149–150 refer to the following ad.

> ***The Office Writer's Handbook***
>
> is a complete and indispensable handbook for anyone who has to write for business purposes. This book takes you step-by-step through composing and formatting the most common types of business documents, including correspondence, reports, and charts and graphs. In addition, chapters on grammar and punctuation present writing conventions and rules with thorough explanations and illustrative examples. The last section of the book covers the most common writing mistakes and shows you how to avoid them. Each chapter in the book ends with a set of exercises for reinforcement. *The Office Writer's Handbook* is available in both print and e-book versions. Order yours today.

149. Who would probably NOT be interested in this book?

(A) Small business owners
(B) University students
(C) Office managers
(D) Legal assistants

150. What is included in every chapter?

(A) Charts and graphs
(B) Sample documents
(C) Practice opportunities
(D) Grammar quizzes

Questions 151–152 refer to the following text message chain.

Eve Branson, 11:45

First the good news. The meeting with the client went really well.

Jim Comley, 11:46

Great. What's the bad news?

Eve Branson, 11:47

The train is delayed. We left Chicago 30 minutes late.

Jim Comley, 11:49

Could be worse. I can still pick you up at the station.

Eve Branson, 11:51

No, I'll take a cab. I need you to do something else. First, tell Rob I'll be late for this afternoon's staff meeting. My presentation is first on the agenda, so he'll have to move me to the end.

Jim Comley, 11:52

You got it. Anything else?

Eve Branson, 11:54

I asked Millie to prepare some handouts I'll need for the presentation. Please check with her and make sure she has everything ready.

151. Where is Eve now?

(A) At her office
(B) On the train
(C) In Chicago
(D) In a cab

152. Who is Millie, most likely?

(A) Eve's boss
(B) Eve's client
(C) Eve's friend
(D) Eve's assistant

Questions 153–154 refer to the following form.

SPHINX, INC.

Ship to:
The Gray Company
345 Lyceum Lane
Dorchester

Customer #: 40298190	Order #: KY30582	Order Date: November 2

Quantity	Item#	Description	Quantity shipped
2	395	coffee—5-lb can	2
3	453	marking pens, assorted colors, 24/box	3
1	684	paper, multipurpose, white, 8-ream case	1
1	858	envelopes, business size, white, 500/box	1

On Backorder (Most backorders ship in 7–14 days)

3	953	file folders, assorted colors, 100/box	0

153. What kind of business is Sphinx, Inc., most likely?
    (A) Restaurant supplies
    (B) Household supplies
    (C) Office supplies
    (D) Art supplies

154. What will happen in 7–14 days?
    (A) The folders will be sent.
    (B) Payment will be due.
    (C) The entire order will be shipped.
    (D) The customer will receive the order.

Questions 155–157 refer to the following introduction.

The Kaleidoscope Company

September 8, 20—

Guy Williams
Landscape Design magazine
Ottho Heldringstraat 2
1066 AZ Amsterdam
The Netherlands

Dear Mr. Williams,

Thank you for contacting us about advertising in your publication. After careful consideration, we have decided not to place an ad in the December issue. Because of the seasonal nature of our business, we generally spend more of our advertising dollars during the warmer months of the year. We will probably, however, be interested in advertising in your next issue in March, in anticipation of the spring rush. People are more interested in thinking about plants and flowers at that time of year. We will be in touch with you closer to that time to discuss pricing, placement, etc.

We look forward to doing business with you.

Sincerely,

Ella Dubois

Ella Dubois

155. What kind of business is the Kaleidoscope Company, most likely?

(A) Publishing
(B) Gardening
(C) Advertising
(D) Photography

156. The word "contacting" in line 1 is closest in meaning to

(A) accepting.
(B) reminding.
(C) explaining to.
(D) communicating with.

157. How often does *Landscape Design magazine* come out?

(A) Once a week
(B) Once a month
(C) Every other month
(D) Four times a year

Questions 158–160 refer to the following introduction.

Darla K. Wise received her BA degree from Arizona State University in 1995 and her Doctorate of Jurisprudence from Harvard University in 2002.

She represented small business owners in New York state for five years before joining the firm of Corman, Hagan, Wallis, and White, where she has been a partner since 2010. Her practice emphasizes contract law and employment issues.

In addition to her legal practice, Ms. Wise has published numerous articles on small business and the law for the layperson. She lectures around the region, her mission being to "educate business owners so that they can make the law work for them." She is a member of the New York Bar Association and the Association of Legal Journalism.

The continuing education foundation of the New York Bar Association is honored to have Ms. Wise speak to us today.

158. What is Ms. Wise's profession?

(A) Lawyer
(B) School principal
(C) Newspaper editor
(D) University professor

159. The word "mission" in paragraph 3, line 2 is closest in meaning to

(A) title.
(B) result.
(C) purpose.
(D) process.

160. What is Ms. Wise doing today?

(A) Applying for a job
(B) Giving a talk
(C) Writing an article
(D) Negotiating a contract

Questions 161–163 refer to the following online chat discussion.

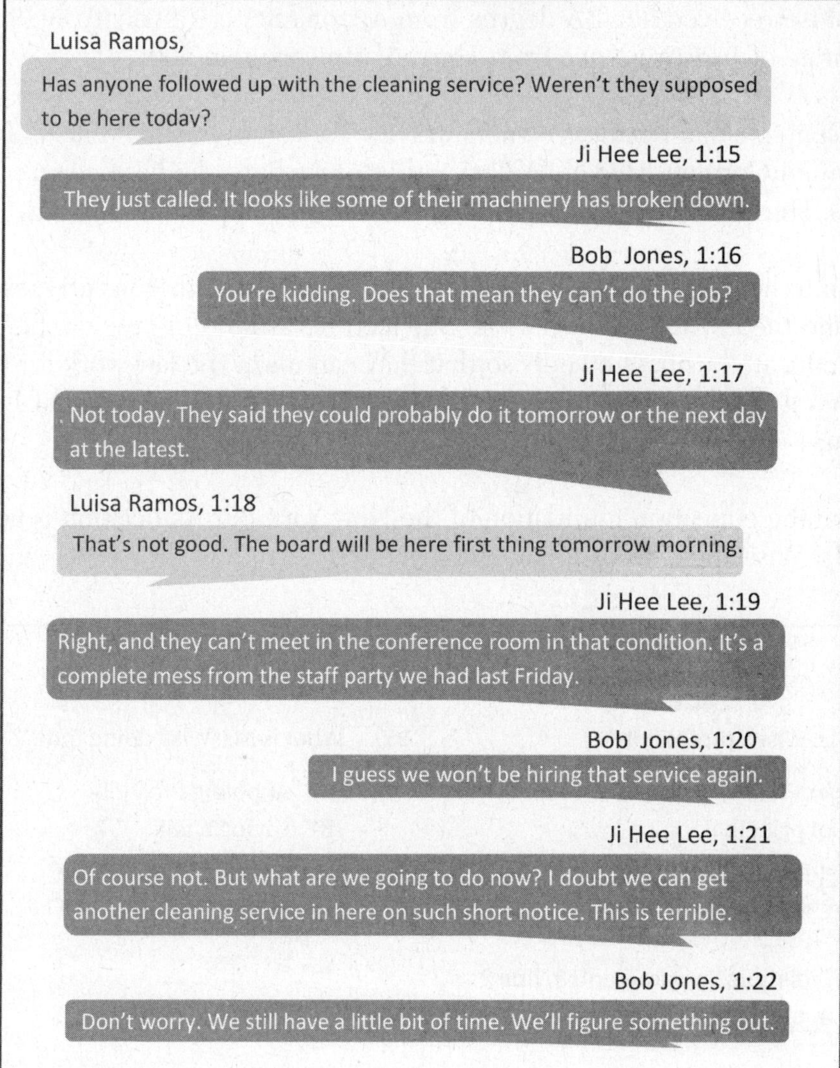
Luisa Ramos,

Has anyone followed up with the cleaning service? Weren't they supposed to be here today?

Ji Hee Lee, 1:15

They just called. It looks like some of their machinery has broken down.

Bob Jones, 1:16

You're kidding. Does that mean they can't do the job?

Ji Hee Lee, 1:17

Not today. They said they could probably do it tomorrow or the next day at the latest.

Luisa Ramos, 1:18

That's not good. The board will be here first thing tomorrow morning.

Ji Hee Lee, 1:19

Right, and they can't meet in the conference room in that condition. It's a complete mess from the staff party we had last Friday.

Bob Jones, 1:20

I guess we won't be hiring that service again.

Ji Hee Lee, 1:21

Of course not. But what are we going to do now? I doubt we can get another cleaning service in here on such short notice. This is terrible.

Bob Jones, 1:22

Don't worry. We still have a little bit of time. We'll figure something out.

161. Why won't the cleaning service do the job today?

(A) Their schedule is full.
(B) The room is too messy.
(C) They didn't get a reminder.
(D) Their equipment isn't working.

162. What will the conference room be used for tomorrow?

(A) A workshop
(B) A staff party
(C) A board meeting
(D) Hiring interviews

163. At 1:22, what does Bob Jones mean when he writes, "We'll figure something out?"

(A) We'll ask someone to help us.
(B) We'll do the cleaning ourselves.
(C) We'll find a solution to the problem.
(D) We'll take some time to think about it.

Questions 164–167 refer to the following article.

Business travelers usually find that they have little time to exercise, especially when their plans suddenly change because of late meetings or delayed flights. But everyone should get regular exercise as much as possible. Fortunately, this is a very reachable goal. Even when a hectic schedule keeps you away from the hotel exercise room, you can still make exercise part of your day. Experts suggest stretching your neck, arms, back, and shoulders while sitting in an airplane seat. In your hotel room, you can stretch your legs and abdominal muscles. Then, you can run in place for a good aerobic workout.

Exercise is not just for your body. It is for your mind as well. The mind-body connection has long been established by medical professionals, and numerous studies have shown that people who exercise regularly perform more efficiently and more effectively than their work colleagues who don't exercise. So, to get ahead of everyone else, make exercise part of your daily routine, even when you are on the road.

164. Who is this article for?

(A) Vacationers
(B) Business people
(C) Airline employees
(D) Overweight people

165. Why is it difficult for travelers to get exercise?

(A) The exercise rooms in hotels are inadequate.
(B) Their schedules change unexpectedly.
(C) There are no places to exercise.
(D) They don't like to exercise.

166. Where does the article suggest exercising?

(A) In a car
(B) At meetings
(C) In the hotel lobby
(D) In an airplane seat

167. According to the article, what is a benefit of exercise?

(A) Weight loss
(B) Feeling younger
(C) Improved work performance
(D) Better relationships with colleagues

Questions 168–171 refer to the following report.

> Food products currently account for the largest portion of our country's agricultural exports, having taken over the lead from natural fibers and dyes, traditionally our major exports. The value of these exports has increased in recent years, with the greater interest among international consumers in exotic fruits and vegetables. [1] Currently, over one million hectares is being cultivated for the purpose of growing food products specifically for the international market. [2] Our low nighttime temperatures, combined with the fact that we have adequate rainfall throughout the year and plenty of sunshine, gives us a competitive edge over growers in other regions. [3]
>
> Our exports of native tropical fruits and vegetables have increased from less than 10% to close to 40% of total agricultural exports in the last five years, and growth is expected to continue. However, we continue to anticipate new food trends over the next decade and will be ready to respond as the market changes. [4]

168. What is exported the most?

(A) Dyes
(B) Fibers
(C) Fruits and vegetables
(D) Prepared food products

169. Why has the value of these exports increased?

(A) Increased grower expertise
(B) Not enough supply for the demand
(C) Poor growing conditions in other regions
(D) More interest from people in other countries

170. What is expected to happen in the next few years?

(A) Increase in prices
(B) Changes in food fashions
(C) Removal of market regulations
(D) Improvement of agricultural methods

171. In which of the positions marked [1], [2], [3], and [4] does the following sentence best belong?

"Our growers have responded enthusiastically to the rising demand."

(A) [1]
(B) [2]
(C) [3]
(D) [4]

Questions 172–175 are based on the following webpage.

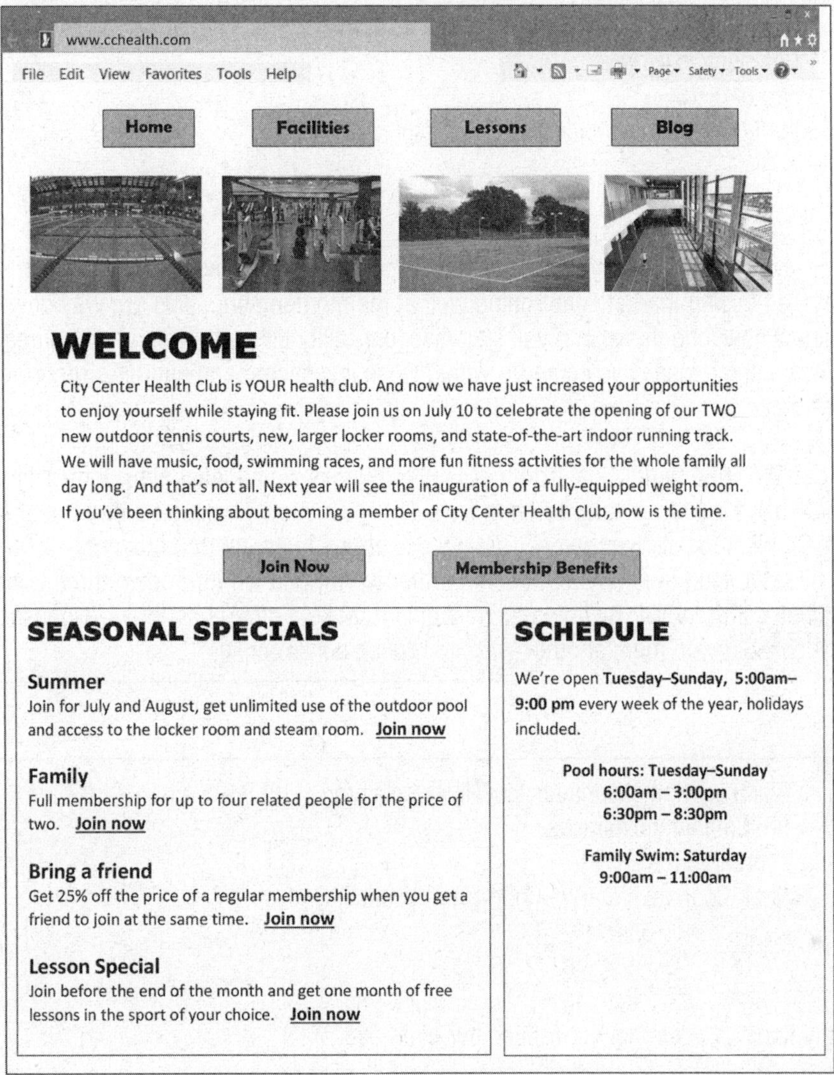

www.cchealth.com

File Edit View Favorites Tools Help

Home | Facilities | Lessons | Blog

WELCOME

City Center Health Club is YOUR health club. And now we have just increased your opportunities to enjoy yourself while staying fit. Please join us on July 10 to celebrate the opening of our TWO new outdoor tennis courts, new, larger locker rooms, and state-of-the-art indoor running track. We will have music, food, swimming races, and more fun fitness activities for the whole family all day long. And that's not all. Next year will see the inauguration of a fully-equipped weight room. If you've been thinking about becoming a member of City Center Health Club, now is the time.

Join Now | Membership Benefits

SEASONAL SPECIALS

Summer
Join for July and August, get unlimited use of the outdoor pool and access to the locker room and steam room. **Join now**

Family
Full membership for up to four related people for the price of two. **Join now**

Bring a friend
Get 25% off the price of a regular membership when you get a friend to join at the same time. **Join now**

Lesson Special
Join before the end of the month and get one month of free lessons in the sport of your choice. **Join now**

SCHEDULE

We're open **Tuesday–Sunday, 5:00am–9:00 pm** every week of the year, holidays included.

Pool hours: Tuesday–Sunday
6:00am – 3:00pm
6:30pm – 8:30pm

Family Swim: Saturday
9:00am – 11:00am

172. What is suggested about the health club?
   (A) It is for adults only.
   (B) It is expensive to join.
   (C) It has recently expanded.
   (D) It is in a convenient location.

173. Which sports activity is currently not available at the club?
   (A) Swimming
   (B) Tennis
   (C) Running
   (D) Weight lifting

174. What information is listed on this webpage?
   (A) Membership fees
   (B) Discounted memberships
   (C) Club rules and regulations
   (D) Class schedule

175. When is the pool closed?
   (A) On Mondays
   (B) Every morning
   (C) On holidays
   (D) At noon

Questions 176–180 refer to the following two e-mails.

From: Mark Connors <markconnors@livingsol.com>
Subject: Company expenses
Date: February 13
To: Alana Dorrian <alanadorrian@livingsol.com>

Alana,

I would like you to research ways to reduce our expenses here at Living Solutions. You are aware that the housing market is not doing well at the moment, our sales are way down, and we don't know how long this slump will last. Also, our utility bills are likely to go up again this year. Below are some ideas I've come up with. Please investigate and submit a report to me within one week.

1. Rent: Can we get a better deal from our landlord? If we sign a lease for a longer time period, we could ask for a lower rate. Ask him for a 15% reduction if we sign a three-year lease.
2. Space: Do we need all five rooms? Can we sublet one to another company?
3. Utility bills: We tend to keep these rooms rather warm. Can we turn down the thermostat and still be comfortable? By how much? Would it make a difference to our expenses?
4. Other ideas: Can you think of other ways to reduce our expenses?

From: Alana Dorrian <alanadorrian@livingsol.com>
Subject: Re: Company expenses
Date: February 16
To: Mark Connors <markconnors@livingsol.com>

Mark,

Here are my findings about how to reduce our overhead.

1. I talked to Mr. Stanley. He says the reduction you request is too high for him. However, he is willing to negotiate some reduction in exchange for a longer lease, and he would like you to contact him about it.
2. We don't need all of our rooms. Stavros and Kama have different schedules and are often out showing houses to clients, so they can easily share a room. The advertising firm next door might be interested in renting one of our rooms.
3. I spoke with a Ms. Perkins at the utility company. She said that turning the thermostat down by two or three degrees can save us a good amount of money without sacrificing comfort. She'll send us some figures.
4. I thought a good way to reduce our electric bills would be to encourage all staff to turn off their computers and office lights at the end of every day.

176. What kind of business is Living Solutions?

(A) Architect firm
(B) Real estate sales
(C) House cleaning
(D) Advertising

177. What is the landlord's name?

(A) Mr. Connors
(B) Ms. Dorrian
(C) Mr. Stanley
(D) Ms. Perkins

178. What is indicated about Mr. Stavros and Mr. Kama?

(A) They are employed by a different company.
(B) They need a larger office space.
(C) They work at different times.
(D) They have the same clients.

179. The word "negotiate" in line 3 of the second e-mail is closest in meaning to

(A) discuss
(B) request
(C) avoid
(D) expect

180. What cost-saving idea does Alana suggest?

(A) Moving to a smaller office
(B) Changing the work schedule
(C) Buying energy-efficient computers
(D) Turning off lights when not in use

Questions 181–185 refer to the following flyer and e-mail.

GENERAL HOSPITAL
UPCOMING WORKSHOPS

Workshop 1: Keep Your Heart Healthy **Oct. 8**
We'll talk about how diet and exercise contribute to heart health and sample some heart-healthy snacks.

Workshop 2: Walk for Fitness* **Oct. 10**
We'll practice walking techniques, outdoors if weather permits.

Workshop 3: Healthful Meals** **Oct. 12**
We'll discuss the principles of healthy cooking and prepare and enjoy a few healthful dishes.

Workshop 4: Yoga for Flexibility* **Oct. 15**
We'll practice some basic yoga positions. All levels are welcome.

Workshops are held from 9:00 A.M. until 12:00 P.M. and meet in Conference Room II. All workshops are open to the public, ages 15 and up. You are welcome to take as many workshops as you like. Participation is free unless otherwise noted, but advance registration is required. Please send an e-mail to *workshops@gh.org* to register. Cookbooks, exercise books, and exercise DVDs will be available for sale at each workshop.

*Please wear comfortable shoes and loose clothing.
**A $10 materials fee, payable to the instructor, covers the cost of ingredients. Participants will cook and eat several dishes.

From: Mona Cappadona
Date: November 10
Subject: October Workshops Report
To: Khalid Mahmod

The October workshops were very successful. All together 65 people participated:

Workshop 1–15 people
Workshop 2–12 people
Workshop 3–16 people
Workshop 4–22 people

In light of this success, I recommend offering these workshops again in January with a few minor changes. First, we need to emphasize the need to wear the proper clothing for the exercise classes. Some people showed up for the walking class without the proper shoes and had an uncomfortable experience as a result. Also, we should raise the materials fee for the Healthful Meals class by $2 to make sure we have enough to cover costs. We should also consider finding a larger space for the Yoga class. It seems to attract a lot of people, and the participants really need room to stretch and move. Finally, I think it would be a good idea to provide a telephone number for registration in our advertisement, as there are still people who aren't comfortable using e-mail, and we want to make sure everyone who wants to sign up for our classes can do so easily.

Please let me know what you think of my suggestions.

Mona

181. How much does it cost to take the Walk for Fitness class?

(A) $0
(B) $2
(C) $10
(D) $12

182. Which workshops include eating?

(A) Workshops 1 and 2
(B) Workshops 3 and 4
(C) Workshop 3 only
(D) Workshops 1 and 3

183. Which workshop was the most popular?

(A) Keep Your Heart Healthy
(B) Walk for Fitness
(C) Healthy Meals
(D) Yoga for Flexibility

184. What does Mona want to change about the Yoga workshop?

(A) The fee
(B) The location
(C) The requirements
(D) The number of participants

185. What does Mona suggest including in the flyer?

(A) An e-mail address
(B) A complete schedule
(C) A telephone number
(D) A registration form

Questions 186–190 refer to the following flyer, letter, and e-mail.

JOB FAIR **JOB FAIR** **JOB FAIR**

When? June 15, 9:00 A.M.–5:00 P.M.
Where? The Peacham Hotel
Cost: FREE

Looking for work?
Whether you are just starting out in your professional life or are looking for a way to climb the career ladder, that special opportunity may be awaiting you at the next Business Professional Association's (BPA) Annual Job Fair.

- Talk with representatives from companies from around the country that are hiring now.
- Submit your résumé to hundreds of companies.
- Find out which industries will be hiring the most over the next decade.
- Learn about the best strategies for getting the job you want now.

Exhibit Hall: Open all day. BPA publications, as well as books by leading employment specialists, will be on sale.

Workshops:

9:00 A.M.	Professional Résumé Writing
11:00 A.M.	Interviewing Skills
1:00 P.M.	Researching the Job Market
3:00 P.M.	Job Skills for the 21st Century

Business Professionals Association
P.O. Box 10
North Haversham, MA 01234

March 1, 20–

Dear Member,

As you know, our annual job fair will take place in June. Many of you have already given generously of your time and talents to organize this event. The job fair is a very popular event and has been a huge support for many young job seekers just entering their professional lives. This year we are adding a new component to the event. We will be giving a small series of workshops to help job seekers develop the skills and knowledge they need for a successful job hunt. At this time, we are asking members to consider whether they might be interested in leading one of these workshops. The schedule is attached. Please contact me if you would like to lead a workshop or would like more information.

Thank you.

Bill Smithers

Bill Smithers
Job Fair Chair

From: Estelle O'Hara <estelleoh@bigbucks.com>
Subject: Workshop
Date: March 6
To: Bill Smithers <bsmithers@industrial.com>

Hi Bill,

I saw your letter about the Job Fair workshops. I would be more than happy to help out. I well remember the time when I was a recent college graduate looking for my first job in finance, and now I work with one of the biggest investment firms in the country. So, I am happy to help young people get started. I can lead the résumé writing workshop for you. I have several ideas for how I would approach it, but please let me know if there is anything particular you would like me to include.

Thanks.

Estelle

186. What is something you CANNOT do at the job fair?

(A) Learn about job opportunities
(B) Prepare for interviews
(C) Get a free meal
(D) Buy a book

187. The word "strategies" in line 9 of the flyer is closest in meaning to

(A) skills.
(B) methods.
(C) resources.
(D) knowledge.

188. What is suggested about the workshops?

(A) They are difficult to organize.
(B) They require a lot of preparation.
(C) They have not been given in the past.
(D) They are the most popular part of the job fair.

189. What is indicated about Estelle O'Hara?

(A) She runs a résumé-writing service.
(B) She has just started out in her career.
(C) She is on the job fair organizing committee.
(D) She is a member of the Business Professionals Association.

190. What time will Estelle O'Hara give her workshop?

(A) 9:00 A.M.
(B) 11:00 A.M.
(C) 1:00 P.M.
(D) 3:00 P.M.

Questions 191–195 refer to the following webpage, review, and e-mail.

www.urbaninn.com/directions

File Edit View Favorites Tools Help

Home | Rooms | Reservations | Things to Do | Directions

GETTING HERE

We're located at 155 Riverside Avenue
Across the street from Riverside Academy.

SUBWAY

Take the green line to Riverside. Exit the station and walk north on Riverside Avenue for five blocks.

BUS

Take the #45 bus to the corner of Riverside Avenue and West Street. Walk up Riverside Avenue for ½ block.

We also run a hotel shuttle to pick up guests at the train station. Please let us know in advance if you will require this service.

If you are arriving in the city by plane, it's easiest to take a taxi from the airport.

I travel frequently for business and have stayed in a lot of hotels but few compare with the Urban Inn. I know a lot of reviewers don't like it because it's not right downtown, but it's an easy ten-minute bus ride to Main Street and all the stores and businesses, and because of the location, the Urban charges significantly less than the downtown hotels. On top of all this, the staff couldn't be nicer, the décor is delightful, and the rooms are very comfortable.

Lorena Schultz

From: Alex Rivera <alexrivera@landover.com>
Subject: Trip
Date: November 25
To: Lisa Sampson <lisas@howdy.com>

Hi Lisa,

The trip is going well, so far. My plane got in on time, and I had no problem getting to the Urban Inn. It's not a bad place, and mostly it's what that review says it is. It's really easy for me to get to my downtown meetings by bus. The staff is great, and the place is nice looking. But I can't say I agree with the reviewer about the rooms, at least not entirely. The first night, I woke up in the middle of the night needing some extra blankets, but there were none. However, when I complained to the manager the next day, she immediately moved me to another room, provided me with a down quilt, and now everything is fine. I am sure I will enjoy the rest of my stay here.

Alex

191. What is close to the hotel?

(A) The train station
(B) The airport
(C) A school
(D) Stores

192. What does the reviewer say about the hotel?

(A) Its staff is unfriendly.
(B) It's inexpensive.
(C) It's hard to get to.
(D) It's in a bad location.

193. The phrase "on top of" in line 6 of the review is closest in meaning to

(A) added to.
(B) in spite of.
(C) because of.
(D) the best part of.

194. How did Alex probably get to the hotel?

(A) Subway
(B) Bus
(C) Hotel shuttle
(D) Taxi

195. What does Alex imply about his first night at the hotel?

(A) The room was cold.
(B) The hotel was too noisy.
(C) The bed was comfortable.
(D) The manager was unhelpful.

Questions 196–200 refer to the following notice, e-mail, and schedule.

The Umpleton Company

This summer we are inaugurating an internship program in information technology. Both graduate and undergraduate students are eligible to apply. Internships will begin in June and July and last 10–15 weeks, depending on the circumstances of each intern.

Interns will work on projects in areas such as networking, business software, website development, and computer administration, according to individual interests. Students who speak a second language are encouraged to apply and will be assigned to work on our global communications project.

Spaces are limited and preference will be given to employee's children and relatives. Contact interns@umpleton.com to apply.

From: Jon Samuels <jon@gomail.com>
Subject: Internship program
Date: March 18
To: Umpleton interns <interns@umpleton.com>

I am interested in applying for an internship in information technology. My mother, who is an electrical engineer at Umpleton, told me about this opportunity.

I am a junior at Eastland University, majoring in business administration. I am also very interested in information technology and am considering pursuing graduate studies in this field. I will be leaving for Korea at the end of this semester, as soon as I have finished my exams. I will spend a couple of weeks there visiting relatives and brushing up on Korean, which is my second language. I am available to start the internship in early June, as soon as I return from my trip, and could work until the beginning of the fall semester.

Please send me an application for the program. Thank you.

Jon Samuels

Eastland University

CALENDAR

Spring Semester: January 19–May 15
Last day to drop classes: February 2
Exam week: May 11–15
Graduation weekend: May 16–17

Summer Session: June 1–August 14
Last day to drop classes: June 15

Fall Semester: September 14–December 11
Last day to drop classes: September 28
Exam week: December 7–11

196. Why will Jon be given preference over other applicants?
   (A) His mother works at Umpleton.
   (B) His major is business administration.
   (C) He is planning to go to graduate school.
   (D) He is a student at Eastland University.

197. What does Jon plan to study in graduate school?
   (A) Korean culture and history
   (B) Information technology
   (C) Electrical engineering
   (D) Communications

198. What project will Jon probably be assigned to work on?
   (A) Networking
   (B) Business software
   (C) Website development
   (D) Global communications

199. What will Jon do in May?
   (A) Apply to graduate school
   (B) Start his internship
   (C) Go to Korea
   (D) Graduate

200. When would Jon finish his internship?
   (A) June
   (B) July
   (C) August
   (D) September

This is the end of the test. If you finish before time is called, you may go back to Parts 5, 6, and 7 and check your work.

ANSWER KEY
TOEIC Practice Test

LISTENING COMPREHENSION

Part 1: Photographs

1. **B**	3. **D**	5. **A**
2. **A**	4. **C**	6. **C**

Part 2: Question-Response

7. **C**	14. **B**	21. **A**	28. **B**
8. **A**	15. **C**	22. **B**	29. **B**
9. **B**	16. **A**	23. **C**	30. **C**
10. **A**	17. **A**	24. **A**	31. **A**
11. **C**	18. **B**	25. **C**	
12. **B**	19. **C**	26. **B**	
13. **A**	20. **B**	27. **A**	

Part 3: Conversations

32. **C**	42. **A**	52. **D**	62. **B**
33. **B**	43. **D**	53. **C**	63. **A**
34. **A**	44. **C**	54. **D**	64. **D**
35. **C**	45. **A**	55. **A**	65. **D**
36. **D**	46. **C**	56. **C**	66. **A**
37. **A**	47. **B**	57. **B**	67. **B**
38. **C**	48. **D**	58. **B**	68. **C**
39. **B**	49. **D**	59. **A**	69. **B**
40. **B**	50. **A**	60. **C**	70. **C**
41. **D**	51. **B**	61. **D**	

Part 4: Talks

71. **B**	79. **B**	87. **C**	95. **D**
72. **A**	80. **B**	88. **D**	96. **C**
73. **D**	81. **A**	89. **B**	97. **A**
74. **A**	82. **A**	90. **A**	98. **C**
75. **C**	83. **D**	91. **D**	99. **D**
76. **D**	84. **C**	92. **B**	100. **C**
77. **C**	85. **B**	93. **A**	
78. **D**	86. **A**	94. **B**	

ANSWER KEY
TOEIC Practice Test

READING

Part 5: Incomplete Sentences

101.	A	109.	A	117.	B	125.	A
102.	D	110.	B	118.	A	126.	D
103.	B	111.	C	119.	A	127.	B
104.	C	112.	D	120.	C	128.	B
105.	D	113.	B	121.	B	129.	A
106.	A	114.	A	122.	C	130.	C
107.	C	115.	C	123.	C		
108.	B	116.	D	124.	B		

Part 6: Text Completion

131.	B	135.	B	139.	B	143.	A
132.	C	136.	C	140.	A	144.	D
133	C	137.	A	141.	D	145.	B
134.	A	138.	D	142.	B	146.	C

Part 7: Reading Comprehension

147.	D	161.	D	175.	A	189.	D
148.	A	162.	C	176.	B	190.	A
149.	B	163.	C	177.	C	191.	C
150.	C	164.	B	178.	C	192.	B
151.	B	165.	B	179.	A	193.	A
152.	D	166.	D	180.	D	194.	D
153.	C	167.	C	181.	A	195.	A
154.	A	168.	C	182.	D	196.	A
155.	B	169.	D	183.	D	197.	B
156.	D	170.	B	184.	B	198.	D
157.	D	171.	A	185.	C	199.	C
158.	A	172.	C	186.	C	200.	D
159.	C	173.	D	187.	B		
160.	B	174.	B	188.	C		

Answer Key for Lessons 1–50

Lessons 1–5 General Business

Lesson 1: Contracts

Words in Context:

1. establish	7. determine
2. agreement	8. provide
3. parties	9. resolve
4. specifies	10. engaging
5. obligates	11. abide by
6. assurance	12. cancel

Word Practice:

1. B	7. A	13. D	19. D
2. A	8. A	14. B	20. A
3. A	9. B	15. D	21. B
4. C	10. A	16. D	22. C
5. A	11. A	17. A	23. A
6. D	12. B	18. B	24. D

Lesson 2: Marketing

Words in Context:

1. product	7. current
2. market	8. inspiration
3. persuaded	9. convince
4. consumers	10. compared
5. attract	11. competes
6. satisfied	12. fad

Word Practice:

1. C	7. D	13. A	19. D
2. A	8. C	14. D	20. B
3. B	9. B	15. B	21. A
4. C	10. C	16. B	22. C
5. D	11. A	17. C	23. D
6. A	12. C	18. A	24. B

Lesson 3: Warranties

Words in Context:

1. promise	7. covers
2. required	8. implies
3. frequently	9. expire
4. consider	10. protect
5. characteristics	11. reputations
6. variety	12. consequences

Word Practice:

1. A	7. B	13. C	19. D
2. B	8. A	14. A	20. A
3. A	9. D	15. D	21. D
4. C	10. D	16. A	22. D
5. B	11. B	17. B	23. B
6. A	12. D	18. C	24. A

Lesson 4: Business Planning

Words in Context:

1. develop	7. evaluation
2. primary	8. offered
3. avoid	9. risks
4. substitute	10. gathering
5. strengthen	11. demonstrate
6. strategy	12. address

Word Practice:

1. A	7. A	13. D	19. B
2. A	8. B	14. C	20. C
3. B	9. B	15. A	21. A
4. D	10. A	16. D	22. B
5. A	11. A	17. A	23. A
6. B	12. C	18. C	24. D

Lesson 5: Conferences

Words in Context:

1. associations	7. arrangements
2. get in touch	8. accommodate
3. take part in	9. hold
4. sessions	10. overcrowded
5. attending	11. location
6. select	12. register

Word Practice:

1. D	7. A	13. A	19. A
2. B	8. D	14. A	20. B
3. B	9. A	15. D	21. B
4. C	10. B	16. A	22. C
5. D	11. C	17. D	23. D
6. C	12. B	18. C	24. A

Word Review #1

1. C	6. B	11. D	16. C
2. D	7. A	12. B	17. B
3. D	8. B	13. C	18. D
4. D	9. A	14. B	19. C
5. A	10. A	15. A	

Lessons 6–10 Office Issues

Lesson 6: Computers and the Internet

Words in Context:

1. shut down	7. duplicate
2. warning	8. ignore
3. figure out	9. display
4. access	10. failed
5. search	11. allocate
6. deleted	12. compatible

Word Practice:

1. C	7. B	13. B	19. D
2. A	8. C	14. B	20. C
3. A	9. D	15. C	21. C
4. D	10. A	16. B	22. D
5. A	11. B	17. A	23. B
6. C	12. B	18. D	24. D

Lesson 7: Office Technology

Words in Context:

1. in charge	7. initiates
2. durable	8. stays on top of
3. affordable	9. recurring
4. reduce	10. provider
5. capacity	11. as needed
6. physical	12. stock

Word Practice:

1. A	7. D	13. B	19. C
2. B	8. B	14. D	20. A
3. C	9. C	15. B	21. C
4. D	10. D	16. A	22. D
5. B	11. C	17. C	23. B
6. A	12. A	18. D	24. A

Lesson 8: Office Procedures

Words in Context:

1. appreciation	7. verbalize
2. made of	8. practices
3. reinforced	9. outdated
4. casually	10. been exposed to
5. code	11. brought in
6. ran out of	12. glimpse

Word Practice:

1. B	7. A	13. D	19. D
2. C	8. B	14. A	20. B
3. C	9. C	15. B	21. C
4. B	10. A	16. C	22. B
5. A	11. B	17. C	23. C
6. D	12. B	18. A	24. A

Lesson 9: Electronics

Words in Context:

1. sharply	7. stored
2. networks	8. revolutionized
3. facilitated	9. devices
4. processing	10. skills
5. popular	11. technical
6. software	12. replaced

Word Practice:

1. C	7. A	13. A	19. C
2. C	8. C	14. C	20. B
3. B	9. D	15. A	21. D
4. A	10. D	16. B	22. B
5. C	11. D	17. A	23. A
6. D	12. B	18. C	24. B

Lesson 10: Correspondence

Words in Context:

1. proofed	7. express
2. revision	8. distributed
3. beforehand	9. layout
4. assemble	10. mention
5. folding	11. complicated
6. courier	12. petition

Word Practice:

1. C	7. A	13. A	19. D
2. B	8. B	14. B	20. D
3. C	9. D	15. C	21. C
4. B	10. A	16. D	22. A
5. C	11. B	17. C	23. B
6. C	12. A	18. A	24. C

Word Review #2

1. C	6. A	11. D	16. B
2. D	7. B	12. B	17. D
3. B	8. B	13. D	18. A
4. D	9. C	14. A	19. B
5. B	10. B	15. C	

Lessons 11–15 Personnel

Lesson 11: Job Advertising and Recruiting

Words in Context:

1. time-consuming	7. candidates
2. match	8. qualifications
3. recruit	9. coming up with
4. accomplishments	10. profile
5. bring together	11. commensurate
6. abundant	12. submit

Word Practice:

1. D	7. D	13. B	19. D
2. A	8. A	14. A	20. B
3. B	9. A	15. A	21. C
4. D	10. C	16. B	22. A
5. C	11. A	17. D	23. D
6. A	12. A	18. A	24. C

L4sson 12: Applying and Interviewing

Words in Context:

1. experts	7. apply
2. confidence	8. backgrounds
3. weaknesses	9. interview
4. constantly	10. called in
5. follow up	11. present
6. abilities	12. hesitant

Word Practice:

1. A	7. D	13. D	19. D
2. A	8. B	14. B	20. C
3. C	9. B	15. A	21. C
4. B	10. D	16. A	22. D
5. D	11. C	17. B	23. A
6. A	12. A	18. C	24. D

Lesson 13: Hiring and Training

Words in Context:

1. conducted	7. update
2. rejected	8. keep up with
3. successfully	9. set up
4. generate	10. mentor
5. hires	11. look up to
6. training	12. on track

Word Practice:

1. B	7. D	13. A	19. A
2. A	8. B	14. D	20. B
3. B	9. D	15. B	21. D
4. D	10. B	16. A	22. A
5. A	11. B	17. D	23. D
6. B	12. C	18. D	24. C

Lesson 14: Salaries and Benefits

Words in Context:

1. negotiated	7. flexibility
2. benefits	8. basis
3. compensated	9. raise
4. delicate	10. retirement
5. aware	11. eligible
6. wage	12. vested

Word Practice:

1. C	7. A	13. B	19. A
2. B	8. A	14. B	20. C
3. A	9. B	15. A	21. B
4. D	10. D	16. A	22. A
5. C	11. C	17. C	23. D
6. B	12. C	18. C	24. A

Lesson 15: Promotions, Pensions, and Awards

Words in Context:

1. recognizes	7. obvious
2. contributions	8. look to
3. achievements/merits	9. praised
4. promotions	10. value
5. merits/achievements	11. look forward
6. loyalty	12. dedicate

Word Practice:

1. C	7. B	13. C	19. A
2. A	8. C	14. B	20. C
3. C	9. C	15. A	21. D
4. D	10. C	16. B	22. B
5. C	11. C	17. D	23. A
6. A	12. C	18. B	24. B

Word Review #3

1. A	6. C	11. A	16. D
2. A	7. B	12. B	17. C
3. B	8. B	13. D	18. B
4. C	9. D	14. D	19. C
5. D	10. B	15. A	

Lessons 16–20 Purchasing

Lesson 16: Shopping

Words in Context:

1. bear	7. exploring
2. behavior	8. bargains
3. mandatory	9. checkout
4. strictly	10. trend
5. items	11. merchandise
6. expand	12. comfort

Word Practice:

1. C	7. B	13. A	19. B
2. B	8. C	14. C	20. C
3. B	9. D	15. C	21. B
4. A	10. C	16. C	22. A
5. B	11. A	17. C	23. D
6. D	12. D	18. C	24. A

Lesson 17: Ordering Supplies

Words in Context:

1. consistent	7. prerequisite
2. stationery	8. smooth
3. obtain	9. functioning
4. diverse	10. enterprise
5. maintaining	11. source
6. essential	12. quality

Word Practice:

1. C	7. B	13. C	19. B
2. C	8. A	14. B	20. A
3. C	9. B	15. A	21. C
4. B	10. C	16. B	22. D
5. D	11. C	17. A	23. A
6. D	12. C	18. D	24. D

Lesson 18: Shipping

Words in Context:

1. integral	7. carrier
2. catalog	8. inventory
3. shipping	9. sufficient
4. minimize	10. fulfill
5. receive	11. on hand
6. accurate	12. supplies

Word Practice:

1. C	7. D	13. A	19. D
2. A	8. D	14. C	20. D
3. A	9. A	15. B	21. A
4. A	10. A	16. B	22. C
5. B	11. C	17. D	23. B
6. C	12. A	18. A	24. C

Lesson 19: Invoices

Words in Context:

1. efficient	7. imposed
2. compiled	8. dispute
3. charges	9. discount
4. customer	10. mistake
5. estimated	11. rectified
6. terms	12. promptly

Word Practice:

1. A	7. C	13. D	19. C
2. A	8. D	14. A	20. C
3. C	9. C	15. A	21. D
4. D	10. B	16. D	22. B
5. C	11. B	17. A	23. A
6. C	12. C	18. D	24. C

Lesson 20: Inventory

Words in Context:

1. verifies	7. automatically
2. crucial	8. scanning
3. installed	9. reflect
4. running	10. tedious
5. subtracts	11. discrepancies
6. adjusted	12. disturbances

Word Practice:

1. A	7. D	13. D	19. B
2. A	8. D	14. D	20. B
3. C	9. B	15. A	21. C
4. B	10. B	16. A	22. B
5. B	11. A	17. D	23. C
6. D	12. A	18. A	24. A

Word Review #4

1. A	6. C	11. D	16. B
2. B	7. B	12. B	17. A
3. A	8. A	13. A	18. C
4. A	9. D	14. C	19. D
5. C	10. B	15. D	

Lessons 21–25 Financing and Budgeting

Lesson 21: Banking

Words in Context:

1. transact	7. restrict
2. borrow	8. take out
3. mortgages	9. balance
4. cautious	10. deductions
5. down payment	11. accept
6. dividends	12. signature

Word Practice:

1. D	7. B	13. B	19. A
2. A	8. A	14. C	20. C
3. C	9. C	15. D	21. B
4. D	10. A	16. C	22. D
5. A	11. B	17. B	23. A
6. A	12. B	18. B	24. C

Lesson 22: Accounting

Words in Context:

1. accumulated	7. accounting
2. budget	8. building up
3. clients	9. turnover
4. outstanding	10. reconcile
5. profitable	11. debt
6. audited	12. assets

Word Practice:

1. A	7. C	13. B	19. D
2. B	8. B	14. C	20. B
3. A	9. A	15. C	21. B
4. D	10. D	16. B	22. C
5. C	11. A	17. D	23. D
6. A	12. B	18. C	24. B

Lesson 23: Investments

Words in Context:

1. invest	8. long-term
2. resources	9. fund
3. wise	10. attitude
4. portfolio	11. conservative (or aggressive)
5. pull out	12. aggressive (or conservative)
6. return	
7. committed	

Word Practice:

1. A	7. D	13. A	19. C
2. A	8. B	14. C	20. B
3. C	9. A	15. D	21. C
4. B	10. C	16. B	22. B
5. A	11. B	17. C	23. A
6. D	12. A	18. D	24. D

Lesson 24: Taxes

Words in Context:

1. prepares	7. refund
2. deadline	8. calculated
3. fill out	9. owe
4. filed	10. gave up
5. spouse	11. withhold
6. joint	12. penalized

Word Practice:

1. D	7. A	13. D	19. D
2. A	8. D	14. B	20. B
3. C	9. A	15. C	21. C
4. B	10. A	16. C	22. D
5. D	11. B	17. C	23. A
6. D	12. B	18. B	24. D

Lesson 25: Financial Statements

Words in Context:

1. level	7. yield
2. target	8. translate
3. forecasts	9. realistic
4. overall	10. perspective
5. projected	11. detailed
6. desired	12. typical

Word Practice:

1. A	7. C	13. A	19. B
2. C	8. C	14. D	20. A
3. A	9. B	15. A	21. C
4. B	10. C	16. D	22. A
5. C	11. C	17. A	23. B
6. D	12. B	18. A	24. D

Word Review #5

1. A	6. C	11. B	16. C
2. B	7. D	12. D	17. A
3. D	8. A	13. C	18. B
4. B	9. D	14. D	19. A
5. C	10. D	15. B	

Lessons 26–30 Management Issues

Lesson 26: Property and Departments

Words in Context:

1. disruptive
2. adjacent
3. lobby
4. inconsiderate
5. collaboration
6. hampered
7. move up
8. scrutinized
9. opting
10. conducive
11. concentrate
12. open to

Word Practice:

1. A	7. D	13. C	19. D
2. A	8. C	14. A	20. A
3. C	9. A	15. C	21. C
4. D	10. B	16. B	22. D
5. B	11. B	17. C	23. B
6. C	12. A	18. A	24. C

Lesson 27: Board Meetings and Committees

Words in Context:

1. waste
2. agenda
3. matters
4. goals
5. lengthy
6. adhered to
7. brought up
8. priority
9. go-ahead
10. periodically
11. progress
12. concluded

Word Practice:

1. D	7. A	13. C	19. B
2. C	8. D	14. B	20. C
3. C	9. A	15. B	21. D
4. D	10. A	16. D	22. B
5. B	11. A	17. C	23. A
6. C	12. B	18. A	24. C

Lesson 28: Quality Control

Words in Context:

1. conform
2. defects
3. garment
4. inspect
5. throws out
6. enhance
7. repel
8. take back
9. brand
10. uniform
11. wrinkle
12. perceive

Word Practice:

1. C	7. D	13. C	19. D
2. B	8. B	14. C	20. B
3. B	9. D	15. A	21. D
4. D	10. C	16. A	22. C
5. A	11. C	17. C	23. A
6. B	12. A	18. B	24. B

Lesson 29: Product Development

Words in Context:

1. anxious
2. decade
3. supervisor
4. responsible
5. logical
6. systematic
7. ascertain
8. solve
9. researched
10. examining
11. experiments
12. assume

Word Practice:

1. B	7. D	13. B	19. A
2. C	8. C	14. B	20. A
3. A	9. B	15. B	21. D
4. A	10. A	16. C	22. C
5. C	11. A	17. D	23. D
6. B	12. C	18. B	24. A

Lesson 30: Renting and Leasing

Words in Context:

1. apprehensive
2. lease
3. occupancy
4. indicator
5. fluctuations
6. due to
7. condition
8. lock (themselves) into
9. get out of
10. circumstances
11. subject
12. tenant

Word Practice:

1. A	7. D	13. C	19. D
2. B	8. B	14. B	20. A
3. A	9. B	15. C	21. D
4. D	10. B	16. A	22. B
5. D	11. A	17. A	23. C
6. B	12. D	18. C	24. A

Word Review #6

1. C	6. D	11. A	16. C
2. A	7. D	12. B	17. A
3. C	8. C	13. C	18. C
4. A	9. B	14. B	19. D
5. C	10. D	15. D	

Lessons 31–35 Restaurants and Events

Lesson 31: Selecting a Restaurant

Words in Context:

1. secure	7. appeal
2. relies	8. delicious
3. guidance	9. majority
4. suggestion	10. compromise
5. subjective	11. mix
6. daring	12. familiar

Word Practice:

1. A	7. A	13. D	19. B
2. A	8. B	14. C	20. B
3. A	9. C	15. A	21. D
4. B	10. B	16. B	22. A
5. C	11. C	17. C	23. B
6. D	12. D	18. D	24. C

Lesson 32: Eating Out

Words in Context:

1. randomly	7. complete
2. foreign	8. judged
3. patrons	9. excite
4. predict	10. flavor
5. remind	11. ingredients
6. mix up	12. appetites

Word Practice:

1. B	7. D	13. C	19. A
2. B	8. C	14. A	20. D
3. C	9. C	15. D	21. A
4. A	10. A	16. D	22. C
5. B	11. C	17. B	23. B
6. D	12. D	18. B	24. B

Lesson 33: Ordering Lunch

Words in Context:

1. falls to	7. settled
2. burdensome	8. delivered
3. multiple	9. pick up
4. narrow	10. impress
5. individual	11. elegant
6. commonly	12. reasonably

Word Practice:

1. A	7. C	13. A	19. D
2. A	8. A	14. B	20. B
3. B	9. C	15. C	21. A
4. D	10. D	16. A	22. D
5. C	11. C	17. D	23. A
6. B	12. B	18. A	24. C

Lesson 34: Cooking as a Career

Words in Context:

1. outlet	7. methods
2. drawn	8. themes
3. profession	9. accustomed
4. demanding	10. relinquish
5. influx	11. culinary
6. incorporate	12. apprenticeship

Word Practice:

1. A	7. C	13. B	19. B
2. C	8. D	14. B	20. A
3. B	9. D	15. A	21. D
4. C	10. D	16. B	22. C
5. A	11. D	17. D	23. A
6. B	12. C	18. C	24. D

Lesson 35: Events

Words in Context:

1. event	7. regulations
2. coordinated	8. lead time
3. site	9. ideally
4. stage	10. assist
5. exact	11. proximity
6. dimensions	12. general

Word Practice:

1. D	7. D	13. A	19. A
2. B	8. B	14. C	20. D
3. C	9. A	15. B	21. A
4. B	10. C	16. D	22. D
5. C	11. A	17. A	23. B
6. C	12. B	18. C	24. C

Word Review #7

1. C	6. C	11. C	16. B
2. D	7. C	12. A	17. C
3. B	8. C	13. D	18. D
4. A	9. D	14. B	19. A
5. D	10. B	15. D	

Lessons 36–40 Travel

Lesson 36: General Travel

Words in Context:

1. agent	7. embarkation
2. valid	8. board
3. itinerary	9. depart
4. delayed	10. beverage
5. prohibited	11. announcements
6. luggage	12. claims

Word Practice:

1. A	7. B	13. A	19. B
2. A	8. B	14. B	20. C
3. B	9. A	15. A	21. B
4. D	10. D	16. A	22. B
5. C	11. C	17. C	23. D
6. A	12. B	18. C	24. D

Lesson 37: Airlines

Words in Context:

1. deal with	7. prospective
2. expensive	8. situation
3. substantial	9. excursion
4. economical	10. equivalent
5. scenery	11. extending
6. destination	12. distinguishable

Word Practice:

1. D	7. B	13. A	19. B
2. C	8. A	14. D	20. D
3. C	9. B	15. B	21. B
4. C	10. D	16. D	22. D
5. B	11. A	17. B	23. A
6. A	12. C	18. C	24. C

Lesson 38: Trains

Words in Context:

1. relatively	7. operate
2. punctual	8. remainder
3. fares	9. duration
4. directories	10. deluxe
5. comprehensive	11. offset
6. remote	12. entitle

Word Practice:

1. C	7. D	13. B	19. A
2. A	8. C	14. C	20. C
3. B	9. A	15. B	21. B
4. D	10. C	16. B	22. D
5. A	11. A	17. D	23. A
6. B	12. A	18. A	24. D

Lesson 39: Hotels

Words in Context:

1. preclude	7. quoted
2. rates	8. service
3. reservations	9. expect
4. advance	10. housekeeper
5. notify	11. chains
6. confirm	12. check in

Word Practice:

1. C	7. A	13. C	19. D
2. B	8. B	14. A	20. D
3. A	9. D	15. B	21. B
4. D	10. C	16. A	22. A
5. C	11. B	17. C	23. C
6. A	12. D	18. D	24. C

Lesson 40: Car Rentals

Words in Context:

1. tempted	7. license
2. nervous	8. confusing
3. coincided	9. intended
4. disappointment	10. tier
5. guaranteed	11. request
6. contacted	12. thrill

Word Practice:

1. C	7. D	13. C	19. B
2. B	8. C	14. D	20. C
3. B	9. A	15. A	21. B
4. D	10. D	16. B	22. A
5. D	11. A	17. C	23. D
6. C	12. A	18. A	24. B

Word Review #8

1. D	6. D	11. B	16. B
2. C	7. A	12. A	17. D
3. A	8. C	13. D	18. A
4. D	9. D	14. C	19. B
5. C	10. B	15. A	

Lessons 41–45 Entertainment

Lesson 41: Movies

Words in Context:

1. continues	7. successive
2. entertaining	8. range
3. disperse	9. combines
4. influence	10. released
5. descriptions	11. attain
6. represent	12. separate

Word Practice:

1. A	7. B	13. B	19. D
2. C	8. C	14. D	20. C
3. A	9. A	15. B	21. B
4. D	10. A	16. D	22. B
5. A	11. C	17. A	23. A
6. C	12. A	18. C	24. D

Lesson 42: Theater

Words in Context:

1. created	7. experiences
2. elements	8. dialogue
3. performance	9. rehearsal
4. occurs	10. audience
5. approach	11. reviews
6. action	12. sell out

Word Practice:

1. A	7. D	13. C	19. B
2. B	8. D	14. A	20. B
3. C	9. B	15. B	21. A
4. B	10. B	16. A	22. D
5. A	11. A	17. C	23. C
6. D	12. D	18. B	24. D

Lesson 43: Music

Words in Context:

1. reason	7. disparate
2. available	8. urge
3. category	9. instinctive
4. taste	10. lively
5. divided	11. favorite
6. broad	12. relax

Word Practice:

1. D	7. C	13. B	19. A
2. A	8. A	14. D	20. C
3. C	9. D	15. B	21. B
4. B	10. C	16. C	22. B
5. C	11. A	17. D	23. D
6. A	12. D	18. B	24. C

Lesson 44: Museums

Words in Context:

1. admire	7. criticism
2. spectrum	8. schedule
3. responded	9. leisure
4. expressing	10. collected
5. significant	11. specialize
6. fashion	12. acquire

Word Practice:

1. B	7. A	13. C	19. C
2. C	8. B	14. D	20. D
3. C	9. A	15. B	21. B
4. C	10. C	16. D	22. C
5. B	11. C	17. A	23. A
6. D	12. A	18. A	24. D

Lesson 45: Media

Words in Context:

1. subscribes	7. assignments
2. political	8. decisions
3. thoroughly	9. impact
4. constitutes	10. links
5. disseminated	11. constant
6. investigative	12. in-depth

Word Practice:

1. C	7. C	13. B	19. A
2. C	8. C	14. B	20. D
3. A	9. D	15. A	21. A
4. B	10. C	16. C	22. D
5. B	11. D	17. B	23. B
6. D	12. B	18. D	24. A

Word Review #9

1. D	6. A	11. D	16. A
2. B	7. B	12. C	17. B
3. C	8. C	13. A	18. C
4. D	9. B	14. B	19. D
5. A	10. B	15. C	

Lessons 46–50 Health

Lesson 46: Doctor's Office

Words in Context:

1. annually	7. assessment
2. effective	8. instruments
3. diagnosing	9. manage
4. preventing	10. recommend
5. appointment	11. refer
6. record	12. serious

Word Practice:

1. A	7. B	13. A	19. D
2. C	8. A	14. B	20. A
3. B	9. B	15. A	21. C
4. C	10. D	16. C	22. D
5. C	11. A	17. A	23. B
6. D	12. D	18. C	24. A

Lesson 47: Dentist's Office

Words in Context:

1. aware	7. irritates
2. catch up	8. illuminates
3. regularly	9. overview
4. encourage	10. evident
5. habit	11. restores
6. position	12. distraction

Word Practice:

1. B	7. B	13. B	19. C
2. C	8. C	14. C	20. D
3. A	9. D	15. B	21. A
4. A	10. D	16. B	22. D
5. A	11. C	17. D	23. B
6. C	12. A	18. C	24. C

Lesson 48: Health Insurance

Words in Context:

1. concerns	7. suitable
2. personnel	8. emphasize
3. policy	9. alternatives
4. portion	10. regardless
5. treatment	11. aspect
6. reimbursement	12. incurs

Word Practice:

1. A	7. A	13. B	19. C
2. C	8. B	14. D	20. B
3. B	9. D	15. B	21. A
4. D	10. A	16. C	22. B
5. D	11. C	17. A	23. B
6. B	12. C	18. B	24. D

Lesson 49: Hospitals

Words in Context:

1. mission	7. procedures
2. pertinent	8. surgeon
3. results	9. escort
4. authorization	10. accompany (or escort)
5. identification	11. statement
6. admission	12. designated

Word Practice:

1. D	7. A	13. D	19. C
2. C	8. C	14. C	20. A
3. A	9. B	15. A	21. C
4. D	10. B	16. D	22. C
5. A	11. A	17. B	23. A
6. C	12. B	18. B	24. B

Lesson 50: Pharmacy

Words in Context:

1. consulting	7. factors
2. control	8. sense
3. samples	9. interactions
4. volunteers	10. monitor
5. limit	11. potential
6. convenient	12. detection

Word Practice:

1. C	7. B	13. A	19. B
2. C	8. A	14. B	20. A
3. B	9. B	15. C	21. B
4. A	10. B	16. A	22. C
5. B	11. D	17. A	23. D
6. D	12. A	18. D	24. D

Word Review #10

1. D	6. D	11. C	16. D
2. A	7. A	12. A	17. B
3. D	8. B	13. A	18. C
4. A	9. A	14. D	19. C
5. C	10. D	15. B	

Word Index

The number indicates the lesson in which the word is taught.

PHRASAL VERBS

IDIOMS

Track Listing

Track Number	Track Title
1	Introduction
2	Lesson 1: Contracts
3	Lesson 2: Marketing
4	Lesson 3: Warranties
5	Lesson 4: Business Planning
6	Lesson 5: Conferences
7	Lesson 6: Computers and the Internet
8	Lesson 7: Office Technology
9	Lesson 8: Office Procedures
10	Lesson 9: Electronics
11	Lesson 10: Correspondence
12	Lesson 11: Job Advertising and Recruiting
13	Lesson 12: Applying and Interviewing
14	Lesson 13: Hiring and Training
15	Lesson 14: Salaries and Benefits
16	Lesson 15: Promotions, Pensions, and Awards
17	Lesson 16: Shopping
18	Lesson 17: Ordering Supplies
19	Lesson 18: Shipping
20	Lesson 19: Invoices
21	Lesson 20: Inventory
22	Lesson 21: Banking
23	Lesson 22: Accounting
24	Lesson 23: Investments
25	Lesson 24: Taxes
26	Lesson 25: Financial Statements

Track Number	Track Title
27	Lesson 26: Property and Departments
28	Lesson 27: Board Meetings and Committees
29	Lesson 28: Quality Control
30	Lesson 29: Product Development
31	Lesson 30: Renting and Leasing
32	Lesson 31: Selecting a Restaurant
33	Lesson 32: Eating Out
34	Lesson 33: Ordering Lunch
35	Lesson 34: Cooking as a Career
36	Lesson 35: Events
37	Lesson 36: General Travel
38	Lesson 37: Airlines
39	Lesson 38: Trains
40	Lesson 39: Hotels
41	Lesson 40: Car Rentals
42	Lesson 41: Movies
43	Lesson 42: Theater
44	Lesson 43: Music
45	Lesson 44: Museums
46	Lesson 45: Media
47	Lesson 46: Doctor's Office
48	Lesson 47: Dentist's Office
49	Lesson 48: Health Insurance
50	Lesson 49: Hospitals
51	Lesson 50: Pharmacy

TOEIC Practice Test

Track Number	Track Title
52	Part 1: Photographs
53	Part 2: Question-Response
54	Part 3: Conversations
55	Part 4: Talks